	DATE DUE		

A HEARTBEAT AWAY

THE INVESTIGATION AND RESIGNATION

A Heartbeat Away

OF VICE PRESIDENT SPIRO T. AGNEW

Richard M. Cohen
Jules Witcover

A WASHINGTON POST BOOK

THE VIKING PRESS NEW YORK

Copyright © 1974 by Washington Post Company
All rights reserved
First published in 1974 by The Viking Press, Inc.
625 Madison Avenue, New York, N.Y. 10022
Published simultaneously in Canada by
The Macmillan Company of Canada Limited
SBN 670-36473-8
Library of Congress catalog card number: 74-28
Printed in U.S.A.

To Barbara
and
to Paul, Amy, and Julie

The prisidincy is th' highest office in th' gift iv th' people. Th' vice-prisidincy is th' next highest an' th' lowest. It isn't a crime exactly. Ye can't be sint to jail f'r it, but it's a kind iv a disgrace. It's like writin' anonymous letters.

—Mr. Dooley (Finley Peter Dunne)

Acknowledgments

Accounts of historic events obviously benefit from the passage of time and the perspective it lends. In attempting the telling at once of this piece of American history, as the investigation of political corruption in Maryland was still in progress, we have knowingly sacrificed that benefit. Yet there is a great advantage in contemporary treatment of history if the writer is fortunate enough to obtain the cooperation of principal players in the drama. First-hand witnesses whose recollections are clear and pointed, and who have documentation to reinforce their accuracy, are more valuable than any printed source material. In trying to put down in some detail the story of the first forced resignation of an American Vice President, we have had the good luck to receive such cooperation from many of the major figures in the case: in the Department of Justice in Baltimore and Washington, the lawyers, staff, and friends of Spiro T. Agnew, and within the White House. Most have requested anonymity, and therefore to all of them as a group we express our gratitude.

The writing of this book in the relatively short time since the resignation was possible only because of the generosity and understanding of our editors at *The Washington Post,* especially Benjamin C. Bradlee, Howard Simons, Harry Rosenfeld, and Richard Harwood. We are particularly indebted to Claudia Nevins, who researched and helped to edit the book with skill and dedication; to Elisabeth Sifton, our editor at The Viking Press, whose impressive editing talents were invaluable; to William Dickinson, director of The Washington Post Writers Group; to our agent, David Obst; to Jenny Edelman, who typed most of the manuscript; and to the library staff of *The Washington Post.* Finally, we thank our wives, Barbara and Marian, who read the manuscript with the critical eyes of professional editors and made constructive suggestions.

R.M.C. and J.W.

Washington, D.C.
February 1974.

Contents

A HEARTBEAT AWAY

1 My Kind of Man

On January 15, 1973, five days before the second inauguration of President Richard M. Nixon and Vice President Spiro T. Agnew, the eyes of the nation's political community were focused on a courtroom in Washington, D.C. There, four men arrested in the break-in of the Democratic National Committee headquarters at the Watergate complex—Bernard Barker, Virgilio Gonzalez, Eugenio Martinez, and Frank Sturgis—pleaded guilty to conspiracy. Their pleas were to have been the final act in an embarrassment that the Nixon-Agnew administration, in the full flush of 1972's landslide victory, hoped to put behind it. On that same Monday, however, another scene was unfolding in nearby Baltimore that was destined to inject an entirely new element into the equation of Watergate—the question of presidential succession in time of national crisis.

The unwitting catalyst in this unforeseen development was an old friend and business associate of Agnew named Lester Matz. During the morning, Matz arrived in the lobby of downtown Baltimore's Mercantile Building for an appointment with a lawyer. Matz was extremely nervous. He walked into the elevator, turned, punched number 18, and watched the elevator's polished metal doors close in front of him. As the car rose to the law offices of Venable, Baetjer and Howard, the glistening doors reflected the image of an athletic-looking man, tanned the year round by the sun of Saint Croix, where he and his friend Ted Agnew had bought condominiums, and trim from the ski slopes of Aspen, where he maintained an apartment.

At the law firm's reception desk, the dapper Matz asked for Joseph H. H. Kaplan, whom he had never met. Up to now, his dealings with the firm had been restricted to corporate and tax law, and Kaplan had nothing to do with those matters. He was in the litigation division, his specialty was trial work, and his experience included two and a half years' service as an assistant United States attorney. That specialty and that experience were what Lester Matz, friend of Spiro T. Agnew, needed very much on this day.

In dress and demeanor, the two men could not have been less alike. Matz, flamboyant and outgoing, affected the mod look— the latest double-knit suits, wide lapels, and flap breast pocket. The lawyer who greeted him was pale and boyish-looking, his hair parted in the best prep-school fashion. His suit, too, was conservative—dark, double-breasted. Matz, forty-nine, was trying to look younger. Kaplan, thirty-six, was trying to look older.

Matz handed Kaplan a subpoena *duces tecum,* issued in the name of a special federal grand jury that had recently been impaneled in Baltimore. It called for the engineering firm of Matz, Childs and Associates, Inc., to produce certain corporate records. Kaplan was not surprised that the firm had received a subpoena. Every lawyer in town had heard by then that George Beall, the U.S. attorney for Maryland, was investigating kickbacks in Baltimore County, with the objective of indicting Dale Anderson, the county's Democratic executive and political boss. Reaching for a yellow legal pad, Kaplan jotted notes as the extremely agitated Matz told his story.

The records, Matz admitted at once, would indicate that his engineering firm had been generating cash for the purpose of kicking back 5 per cent of its fees for county public-works projects to Baltimore County politicians. It was an old, familiar story, and Kaplan had a ready strategy to deal with it. The government, he explained to Matz, was not interested in making a case against Matz or his partner, John Childs. What the government wanted was information to use against higher-ups. Kaplan's advice was orthodox and blunt: tell the government everything. Withhold nothing. Then the U.S. attorney, as was the custom, would offer Matz and Childs immunity from prosecution. All they had to do was be absolutely candid and agree to testify as government witnesses at any subsequent trial.

Matz was hesitant. "Do I have to tell them everything I know?" he asked.

Yes, Kaplan said, he did. If the prosecutors discovered that he had withheld any information, the immunity grant would be voided and he would be prosecuted with a vengeance.

In that case, Matz replied uneasily, he could not cooperate.

Why couldn't he? the perplexed Kaplan demanded.

"Because," Matz blurted out, "I have been paying off the Vice President."

For the rest of that morning, as Joe Kaplan sat stunned, Lester Matz related a story that before long would jolt a nation nearly inured to shock after the many months of revelations in the Watergate case. It was—unlike the Watergate chronicle of arrogance, excess, and stupidity in high places that defied imagination—a story of old-fashioned graft and greed practiced by the one man regarded more than most as the epitome of righteousness in American politics. Systematically since 1962, the year Agnew became executive of Baltimore County, Matz had been making cash payments to him in return for county public-works contracts. The arrangement had continued after Agnew became governor of Maryland in 1967, except from that point on the *quid pro quo* involved state contracts. In fact, Matz had made payments to Agnew even after his election as Vice President. On one occasion, he had visited Agnew in an office he then occupied in the basement of the White House, and there handed him an envelope containing about $10,000 in cash.

Matz, having concluded his story, asked to use a phone. Kaplan led him to one in the outer office, and from there Matz made two calls to close associates of Agnew. He was in trouble and something had to be done. Agnew must somehow stop this blasted investigation. But the Vice President was very busy. It was a period of intense activity for him. In just five days he would be inaugurated for his second term and would then leave almost immediately for the Far East as a presidential emissary extraordinary.

After Matz left the office, Kaplan remained in his chair. The lunch hour came and went and still the young lawyer sat there, tumbling Matz's admissions over and over in his head. The six clocks in his office—three of them pendulum models—ticked off the time, ringing the hours as they passed. Finally, at five o'clock, Joe Kaplan went home. He said little to his wife, telling her only that there was trouble at the office. He went to bed but not to sleep. That night he experienced the first of many episodes of insomnia. Payoff in the White House itself! It made him sick.

All over Baltimore that third week in January, other consulting engineers and architects rushed to the offices of the city's available legal talent, advised by some cold and blunt-talking assistant U.S. attorneys that they should retain counsel "familiar with the federal criminal code." The first subpoenas of nearly one thousand were being served, all bearing the name of assistant U.S. Attorney Russell T. Baker, Jr., and all issued in the name of a special federal grand jury.

George Beall, the thirty-five-year-old U.S. attorney for Maryland, was papering the Baltimore metropolitan area with subpoenas, attempting, or so it was rumored, to prove at the bar of justice what was already no secret in the state of Maryland: Baltimore County public officials were receiving kickbacks. Already, there were rumors that Agnew was involved, indeed that he was Beall's principal target. Beall turned away the questions with the facts. The investigation was directed at Baltimore County and Agnew had not been county executive since 1966—seven years before—two years past the statute of limitations.

The special federal grand jury had been impaneled on December 5, 1972, and its task was twofold: to investigate police corruption in Baltimore City and political corruption in Baltimore County. Of the two, Beall seemed more interested in the latter. On December 11, he, Baker, and Robert Browne, the chief of intelligence for the Internal Revenue Service's Baltimore division, took the Metroliner to Newark to spend a day learning from a master.

The man the Baltimoreans went to see was probably the nation's foremost racket-buster, the U.S. attorney for New Jersey, Herbert Jay Stern. In nearly eight years in his job, he had brought at least a dozen prominent New Jersey political figures to account for various kinds of corruption and graft, and in his zeal for law enforcement he had a special relish for going after the big fish. That was what George Beall, too, was setting out to do, with Democrat Dale Anderson as his prime target. Beall didn't realize then that the investigation for which he was seeking Stern's advice would go much higher.

Confident and free with his advice, Stern lectured the inexperienced Beall on how it was done. Move quickly, he advised. Subpoena the county's records and simultaneously subpoena the records of the firms that do the most business with the county. When you have the records, look for the tell-tale bookkeeping signs that indicate cash is being generated. Large amounts of cash, Stern said, should be a red flag: in a credit-card and checkbook society there is no need for large amounts of cash. He recommended that Beall adopt his own rule of thumb that a cash flow of $2000 was sufficient reason by itself for further investigation. Beall, scaling his figures to the less populous state of Maryland, used the figure of $500.

Another bit of advice picked up in New Jersey was discarded when it was misapplied in Maryland. Stern recommended that the subpoenas be served with authority. Two of the Baltimore IRS agents, using what they thought were Stern's methods, began to serve subpoenas like bricks through a window. The agents hit hard: "Here's your subpoena," they would say. "I want you to know you're in a hell of a lot of trouble." With that, they would recite the suspected violations, the maximum penalty for each, and conclude with a message straight from a Cagney film—cooperate, or else!

The predictable result was a howl of protests from the subpoenaed firms' lawyers. Beall, horrified, put his agents on a tighter leash, but the damage had already been done. From then on, the investigation was haunted by charges that it was being improperly conducted by overzealous government attorneys—charges that later the White House would demand answers for.

On January 4, Baker sent out his first wave of subpoenas—twenty-seven to the firms doing the most business with Baltimore County and the twenty-eighth to the county government itself. Then he waited, hoping that Stern's predictions would come true and that he would soon discover kickbacks in the county's construction industry. But Baker would have been in for a long wait had the subpoenas all gone to construction firms. No unusual cash flow was found in any of them. It so happened, however, that one of the twenty-seven top firms receiving government business was an architectural company. This was in itself unusual, but in addition, there in the books of Gaudreau, Inc., a largely family-owned company headed by Paul Gaudreau and his brothers, Robert Browne's IRS agents found the cash they were looking for. Almost by accident, the prosecutors who had plunged into what amounted to a fishing expedition in the wrong industry suddenly stumbled on a key to another world of corruption—smaller but still numerous contracts for architectural and engineering work that were let not by public, competitive bidding but by private negotiation with public officials.

On January 11, Baker, who handled most of the paper work, authorized a new wave of subpoenas, this one to wash on all those engineers and architects who dealt directly with Baltimore County officeholders to get county business. The next day, a Friday, an IRS agent served a subpoena on the consulting engineering firm of Matz, Childs and Associates, demanding that the corporation produce its books. Neither John Childs nor Lester Matz was at work that day, so it was not until the next Monday that Matz, the president of the firm, went to see his lawyer, Kaplan.

Nothing in Joe Kaplan's thirty-six years had prepared him for what Matz told him that day. Kaplan was not one of Baltimore's foremost criminal lawyers, certainly not nearly so experienced or canny as some of those he would soon be working with. He was better known in Baltimore for his close association and friendship with the state's former U.S. attorney and Democratic senator, Joseph D. Tydings, under whom he had served in the early 1960s as an assistant U.S. attorney, and in 1970 as his campaign treasurer in Tydings' doomed re-election effort. The winner, by a scant 29,000 votes, was J. Glenn Beall, Jr., the son of the Republican senator whom Tydings had defeated six years before.

The young Beall, a freshman congressman, had evened the score for his aging father, but he had done so with an infusion of White House funds—at least $200,000 worth, much of it used to buy the loyalties of Baltimore Democratic clubs, whose members detested the aloof Tydings. In addition to the White House money—raised nationally from the basement of a Washington town house—Beall was the beneficiary of White House advice, a White House-directed smear campaign against Tydings, and last-minute campaign forays into Maryland by both President Nixon and Vice President Agnew. In the end, Beall was justly claimed by the White House as its own creation, its most spectacular success of 1970.

That same year, his youngest brother, George, was named to succeed the crusading Stephen Sachs as U.S. attorney for Maryland Beall's qualifications were little more than the requisite law degree, a close personal friendship with the state's senior Republican senator, Charles McC. Mathias, Jr., and the name Beall. He took office on August 18, declaring he would wage war on narcotics peddlers and environmental polluters.

The brother of Senator Beall, Kaplan believed, would hardly prosecute Spiro T. Agnew, Vice President of the United States and titular head of the Maryland Republican Party. It would be political fratricide of the meanest sort, an unthinkable crusade for the cavalier Justice Department that John N. Mitchell had handed over to Richard Kleindienst in the pre-Watergate spring of 1972. Moreover, what Matz had to tell was the sort of dynamite information that could buy immunity from prosecution at any stage of investigation. Matz, Kaplan told him, could hold his counsel while the government built a case. If and when the government held the cards, Matz could strike a deal.

Kaplan's reasoning seemed sound to Matz. Anyway, his friend, Ted Agnew, in his own self-interest, would see to it that the investigation did not get off the ground. It was, Matz said at the time, the best thing for the country that it did not. He declared, though, that he would rather go to jail than add to the woes of an already troubled nation by implicating the Vice President. Friendship apart, the best thing for him to do for his country was to keep his mouth shut, he said. But there was friendship, too, and an association that went back more than ten years. Matz had courted Agnew in 1961, and had donated $500 to his 1962 campaign for county executive; both Matz and Childs hoped that with a friend in the county seat of Towson their firm would receive the public-works contracts that up to then had been denied them. They were right; their friend rewarded them with the long-sought contracts. All he asked was 5 per cent of their fees, an expense both men thought was only fair.

Years before, Matz had learned his lesson. As he told the story, his engineering firm and two others had formed a consortium to negotiate a public-works contract in nearby Anne Arundel County. Matz, trained at the Johns Hopkins University and proud of his talents, worked hard for that contract, drafting his plans meticulously and presenting them with the preparation of a doctoral candidate taking his oral examinations. He was rewarded with a note telling him that the contract had been let to one of the other firms in the consortium. Matz henceforth would often reach for his wallet before bothering to reach for his slide rule.

Now Matz's firm prospered. He rented an apartment in Aspen, Colorado, to indulge his love of skiing and purchased a condominium on Saint Croix in the Virgin Islands, near the one bought by Agnew. He became a man of wealth and substance, a first vice president of the Chazic Amuno synagogue, a *mensch* who honored the Jewish tradition of charity by sharing his wealth with his less fortunate coreligionists in Israel. In 1970, his charities cost him $90,000. The year before, a different tradition had cost him at least $10,000, for it was in 1969 that he had placed that sum in an envelope and handed it to the Vice President of the United States.

At the time Matz told his story to Kaplan, his friend Agnew was nearly at the pinnacle of American political power. In just five days, Richard Milhous Nixon, the son of midwestern Quakers, and Spiro Theodore Agnew, the son of a Greek immigrant, would be sworn in for a second term after one of the largest landslide electoral victories in American history. As a team, they had lost only Massachusetts and the District of Columbia, which, after all, were two bastions of Democratic liberalism. In every other quarter of America, and especially in that segment that had come to be known as Middle America, the Nixon-Agnew ticket had been the resounding choice.

In the orthodoxy of American politics, it is axiomatic to look upon the second man on a national ticket, even when he is the incumbent Vice President, as a sort of political barnacle going along for the ride. Americans vote for or against the head of the ticket, not for or against his running mate. In the 1972 election the Republican landslide was fashioned indisputably on two factors—Nixon's record in foreign policy, and the public rejection of Democrat George McGovern, who coupled an unpopular foreign policy with a domestic policy tailored chiefly for minorities. As in 1964, when Lyndon B. Johnson achieved a landslide out of widespread public rejection of Barry Goldwater, Americans voted for or against the front man and took what they got in his running mate.

Yet, for all that, it could be argued that more than most vice-presidential candidates Ted Agnew probably contributed to the dimensions of the 1972 rout of the Democrats. In the first place, the Vice Presidency itself was a focus of attention in this campaign; the hapless McGovern had chosen Senator Thomas F. Eagleton as his running mate and then scuttled him when Eagleton acknowledged episodes of mental illness. Agnew seemed to stand in contrast to Eagleton, having exhibited over the previous four years an imposing stolidness in the public spotlight as the point man for the Nixon administration.

In that first Nixon administration, the former governor of Maryland had emerged as the spokesman of middle-class America, more so even than Nixon himself. Indeed, he had been selected by the President as the man to rally the "great silent majority" who felt put upon by the loud dissenters in the land. To such degree did Ted Agnew succeed in the assignment that Nixon in a sense became a hostage to his own Vice President. Thoughts of replacing him on the 1972 ticket with John B. Connally, Jr., of Texas were banished by the strength of the constituency Agnew could muster. While it was not possible to measure precisely how much of that constituency Agnew delivered in 1972, there was one clear yardstick of the man's political muscle: in the wake of the Nixon-Agnew landslide, he was already the man to beat for the 1976 Republican presidential nomination. In 1972 as in 1970, Agnew bore the political burden in the Nixon administration, taking the fight to the Democrats as chief surrogate for an otherwise occupied President, just as Nixon himself as Vice President had done for President Dwight D. Eisenhower in 1954 and 1958. He labored loyally in the party vineyards, and he, like Nixon in 1960, was in a position to reap the ultimate reward.

If it was true, as Nixon suggested, that the country was on the brink of a historic shift of party allegiance among the middle class, the obvious beneficiary of that shift was the voice of Middle America: Spiro T. Agnew. Like Nixon, he was a controversial figure. He had his love cult and his hate cult, but members of each were likely to give him an edge not often or readily allowed Nixon—they saw Agnew as a man of candor. His reputation, indeed, was built on his habit of saying how he felt, no matter what. In a nation suspicious of doubletalking politicians, that alone rallied an army of believers to his side.

Back in Baltimore County, however, there was at least one Agnew admirer who sensed a touch of demagoguery in the Vice President's attacks on the press, student dissidents, and liberals as destructive or disloyal. On February 1, 1970, Lester Matz wrote his friend a nine-page letter in which he reviewed six of

Agnew's recent speeches and suggested changes that he thought would mollify Agnew's critics.

The speeches, Matz wrote, were not well received in the Jewish community, where some people were now suggesting that Agnew was an anti-Semite: "You must remember that many of these people do not know you as I do—and as your other Jewish friends know you." Next, he took Agnew to task for his attacks on the news media and the Eastern intellectual community: "Your constant attacks on the northeastern liberal news media and . . . an entire intellectual community in the northeast is [sic] too general—and I think offensive to many who might otherwise be 'Agnew' people.

"For instance, my son, Harry (the one with limited vision whom you've met) attends Park School in Baltimore. If the student view mirrors the parents' view—they are all anti-Agnew except for Harry who is constantly taking your side in conversations and debates in school. . . ."

Matz thought that Agnew's attacks on students could prove costly politically, and he suggested that the Vice President temper his speeches by abandoning the generalities. Citing specific lines in Agnew's speeches, Matz recommended changes: "There are *some* students who go to college . . . To a *relatively small group* of dissidents . . . There are *some* students . . . a *few . . . relatively small*." Matz reminded Agnew that he was a skier and went on to describe his political talks with the many students he met on the slopes. "I am constantly defending your remarks and position on various issues. These students—now 18 to 21—will be 24 to 27 and will be voting when and if you run for President."

In a postscript, Matz concluded with the words of a political song written for Agnew during his 1966 campaign for governor. It was almost as if he wanted to remind the Vice President of the days when he had been a less contentious politician and the adopted darling of Maryland's liberal community. "Ted: I really honestly and sincerely feel my comments to be generally true. Please give them your serious consideration—and remember—'My kind of man—Ted Agnew is.'"

Agnew never answered that letter, nor did he temper his political rhetoric. Without apology he continued to hammer at the perceived enemies of Middle America, and by January 1973 he was a man near the very top of the political world. Although he clearly relished his associations with the famous, he was not one to forget his old friends. Two nights after his re-election, Agnew had been the guest of honor at a special party commemorating not only the victory at the polls but his fifty-fourth birthday as well. About 300 of the Vice President's best friends were invited for drinks and buffet supper in the Cotillion Room of Washington's Sheraton Park Hotel, where the Agnews lived. Frank Sinatra was there, and Barbara Marx, wife of Zeppo Marx, and Rod Laver, the Australian tennis star. These were people who had not been on the Agnew social calendar ten years earlier, when he first became executive of Baltimore County; but there were others present who had been. In fact, the host for the evening was an old Baltimore chum, I. H. Hammerman II, called Bud, a wealthy real-estate developer and mortgage broker.

It was appropriate that Hammerman would be the man who picked up the tab for his friend Ted. Bud Hammerman had practically made a career of taking care of Ted Agnew. And before the next year was out it would be known that Bud Hammerman had paid for Agnew's expensive and finely tailored suits, that he had given him cash when he needed it, that he had financed many of his trips around the country, and, most significantly, that he had been a middleman in a bribery scheme that brought Ted Agnew down. Who more suitably would wine and dine the Vice President of the United States on this auspicious occasion? Bud Hammerman had always been around, looking out for Ted Agnew and in the process looking out for himself, and he intended to stay around for a long time to come. It was not too far-fetched that in another four years he might be hosting the President-elect at a similar party.

Other old Agnew friends from Maryland days were still in close contact with the Vice President. One of them was, of course, Matz. By the most curious happenstance, on February 1, eleven days after Agnew began his second term of office, another lawyer who said he had been asked to represent Matz called on George

Beall. He was George White, the Vice President's own legal counsel and friend.

White's purpose was simple enough, but it was expressed in the code that lawyers sometimes use when they are trying to get information. In being asked to represent Matz, White told Beall, he was worried about a possible conflict of interest. He was, after all, the Vice President's personal attorney and close adviser. Decoded, his question was clear: was Agnew under investigation?

Beall told White that representing Matz would pose no conflict: Agnew was not under investigation. Beall was after the *current* Baltimore County political leadership, and Agnew had not been a part of that leadership since 1966. Even assuming that Agnew had done something wrong, he was protected by the statute of limitations.

Nevertheless, White said, he was worried that the newspapers would seize upon the investigation and make an effort to drag Agnew into it. They hated Agnew and would try through innuendo to link him to the investigation. Beall assured White that he would do everything possible to protect the Vice President's good name. White thanked the young prosecutor, and then, almost as an afterthought, he added that he had decided not to represent Matz after all.

At the time of White's visit, rumors indeed were sweeping Baltimore that Agnew was being implicated in the investigation. The rumors persisted—even though the U.S. attorney was of the Vice President's own party. So Beall moved quickly. On February 6, he went to see his boss, the Attorney General of the United States, Richard Kleindienst. Beall told Kleindienst he wanted to alert him that rumors saying Agnew was involved in the Baltimore County investigation were false.

Only three days later, on February 9, Kleindienst called back. Agnew, worried, had called him to complain that Beall's investigation into political corruption in Baltimore County had the potential to embarrass him. Echoing what White had said, Agnew argued that the press would have a field day intimating that the scandals of the present county executive, Dale Anderson, had their genesis in the administration of his predecessor. Moreover, he had reason to believe that one of Beall's assistants, Barnet D. Skolnik, was intent on political mischief. After all, Skolnik had been on the staff of the 1972 presidential campaign of Edmund S. Muskie.

Beall repeated the same assurances he had already given Kleindienst. Nothing had changed. Agnew was protected both by the statute of limitations and by a total lack of evidence that he had ever accepted kickbacks. As for Skolnik, Beall protested, he was his most experienced man, a gifted prosecutor. He agreed, however, to Kleindienst's suggestion that Skolnik assume a "low profile" and refrain from interviewing witnesses who were once close to Agnew.

Beall hung up the phone and later in the day reported Agnew's call to Kleindienst to his three assistants—Baker, Skolnik, and Ronald S. Liebman. The Vice President, Baker suggested, was "acting like a guilty man." This remark drew quizzical looks from his colleagues.

"We're going to get Agnew," Baker said.

The others laughed.

2 Creature
of Suburbia

Ten years before the triumphant re-election of President Nixon and Vice President Agnew, a gambling man could have written his own odds on the chances that these two men, or either one of them, would be at the apex of political power in the United States in 1972.

Richard Nixon, who had enjoyed the heady trappings of high office as Vice President under Eisenhower and had reached for and barely missed the Presidency in 1960, was at rock-bottom on election night 1962. Seeking to avoid a rematch with John F. Kennedy in 1964 and to position himself for a second try in 1968, he had run for the governorship of California and lost. It was a rank humiliation that the usually self-disciplined Nixon could not bear, and the depth of his bitterness spilled out in his famous "last press conference" harangue at his adversaries in the news business. *Time* magazine expressed the accepted wisdom of the early 1960s when it proclaimed, "Barring a miracle, Nixon's public career has ended."

On the night of Nixon's great debacle, Agnew by contrast was at the high point of an undistinguished, small-time career in politics. Having run for public office only once before—a local judge-ship—and lost, he was now celebrating his very first election victory, as county executive of Baltimore County. Like most political successes in Agnew's career, this one was a fluke, due principally to a deep and acrimonious split in the county's Democratic ranks and Agnew's eye for opportunity.

Five years earlier, after working for the re-election of a Republican congressman and for county charter reform, he had been rewarded with a one-year appointment to the county zoning board of appeals, which reviewed zoning decisions critical to the nature, scope, and pace of suburban growth. The job paid only $3600 but Agnew took it. As a lawyer who had not succeeded in private practice, bouncing in and out of a series of jobs and small law firms, teaching in a law school at night, he had seized upon politics as a vehicle to lift him out of mediocrity and obscurity. He was not the sort of man who would rest content with the indifferent pattern of his earlier years: a chemistry major drop-out at Johns Hopkins; an assistant underwriter for an insurance company and simultaneously a student at the University of Baltimore Law School; a service company commander in Europe in World War II; a clerk-trainee in a Baltimore law firm; an insurance investigator and claims adjuster; an assistant personnel manager and glorified store detective for a Baltimore supermarket chain; a union contract negotiator.

The job for the supermarket chain, run by four brothers named Schreiber, is particularly interesting in light of Agnew's later prominence as the embodiment of and spokesman for the law-and-order society. Part of his time was spent as a one-man unofficial prosecutor and judge for suspected shoplifters in the stores. Customers caught red-handed were taken to his small office and interrogated by Agnew, "broken down," and obliged to pay for whatever they had taken. Carl Gleitsman, another worker at Schreibers who shared the office with Agnew, later provided this description of the approach Agnew used: "Now you took this item. We saw you take it. We know you had it. We told you where it was and what the item was and what pocket you had it in. So you know you're in trouble. Now, we're not trying to give you any trouble, all we want you to do is pay for it, give us a release [protecting the store against a later charge of false arrest], and promise us you won't do it again. If you do that, why, nobody need know anything about it except you and me. If you don't want to do that, then you're going to force me to call the police. . . . " It is not surprising that when the power of public office came into his hands, Ted Agnew would earn a reputation as a hard man on those who transgressed the law.

On the county zoning appeals board, Agnew applied himself diligently and in 1958 was reappointed for a full three-year term, becoming chairman when the incumbent quit out of boredom. But he was, alas, a Republican in an overwhelmingly Democratic county, and a vocal and contentious one, so when the Democrats won all seven seats on the county council they decided to replace him. Agnew raised such a squawk that, although he failed to save his seat on the board, he managed to portray himself as the victim of underhanded politics. Hoping to capitalize on that, he first went to his party's county leaders and sought the Republican nomination for Congress. When they turned him down, he agreed to run for county executive. Such was the state of the Republican Party in Baltimore County in 1962 that it would turn to a man who had been defeated in his only previous political race, for an obscure local judgeship, to be its county standard-bearer.

As was to happen so often in Agnew's career, however, the opposition played into his hands. A bitter primary battle between two former political allies split the Democratic ranks and allowed Agnew to sneak through. At forty-three, he most certainly had reached the zenith of his political career, precisely when Richard Nixon, at forty-nine, had reached his nadir.

It was in all ways appropriate that Spiro Agnew should get his start in politics in suburbia. A city boy, he had found Baltimore less than responsive to his talents. To practice law at the culmination of his many job switches, he rented space for a desk in somebody else's downtown Baltimore office. He might have remained mired there indefinitely had not Lester Barrett—an older lawyer and counselor to the ambitious but stalled Agnew—been named a county judge and moved to Towson, the Baltimore County seat. Agnew; his partner at the time, Sam Kimmel; and a third friend and lawyer, George White, moved out on Barrett's heels and opened a small office of their own across the street from the county courthouse.

It had been Barrett, rather than any great ideological pull, who had brought Agnew into the Republican Party in the first place. In a county with a four-to-one Democratic registration bulge, Barrett had provided pragmatic advice when Agnew, right after World War II, asked him how a young man got started in county politics. Become a Republican, Barrett had told him: the field of competition is smaller, and although the odds on winning public office are longer, there are other benefits, not the least of which is the law business Republican contacts can bring. Agnew followed that advice in 1946, and hence was already in the party of property-owners when he left the city in 1947 and bought a small house in Lutherville, near the county seat. Then, and later, when he moved to Towson, Agnew led a joiner's life—Kiwanis, Parent-Teacher Association, Thursday-night bowling, Saturday-night neighborhood socializing, Sunday afternoon at the Baltimore Colts' games. It was a life of mutual dependency or, put less elegantly, of mutual back-scratching.

For a lawyer especially, suburban togetherness spelled career opportunity. The county in the late 1940s and early 1950s had only recently awakened from rural sleepiness and was experiencing the post-World War II housing and population explosion into suburbia. It was a national phenomenon, but there was a special geographical factor here that fired the county's growth. Baltimore County surrounds but does not include the city of Baltimore. By the mid-1950s, the city had a black population of about one third (now more than half); when the postwar white flight to the suburbs took place in all directions, the result was not the usual redistribution of population by race within a county, but a wholesale abandonment of the city by whites into a separate governmental entity, the city-less suburban county. In the most exact sense, the Baltimore County to which Spiro Agnew moved, and in which he charted and achieved his first political success, was a white noose—96 per cent white—around a black inner city.

Into this white noose poured not only new residents but also all the business interests customarily poised to capitalize on community growth: the real-estate agents, the land speculators, the road builders, the engineers, the architects, the construction giants, and the army of contractors and subcontractors whose men, machines, and materiel convert rural America into suburban sprawl. And wherever there is land disposal and acquisition, bids for rezoning, the pursuit of construction permits and large government contracts for roads and buildings, there must be lawyers to draw up, shuffle, and sign the papers that give legality to the transformation of the countryside; lawyers, and officeholders to decide which contract applicants are to be rewarded with the work. This was the environment in which Agnew sought a new start after the career stalemate he had been trying to break for so long in the city, and this was the political climate in which his effort finally bore fruit.

In his post on the county zoning board of appeals, Agnew received an education on the economics and the opportunities of suburban growth. Among those who helped his learning process was the deputy chief engineer and later assistant director of public works for Baltimore County, a man named Jerome B. Wolff. They worked closely together then and later in Agnew's public career in the granting of certain government contracts.

The three-member zoning board—two Democrats and one Republican—was established under a new county charter as a buttress for the public against the avarice of the builders and developers, to whom a favorable rezoning could mean millions of dollars of profit. Spiro Agnew took to the job with zest and optimism. "It was really a quasi-judicial position where we actually made the record in zoning cases and other appeals for the courts," he said later, "and it was good for my law practice to have the prestige connected with this."

According to those who served with him, Agnew performed his duties with fairness, and as the lone Republican became a favorite of the *Baltimore Sun* papers. He forever railed against what he saw as laxness against zoning violators. Contentiousness and righteousness came to be the man's trademarks, trademarks that stayed with him throughout his political career.

Yet for all Agnew's righteousness, he demonstrated from the start in public life a peculiar sense of propriety. Right after his election as county executive, he telephoned his Republican replacement on the zoning appeals board late one night to discuss an appeal brought by one of his clients who had been a major financial backer in the recent county executive race. The appeal concerned a potentially lucrative rezoning needed to build an apartment house in the suburban town of Pikesville—against the wishes of homeowners in the area. The board member, Charles Steinbock, Jr., some years later charged that Agnew "telephoned me and asked me to grant the petition. I told him I decided cases solely on the evidence presented at the hearings, and that the evidence did not warrant classification. He then had [an associate] call me and asked me to grant the rezoning for the good of the Republican Party. I told him I was not on the board for the good of any party and promptly denied the petition. . . . In my five years on the board, he was the only county official or employee to attempt to influence my decisions."

When Steinbock made the allegation, Agnew acknowledged the call, but he dismissed it—in a phrase he was to use later concerning other allegations about him as governor of Maryland—as "common practice" among lawyers trying to speed up zoning decisions. "After my election [as county executive], I obviously had to give up my law practice. But my client was pressing me, so I called Steinbock and asked him if he could accelerate a decision. . . . It was simply to obtain information about future hearing dates for the drawn-out testimony. . . . I at no time suggested how he should decide it." There was some dispute about whether Agnew had actually taken office as county executive at the time of his phone call to Steinbock, or was county executive-elect. But, either way, the call demonstrated a certain insensitivity that was to surface repeatedly through Agnew's public career.

On another occasion as county executive, he secretly designated three Republicans, one of them an old Kiwanis buddy, as insurance "brokers of record" for Baltimore County, making them exclusive agents for a planned multimillion-dollar life- and health-insurance plan for county and school-board employees. The designation assured each of the three men huge commissions on the plan, for which county open-bid specifications had gone out to sixty companies and brokers with no mention that there were brokers of record. Their existence surfaced only when the three agents blessed by Agnew began to flash copies of a letter of authority to start cashing in on the business. Even when confronted at a private meeting of the county council with rumors about the three anointed brokers, Agnew through a spokesman flatly denied them. A member of the Baltimore city insurance advisory board who happened to be a sales representative for a large insurance company, complained: "If this isn't discrimination, nothing else is." To which Agnew irately replied: "The big brokers are putting the heat on the companies." In time, he finally conceded that the appointments had been made, and that they were nothing more than political patronage. But he insisted on a distinction that to him at least was important—the same kind of distinction he was to make as Vice President when confronted with allegations that he had favored contractors who had given him cash "gifts." "Bear in mind," County Executive Agnew said of the insurance brokers of record, "these are not just people picked to be the recipients of a political largess. These are full-time insurance men." The critical point, in other words, was the qualification of the designees to perform the task, not the fact that their designation was a political payoff.

In giving this particular explanation, Agnew said he was doing so to "correct the outrageous distortions and improper inferences" made against him. This moral indignation was an Agnew tactic developed and honed in the minor leagues of suburban politics; it was to become a standard weapon in his oratorical arsenal later on, when the stakes and the rewards were infinitely greater. Finally, there was in this episode another element that came to be part of Agnew's public identity: a striking unwillingness readily to acknowledge error or misjudgment and correct it. "If I had it to do all over again," Agnew told reporters afterward, "I'd never have appointed brokers of record. But to back off now would be tantamount to an admission of lack of integrity, and there is no impropriety here."

Integrity—that was the characteristic that Agnew sought above all else to convey as a public official. But successful as he was in doing so in his four years as county executive, by 1966 he appeared to be at the end of the road politically. Baltimore County was still overwhelmingly Democratic, and one of the two Democratic chieftains (whose intraparty war had enabled Agnew to win the first time) had died. The Democrats were on the mend. So Agnew looked elsewhere for his future. He was, after all, the ranking Republican officeholder in Maryland, and by this time he had some rich and influential friends to share his hours. They were men like Bud Hammerman, Lester Matz, and John Childs; J. Walter Jones, Jr., a wealthy Towson real-estate man; and Tilton Dobbin, president of the Maryland National Bank. These friends had more than a social interest in Agnew; he was a political property of value and it was in their interest as well as his own that the property be preserved. Jones, Matz, and Childs all did considerable business with the county, and it was most helpful to know the man in charge.

Once again, the Democratic Party's talent for political cannibalism worked to Agnew's great advantage. Three Democrats sought their party's gubernatorial nomination in a bitter primary, while Agnew ran uncontested in the Republican primary. To the state's utter astonishment and great embarrassment, the two principal Democratic candidates, state Attorney General Tom Finan and Congressman-at-large Carleton R. Sickles, canceled each other out and the third man, the ultraconservative, segregationist George P. Mahoney, a perennial loser, sneaked in. A wealthy road contractor, Mahoney had money and the issue of the white backlash in his favor—and he parlayed them into the nomination.

Agnew, whose performance on civil-rights issues as county executive had marked him as a mild conservative or moderate, suddenly found himself the darling of Maryland's Democratic liberals. He was the last line of defense against redneckism in Annapolis, and they flocked to his support. Aware of this shift, Agnew after a sluggish start campaigned aggressively against

Mahoney, whom he characterized as a throwback to the Dark Ages. He accused Mahoney (who ran on the transparently racist slogan "A Man's Home Is His Castle—Protect It") of conducting a "yellow, skulking, slinky campaign" and of being tied to the Ku Klux Klan. "There is no middle ground in this election," he told the voters. "The electorate of Maryland must choose between the bright, pure, courageous flame of righteousness or the evil of a fiery cross." And on election day, by 81,775 votes, they chose the bright, pure, courageous flame of Spiro T. Agnew to light the governor's mansion in Annapolis for the next four years.

Agnew's victory was based on more than rhetoric. Secretly, he had negotiated a deal with Richard Schifter, chairman of the liberal Montgomery County Democratic organization, that resulted in the establishment of a Democrats for Agnew organization in the state's wealthiest county. Schifter's and Agnew's representatives hammered out a four-point agreement under which Agnew allowed the local Democrats to review in advance all his position papers, promised not to campaign for the local Republican ticket, assumed full responsibility for financing the Democrats for Agnew organization, and promised the local organization patronage appointments.

Agnew honored his part of the agreement. In return, the Democratic organization established the bogus committee, and Agnew carried the county. The patronage agreement eventually lapsed, not because Agnew welshed, but because the Democrats found the relationship too cozy and politically compromising.

Though Mahoney, not Agnew, clearly was the issue in the Maryland gubernatorial race, the 1966 campaign contributed some revealing insights into the workings of the Agnew mind. Just before his surprise nomination, a story broke charging that Mahoney had been offered a huge bribe by the state's slot-machine interests, who were fighting a 1963 act of the state legislature that required phasing out all slots in four southern Maryland counties by mid-1968. Mahoney immediately denied the allegation. But Agnew, seizing a chance to demonstrate his purity, revealed that he in fact had been offered $200,000 in campaign contributions by the same slot-machine interests. "On three separate occasions

I was approached with deals involving the slot machines," he said. "The offer at first was $20,000, then went to $75,000, and not two weeks ago it jumped to $200,000. All I had to do was agree not to oppose or veto legislation which might pass the general assembly extending the life of the machines. I told those who approached me on the deals that I didn't even want to talk to the slot people."

The account shook the electorate much more than it seemed to affect Agnew. Three times, attempts had been made to bribe a public official seeking the governorship of the state, and three times he had simply ignored the attempts and kept them to himself. The Baltimore County state's attorney, Frank Newell, said Agnew had a public duty to tell all, but Agnew said he had no intention of revealing the names of those who had approached him. He didn't consider that "there was any criminal act unless a definite offer is made by the person who is making the bribe." The approaches were made, he said, "by an innocent person" acting as an intermediary, relaying the offer "second or third hand." Newell was incredulous. If a genuine offer was made, it was an "attempted bribe," he argued; and Agnew was only "compounding the action by remaining silent." But Agnew saw it otherwise. "Literally hundreds of people come up with similar suggestions during a campaign," he said. "I'm sure they've been made to every candidate."

To admit to having been offered a bribe three times and to having failed to report it was an incredible *gaffe* for a man seeking high public office. It demonstrated the kind of naïveté that one might expect of a political neophyte, and Agnew indeed often seemed an amateur in the game of politics that was played so hard and fast in Maryland. So in the end the incident only contributed to his image as a man somehow set apart from—even above—the sweaty, earthy grapplers in the political pit. In this bribe incident Agnew saw shady activity in politics as common practice, and hence there was no need to report it unless it was blatant. "Unless someone can show me that a crime was committed, I am not going to reveal his name," he insisted. "Nobody sat down in front of me with a suitcase full of money." He never did name the individual he said had approached him. (But in August 1973, when Agnew was first notified he was under federal investigation for possible violation of laws governing bribery and other crimes, he told a press conference that he had once been offered a "bribe." Presumably the reference was to this incident.)

The same peculiar sense of what constitutes impropriety by a servant of the people also surfaced in the disclosure that in June 1965 Agnew and nine other men had bought for $267,000 a 107-acre tract of land in Anne Arundel County, where a second Chesapeake Bay crossing was planned, parallel to the existing bridge. (The purchase was made six months after Democratic Governor J. Millard Tawes announced the plans for the new bridge.) Agnew argued that there was no conflict of interest here, because he had not been a declared candidate for governor at the time of purchase, and the land was not within his jurisdiction as Baltimore County executive. But this explanation glossed over the real grounds for a charge of conflict of interest: several of Agnew's partners in the land deal were men who did considerable business with Baltimore County, or who were large contributors to the gubernatorial campaign. Three of them—Jones; Harry Dundore, Sr., the wealthy head of a large machine shop; and Leonard C. Gerber, an official of McCormick and Company—were fellow directors with Agnew of the Chesapeake National Bank (a post Agnew acquired when he first became county executive and retained when he became governor, with his name conspicuously going to the head of the list of directors on the bank's letterhead). The others were Matz; Childs; Ernest Issel, another McCormick official; Robert O. Crampton, president of the Schilling spice firm of San Francisco, a McCormick affiliate; Allen C. Jackson, advertising director of the *Annapolis Evening Capital*; and Harry T. Solomon, a Westinghouse Corporation executive. Agnew disclosed that his share of the package had cost him $5,000 in cash, plus mortgages and a personal loan that brought his total investment to $34,200.

Of the arrangement, Agnew said: "I see no impropriety of any kind in holding property outside my jurisdiction. . . . I will certainly sell it if I am elected. . . . I don't expect you to believe it but when this transaction was being worked out, not one of us said anything about the parallel bridge. It didn't occur to us." Nor, evidently, did it occur to Agnew that there might be something wrong with the Baltimore County executive joining in a land-deal partnership with a man like Jones, who had received in excess of $24,000 for county land-appraisal work in the two previous years or about half of all the money spent by the county for that purpose. Or Matz and Childs, whose activities as consulting engineers were to be part of a much bigger story in the life of Spiro Agnew eight years later.

One of Agnew's closest associates in Towson, Ormsby S. (Dutch) Moore, himself a real-estate man, said later of the furor over the land-purchase partnership: "The whole thing bad about the deal . . . was that Ted was in a deal with Walter Jones, who was doing business with the county. . . . Strictly from the viewpoint of two men, Lester Matz and Walter Jones . . . Ted could call the shots on the contracts with respect to the type of business these two men do. Walter does appraising business, and it's a type of patronage. In other words, any professional appraiser can come into the county and request business. It's up to the county to decide . . . and obviously the department heads look to the administrative officer or the county executive for some guidance in whom to select."

Agnew, under the pressure of disclosure, finally announced he had decided to sell the land, all the while insisting there had been no conflict of interest in its purchase. The land had "excellent industrial potential" and he had bought it for that reason alone, "as proven investment for my family's future." When his share was put up for auction along with Jones's slice a year later, however, this "excellent industrial potential" produced only one bid—from the other partners in the deal. They paid $13,200 more than Agnew's original cost for it.

In Annapolis, many of the same figures who had introduced Ted Agnew to the ways of business-and-politics in suburbia were there beside him as he moved on to a larger and more important playing field. Foremost among them again was Jones, a man who knew how to live well. He had a comfortable boat tied up in the Annapolis harbor, and the new governor often spent quiet nights aboard, basking in the attention accorded him by all the other Walter Joneses of the business-and-politics fraternity in the state capital. Jones, a connoisseur of wines, had a wine cellar built for the new governor in the basement of the executive mansion, and he and other members of the fraternity stocked it for him. Unlike previous governors who had risen over the legislative route, or had spent a great deal of time in State House politics, Agnew had few cronies in the state legislature and little desire to develop any. He continued to surround himself with businessmen, as he had in Towson. Veterans of the Annapolis legislature regarded him as aloof, maybe a bit snobbish, but few saw any venality in his preference for men of the business world. "Ted was an honest guy," one of his Annapolis associates said later, "but there always seemed to be people around him who were in business. Being governor, you didn't have to do anything, you just had to be there. Having it known you were close to him was enough." "He wasn't corrupt," said another, "but he allowed himself to be used by the people around him."

For all his standoffishness with the legislators, Agnew won their respect by running a tidy operation, lobbying a new constitution through a state convention (it was rejected by the voters, to Agnew's dismay), and advancing programs in water pollution, housing, highway construction, mental health, and alcoholism. He had come into office, thanks to George Mahoney, with a liberal image, and it stayed with him, though his programs could not in truth be described as much more than moderate.

Outside Maryland, Agnew remained unknown to the general public. But he soon became recognized among the nation's other governors as a particularly articulate and serious-minded member of that exclusive club. At the several governors' conferences that punctuate the political year and bring state leaders and political writers to some of America's more attractive watering holes, he impressed his fellow governors with his polished appearance and vocabulary, and with his good fellowship on the golf course and the tennis court.

What probably sustained his image as a liberal above all else—while bringing into question his political acumen—was his repeatedly declared admiration for Governor Nelson A. Rockefeller of New York. In April 1967, ignoring Rockefeller's public pledge that he would not seek the Presidency in 1968, Governor Agnew announced his intention to dissuade Rockefeller and work for his nomination. His ardor grew steadily, leading some who thought of Rockefeller as nothing more than a perennial windmill-tilter in national politics to conclude that Agnew was simply an opportunistic climber, hoping by his solicitude toward one of America's richest and most influential men to parlay his own almost accidental rise in politics into a well-paying and prestigious resting place after he left Annapolis.

Agnew's confidence that Rockefeller could be talked into running rose in direct proportion to the decline of George Romney, Rockefeller's own choice as candidate for 1968. On the afternoon of March 21, 1968, by which time Romney was finally out of the running, Agnew settled in front of a television set in his office, with reporters around him, to watch what he and just about everybody else expected would be Rockefeller's announcement of candidacy. But the New York governor, to Agnew's great embarrassment, instead announced that he would *not* run. It was shortly learned that before going on television Rockefeller had tried to reach Agnew by phone to break the news personally, but had failed. What Agnew construed to be unforgivable thoughtlessness drove him in his humiliation and anger into the political arms of Richard Nixon, and he was on his way. Nixon and Agnew met in New York, were mutually impressed, and Agnew soon was working for Nixon's nomination. In his official duties, too, Agnew began to make moves that would make him attractive to a man like Nixon shopping for a running mate. In the next few weeks, Agnew dealt harshly with three major incidents involving Maryland blacks—a student boycott at Bowie State College, a sit-in outside his office, and the Baltimore riots after the assassination of Dr. Martin Luther King, Jr. The "liberal" governor of Maryland suddenly was perceived as what he always had been—a rigid authoritarian. One of Nixon's chief aides, the conservative Patrick

J. Buchanan, gave newspaper clippings to Nixon about Agnew's tough handling of these incidents—and the rest is history.

At the Republican national convention in Miami Beach that summer, Agnew—who earlier had worked diligently to bring the Maryland delegation in for Rockefeller—labored just as diligently to switch it to his new choice, Nixon. He rented a suite at the Sans Souci Hotel and summoned the ten remaining recalcitrant Rockefeller delegates. One of those he tried to persuade to bolt for Nixon was a young man named George Beall, then an Agnew-appointed attorney for the Baltimore liquor board. Just a few months earlier, Agnew had asked Beall to join the Maryland Committee for Rockefeller. Now he asked him to switch; if he could not deliver his own delegation to Nixon, Agnew said, he would be publicly humiliated. His reputation and political future were on the line.

Beall, a comer with political ambitions of his own, said he was publicly committed to Rockefeller and saw no way he could renounce the man now. Think it over, Agnew told him. And while he was mulling over his choice for the presidential nomination, he could also think about the post of people's counsel—a lawyer who represented the public before the state's regulatory agencies. The job was then vacant.

Beall, confused and torn between his commitment to Rockefeller and his own aspirations, very much wanted the well-publicized job of people's counsel. He called his father, the former senator then living in retirement in Frostburg, Maryland. Young Beall characterized Agnew's offer as a "subtle bribe." The old senator was amused. "Subtle, hell," he said. In the end, George Beall was one of eight Marylanders who cast his ballot for Rockefeller. He never became people's counsel.

As matters turned out, however, Ted Agnew did not need George Beall's delegate vote for Nixon. Weeks before the convention, according to insiders, Nixon had all but decided on this cool, no-nonsense man from suburbia as his running mate. A series of convention meetings among Republican leaders to discuss the Vice Presidency was little more than a façade; after a brief flirtation with the prospect of selecting his old California crony, Robert Finch, Nixon settled on Agnew. The grateful unknown told reporters: ". . . I agree with you that the name of Spiro T. Agnew is not a household name. I certainly hope that it will become one within the next couple of months." These were words that would come back to haunt him, but no more so than those Richard Nixon uttered about Agnew at a press party after the convention. "There is a mysticism about men," he said. "There is a quiet confidence. You look a man in the eye and you know he's got it—brains. This guy has got it. If he doesn't, Nixon has made a bum choice."

In the ensuing campaign, and in nearly five years as Vice President, Agnew became perhaps the most controversial of all the men who have stood a heartbeat away from the Presidency. Through it all, he remained essentially the same creature of suburbia he was when Nixon plucked him from relative obscurity—a product of postwar middle-class values, hopes, and dreams. One of his greatest disappointments as Vice President was that Nixon did not involve him importantly in domestic affairs, did not make use of his knowledge of local- and state-level government and the skills he had developed in Towson and Annapolis. Instead, he became the voice of suburbia—a sleek, articulate, confident spokesman for the middle class, for all those who had labored to get what they had, for all those determined to hold onto it. If his talents and training were not tapped in the Nixon administration, something else out of his suburban experience was: the attitudes and the biases he formed and nurtured at those Kiwanis luncheons, PTA meetings, Saturday-night get-togethers, Sunday Colt games. He became the front man for the silent majority; for all the churchgoers, all the taxpayers, all the flag-respecters who constituted the real America, but who were blotted out of the national consciousness by the frenzied behavior of those who sought to tear America down.

By November 1972, when the American electorate was called to choose between the team of Richard Nixon and Spiro Agnew and the team of George McGovern and R. Sargent Shriver, it was no contest. Vice Presidents seldom are thought to have any real effect on the outcome of national elections, and perhaps Agnew did not either; but he had developed by this time such a strong constituency in Middle America that Nixon could have no thought of replacing him. To a vast segment of the American citizenry, he was "Spiro Our Hero." He was tough and he was outspoken; but more than that, he was in the eyes of his legions of admirers the personification of Middle American values—a man of honesty and integrity. This is what he had insisted he was, ever since those first days on the Baltimore County board of zoning appeals, and that is what they believed of him.

And because they believed so strongly, because they believed so thoroughly, the things they were soon to hear about what their hero had been up to in those days of suburbia were at first incomprehensible and, in the end, shattering.

3 Maryland, My Maryland

In the midst of Spiro T. Agnew's final great crisis as Vice President, he called Christian Kahl, his Democratic predecessor as executive of Baltimore County, and invited him to Washington for a chat. Kahl, sixty-eight years old and recently retired from a sinecure in the state's department of employment and social services, boarded a southbound train and visited with Agnew in the Old Executive Office Building, an imposing, brooding structure that is part of the White House compound.

As Kahl later recounted the conversation, Agnew complained of being investigated for accepting campaign contributions in a timeworn and acceptable manner. "Chris, they're trying to get me for something that has been going on ever since this country was founded," Agnew said.

In Baltimore County and in Maryland, the political habitat of both Agnew and Kahl, there certainly could be no denying the tradition of the open hand and the greased palm. To comprehend how it could be that Agnew looked upon the catastrophe befalling him as gross injustice, one needs an understanding of the environment from which he sprang—an environment in which corruption was indelibly woven into the political fabric.

All the way back to the first of Baltimore County's post-Civil War political bosses, there stretched an unbroken line of Democratic succession, older than some of the royal houses of Europe and, in its way, equally adept at plunder. The first of these bosses was Joshua Frederick Cockey Talbott—Marse Fred, in the Southern fashion—who beginning in 1871 ruled Baltimore County first from Towson as the state's attorney and later from Washington as a congressman. When he died in 1918, the county's reigning Democratic organization was handed down to Harrison "Rolling Thunder" Rider, then to Jim Kelley, H. Street Baldwin, Michael "Iron Mike" Birmingham, and finally Kahl himself. Kahl's split with the tyrannical Birmingham paved the way for the victory of Ted Agnew, a Republican with the rhetoric of a reformer and, like so many of the new residents of the county, an *Ausländer* from Baltimore City.

Kahl was the last of the genuine articles—a native of the county and a man steeped in its vaguely Southern folkways. Yet he could sympathize with his Republican successor that day in the Old Executive Office Building, because Agnew—a fellow politician, after all—was talking about campaign contributions, or so Kahl reported, and not bribes to line his own pocket. The accepted rules of politics in Baltimore County stipulated, Kahl later observed, that such money under no circumstances was to be used for personal enrichment.

Still, Agnew had not been the first to flout the rules. If anything, the recent history of Maryland—and especially Baltimore County—indicated they were honored more often in the breach. One rule that was nearly always adhered to, however, was the rule of silence. The politician in good standing kept his mouth shut and was saluted as a "stand-up guy." The stand-up guys had gone off to jail gracefully, served their time, and come back to the state with a parole and seemingly undiminished stature. A. Gordon Boone, for instance, was speaker of the Maryland House of Delegates in 1963 when he was indicted in connection with a scandal in the state's savings and loan industry. Boone left the legislative chamber with the cheers of his fellow legislators ringing in his ears. On the occasions when the former speaker and ex-con revisited the state capital he was treated not as a pariah who had squandered the trust the public placed in him, but rather as a celebrity. Boone was toasted at the bar of the Maryland Inn, and his table was always crowded with lawmakers listening in rapt fascination to the raconteur spinning tales of the good old days. Gordie Boone, it was said, took the rap for others. He was, bless his heart, a stand-up guy.

Boone was only one of a prominent line of Baltimore County politicians to run afoul of the law. In 1972, Boone's former law partner Daniel B. Brewster was convicted of accepting an illegal gratuity while serving in the United States Senate. Brewster, too, made his home in Baltimore County and rose through the dominant Democratic organization that later weathered four years of Agnew rule in Towson and regained the county executiveship under Dale Anderson. By the summer of 1973, Anderson, too, was in trouble. Boss of all the bosses in the county and a former Democratic national committeeman, he was indicted on forty-three counts, involving bribery, extortion, conspiracy, and tax evasion. His response was simultaneously to proclaim his innocence and his intention to seek re-election. He pledged at a packed synagogue rally in the midst of the 1973 Middle East war that if he had accepted the bribes the government accused him of taking, he would have donated every last cent to the State of Israel. No such pledge was heard from Samuel Green, Jr., Baltimore County's state's attorney, whose indictment around the same time included the charge that he accepted a "carnal bribe" from an accused shoplifter and then reduced the charges against the young lady. Green, apparently, had nothing to offer the Jewish state.

If the evidence against Agnew and the indictment of Anderson are accepted at face value, then Baltimore County had somehow weathered eleven straight years of corrupt political rule and contributed mightily to Maryland's growing reputation as a state of lackadaisical morality. But the county's contribution, though significant, was by no means exceptional. The other sections of the state pitched in, too, adding scandal after scandal until Maryland, once known almost exclusively for fine horses, abundant seafood, and the star-spangled banner that had flown over Fort McHenry, was suddenly challenging such citadels of corruption as New Jersey, Massachusetts, and Illinois for first place in the rogues' gallery of states. President Nixon in November 1973 privately told a group of senators that Agnew's transgressions had been in the Maryland tradition. The sole listener to challenge that remark was the state's senior senator, Charles McC. Mathias, Jr. He received a perfunctory presidential apology.

The President appeared, however, to be on solid ground. Prince George's County had by the 1970s earned a reputation as a developer's paradise, where zoning restrictions fell at the drop of an influential name or, as the U.S. attorney's office documented in back-to-back trials, the offering of a few gifts. In the southern Maryland counties of Charles, Anne Arundel, Calvert, and St. Mary's the great yearning—as enunciated by the politicians from the area—was for the return of the cherished slot machines that somewhere along the line had replaced tobacco as the cash crop of the area. In Anne Arundel County, home to the U.S. Naval Academy and the state capital of Annapolis, the county executive, a Republican named Joseph Alton, acknowledged in 1973 that he, too, was under investigation in the mushrooming kickback scandal. Alton insisted—in an observation most revealing of the mind of a Maryland politician—that while he had probably done some indictable things in his time, he had never done anything wrong!

Across the Chesapeake Bay on the Eastern Shore, the largely conservative residents of this Dixie stronghold had scandals of their own. Their Democratic congressman, Thomas Johnson, had gone to jail in 1970 for his role in the ubiquitous savings-and-loan scandal of the 1960s. His replacement, Rogers C. B. Morton, managed to make it into President Nixon's cabinet as Interior secretary without a blemish attached to his towering form and reputation. But Morton's hand-picked successor, William O. Mills, was not so fortunate. A consummate Rotarian plagued by a succession of personal misfortunes, he was revealed in the Watergate hearings as having received and never reported $25,000 in cash from President Nixon's campaign organization. Mills, apparently unable to reconcile his financial sleight of hand with his Community Chest image, walked out to his stables the morning of May 24, 1973, and fatally wounded himself in the chest with a shotgun, leaving a Republican vacancy in Congress and another blotch on the state's already stained reputation.

In early July 1973, the Watergate hearings in Washington broke yet another Maryland scandal. A fund-raising committee in 1972 had secretly borrowed about $50,000 in cash from the Finance Committee for the Re-Election of the President for the sole purpose of inflating the proceeds of a testimonial gala for the Maryland GOP's favorite son, Spiro T. Agnew. The Vice President, who had troubles aplenty by then, was never implicated in this particular financial chicanery and it seemed he did not even know to what lengths his admirers had gone in an effort to make him appear the formidable fund-raiser. The Salute to Ted Agnew Night Committee was eventually convicted of playing fast and loose with the state's nearly atrophied campaign laws. (A fired-up Anne Arundel County grand jury, having disposed of the Salute to Ted Agnew Night investigation, turned its attention to more Watergate-related disclosures, launching an investigation into Senator J. Glenn Beall's spending of an undisclosed $140,000 in cash during his 1970 campaign. It concluded that he had done so legally.)

For all the misdemeanors being committed out in the provinces, the port city of Baltimore—the state's only city of any consequence—remained Maryland's unchallenged capital of political vertigo, a place where even orthodox political activities seemed to be conducted before a fun-house mirror. Even by Maryland standards the city stood alone. It even had its own accent—or accents—and it was the city that saw no future in Babe Ruth, that horrified even Edgar Allan Poe, and whose major literary figures, H. L. Mencken and Ogden Nash, were eccentrics. The city was forever playing the role of dead-end kid.

In the 1973 legislative session alone, two of Baltimore's state legislators were indicted, one—Senator Clarence Mitchell III—on the pedestrian charge of failing to pay his income taxes for four straight years, the other—Delegate James A. (Turk) Scott—for his attempt to import heroin from New York. Scott, appointed by the local Democratic organization to fill a vacancy in the House of Delegates, was flushed out of the State House in Annapolis by U.S. marshals armed with weapons, a subpoena, and a healthy dose of chutzpah. As the marshals surrounded the legislative chamber, Scott received a note warning him of his imminent arrest. He bolted from his desk and within minutes was racing down an Annapolis street with reporters, onlookers, and the intrepid marshals in frantic pursuit. He was finally cornered a block from the historic State House and taken to Baltimore for arraignment. About three months later, he was found shotgunned dead at close range in the basement parking garage of his Baltimore apartment house.

Scott had been a virtual unknown. When he was arrested, no one seemed to know his background or even his politics. What was known was that he once owned a tavern, had become popular in the neighborhood, worked for the local Democratic organization, and was deserving of reward. While in the House he refrained from speaking and voted, so it was said, as instructed.

The same could not be said, however, for State Senator Frank McCourt. Arrested and jailed in New York in early 1968 on charges of possessing hashish, he was bailed out by a group of the senatorial old guard and escorted back to Annapolis, where his vote was considered crucial to the defeat of the bill that would have outlawed slot machines. Once there, though, he refused to vote. In the end, his vote was not needed, but neither, the organization and the voters decided, was he. McCourt was dropped from the ticket and defeated in the 1970 Democratic primary—the same year he was acquitted on the hashish charge.

Yet the city's voters were willing to condone almost any other kind of political behavior. In many sections of the city, the expression "conflict of interest" engendered nothing but expressions of puzzlement, as if the speaker had just lapsed into a foreign tongue. Protected by the organization, the city's old-line legislators were free to vote—or trade their vote—any way they saw fit.

In 1973, State Senator Joseph J. Staszak, the owner of a tavern that did a brisk trade in bottled liquor and beer, became the principal floor leader for a bill to outlaw the discount selling of beer, wine, and liquor. When Staszak was asked if his actions did not constitute a conflict of interest, he responded, "How does this conflict with my interests?"

On issues of great public concern, not even the organization was immune from pressure. On the rare occasions when such issues were raised—a rent-control bill, a bill to set the ceiling on interest rates—the organization types became populists, and not even the governor and his apparently inexhaustible supply of race-track passes could keep them in line. With most legislative measures, though, this was not the case, and it was not unusual to see the governor's lobbyists closeted with a senator in the men's room off the Senate chamber, handing over track passes or promising that the next patronage job would be his.

As for Democratic Governor Marvin Mandel, by 1973 he had troubles of his own. An undemonstrative man of consummate legislative skills, he shocked the state on July 3 when he announced that he had left his wife of thirty-two years and would marry a southern Maryland divorcee with four children. Almost immediately, his wife, Barbara, issued an announcement of her own. Her husband, she declared, was overworked and in need of psychiatric care; a divorce was out of the question. With that, she dug in at the state-owned Executive Mansion across the street from the State House, forcing Mandel first to an Annapolis hotel and later to a subleased garden apartment. It was not until winter that the scorned woman relented and moved to Baltimore.

Mandel, too, was a Baltimorean to the core. Reared by the organization and educated to the political facts of life at the precinct level, he established himself as the state's dominant politician.[1] He had come up through the legislature, becoming speaker of the House of Delegates in 1963 and then in 1969 the choice of the

---

[1] Like the long-time comptroller of the state, Louis Goldstein, he was Jewish. Maryland, interestingly, ranks second among all states in its percentage of Jews; the estimated Jewish population is 4.68 per cent of the total. New York is first, with 13.79 per cent.

legislature to succeed Agnew. In 1970, he won election on his own, first scaring away all primary opposition—including R. Sargent Shriver—and then vanquishing Agnew's hand-picked candidate, C. Stanley Blair. Mandel carried twenty-two of the state's twenty-three counties and was only deprived of the twenty-third—Garrett—by some ninety votes. Naturally, he swept Baltimore City. In both 1969 and 1973 he offered Maryland a signal lesson of the power of incumbency, collecting first $639,973 and then $917,020 at two dinners in Baltimore's cavernous Civic Center. Typically, most of the money came from individuals and firms that either relied on the state for business or were regulated by the state, especially engineering and architectural firms. But Governor Mandel, under a new policy, later returned $59,750 in contributions from consulting engineers doing business with the state.[2]

Returned donations notwithstanding, it was accepted that if one wanted to do business with the state one had to pay for services or contracts that in some other states were awarded either by random selection or by merit. In Maryland, and especially in Baltimore, political contributions were considered part of the overhead, like the monthly bill from Baltimore Gas and Electric.

Baltimore had been cynically political from its earliest years, when in 1730 it was established by legislative fiat as a market place and port. Within a short time, the city had developed a brawling, pugnacious, and laissez-faire character that it has never lost.

By the middle of the nineteenth century, Baltimore had already been dubbed "Mob Town" for the frequency with which the outraged citizenry rose up and took into their hands either newspaper editors or public servants, depending on the grievance of the moment. In 1858, the Know-Nothing Party had singular success in both Baltimore and Maryland, gaining control of the city government and the state legislature. Democrats or other voters

---

[2] Mandel's fund-raisers, exhibiting all the subtlety of hit-men for the Mafia, also managed to wrangle $500 donation from the Maryland Workshop for the Blind, which maintained snack bars in some of the legislative buildings. Mandel returned the donation.

of questionable allegiance were locked in the basements of homes —"coops"—and held there until the election was over, lest they exercise their franchise in an unpredictable manner. One of those to have the honor of spending election day in a Baltimore "coop" was Edgar Allan Poe. Any citizen who turned to the police for protection was going from the frying pan to the fire. So corrupt was the municipal constabulary that when the Democrats regained control of the state legislature in 1862, they vested control of the Baltimore police department in the governor's office, where it remains to this day. As for the Know-Nothing Party, its stand on slavery—a *status quo* position that seemed to appeal to Marylanders—accounted for the party's survival in the state long after it had become an historic curio elsewhere in the young nation.

With the onset of the Civil War, Baltimoreans lost little time living up to their reputation as brawlers. Union troops passing through the city on their way to battlefields to the south unexpectedly found their first fight in Baltimore. Only the city's strategic importance as a railhead and Maryland's position as the District of Columbia's northern neighbor kept the state and city in the Union and on the winning side. Maryland, though, was reluctantly loyal; it was occupied by Union troops and remained under martial law until the collapse of the South.

By the middle of the twentieth century, Baltimore was no longer a Southern city. It had become a typically Northern, industrial metropolis, the largest big city south of the Mason-Dixon Line (it forms the northern boundary of Baltimore County), and an immigrant center much like New York or Philadelphia—Balkanized along religious and ethnic lines, with a neighborhood or two for each nation of Europe and a political boss to go with it. By 1950, the immigrants in steerage and the hillbillies coming over the Appalachians in search of jobs in steel plants and apartments with steam heat had swollen the city's population to nearly a million. Baltimore then was the sixth largest city in the nation and held nearly half the people who lived in the Free State of Maryland.

The city, like the rest of the state, was heavily Democratic. Except in the old pro-Union strongholds in the mountainous far-western counties and some black enclaves on the Eastern Shore, Republicans were rare. Between 1867, when the state adopted its post-Civil War constitution, and 1974, Marylanders elected eighteen governors, and only four of them were Republicans. During that same period, Republicans controlled only one state Senate—in 1898—and the House of Delegates just three times. In Baltimore County, Agnew's election as county executive in 1962 sent historians scurrying for the record books. The best estimate was that he was the first Republican chosen to head the county government since at least the turn of the century.

Maryland's political history is therefore similar to the history of other Southern or border states. When it came to political allegiance, the city and the countryside were one. Unlike Illinois, there was no downstate vote to offset the achievements of the upstate big city machine; unlike New York, there was no upstate Republican vote to narrow or possibly cancel the margin of the Democratic victory in the metropolis. In Maryland it was simple: whoever won Baltimore more than likely took the state. Because the entire state was Democratic, the primary and not the general election was more often the main event. Whoever could control Baltimore in a low-turnout Democratic primary would control the state of Maryland from Annapolis.

But Baltimore would not come cheaply. Even by the time of the Civil War the city had seized upon election day not as a civic occasion but as a Mardi Gras of sorts. With the mobs kept in place by the gubernatorially controlled police, a different tradition arose. In 1870, Maryland's black population was enfranchised and that political milestone was soon followed by another: the wholesale buying of votes, for the Democrats paid blacks to stay away from the polls because almost to a man they were loyal to the party of Lincoln. From there, it was a just a matter of time before the political bosses discovered that whites, too, could be paid to vote or not vote. And in the city of Baltimore, attracting large numbers of European immigrants (among them Theodore Spiro Anagnostopoulos of Greece, who was later to shorten his name to Agnew), the politicians found many who would take money for their vote, work at the polls on election day, or sit on their hands. They would do, in short, whatever the local Democratic political bosses required of them, in the hope the organization would reward their diligence with a city job or, at the very least, a dignified burial in the New World.

By the time Agnew came home from the European theater in World War II, Baltimore was carved into more independent political duchies than the continent he had just marched across. Each one was tied to the next through an intricate set of feudal relationships. Above the ward bosses stood other bosses, and above them stood the power-brokers, men of keen organizational ability able to hold the whole mishmash together through constant arbitration and delicate negotiations. Occasionally, the supreme organizational chieftain would be an officeholder; more often the boss was a nonofficeholding man of wealth. *Putsch* followed *Putsch*. Alliances came apart over a patronage squabble and new ones formed overnight with the creation of a new Democratic club, sometimes one bearing a national or ethnic title, such as the East Side Polish Club. Whatever the organization chart of the moment, the essential ingredients were money and jobs.

Without money—preferably cash—the organization would dry up, its lubricant gone. Without jobs it had nothing with which to reward the faithful. City Hall and the State House in Annapolis provided the jobs, and candidates for election provided the money. A candidate who could not—or would not—supply the organization with money to handle what were euphemistically called election-day expenses could probably write off his chances in that particular neighborhood. The practice of handing out cash to the organizations had a special Baltimore term—"walking-around money." In other American cities, it was called "street money," but probably nowhere outside a few counties in West Virginia was the practice of dispensing election-day money so openly acknowledged, nor did it play such an important role in politics, as in Baltimore.

Thus, shortly before election day—primary or general—the Baltimore organizations had their hands out. A candidate for governor or mayor would pay an organization for the cost of printing sample ballots, for the salaries of poll workers (usually $15 a day), for car pools, and other costs attendant to a get-out-the-vote effort. But walking-around money also went for the purchase of something else: loyalty. In recent times, $1500 would be enough to buy the loyalty of a state senator, his organization, and, with luck, its votes. A larger amount, sometimes as much as $50,000, would be required for a really powerful boss, somebody like James H. (Jack) Pollack, whose organization, once rooted in the largely Jewish northwest part of the city, sponsored the early political career of Marvin Mandel. Even in 1972, with Pollack's power decidedly on the wane, the forces of George McGovern felt obliged to do business with him. Shortly before the presidential election, $2500 in cash was walked over to Pollack's political headquarters in the futile hope that the aging political capo could turn out his troops.

What a candidate received for his walking-around money was open to question. In some cases, undoubtedly, he got his money's worth—a genuine attempt by the organization to deliver the vote. In a close election, a $1500 investment could make the difference between victory and defeat. In other cases, however, the candidate was simply sold out. The organization took his money, showed him the sample ballots with his name grandly printed at the top, and then, as soon as he was out the door, proceeded to flush them into the municipal sewer system. At the same time, "double dipping"—taking money from two opposing candidates—was not unheard of. Nor was it particularly surprising when the money simply disappeared. Some candidates tried to make the organization account for the money by sending them checks that at least would bear the endorsement of the chieftain. Hubert H. Humphrey, for instance, used checks in Baltimore in 1968 when he ran for President. Barbara Mandel, the governor's wife, cashed an $8000 check to her husband's organization at the race track, so that the walking-around money could be doled out in cash.

Whatever the long-term insidious effect of the quaint Baltimore tradition, it was indisputably expensive. In 1970, J. Glenn Beall, Jr., poured at least $60,000 into Baltimore on election day in unseating Democratic Senator Joseph D. Tydings, the former U.S. attorney who was anathema to the old-line organizations.

Many of the Democratic clubs, caring nothing about so lofty an office as U.S. senator—he appoints no inspectors, no members of the liquor board, and dispenses no race-track passes—simply cut Tydings from the sample ballot. Then they watched in smug satisfaction as the Democratic reformer went down to a narrow defeat. The Tydings loss, though, may have been the organizations' last hurrah. Political change was coming to Baltimore, too. The organizations over the years had been losing their constituents to the suburbs and their patronage to civil service. Not many men would spend a cold November day any more stamping their feet outside a polling place, handing out sample ballots in exchange for $15 and the long-shot chance that the organization would come through with some no-show city job.

Still, walking-around money remained a Baltimore institution if only because no reform-minded candidate seemed willing to challenge the tradition and conclusively prove what many suspected: that the political organizations were impotent. So the practice continued, accepted in the highest councils of American politics. Humphrey enriched Baltimore's election-day economy by about $80,000 in 1968 and narrowly carried Maryland. George McGovern spent about half that amount in 1972 for the privilege of being double-crossed by some of the same organizations that had lined up on election eve pledging fealty to the Democratic ticket. State Senator Verda F. Welcome, a black Baltimore Democrat with a record of civil-rights leadership, suffered little criticism in 1970 when she admitted that the congressional candidate she endorsed had won her heart by paying her more than his rival offered. Nobody batted an eye. After all, some argued, wasn't it better to spend the money in this fashion than to pay a New York advertising firm for a thirty-second television spot? When a traffic light needed fixing, whom could the people turn to after an election—the local boss or some account executive on Madison Avenue?

Still, walking-around money corroded the politics of the city and the state. To many citizens, it seemed that anything was for sale—elections and everything that came with them. There was money on the move in Baltimore, and if a Ted Agnew growing up in the city had not heard the stories about how some of the cash stuck to fingers along the way, he was not keeping his ears open.

For any candidate or officeholder, walking-around money was an enormously expensive campaign burden. In addition to the usual campaign costs—media advertising, salaries, mailings, polling, and the like, a Maryland candidate somehow had to come up with his street cash. In the end, some politicians apparently did so by stretching the rules—by accepting donations over the legal limit and "encouraging" contributions from persons and firms that did business with the state—such as consulting engineers. Over the years, it became accepted in Maryland (and some other states) that the men who made money from the state ought to pay some dues. In many cases, there was nothing illegal in the practice. The state needed the talents of consulting engineers, and if the governor gave a job to a campaign contributor who was qualified as well, who suffered? An Ohio politician called it the "parking-meter syndrome": "Look, you're on the city council and your city needs $400,000 worth of parking meters. Four companies make parking meters, and there isn't a dime's bit of difference between them. Whom do you pick? You give the contract to your friend—the guy who gave to you."

The most essential element of the parking-meter syndrome was one that Spiro T. Agnew adhered to religiously while he was Baltimore county executive and then governor. In no case, he always stressed, did he ever award a contract to an unqualified engineer. In every case, he chose among equals; he chose his friends. In this respect, Agnew was following another Maryland tradition. Already it was well established that whatever largess government had to offer would be bestowed on only the politically deserving. Thus, it was no accident that the state's politicians were often positioned to receive this bounty: they were often in the insurance or real-estate business. If the state required a performance bond for a highway project, arrangements for the bond were usually handled by a politically well-connected insurance agency. Similarly, real-estate or legal work flowed to the real-estate or legal firms that were politically deserving. Private businesses setting their sights on a state contract were encouraged to place their legal or insurance work with the same firms.

To a great extent, the politics of Agnew's Baltimore County were not much different from the politics of the city it surrounded. Unlike some of the other suburban Maryland counties, the old Democratic courthouse organization was never displaced by the new suburbanite passion for open meetings and issues. Instead, it merged with the political clubs moving out from the city in the wake of their constituencies. Along the southern and eastern rim of the county, suburbia was indistinguishable from the city; the neighborhoods had simply rolled across the border. Here, in the tightly compacted blue-collar areas, the Democratic organization established its base. Aligned with the old, rural courthouse crowd, it managed to control the county council through the at-large election of county councilmen. Pluralities built in each of the county districts pushed aside the feeble resistance of the up-county Republicans and reform-minded liberals. Sectors that sent independent legislators to the state capital were frustrated when it came to seating a representative on the county council in Towson.

Moreover, Baltimore County, like Maryland's twenty-two other counties, had long been accustomed to boss rule stemming from the legislative malapportionment that plagued most states prior to the Supreme Court's 1966 one-man, one-vote decision. Until then, every Maryland county—regardless of population—had a single state senator in Annapolis. All the governor's patronage flowed through him. Senatorial courtesy provided that a state senator could veto any appointment for his county, possibly a job for which a loyal party worker had waited for years. Enhancing the senator's power was Maryland's peculiar form of local government. Until the mid-1950s, none of the major counties enjoyed "home rule," and most local issues had to be settled in the legislature in Annapolis. Again, senatorial courtesy prevailed. The salary of the sheriff, the route of a proposed road, the hours during which liquor could be sold—all these and many more issues were in the province of the county's legislative delegation. As a result, a state senator like James A. Pine of Baltimore County could not be ignored. Until the Supreme Court reduced his power, he was virtually the viceroy of his county, and as of 1973 he still remained the single most important element in the organization Dale Anderson had fashioned after Agnew had gone on to bigger and better things in Annapolis. Pine had yet another connection with Anderson. In the winter of 1973, he was accused by the government of accepting money allegedly extorted by Anderson—probably, officials said, to provide his own organization with walking-around money.

These two factors—the rule of the political squires from the rural courthouses, and the dominance of the organization in Maryland's only major city, combined to produce politics that, if judged only by appearances, seemed almost sordid, combining the worst of the Northern big city machine with the worst of the Southern courthouse tradition. Yet, for a time, it worked fairly well. Somewhere along the line, though, the organizations turned rapacious and the courthouse politicians fell victim to attorneys practicing the exotic specialty of zoning law. You could hardly cheat a neighbor whose farm had been in the family for generations, but you could soak the strangers who were moving into new housing developments.

At least for Spiro T. Agnew, Maryland's Southern traditions—and anxieties—proved providential. His 1966 gubernatorial victory was almost entirely fashioned out of the schism within the Democratic Party produced by the unexpected primary victory of the segregationist George Mahoney. Also, the primary and general elections of that year left the Democratic reform movement weak and divided. In 1964, building on new constituencies in Montgomery County and other parts of the state rapidly being populated with northern immigrants, Maryland's liberal reform movement had established a bridgehead with the senatorial election of Joseph Tydings, the crusading former U.S. attorney and Kennedy protégé. Two years later, this wing of the party largely supported the gubernatorial candidacy of Congressman-at-large Carleton Sickles, seemingly a certain winner until he was wiped out by Mahoney in the primary. Sickles had made the mistake of allowing reform to become confused with a civil-rights issue—

open housing—and suffered a fate common to Southern reformers. In 1970, what was left of the reform movement was dealt a double setback—the defeat of Tydings and the victory of Marvin Mandel, speaker of the House and a Baltimorean with solid clubhouse credentials.

So Maryland escaped the reformist purges that periodically sweep other states clean. Even the Republican administration of Governor Theodore Roosevelt McKeldin in the 1950s had been characterized by the lurking presence of reassuring aides from the Democratic clubhouses of Baltimore. Aside from McKeldin, just about the only break in the steady rule of the conservative Democratic coalition in Baltimore County and Annapolis was the election of Agnew—a strictly personal triumph that left the Towson Courthouse and the Annapolis State House in control of Democratic majorities.

In either place, a man did not have to be long on the scene before he sensed that something was in the air. The aroma of corruption was always present. Just before Agnew took over in Towson, the county had been rocked by the "Tar-Baby Scandal"— a run-of-the-mill pea game in which asphalt suppliers shortweighted the county and then split the profit with county officials. Statewide, Maryland was in the throes of a major savings-and-loan scandal. Any young Republican lawyer coming of age in Baltimore County with his nose pressed against the glass of politics could know the stories, the constant rumors of payoffs, the references to others as "bag men." One day spent in the legislature and a bystander could see that something was amiss. Bills mysteriously became lost or were locked in the safes of committee chairmen. Whole delegations switched positions as if controlled by a puppeteer somewhere offstage. Vote-trading was endemic, and "taking a walk" before a critical vote was as routine as seeing the state police combing the legislative compound, the men's rooms, and the nearby bars for missing lawmakers whose votes were needed.

But in Towson and Annapolis Ted Agnew seemed to radiate integrity. This was deceptive, however—in neither place was he the reformer he pretended to be and the media mistook him for.

True, he was a Maryland exotic—a Republican from suburbia who eschewed nights in political clubhouses for the camaraderie and ritual of the Kiwanis. And unlike Christian Kahl, his predecessor in Towson, or Millard Tawes, his predecessor in Annapolis, he came to office beholden to no organization. Instead, he reported to the people, taking his case frequently and forcefully to the same media he would later attempt to chase from the temple. He was trim, neat, and polished. Even his accent was only vaguely Baltimorean, nothing compared to the area's second American language, in which Baltimore came out "Balamore," Calvert became "Kulvert," "Maryland, My Maryland" sounded like "Muralan, Ma Muralan," and the municipal constabulary was referred to as "the poleeces." Agnew was a man of precise diction and esoteric words. In a Maryland where one state legislator rose to say, "This debate has degenerated to a matter of principle," and where one Baltimore mayor had to take speech lessons so he could be understood, Agnew stood out like an Edward Everett Horton of the Chesapeake. He was dignified, too. It would be hard to imagine him joining the boys in Annapolis for a spree with the girls who annually flock to the legislative session like sparrows returning to Capistrano. Nor could anyone imagine him introducing a "bell ringer"—a bill designed strictly to encourage certain interests to pay off—or join his fellow lawmakers on Saint Patrick's Day in a wandering rendition of "Danny Boy," to be followed by a night on the town.

No, Spiro Agnew was a cut above that sort of thing, a breed different from the organization types who ate salami sandwiches at their desks in the legislative chambers and belched into open microphones while defending the rights of "the little man." Agnew was different. Or so it seemed.

4 The Boat Is Leaving

Early in the winter of 1973, there was not a hint on the nightly television news that the world of Spiro T. Agnew was slowly coming apart. In late January and early February, American television viewers were witnessing Agnew the diplomat, speaking softly after having wielded a big, partisan stick for the GOP in the recently concluded campaign. By fiat, Agnew was a presidential emissary, off in the Far East conferring with heads of state on the weightiest of matters—"substantive discussions," White House press secretary Ronald L. Ziegler called them in announcing the tour.

In Saigon Agnew discussed postwar relations with South Vietnamese President Nguyen Van Thieu, and in Phnom Penh he conferred with Cambodian President Lon Nol. Agnew concluded his trip in the Philippines, thanking the government for its assistance in the repatriation of American prisoners of war. Returning home, he was greeted with none of the criticism that had marred his earlier foreign assignments. No longer did American newspapers staff an Agnew trip to report on the blunders of the innocent from Towson. The former provincial from Baltimore County had acquitted himself well. Spiro T. Agnew, the world could see, was a statesman.

What the world did not know, however, was that he was also a man in trouble. By late February, as he learned of the progress of George Beall's investigation, Agnew asked his aide John Damgard to compile a list of all his contacts with Lester Matz since he became Vice President. Agnew himself took his concerns to the very top of the Justice Department and called Attorney General Richard Kleindienst. The attorney general wasted little time communicating the Vice President's anxieties to Beall in Baltimore. Beall commiserated and understood. However, his assistant, Tim Baker, viewed things differently. In repeated arguments with his colleagues, Baker maintained that Kleindienst's calls represented the tentative probings of a man with something to hide. He didn't know what that something was, Baker admitted, but possibly—just possibly—there was a skeleton in Agnew's closet that would come popping out if Baltimore County were thoroughly house-cleaned. Possibly, he conjectured, Agnew had once accepted illegal campaign contributions while he was county executive.

Barney Skolnik, the most experienced and therefore the most influential of the assistant U.S. attorneys assigned to the Baltimore County investigation, greeted Baker's prediction with friendly ridicule, scoffing at the notion that Agnew was a petty crook who would be exposed to the world by a quartet of young prosecutors in Baltimore. In the real world such things did not happen. Skolnik had hauled in some big fish in his time—a senator, two congressmen, and a handful of local politicians—and therefore could speak with authority: each one of those prosecutions had required months of painstaking work; to think that Agnew's head would be serendipitously served up in the midst of the ongoing Baltimore County investigation was sheer fantasy.

Baker, after a while, retreated before the strength of this fast-talking New Yorker's logic, unable to summon up a more convincing argument than that Agnew was "acting like a guilty man." Still, he clung to his suspicions, sitting silently as his Agnew prediction became a stock joke among his colleagues. Ronald Liebman, too, joined in, altering one of the comic routines he had memorized when he was a drummer on the borscht circuit of the Catskill Mountains. Skolnik and Liebman, two prosecutors with a ready wit, worked him over, leading him from one straight line to the next until he was dizzy.

Among the three, Baker, the son of one of Baltimore's leading real-estate men, was the odd man out. Tall, blond, wealthy, and secure by birth, there was no public school in his past; it was a prep school, then Williams College, and finally Harvard Law. But after Harvard, Tim Baker broke the pattern. Instead of a secure position in a Baltimore or New York law firm, Baker and his wife, Betsy, joined the Peace Corps and spent two years in Liberia. When they returned to Baltimore, Baker had two job offers. The first was from Stephen Sachs, the former U.S. attorney who had since gone into private practice, the second from the new U.S. attorney, George Beall. He asked Sachs for advice and wound up accepting the job with Beall, a choice Baker never regretted.

From the day Baker signed on in August 1971, he became Skolnik's protégé at corruption trials. They formed an odd pair: Skolnik, irrepressibly sloppy and lackadaisical except when fired up by something that interested him; Baker, a disciplined worker of nearly compulsive work habits. Together they were energized by the importance and drama of their work, and they had a great time at it. Even in the grand jury room they happily, sometimes even playfully, complemented each other. First Baker would politely interrogate a witness, softening him up. When he finished, he would turn to Skolnik and whisper, "Go get him, Tiger." It was a variation of the nice-guy, bad-guy routine detectives used when questioning suspects in a station house.

As Baker learned his new business, his admiration for Skolnik grew. Eventually, he began to talk like his mentor, picking up whole phrases from him. You could talk to one, then the other, and hear the same speech almost in duplicate.

Ron Liebman, too, looked up to Skolnik. Like Baker, he was a Baltimorean; unlike his colleague he was the product of the city's public schools, Western Maryland College, and the University of Maryland Law School. Liebman, though, was better than his schooling—a fact apparent to one of Baltimore's leading criminal law firms, Melnicove, Greenberg and Kaufman, which hired him after he had completed a clerkship under Judge R. Dorsey Watkins of the U.S. District Court. Liebman also had applied to Beall for a job and seized the opportunity to join the federal prosecuting team when a vacancy occurred in August 1972. His law firm allowed him to leave with its blessing, believing he would be a better and more experienced lawyer after a term as an assistant U.S. attorney. In Liebman, Skolnik had another disciple in the making. With the start of the Baltimore County investigation, Skolnik asked Beall for Liebman's services. At first, the self-described rookie simply watched Skolnik and Baker. In the interrogation room and before the grand jury, he said little and listened a great deal.

By the time Agnew's name was first introduced by Matz, the team of Skolnik, Baker, and Liebman was in place, with Skolnik clearly the leader—and expressing nothing but doubt about Baker's Agnew prophecy. In the months to come, Skolnik clung to this position, summoning all the logic at his command to rebut the growing evidence that the trail of corruption that began in Towson was leading straight to Washington. For as witnesses came in and talked about corruption in Baltimore County, Agnew's name did indeed crop up from time to time, although always in a very soft way; a witness would say the practice of payoffs had gone on for years, and he *thought* Agnew was or *must have been* party to it; some other county official had received money and the witness *had heard* the official was a bagman for Agnew but didn't know for sure himself. To Skolnik this didn't seem to matter all that much, because the statute of limitations had run out on Agnew's Baltimore County years, and besides, who could believe that the Justice Department would permit an investigation of the Vice President of the United States to go forward on such iffy testimony? There was a fantasy flavor to the prospect that Skolnik did not relish. He repeatedly lectured his juniors that if Agnew was out there, he would be flushed out by standard investigatory techniques. Now was not the time for an end run. The business at hand was political corruption in Baltimore County, where, at last, some progress was being made.

While Agnew was en route to the Far East in Air Force Two, Robert Browne's IRS agents were poring over the corporate records hauled out of Baltimore County in January. Daily, the agents combed the books of the subpoenaed corporations, logging incoming and outgoing checks in a methodical search for the slightest hint that cash was being generated. Finally, in the books of the architectural firm of Gaudreau, Inc., the agents struck gold. Shortly after the firm received an installment payment from the county government for the design of a public building, it would issue a check to a corporate officer, and the amount of the check was almost always 5 per cent of the recent installment from the county. This seemed like an unmistakable method for generating cash. The Gaudreau firm, the agents concluded, was probably kicking back 5 per cent of its fees—half as much as the going rate in New Jersey, but still a considerable sum.[1]

The agents promptly reported their findings to Browne, who checked again with his counterparts in New Jersey. The New Jersey IRS was not surprised; engineers and architects were the soft touches of the construction industry and therefore the easiest to extort. Unlike the ruggedly independent builders or any of the building tradesmen, the designers were invariably college-educated men with little or no inclination for a brawl. In addition, they were generally the proprietors of firms with many employees and unlike the builders could not pick up a crew at the union hall, so the loss of a contract could mean layoffs and economic ruin.

Acting on the latest advice from the Garden State and the pattern spotted in Gaudreau's books, Baker authorized a second wave of subpoenas, this time demanding the records of the seven design firms—engineering or architectural—that had done the greatest dollar volume of Baltimore County work during the previous two years. One of the firms subpoenaed in that manner was Matz, Childs and Associates, which like Gaudreau was enjoying a financially rewarding relationship with the county govern-

---

[1] The government later charged that Gaudreau had paid Dale Anderson $23,920 in bribes between November 1968 and March 1972.

ment. And with the latest round of subpoenas disposed of, Baker turned his attention to the president of Gaudreau, Inc.; Paul Gaudreau was to mean as much in his own way to the future of Spiro T. Agnew as Richard Nixon had meant to his past.

Paul Gaudreau, it turned out, was in no mood for a fight. At fifty-nine, he was no longer in good health, having recently been hospitalized for the removal of cataracts. For years, Gaudreau was later to admit, he had been kicking back a percentage of his fees on county contracts. Unlike some of his peers, he had no ready excuse for his actions. He was wrong and he knew it. A religious man, who had received his architectural degree from the Catholic University of America, Gaudreau was also a troubled man. When a second subpoena from Baker arrived asking for his personal records, Gaudreau greeted it like a visit from a priest. His mind set, the architect was determined to purge his soul. There would be no shenanigans from him about testifying. He called his lawyer, Nevitt Steele, a former assistant U.S. attorney and a friend of Skolnik's, and authorized what turned out to be the first deal the prosecutors struck.

Among Baltimore's lawyers, Nevitt Steele enjoyed a unique reputation. In a city that cherished the cabal, Steele was without guile. With Steele, Skolnik would have no need to fence. But Steele was also an experienced lawyer, as familiar as any attorney in Baltimore with Skolnik's methods, especially his pitch to coax potential witnesses into cooperating.

"Look," Skolnik would say, "the boat is filling up. When it does, it will be too late for your client." This meant, to a lawyer, that witnesses had already come forward and were cooperating with the government. The more witnesses who cooperated, the less chance the lawyer's client would have of striking a deal and gaining immunity.

On the day Steele walked into Skolnik's office, however, the prosecutor was at the helm of an empty boat. Not a single witness had come forward; not a single deal had been struck. The harsh fact was that the investigation of Baltimore County corruption, trumpeted in the local press when the government had seized the county's records and hauled them off in a truck, was going nowhere fast. Its unannounced but apparent goal of indicting Dale Anderson was as elusive as ever. Outside the courthouse offices of the U.S. attorney, the street talk was that the investigation was a dud, that the truckload of records was a paper monument to its failure.

But Steele could not have cared less about the conventional street wisdom of the moment. He came straight to the point. "I told my client that the boat was undoubtedly not yet full," he said. Could they make a deal? The startled Skolnik had his first passenger.

Paul Gaudreau in all respects was a dream witness. Aristocratic in bearing, dignified in manner, not only was he likable, he was also believable. A jury, the prosecutors concluded, would accept both the man and his testimony; as for them, they already loved him.

It was January 25 when Gaudreau came to the Baltimore courthouse to admit that he had been kicking back a portion of his fees to William E. Fornoff, the administrative officer of Baltimore County and Anderson's number-one aide. There was no need to hide the architect's presence in the building that day. In Texas, Lyndon B. Johnson was being buried near the Pedernales River he loved, and government workers had been given the day off. Later, though, Gaudreau was treated like the hot property he was. Along with some other valuable witnesses, he was allowed to enter the grand jury room in full view of waiting reporters. With the door closed behind him, Gaudreau was whisked before the panel and was out in thirty seconds. The conclusion seemed inescapable: he was apparently refusing to cooperate.

Gaudreau, the first major witness in a procession of many that eventually led the prosecutors to Agnew, ironically provided the government with information that, if anything, gave Agnew a reprieve. Although Gaudreau had been receiving large public-works contracts in Baltimore County for years, he had not been forced to kick back a portion of his fees until the Anderson administration took over in Towson. He gave the administration of County Executive Agnew nothing in exchange for the contracts he won under Agnew's tenure. So for a while what vague scent of corruption the prosecutors may have sniffed whenever Agnew's name surfaced, seemed to be contradicted by the solid information from Gaudreau.

Although Gaudreau's cooperation with the government remained a secret, lawyers visiting the U.S. attorney's office could sense that something had changed after January 25. If it was only a newly acquired cockiness on the part of the prosecutors, an experienced criminal lawyer soon got the idea that the boat had a first-class passenger. And Gaudreau soon had company. Within days, two of the engineers subpoenaed by Baker signed aboard. Again the revelations were similar. Again it was Fornoff, and again, when the witnesses were asked to provide the names of other engineers who might also be kicking back, the same names surfaced: Matz, Childs and Associates; and Jerome B. Wolff. The name of Wolff would haunt the investigation from the winter day in late January when his name was first mentioned until the muggy summer day in July when his testimony sealed the case against Agnew. Already the two engineers who had joined Gaudreau in cooperating had supplied deeply incriminating information about Wolff.

Among his fellow engineers, the brilliant Wolff was hailed as a genius, and it was at least true that he was nationally recognized for his expertise in the new and complex field of environmental planning. He was both lawyer and civil engineer, able to provide legal and scientific advice to a client concerned about the environmental impact of a particular project. Short, compact, and robust at the age of fifty-nine, Wolff was justly proud of his professional standing, honored that other engineers turned to him when they had a seemingly insoluble problem. He considered himself to be above all a scientist; certainly, he was no mere hack engineer lusting for a municipal sewer contract. His hobby, fittingly, was astronomy; his compulsion, ominously for Ted Agnew, was record-keeping.

To others who were not engineers, Wolff was far better known for a different reason—his long and enduring relationship with Ted Agnew. Thumb out, Wolff had hitched a ride with him from Towson to Annapolis and finally to Washington. In Washington, he held the title of vice-presidential adviser for science and technology until 1970, when he returned to private business.[2] In Annapolis, where he was the Agnew-appointed chairman of the State Roads Commission, Wolff performed a pivotal task—he advised the governor on the awarding of state engineering contracts.

In the winter of 1973, though, what the prosecutors were hearing about Wolff had nothing to do with Agnew. Jerry Wolff was just another engineer, president of Greiner Environmental Systems, Inc., a subsidiary of one of Maryland's largest engineering firms, the J. E. Greiner Co. Wolff's firm, the prosecutors were hearing, was one of those that was kicking back a portion of its fees. Routinely, another subpoena was authorized by Baker. When Wolff received it, he took two actions to protect himself: he called a lawyer—and he sent a message to Agnew.

For the moment, though, Wolff and his significance were lost in the rush of events. The pieces were beginning to fall into place. Skolnik was exhilarated. Dealing up was his game, and now he was beginning to hold some cards. Gaudreau and the engineers would bring in Fornoff, and he in turn would bring in Anderson. From there, who could tell? It meant building a human pyramid, stepping on one man to get to another. That was a game Skolnik relished, and he played it exceedingly well. When things were humming, as they were now, Skolnik would rise from his chair, pace behind his desk, and sing. At Harvard, he had earned spending money as a choirboy. He was no choirboy now.

Since 1968, when he had helped the then U.S. attorney, Steve Sachs, retry former Maryland congressman Thomas Johnson, Skolnik had specialized in ferreting out political corruption. First under Sachs and then under Beall, Skolnik had produced an enviable list of convictions for corruption, including those of senator Daniel B. Brewster of Maryland; congressman John Dowdy of Texas; Jesse Baggett, a former member of the Prince George's County Council; a major builder from the same county, Ralph Rocks; and even a zoning lawyer with whom Rocks and Baggett

---

[2] According to Agnew associates, Wolff was discharged by the Vice President when he learned that his adviser had retained an interest in two engineering companies. Wolff was ordered off the payroll by White House Counsel John W. Dean III, who ruled Wolff had a conflict of interest.

did business. Skolnik got the hapless lawyer, William Kahler, for perjury. By 1973, Skolnik was an acknowledged expert on bribery law, surely one of the most sophisticated and experienced practitioners of this exotic specialty in the employ of the Justice Department. Unlike the bulk of the 1300 other assistant U.S. attorneys in the nation—young men who suffered the relatively low pay for a few years in order to gain the experience in criminal law that would bring handsome dividends in private practice—Skolnik was becoming a career man. Only George Beall's deputy, Paul Kramer, had been in the office longer than he.

As a result of his experience and the nature of the cases he had worked on, Skolnik more than any other assistant U.S. attorney in Baltimore knew the workings of the bureaucratic layer above him —the Justice Department thirty-nine miles away in Washington. In 1970, he and Sachs had had a bruising encounter with that bureacracy, and it had determined to a large extent how the Baltimore outpost of the Justice Department would handle what was soon to become an investigation of the Vice President of the United States. A special federal grand jury under Sachs had attempted to indict a Maryland contractor on charges that he illegally attempted to have the government honor $5 million in claims resulting from work on the Rayburn House Office Building on Capitol Hill. The case was complex, and a political can of worms. Some of the biggest names in Congress were involved —some, the grand jury felt, criminally—and it attempted to indict these. But the grand jury was rebuffed by the Justice Department under John Mitchell, then attorney general. He ordered Sachs not to sign the indictment, rendering it moot; the criminal division of the Justice Department, he said, disagreed with the way Sachs had handled the case and saw no reason for an indictment. But a different explanation was rumored—that Mitchell had killed the indictment for political reasons, hoping to ingratiate the Nixon administration with Russell B. Long, chairman of the Senate Finance Committee, who was involved in the case.

The angry and frustrated grand jurors then attempted an end run. Instead of indicting the members of Congress, they settled on Frenkil, hoping that at his trial the roles of the various congressmen would become public. Again Mitchell stepped in, ordering Sachs to withhold his signature from the indictment. Sachs, a Democrat about to leave office anyway, resigned in protest, turning the grand jury over to his successor, George Beall. After studying the case, Beall also tried for an indictment but was slapped down by Mitchell. The new U.S. attorney finally had to dismiss the grand jury.

Skolnik, who featured himself a bit of a radical,[3] read politics into Mitchell's decision and contracted a skepticism that stuck with him for the duration of the Agnew investigation. As a result, his constant counsel to Beall was to keep the Justice Department ignorant of the investigation until only a blatantly political directive could abort it. By then, of course, Elliot L. Richardson was the attorney general and much had changed at the building on Constitution Avenue.

As a result of his prosecutorial experience, Skolnik was the undisputed leader of the assistant U.S. attorneys assigned to the investigation of political corruption in Baltimore County. Even Beall, just three years his senior, treated him as an equal and relied on his advice every step of the way. Skolnik, reviewing the evidence already assembled, decided that the next thing to do was to bring to terms Lester Matz, his partner John Childs, and Jerry Wolff, none of whom were turning out to be cooperative.

In fact, it was their very lack of cooperation that first aroused the suspicions of the prosecutors. Originally, they had been just three more engineers caught in the net thrown over Baltimore County's engineering industry. More and more, though, the prosecutors were hearing their names. They offered all three immunity from prosecution in return for their cooperation, but when they were summoned before the grand jury, all three invoked their Fifth Amendment rights against self-incrimination. It was a most peculiar performance. By invoking their right against incriminating themselves, all three were in the prosecutors' eyes

---

[3] To his regret, he had been ordered to prosecute the so-called Catonsville Nine, the group of anti-Vietnam War activists who broke into a Selective Service office in May 1971, burning its records with home-made napalm, splashing animal blood on some of them, and scattering others along a nearby railroad track.

admitting they had something to hide. Whatever it was, the prosecutors were determined to find out. Already, there were hints that the firm of Matz, Childs and Associates was worth investigating. Its rapid success in the highly competitive engineering field was reason enough for suspicion.

Of the approximately two hundred engineering firms in Maryland, Matz, Childs was by far one of the most prosperous. Founded in 1955 with only a small nucleus of engineers, the company eighteen years later had more than three hundred and fifty employees and was ranked the ninety-second largest design firm in the nation. In the last decade, more than half of its contracts—231 in all—were awarded by various government agencies, notably those headquartered in Towson. From what the prosecutors had already learned, it seemed doubtful that Matz, Childs and Associates owed its success only to the quality of its work. In Baltimore County, success did not come with hard work alone.

In addition to all that, the corporation's books, now in the hands of Browne's IRS agents, were turning informer. Matz, like Gaudreau before him, stood by helplessly as the seemingly meaningless entries made by anonymous accountants fell into a pattern that told a story. Once again, the IRS agents were finding indications that cash was being generated. What made them suspicious was the way in which the Matz, Childs firm rewarded some of its key employees with bonuses. Nothing can look so suspicious to an IRS agent as a pattern of bonuses. A cooperating employee, an IRS agent knows, can give the bonus back to the firm in cash almost immediately, retaining just enough to pay his income tax on it. In the case of Matz, Childs and Associates, the cash accumulated in this fashion was kept in a wall safe. And the books of Matz, Childs and Associates tantalized the IRS agents for another reason. The firm frequently used the services of a consultant already under investigation as a suspected bag man and money launderer. The agents suspected that the only service this particular consultant provided the firm was a kickback of his fee (less, of course, his percentage).

Taken together, the pattern of bonuses and the steady use of the consultant was a suspicious bundle of information, but it was not hard enough evidence. In order to breathe life into the cold ledgers someone would have to talk. Matz and Childs would not; they had already been before the grand jury and taken the Fifth Amendment. So Baker turned logically enough to the employees themselves, the ones who had been receiving bonuses. On April 10, he subpoenaed six of the highest-ranking employees of the firm and directed them to appear before the grand jury on Thursday, April 12. Then Baker set his trap.

Baker naturally expected that the Matz, Childs employees, like the firm's owners, would invoke the Fifth Amendment before the grand jury. Therefore, he decided to take them before a judge and confer "use immunity" on them. A relatively new legal device enacted by the Nixon administration, use immunity enabled a prosecutor to compel a witness to answer any question put to him before the grand jury, in exchange for which the witness was granted immunity so that anything he admitted to under the line of questioning could not be used against him in any prosecution for a crime. It was a *quid pro quo* that honored the witness's Fifth Amendment right while also compelling him to testify. The witness could still be prosecuted on evidence the government had learned independently. In the case of the Matz, Childs employees, use immunity was a perfect solution. Beall's staff had no interest in prosecuting them. All they wanted was information with which to build a case against Matz and Childs, who in turn might prove instrumental in the investigation of Fornoff and Anderson.

Joseph H. H. Kaplan had been expecting the prosecutors to subpoena the Matz, Childs employees, whom he was now also representing. He advised them to invoke the Fifth Amendment, forcing the government to fish elsewhere for its information. So confident was Kaplan of his defensive parry that he planned to be in Delaware later in the day, attending to the problems of a different client. Kaplan had to break that appointment. While he stood helplessly by, the confused and panicked Matz, Childs employees were whisked before a judge, use-immunized, and escorted by a triumphant Baker into the grand jury room. There, one by one, they confirmed the suspicions of the IRS agents. They had been kicking back their bonuses.

Suddenly, both Lester Matz and John Childs were in very bad trouble—tax trouble, to be precise. Their firm had been deducting the bonuses as wages—a legitimate business expense—but now there was abundant evidence that the bonuses were not salaries at all. The employees themselves were not sure exactly what one would call them. Bribes? Illegal campaign contributions? Cash for the apartment of a mistress? Whatever it was, it was not deductible.

Word of what happened in the grand jury room was soon flashed to Washington. Matz, who all along had been receiving pep talks from Agnew via Bud Hammerman, was no longer confident. Wolff, too, was beginning to feel pressed, knowing that only a steadfast Matz stood between him and total incrimination. Abandoning Hammerman as an intermediary, Wolff sat down and wrote directly to the Vice President in Washington. Choosing his words meticulously in case the letter was read by a vice-presidential aide, Wolff composed what one of the prosecutors later called a "carefully worded scream for help" that left little doubt that it was in Agnew's best interest that the investigation be halted. Having mailed the letter, Wolff destroyed his only copy, reciting it later from memory.

In Washington, Agnew realized—possibly for the first time— that he was being inexorably drawn into Beall's investigation. He did what so many before him had done—he called a lawyer. His choice was Charles W. Colson, President Nixon's former special counsel, who had left the White House just two months before to establish a private law practice in Washington. Now a partner in the law firm of Colson and Shapiro, he had become friendly with Agnew during his White House years. In a way, the two were alike: both were gut fighters of the first magnitude. In a Washington used to "hardball" politics, Chuck Colson stood out because he threw a spitter. (In a famous memo leaked to the press, Colson wrote that he was correctly quoted when he said he "would walk over my grandmother if necessary" to insure the re-election of Nixon.[4])

---

[4] Before Christmas 1973, Colson reported he had found a "relationship with Christ." In March 1974, he was indicted in the Watergate case.

Yet he was not only a political street fighter, but also a tactician. During the 1972 presidential campaign, his assignment had been the special-interest groups—primarily ethnic blocs and labor—that for years had been part of the Democratic coalition and that Colson, aided by the divisive candidacy of George Mc-Govern, helped pry loose for Nixon. These same groups now formed a major part of the constituency that Agnew called his own, one he could rally, if need be, when the chips were down.

But harried and preoccupied with the preparation of his own Watergate defense, Colson could not take on Agnew's case himself. Instead, he and his partner, David Shapiro, approached a third partner, Judah H. Best, and asked him to handle it. It was, the two senior partners told Best, a simple matter of liaison. Get in touch with George Beall in Baltimore, and tell him you represent the Vice President. Tell him that Agnew had heard "cocktail-party rumors" about the investigation and was afraid he might be harmed by prejudicial publicity. Tell him also that the Vice President has no intention of impeding the investigation.

On April 17, five days after the grand jury appearance of the Matz, Childs employees, Judah Best momentarily put aside the legal concerns of his partner Colson, and the preparation of his defense, and called Beall in Baltimore, introducing himself as the lawyer for Vice President Agnew. He arranged an appointment for two days later. Beall was not surprised by the call. He thought it natural that Agnew would retain an attorney. What puzzled him was the firm chosen and especially the reputation of its best-known partner. Why hadn't Agnew chosen local counsel —his friend George White, for instance?

It was not a day, though, for either man to be concerned about the Vice President. The eyes of the nation were on the White House, where the President, after months of ostrich-like behavior on the Watergate scandal, finally had something to say. He announced that after "serious charges" were brought to his attention nearly a month before, he had ordered a new, "intensive" investigation into the Watergate burglary and cover-up. The investigation, the President said, had produced "major developments" and "real progress" in finding the truth about the Watergate break-in. Ziegler, the President's press secretary, capped Nixon's announcement by declaring that all previous White House statements were "inoperative."

The startling White House admissions served only to mask other sordid events unfolding behind the scenes. Already, Nixon was demanding the resignation of his counsel, John W. Dean III, and weighing whether he also would have to sacrifice his two most trusted aides, H. R. (Bob) Haldeman and John D. Ehrlichman. At the Justice Department that very day L. Patrick Gray III, the acting director of the FBI, admitted to Henry E. Petersen, the assistant attorney general in charge of the criminal division, that he had destroyed the files removed from the White House safe of E. Howard Hunt, Jr., one of the original Watergate conspirators.

By the end of April, Gray, Dean, Ehrlichman, and Haldeman along with Attorney General Kleindienst would be gone from the government and a new group would take over. Elliot Richardson would move from Defense to Justice and William D. Ruckelshaus from the Environmental Protection Agency to Gray's old FBI office, and eventually to Justice as Richardson's deputy attorney general. Only Petersen would remain in place, as the government went into a tailspin caused nearly a year before by what Ziegler once called a "third-rate burglary."

Dean, the once-trusted presidential lawyer, was in seclusion, but his version of Watergate was now leaking all over Washington, casting a pall of suspicion over the entire Nixon administration. In all the stories, in all the accusations and allegations that surfaced as members of the White House team began to cannibalize each other, there was no suggestion that Agnew was in the least way connected with Watergate or any of its ramifications. Once again, he had come through clean, growing in stature if only because those around him were diminished by the scandal. More and more he was viewed as the possible savior of the GOP, the one man untarnished by the spreading stain of Watergate.

On April 19, the day Dean escalated his struggle for survival by announcing he would not be the White House's Watergate "scapegoat," Jud Best set out for his appointment with Beall in

Baltimore—and reassurance that Agnew's image would not be sullied by rumors surrounding an investigation that had nothing to do with him. In the office of the U.S. attorney, Best followed his instructions closely, describing Agnew's concern and his willingness to cooperate. Solicitous as usual, Beall assured Best that he would make every effort to see that the Vice President's good name and reputation were not damaged by the investigation. Of course, he had no control over other lawyers or witnesses and could not censor what they might tell the press, but as for the investigation itself, Best could tell his client that he had nothing to worry about. It did not involve Agnew. After fifteen minutes, the two men parted with the understanding that Best would check back from time to time to see if anything had changed.

Upon his return to Washington, Best walked the one and one half blocks from his law office to the Old Executive Office Building and his first meeting with his new client. He reported to Agnew on his meeting with Beall and left. It was the beginning of a long relationship that was to consume Best's spring, summer, and fall. When nine-year-old Stephen Best returned to school four months later, he wrote an essay that told the whole story.

"My father is the lawyer of the Vice President of the United States," Stephen Best wrote. "So we could not go anywhere, but we had a fun time at home. We are planning to go on a trip soon."

5 Say You Gave at the Office

A year before Ted Agnew's name was injected into the Baltimore County corruption investigation by Lester Matz, Barnet Skolnik put down his prosecutorial whip and turned to the no less gentle practice of presidential politics. He quit the office of the U.S. attorney in Baltimore and joined the campaign of Senator Edmund S. Muskie of Maine, which then seemed to be embarked on a smooth and relatively uneventful road to the Democratic nomination. Skolnik had always wanted to be in politics, but he soon realized he had hitched his wagon to a sputtering star. Bogged down writing issue papers in a Washington office, Skolnik left, went to Europe for several months, and in early September 1972 asked for and got his old job back with George Beall. Beall was only too happy to have his ace prosecutor on the team again, but on one condition—that Skolnik shave off the beard he had grown during his brief flirtation with politics and vagabondage. On his first day back, Skolnik went to lunch with Tim Baker, and as they returned from the restaurant, Baker asked him how he thought a certain Maryland political figure then under investigation

69

would feel when he learned that Skolnik, his nemesis, was back on the job.

Skolnik looked at Baker and smiled.

"Terrorized," he said with a laugh.

Baker understood. It was not that Skolnik enjoyed terrorizing potential witnesses or defendants. It was, rather, that Skolnik appreciated the utility of fear. He recognized it as a tool of his trade. Pleasant enough in a social situation, Skolnik could quickly adopt the posture of an inquisitor when in the interrogation or grand jury room. He could question in a way that would bring sweat to a witness' brow and drain blood from his face. Jerry Wolff told others that his "blood froze" when Skolnik grinned and said, "I got Congressman Johnson, and I'll get you." The terrifying element, Wolff said, was the grin. With other witnesses, Skolnik used different techniques. Suddenly, his voice would explode in the witness's face: "Why are you lying to us?" Most lawyers considered it rough but within the bounds of fair play. As stories of Skolnik's methods made the rounds, his reputation grew, until by spring a summons from the prosecutor was greeted in certain quarters of the engineering community like a visit from the Angel of Death. Baker and Liebman, who watched Skolnik in action, took mental notes and attempted to emulate his ways. Baker, for one, was critical of himself for his inability to make his own tough-guy routine appear convincing.

It was therefore understandable that many lawyers with clients being investigated by the U.S. attorney's office preferred to deal with Beall. The U.S. attorney for Maryland was known as a decent man who lacked Skolnik's guile and tenacity. Throughout the spring, it became common practice for a lawyer to try to get alone with Beall, to win from him a concession that Skolnik had earlier rebutted with a laugh. But invariably when the meeting took place, Skolnik would be there, too. The reason was simple: George Beall at the age of thirty-five was a neophyte as a criminal lawyer. Until his appointment as U.S. attorney, he had mostly handled negligence cases for a large Baltimore law firm. Had it not been because of a patronage squabble between his patron, Senator Mathias, and Agnew, he would have come into his job cold. As it was, an internecine struggle for supremacy within the Maryland GOP delayed the appointment for several months, during which time Beall was a frequent visitor to the office of Stephen Sachs, conferring with the outgoing U.S. attorney on cases then under investigation. Beall was, everyone conceded, a quick learner but he had a long way to go.

When Beall finally took office in August 1970, the reporters covering the federal courthouse settled down for what they thought would be a soporific tenure. In a short time, though, Beall proved them wrong. He energetically pursued drug pushers and the industrial polluters of the state's waters; in cooperation with the IRS, he pioneered a technique of bringing drug suppliers to account through the use of tax laws. Slowly, he made a name for himself, although he was forever in the shadow of his late father and his older brother.

In appearance, George Beall was a striking man. Handsome, with a wide, toothy smile and carefully combed hair, he was every inch the son of a senator—poised, articulate, and endowed with what many considered to be excellent political instincts. Yet, for all that, Beall appeared to lack leadership qualities, and it was not surprising that many in Maryland firmly believed that Skolnik was leading him around by the nose. This scenario, however, lacked subtlety. Beall was very much his own man; if Skolnik was leading him, it was because Beall wanted to travel in that direction.

Like Baker and Liebman, Beall began to pick up Skolnik's phrases. Men under investigation were called "bad men." Jerry Wolff was called "a very bad man" because they thought he was significantly more corrupt than most of the other engineers. In a way, the prosecutors employed terms like these to condition themselves for the job at hand—mean, nasty work that often entailed sending a man to jail. It was one thing to dispose of a mugger in that fashion, but quite another thing when it came to men very much like themselves—college-educated, middle class, articulate. These were not street people, but men with roots in the community. The humiliation of jail was total and absolute. It destroyed families, careers, and the men themselves.

The power of the Baltimore prosecutors thus was great. Judges generally abided by the recommendation of the U.S. attorney at sentencing time: if he told the court that the convicted defendant had been cooperative and that jail would be unwarranted, the judge was likely to follow that recommendation; if, on the other hand, the government informed the court that the defendant had been recalcitrant and deserving of jail, the judge was likely to follow that recommendation, too. Thus, when a lawyer entered into negotiations with the government, his primary concern was "final disposition"—jail or no jail. All the rest—attempts to gain immunity from prosecution or an agreement that would allow the client to plead guilty to a lesser charge—was only frosting on the cake. What really concerned the client was jail, the ultimate disgrace.

When a prosecutor ran across an uncooperative witness—men like Matz, Childs, or Wolff—he chased him with a special relish. In the unwritten code of prosecutors, no man could be permitted to thumb his nose at the government, and if he did, the prosecutor detoured his investigation to bring the witness to terms. Then, with the government's case developed, he would hammer at the witness unceasingly, threatening imprisonment and the disgrace that went with it. The potential witness, in John Ehrlichman's phrase, would hang twisting in the wind. Trapped, he would finally decide to cooperate. And once that decision was made— once that line was crossed—there was almost nothing that could drag a witness back to his original position. He became malleable, often zealous, willing to report fact and hearsay.

At that point, the chase ended. The prosecutor who for months had been stalking his man suddenly became his confidant and protector, looking out after his interests and massaging his psyche. Slowly, the prosecutor would rehabilitate the witness he had so recently leveled and prepare him for the moment when he was to appear before a judge and jury and offer his testimony. Instead of a wreck of a man with stuttering voice and trembling hands, the jury would see a confident and—the prosecutor hoped—believable witness.

By April, this process was just beginning for Matz, Childs,

Wolff, and Fornoff. The four had retained some of the best legal talent in Baltimore and were well prepared for a fight. Fornoff, already doomed by the testimony of Gaudreau and others, had hired Stephen Sachs, who in the two years since he had resigned as U.S. attorney had earned a national reputation as a criminal lawyer. (In the Watergate hearings that spring, he represented the former director of the FBI, L. Patrick Gray III.)

Matz and Childs, who had already retained Joseph Kaplan, in February had also hired Arnold Weiner, who was Wolff's lawyer as well. At thirty-nine, Weiner was regarded as Sachs's peer. Since the mid-1960s, when he, too, had been an assistant U.S. attorney working as one of Sachs's chief prosecutors, he had matched wits with Skolnik several times, including the Baggett and Rocks trials. Erudite and worldly, with a love for the cinema and the theater, Arnold Weiner was known as the best deal-maker in Baltimore.

By April, Weiner had emerged as the chief strategist for Matz, Childs, and Wolff. As a lawyer for all three, he had an overview that the prosecution could not hope to obtain for months to come. Unlike the other lawyers, he was working in the half-light of some knowledge, and already he had framed his strategy. Unlike his co-counsel Kaplan, Weiner entertained no doubts that Beall would prosecute Agnew—especially if Skolnik cajoled him into it. He knew that the information his clients had was far from worthless —as Kaplan for a time believed. So he decided on a waiting game. Let the government build its case. For the kind of information his clients possessed, the boat would always come back. Kaplan, though, was becoming uneasy and was counseling Matz to cooperate with the government. The young lawyer was a brooder. Since January, he had been living with an awesome secret and now it was eating at his innards.

Of the two strategies, Matz opted for Weiner's. He, too, appreciated the value of his information. But even more than that, he appreciated that scorn and ostracism would rain upon him for being the man who turned informer on the Vice President of the United States. What seemed to chill Matz even more than a jail term was the prospect of his picture on the cover of *Time* magazine. Even as he began to appreciate that he would eventually have to cooperate, his drift toward making a deal was slowed by his fear of public scorn.

Skolnik, too, was setting his strategy. Matz, Childs, and Wolff intrigued him. Why were the three engineers holding out, refusing to cooperate with the government? Their recalcitrance ran counter to everything Skolnik had learned in his years as an investigating prosecutor. Could it be that they were attempting to shield someone other than Fornoff and Anderson? Could it be that they were paying off a different Maryland politician? The executive of another county? Perhaps even the governor himself? At any rate, what Matz, Childs, and Wolff apparently had in common was a relationship—probably illegal—with Fornoff. And if the paunchy bureaucrat who served as Dale Anderson's chief aide could be brought to terms, he would bring down everyone connected with the suspected bribery scheme—including Matz, Childs, and Wolff, not to mention Anderson himself. So Skolnik announced his strategy: "Turn Fornoff," he said in the jargon of his profession, and he would yield the others.

While Liebman and Baker continued to press the investigation of Matz, Childs, and Wolff, Barney Skolnik turned his full attention to Fornoff and his lawyer, Sachs. With relish, Skolnik took on his old mentor. To Sachs the criminal lawyer he cited the lectures of Sachs the former U.S. attorney. For instance, when Sachs proposed that Fornoff be given blanket immunity in return for cooperation, Skolnik rejected the idea, reminding Sachs of what he himself had once said: You don't give immunity to a major target of an investigation.

This legal tug-of-war was waged between equals. Sachs and Skolnik were experienced and talented, and each had excellent field position. Skolnik by then was ready to indict Fornoff on the basis of evidence supplied by Gaudreau and others, and he wasted little time in hammering that point home. Sachs, though, appeared unimpressed. He, after all, had taught Skolnik how to play the game—especially how to bluff—but, more than that, Sachs knew his client was the linchpin of the cases the government was building against Anderson, and he was determined that the government would pay dearly for the information his client possessed. Just how dearly soon became a matter of the most delicate and protracted negotiations. The government was willing to pay, but it was not willing to offer total immunity. Skolnik, in effect, denied Fornoff the same arrangement he had once been so glad to offer Gaudreau. Sachs understood. For one thing, the time for getting the very best deal—total immunity from prosecution—had already passed. The government had its case, or most of it. Moreover, in the eyes of the prosecutors Fornoff was not deserving of full immunity. He was not, as Gaudreau had been, the victim of extortion; he was the intermediary for the alleged extorter. And the prosecutors were in any case becoming stingy in awarding immunity. After all, there was a trial to be had out of all this work, they hoped, and they had no intention of parading before the jury nothing but witnesses who had bought immunity through cooperation. A defense lawyer did not have to be a whiz to use the argument that such witnesses had manufactured testimony to please the government and, in the process, save their own skins.

Throughout April and into early May, Skolnik and Sachs continued the tug-of-war. Bluff was met with counterbluff, but inevitably Sachs picked up signals that the government indeed had a sound case against his client. What appeared to convince him was a chance conversation he had with Nevitt Steele, the lawyer for Gaudreau. Sachs came away from that encounter certain that his client's position was in fact as perilous as the government was painting it. After conferring with Fornoff, Sachs called Beall and arranged an appointment for three o'clock on the afternoon of May 4.

At the appointed hour, Beall, Skolnik, and Liebman waited expectantly in Beall's office for Sachs. All of them sensed that the moment of surrender was at hand and that the case they had been laboriously building since January was about to reach fruition. Finally, after ten minutes, the door to Beall's office opened a crack. A hand appeared—waving a white handkerchief. With a burst of laughter, the tension broke and Sachs, a mischievous, little-boy smile on his face, entered to accept the terms of surrender. Fornoff had been "turned." He had agreed to plead guilty to a tax-evasion felony in exchange for a government recommendation that he not be jailed.

How best to use the suddenly available Fornoff was the next question. When he finally appeared for interrogation, the back-slapping official turned out to be less than a stellar witness. Red-faced, puffy-eyed, and rumpled, he seemed to lack credibility. Whereas Gaudreau spoke with sincerity and authority, Fornoff used the jargon of a bureaucrat giving a citizen the run-around at the motor vehicle bureau. Yet his information was golden. He provided a virtual blueprint of the alleged Baltimore County kickback scheme, integral parts of which, Fornoff testified, were the engineering firms of Matz, Childs and Associates and Greiner Environmental Systems, Inc.

For a time, the prosecutors considered "wiring" Fornoff—sending him off to talk to his erstwhile collaborators in the kickback scheme wearing a hidden tape recorder. But they discarded the idea, deciding that Fornoff was of more value to them publicly exposed as a cooperating witness. They would mount a full-scale public-relations spectacle, at which Fornoff, the man who had been central to much of Baltimore County's corruption, would publicly plead guilty to a felony. It would be a signal to everyone concerned that everything Bill Fornoff knew was now in the files of the U.S. attorney's office.[1] Fornoff would "shake the trees" and out would tumble a host of possible witnesses, including Wolff, Matz, and Childs.

Weiner and Kaplan kept a nervous eye on Fornoff, knowing he could harden the case against their clients Matz, Childs, and Wolff. They continued to hold out, waiting until events—if they ever came—might force them to the negotiating table. If the government ever tripped over the dark secrets their clients possessed, the lawyers would work a deal, if possible. If the information never came out, they would take their secrets with them to their graves. Such were the rules. Their primary obligation was to their clients—not to history.

---

[1] The government later charged that Matz, Childs had kicked back $5600 to Fornoff and Anderson between 1970 and 1972. Greiner Environmental, the government alleged, had kicked back $1750 over the same period.

During the spring, Matz and Wolff continued to send periodic messages to Vice President Agnew through Bud Hammerman. The responses coming back from Washington were always the same: Hold out, don't talk, the Vice President will fix things. At one point, Hammerman reported that Beall would be promoted, taking his plague of an investigation with him. But meetings between Hammerman and Agnew became less frequent as the spring warmed into an early Maryland summer. One of the last occurred on the sands of Ocean City, Maryland, where the two of them walked along the beach, their conversation muffled by the surf. Still, Hammerman retained his long-standing invitation to visit the Agnews in the $190,000 home they had purchased in the Washington suburb of Kenwood, Maryland.

Judah Best was also staying in touch. As he had arranged, he called Beall periodically to inquire if any change in the investigation had affected Agnew's status. The answer was always no. But in mid-May, Best decided it was time for another face-to-face meeting with Beall, for he was incensed by rumors his client had heard. Best told Beall that Baker had been overheard at a party saying that the prosecutors were breathing down Agnew's neck. This was no way to conduct an investigation! Beall had his standard reply: the Vice President was not under investigation. (Beall did not say so, but, if anything, the information from Fornoff indicated that the investigation would veer away from Agnew. Fornoff had testified that the kickback scheme had been conceived *after* Agnew left Towson.) But Best was apparently unconvinced. When he returned to Washington, he advised Agnew to prepare a log of all visits he had had from Hammerman, Matz, and other engineers. Agnew communicated Best's suggestion to his aide, John Damgard. When the laborious task was completed, the logs filled a bookcase that lined a wall in Damgard's office. It contained, at Agnew's insistence, not only all the visits of the engineers to his office, but also a record of every trip Agnew had made to New York when accompanied by Hammerman.

On the very same day that Best called on Beall, the first published reports had appeared concerning the Baltimore County investigation. That morning's *Washington Post* contained a front-page story saying that Dale Anderson, "one of Maryland's most powerful Democrats, has been notified by federal officials that he is under investigation," that the investigation also involved several persons who had formerly worked in the administration of County Executive Agnew and others who had been associated with Agnew. "Despite this fact, sources in Baltimore, Washington, and Towson, the seat of Baltimore County, have stated categorically that the Vice President himself is in no way involved in the investigation and that widespread rumors to the contrary are without foundation."

The "widespread rumors" mentioned in the *Post* story were in fact what had prompted the newspaper to look into the Baltimore County situation in the first place. Maryland had been abuzz for some time with reports that Agnew was under investigation and that the probe of Anderson was actually a ruse to throw the press off the track. The rumors had circulated freely during the recently concluded legislative session in Annapolis and had made their way west to Washington. But the *Post* had more than rumors to go on. Bob Woodward, who along with Carl Bernstein had won a Pulitzer Prize for *The Washington Post* on the Watergate story, had been told by his most trusted source—a government official whom he code-named "Deep Throat"—that FBI files contained apparently unverified allegations that Agnew had accepted a bribe while Vice President.

Woodward's information, as usual, was specific. Agnew had taken the money in cash and placed it in a desk drawer. The amount was $2500. The Baltimore grand jury, the source added, was heading Agnew's way and the Vice President was in fact its target. This seemingly preposterous information was received in April, nearly a month before the prosecutors acknowledged getting the first veiled hint that Agnew had taken kickbacks, and nearly two months before they learned anything specific. At the time, it was not clear if the FBI's files merely documented one of Maryland's recurring rumors—that Agnew had once taken a bribe—or whether the Bureau was simply feeding its ravenous files the same "cocktail-party chatter" about the investigation that Agnew and others were hearing.

The evidence from the start was contradictory. Many, even at that early date, firmly believed that Agnew was the ultimate target of the investigation. Just as many others, however, scoffed at the notion, arguing convincingly that George Beall, a Republican U.S. attorney, had neither the temerity nor the sagacity to investigate his party's second-highest-ranking member. Governor Marvin Mandel, for one, expressed his belief that the investigation was a Nixon administration plot to embarrass Maryland's Democratic administration. "Look at the indictments when they come down and see who is indicted and who is not indicted," he warned.

Logic, of course, was on Mandel's side. But in Washington that spring and summer, the Senate Watergate hearings and other daily revelations strongly suggested that Nixon's administration played by a set of rules governed by no logic at all. Looking at politics through the kaleidoscope of Watergate, anything and everything seemed possible. If it made no sense for a Republican U.S. attorney to hunt a Republican Vice President, then it also made no sense for the same party to risk an impending electoral landslide on a burglary of the opposition's party headquarters. To the unsophisticated, Watergate may have seemed to be nothing more than politics as usual. But the politically sophisticated were horrified. Even in the street brawl of American politics, there had always been rules. The political process, notwithstanding how it looked to outsiders, was normally governed by restraint. Now, however, restraint had become a quaint term, a Victorian relic. An administration that could burglarize, wiretap, and then attempt to cover the whole thing up under the rubric of national security could just as easily initiate an investigation of its Vice President to make way for another person more to the President's liking.

Adding to the general confusion was the nature of the man Agnew himself. For years, rumors had circulated in Maryland that Agnew accepted bribes, but then, the same sort of rumors circulated about many politicians. Moreover, Agnew, after all, was, well, Agnew. Not only was he set apart from the normal run-of-the-mill politicians Maryland had given to the world but almost alone among the major figures of the Nixon administration, he had been left untouched by Watergate. Any rumors of misconduct collided with the Agnew image and disintegrated. Every trail, every incident of alleged impropriety gave out either from lack of evidence or from the strength of the denunciations that came from Agnew. Ted Agnew may not have been a liberal's idea of a hero, but then he was no whore either. More than most politicians, one had to concede, Agnew had integrity.

If this view persisted long past the time when some in Maryland knew better, it was due in no small part to the efforts that Beall and his staff made to disguise the turn their investigation was about to take. Beginning in May and continuing until the very day when news that Agnew *was* under investigation surfaced in *The Wall Street Journal* and *The Washington Post,* the prosecutors repeatedly lied to the press. The Vice President of the United States was under investigation? Absurd, they said. And who could disagree with that?

Arnold Weiner was one who knew better. But Weiner could not have cared less about Agnew. He was being paid by Wolff, Matz, and Childs to look after *them,* and he was scrambling to keep them out of jail. Repeatedly, he attempted to deflect Skolnik, minimizing the importance of his three clients. Even when it came to the questions posed by the admitted kickbacks of the Matz, Childs bonuses, Weiner had a ready answer: "It's just campaign contributions. . . . It's a big nothing. It's no case." Skolnik, however, was not persuaded. Weiner was protesting too much.

Kaplan, meanwhile, was doing some probing of his own. He was in frequent touch with Baker, often discussing some of the Matz, Childs corporate records the government had seized months before and the firm wanted returned. On Friday, May 18, Kaplan made another of these routine calls to Baker, giving him no hint that he was about to blurt out the secret that had been weighing upon him since January. Baker reminded Kaplan that his clients were certain to be indicted. Kaplan didn't flinch. Both Matz and Childs were aware of that possibility, he replied, and in fact were reconciled to it. They had always been prepared to cooperate with the government, but they had nothing the government would consider of value. Anyway, what they *did* have to say, the government would not be willing to hear.

Baker reacted as if Kaplan had slandered him. What did Kaplan mean by that? Both Matz and Childs had been offered immunity months ago, and it was Kaplan who had rejected the idea. Kaplan cut right in as if Baker had not said a thing. He seemed eager to say his piece. Matz and Childs were in a position to incriminate Fornoff, but that information was probably worthless now. From what he had been hearing, the government already had more than enough evidence to indict Fornoff. As for Anderson, his clients had no information to offer.

Then, without the slightest fanfare, Kaplan dropped the bombshell. The only person his clients were uniquely in a position to incriminate was—the Vice President of the United States! The government undoubtedly would not be interested in that sort of information.

Baker was outraged at this suggestion that the Justice Department would retreat in the face of an investigation of the Vice President. After all, he had been the one who had insisted for months that Agnew was camouflaging some crime behind his protestations. Now, rather than reacting with shock, he was indignant. The Baltimore U.S. attorney's office, Baker sternly lectured Kaplan, was nonpartisan. It was prepared to investigate and prosecute all federal crimes. Period. Then, as if suspecting that he was being duped, Baker reminded Kaplan that Agnew had not been executive of Baltimore County since December 1966. The statute of limitations would bar prosecution for any crimes committed during that period.

Kaplan thought maybe Baker had missed the point. Certainly his clients had information about Agnew when he was county executive, he said, but their dealings did not cease when Agnew became governor or, in fact, Vice President.

Baker fought to contain his excitement, but he invoked Skolnik's first rule: Don't alert a lawyer to the fact that his client has information you desperately want. He played it cool, steering the conversation back to the mundane. He made the routine assurances that the U.S. attorney's office would make every effort to protect the Matz, Childs firm, but that it could not be held accountable for what appeared in the newspapers. If Matz, Childs suffered economic losses because of bad publicity, he would be sorry, but helpless to do anything about it. Kaplan said he understood; he would consult with his clients and report back, probably on Monday. Baker said that would be fine and then applied one final squeeze: Matz and Childs would soon be indicted, he warned again, and hung up the telephone.

Then Baker erupted. Leaping from his chair, he crossed the common reception room shared with his colleagues and rushed into Liebman's office. "Get into Skolnik's office," he barked, and then he ducked into Skolnik's office himself, Liebman right behind. "Have I got news for you!"

In a rush, Baker spilled out the details of Kaplan's jolting call, ending with a hard pitch for an all-out investigation of Agnew. He had been right in the winter, he said, and he was right now. Skolnik, listening and pacing behind his desk, was not so sure. Instead of the enthusiasm and excitement that Baker had expected of him, Skolnik expressed cynicism and doubt. Maybe Kaplan was talking about campaign violations or some other sort of petty bookkeeping crime. Maybe Kaplan was bluffing. Maybe his clients were lying to him. Still pacing, Skolnik lectured his associates on the harsh realities of investigatory life—how they'd been promised everyone from the Queen of Sheba to the Pope in other investigations.

But Baker was having none of it. "What's wrong with you?" he demanded. "You know I'm right! You know I'm right!"

Indeed, Skolnik, the ultimate skeptic, did know. But he was also awed by Baker's report. Dale Anderson was one thing, but this was the Vice President of the United States. Still, if Agnew were a crook, if, indeed, he had broken a federal law at any time in the last five years, then Skolnik and only Skolnik would get the man—Skolnik and not some special prosecutor zipped in from the

Justice Department; Skolnik and not some hot-shot Brooks Brothers type in the office of a special Watergate prosecutor. This was going to be a Baltimore investigation. It would proceed as usual. There would be no sudden sharp turns to go after Agnew. No need to notify the Justice Department. Just play it by the book. Skolnik issued his orders. Baker would handle Kaplan from now on. He was to keep the pressure on. If Agnew was out there, they would get him by keeping the pressure on Matz, Childs, and Wolff.

With that settled, the three prosecutors marched down the hall to report to Beall. Baker told him of the conversation with Kaplan. The U.S. attorney smiled, recalling Baker's prophecy. Then Skolnik took over, arguing as he had with Baker: keep up the pressure, George, keep hammering at Matz and soon enough he will serve up Agnew. Beall agreed, and the four prosecutors parted company for the weekend.

By now they all knew that a cover-up of a potential Agnew investigation was out of the question. They had agreed that the new attorney general was sincere when he defined his mandate as the restoration of confidence in the Justice Department. Besides, the Nixon administration, reeling from Watergate blows, was incapable of either ordering them off Agnew's trail or taking the investigation away from them.

As for Agnew himself, none of the prosecutors was entirely shocked to learn—even in this veiled fashion—that the Vice President might be a crook. Since February the evidence had been building that Agnew might have taken kickbacks while serving as executive of Baltimore County. What surprised them, they later recalled, was that they had not thought to look at Agnew's years as governor. Looking back in their notes and straining their recollections, they could summon tidbits of information learned months before that hinted at Agnew's corruption. One of them could recall, for instance, the time in February when a witness asked, "You're not interested in ancient history, are you?" Now the question made some sense.

For all of them it seemed to be a very long weekend, an inconvenient interruption. Liebman, in his twentieth-floor apartment overlooking Baltimore's commercial center, confided in his wife, Simma, and spent the next two days deep in thought. If the signals from Kaplan were being read correctly, then Ronald Stanley Liebman was about to investigate the Vice President of the United States. Not bad for a self-described rookie with less than a year of investigatory experience under his belt. Simma, an artist, eventually abandoned her attempts to talk to her husband and returned to her painting. Liebman sat and thought.

In Columbia, Maryland, Tim Baker also passed an anxious weekend. His ability to leave the cares of the job at the office had suddenly deserted him. He confided in his wife, Betsy, and then spent the weekend pacing like a caged animal, acting as if Monday and the return telephone call to Kaplan would never come.

Nancy Beall also found out about Kaplan's telephone call that weekend. She was upset and not quite believing. Her husband was more reflective. Fate had just handed George Beall a monster of an investigation, and he knew it was going to make him or break him.

Monday finally arrived. With Skolnik at his side, Baker called Kaplan to implement the instructions he had received on Friday. He had discussed their Friday conversation with Beall, Baker told him, and was authorized to say that the Maryland U.S. attorney's office was prepared to investigate federal crimes committed by anyone. He realized that Matz and Childs had difficult decisions to make, but the government was under no circumstances prepared to grant them a period of grace. Their indictments were imminent.

Kaplan protested. He had conferred with his clients over the weekend and they were both concerned about the "national implications" of the information they possessed. They were worried lest the downfall of Agnew, added to the national trauma of Watergate, prove to be more than the nation could endure. This was no mere political figure they were talking about. The subject of the discussion was the Vice President.

Well, Baker replied, both Matz and Childs would have to have faith in the American criminal-justice system. They were in no position to worry about what effect the investigation would have

on the government's ability to function. If they refused to cooperate, the government would have only one recourse—to make a
case against them, haul them before a judge, immunize them,
and compel them to talk about Agnew before a grand jury.

For the next two weeks and through the Memorial Day holiday,
Baker and Kaplan continued to fence by phone. Meanwhile,
events were unfolding elsewhere that were to set the course of
the Agnew investigation and its eventual resolution. On May 18,
the day Kaplan called Baker, Archibald Cox was nominated as
the special Watergate prosecutor. Three days later, Cox defined
his mandate in terms that quickly enhanced the importance of
the Vice Presidency: if necessary, Cox said, he would follow the
Watergate investigations into "the Oval Office."

Matz and Childs, with an eye on the events in Washington, had
cause to worry about the effect their testimony would have on an
already troubled nation. But the two engineers had more mundane
concerns.

They were afraid they would look like turncoats, men who had
squealed on their friends. They requested, and received, assurances that they would be given "use immunity" so it would
appear they had been compelled to testify. Another worry was
that Wolff might not cooperate, leaving them to face Agnew on
their own. That would be an uneven confrontation, a swearing
contest between two admittedly corrupt engineers and the Vice
President of the United States. Lastly, they feared that if they
admitted all their transactions they would implicate politicians
with whom they had nothing but honest dealings but who might
not have reported legitimate campaign contributions they had
made. If the politicians disowned the contributions, again Matz
and Childs would look like liars. Over the weeks, Baker met one
objection after the other and disposed of them.

Finally, Kaplan played what appeared to be his trump card.
His clients, he said, were prepared to be indicted. They had discussed the possibility with their families and were ready, stoically,
to go to jail. Baker laughed at the transparent ploy.

There was little cheer, however, in the Matz household—a
ranch-style house not far from Jerry Wolff's in the Baltimore

County area of Stevenson. His attorney's word notwithstanding, Lester Matz was far from reconciled to an indictment. He was not, after all, a criminal. What bank had he held up? What woman had he raped? He had done what was necessary to do. He had not created the system. In Kaplan's presence Matz had repeatedly said, "The United States of America versus Lester Matz," and shuddered. It was a travesty. He had fought for his country in the war. He loved his country. Now it was threatening him with jail.

One of those in whom the panicked engineer confided in those gloomy days was his son Harry, who now was past the days when he took the Vice President's side in school debate. His advice to his father was simple: Cooperate. Slowly Matz was coming around to agree with him. No longer was he Agnew's friend. The chummy days in Baltimore County were now just a fond memory. Agnew had gone on to other things, other friends. Agnew, moreover, was cool, aloof. You could know him, but it was hard to be really fond of him.

While Lester Matz and Jerome Wolffe wrestled with their options, the prosecutors prepared a surprise they hoped would force both men to terms. Fornoff, by now fully interrogated, was about to make his debut as a government witness. On Friday, June 1, Beall's staff alerted news organizations in Baltimore and Washington to have reporters on hand the next Monday for an important event in the Baltimore courthouse.

It was a carefully planned extravaganza. From the door behind the dais where Judge Alexander Harvey was sitting, William Fornoff strode to the defendant's table. Baker rose and read what the government claimed it would have proved had Fornoff gone to trial. Fornoff, Baker said, "on many occasions" since 1967 "received substantial quantities of money, in cash, from various businesses that had contracts with Baltimore County and wished to acquire such contracts in the future, or both. All such cash received by Mr. Fornoff was delivered by him to another public official in Baltimore County." He was being charged with interfering with IRS agents in the performance of their job (an obscure provision of the criminal code that Baker had discovered in his research). Baker then filed a sealed document with the court that contained the fruits of the months of negotiations between Sachs and Skolnik. The government recommended no jail for Fornoff. Baker returned to his seat.

"Do you admit that these facts actually happened?" Judge Harvey asked Fornoff.

"Yes, sir," Fornoff replied.

"Have there been any threats or pressures exerted to enter this plea of guilty?"

"No, sir."

The tree had just been shaken.

Within moments, as the wire services flashed the news to Baltimore's radio stations, Baltimore County was feeling the shock tremors. Fornoff had just admitted receiving bribes on behalf of another public official. No one could fail to fill in the missing name: Dale Anderson. Fornoff had also told the prosecutors who had bribed him. Again those in the know had little trouble supplying the missing names: Matz, Childs, and Wolff had to be included in that select set.

Skolnik walked out of the courtroom wearing a mischievous grin.

The very next day, the first harvest began to come in. To no one's surprise, one of Beall's first calls was from Kaplan. His clients had decided that in "the national interest" they ought to explore the possibility of a deal with the government. He asked for an appointment later that same day, and by three o'clock he and Weiner were in Beall's office. Ten minutes later, Beall asked Skolnik, Baker, Liebman, and deputy U.S. Attorney Paul Kramer to join the meeting.

Kaplan did the talking. His clients, concerned as they were about the national interest, were now prepared to see what the government was willing to offer in exchange for the information they possessed about a "high federal official." What they would like, he said, was a pledge of immunity from prosecution.

No deal, Skolnik snapped. Immunity would not even be discussed until the government had a better reading of what sort of information Matz, Childs, and Wolff possessed. So Kaplan began to drop some enticing hints. The information his clients possessed would provide the government with a hard case against the "high federal official." It would amount to considerably more than a "swearing match" between two engineers and the "high federal official." It would incriminate others who, in turn, would harden the case even further. The crimes committed by the "high federal official" were committed both before and after he joined the federal government.

To look at the poker faces of the prosecutors in the room, one would have thought that the young lawyer had merely recited the Pledge of Allegiance. But they were determined that Kaplan would have to offer more samples before any bid was tendered.

At that point, Weiner reminded Skolnik that he was not present in his capacity as lawyer for Wolff, but as Kaplan's co-counsel for Matz and Childs. If that was the case, Skolnik said, Weiner would have to leave the room, since Wolff was not being discussed. Then, with Weiner gone, the prosecutors zeroed in on Kaplan.

He had not told them enough, the prosecutors said. What the hell was he talking about, anyway? Some illegal campaign contributions? Did he think that would get his clients immunity? No, Kaplan protested. He was talking about "substantial federal crimes." The case was a strong one. "I'll tell you this. If I were in your shoes, I could win it."

The prosecutors told Kaplan they would have to consider the question of immunity and would respond by mail within the next several days. Skolnik sternly warned him that if his clients failed to cooperate fully, if they lied or withheld a shred of information, any deal would be off and they would be prosecuted with a vengeance.

The meeting had produced nothing in terms of evidence for the prosecutors, but plenty of tidbits. They now knew that Matz and Childs possessed substantive information about Agnew and there seemed to be no pressing statute-of-limitations problems. What, though, were these "substantial federal crimes," and what kind of information did they have about them? Was it hearsay or something else?

Kaplan, too, had scored some points. No longer could the prosecutors dismiss his clients' overtures on the grounds they might be peddling junk. Despite their blank expressions, they must have been impressed, and he was on his way to making a deal. There would be no imminent indictment, as they had threatened. Kaplan would get something for his troubles.

It was not to be full immunity. Beall and his staff, already committed to the strategy of slowly increasing the pressure on the engineers, had no intention of letting up now. It was working too well. A couple of more hammer blows and the engineers might cave in.

On June 7, Beall made his position clear. In identical letters of negotiation written to Matz, Childs, and Wolff, he spelled out the terms under which he would be willing to hear the information they had to offer. First, he would have to hear the information in detail before any deal could be discussed. Second, he did not want to hear anything from the engineers on certain corrupt relationships the U.S. attorney's office was already aware of. In other words, Beall was saying, Don't tell me about your relationship with Fornoff. I already know about that and I don't want to hear it again from you. (In saying this, Beall was trying to avoid tainting the evidence he already had about Fornoff in the event he indicted the engineers and took them to trial. In such a trial, he would not want to have to prove that he had not come by his information during the negotiating process.)

The next day, June 8, he stepped up the pressure even more. "On the basis of [your] extremely limited disclosure," Beall wrote to Kaplan, "you have asked me to indicate if this office would be prepared to grant your clients total immunity in exchange for their cooperation and information. I have concluded that I cannot in the proper exercise of our responsibilities make any representation to you on the basis of limited disclosures." Beall concluded with yet another warning that Matz and Childs were perilously close to indictment. The letter marked the start of a steady correspondence—as many as two letters a day—between Beall and Kaplan, supplementing and often directly following telephone calls or personal visits, and primarily designed to set down on paper the negotiations between them. In the event their talks collapsed, each party wanted to be in a position to document what the ground rules had been for the negotiations.

Kaplan and Weiner were engaged in a most delicate balancing act. On one hand, they were negotiating with the government to get the best possible deal for their clients. On the other hand, they had to explain it all to their clients and educate them quickly in the intricacies of the law. Of the three, Wolff appeared to be the most recalcitrant. He was a lawyer himself, and while he had not made the mistake of attempting to represent himself, he was free to do some backseat driving. And he vacillated. An unrelated event would seem to impede his gradual drift toward accepting a deal. He was a sensitive man, and the months of anxiety had taken their toll; he was, Weiner told the prosecutors at one point, on the verge of suicide. The message back was: Be our guest. Finally, on June 13, Weiner told Beall that Wolff was probably ready to cooperate, and asked total immunity for him. Again, as he had done with Matz and Childs, Beall refused to discuss the possibility until he had detailed information in hand.

So the time had come for Weiner to see Beall alone. Probing to determine how hard a case the government had, Weiner characterized his client as a "victim" of the Baltimore County system, whom in all fairness the government should not be interested in prosecuting. Wolff was a minor figure in the bribery scheme, a virtual nobody who, like other engineers, had been extorted into kicking back a portion of his fees. Beall was unmoved. Wolff was nothing of the sort, he said. He was markedly different from some of the other engineers, and at least as culpable as the public officials he bribed. The meeting ended inconclusively.

By this time, however, Matz and Childs had made up their minds to cooperate. The two engineers signed letters of negotiation, spelling out the terms under which the plea bargaining would proceed and their testimony be heard. On June 21, Kaplan and Weiner met with Beall and his staff to turn over the letters and explain for the first time the meaning of the cryptic phrase "substantial federal crimes."

Ron Liebman was otherwise occupied that day. In a small

courtroom up one flight from Beall's office, he was racing through a final argument to the jury on a case involving theft of government property. Liebman abandoned the embellishments that normally go onto a summation, for his mind was on the events unfolding in Beall's office downstairs. When he concluded, and the judge began to charge the jury, it seemed to the young prosecutor that he was talking like a wound-down record. Liebman fidgeted. Finally, the judge's instructions were done and the jury went to the jury room (where later they voted a verdict of guilty). Liebman bolted from the courtroom, along the hall, and down the stairs. His heart was pounding as he reached Beall's office and threw open the door.

Arnold Weiner was doing the talking, in his high, sing-song voice. Skolnik sat off to the side, his temple bursting with what he later described as the worst headache of his life. Beall, too, had a physical, nearly allergic reaction to what he was being told; his stomach was bothering him. Baker showed no emotion at all. Liebman slipped into his chair like a tardy arrival at a funeral service. Weiner noted his arrival with a nod and continued to talk.

Lester Matz and John Childs met during the 1950s when they both worked as municipal engineers for Baltimore. They formed their own firm in 1955, establishing their offices in an old building at 2129 North Charles Street. Matz, a gregarious fellow, went out to seek clients. He found them in Baltimore County, to which thousands of Baltimoreans were then fleeing. All over the county, fortunes were being built as farms made way for housing tracts and sewers and roads were constructed—a heady sight, a Comstock Lode of opportunities for an engineer. One of the major developers was Bud Hammerman, whose father, Sam, had founded the S. I. Hammerman Organization, a real-estate conglomerate. Another was Wolff, then an engineer in private practice. Before long, the three—Matz, Hammerman, and Wolff—established a business relationship.

The firm of Matz, Childs began to prosper. As a new and politically unconnected firm, however, it received none of the county's public-works contracts. Despite repeated attempts to break into the favored circle of firms that did, Matz, Childs and Associates remained outsiders, watching with mounting chagrin as the contracts flowed to their better-connected rivals. Still, Matz was not idle. By 1960, he had befriended the chairman of the county zoning board of appeals—Spiro Agnew. (Within two years, Matz and Agnew became involved in certain transactions with a man who will be referred to in this book as The Close Associate. Matz made the man's identity known to the prosecutors, but it was not publicly disclosed because the man was not cooperating with the investigation.) When Agnew announced that he would run for county executive, Matz and Childs threw in with him, donating $500 to what appeared then to be a doomed cause. The two engineers genuinely admired Agnew, and of course also hoped that his victory would bring them the contracts they believed they deserved.

Over the next four years, Matz, Agnew, and The Close Associate became even friendlier—visiting in each other's homes and celebrating milestone family occasions together, such as the bar mitzvah of a Matz son. There was also a business relationship. Shortly after Agnew's election, The Close Associate told Matz that the two of them figured to make a lot of money. The comment, though cryptic, was not lost on Matz, and a short time later, they met with Agnew. The new county executive told Matz that he had great confidence in The Close Associate. Matz unscrambled this message to mean that he was supposed to work through The Close Associate. That was fine with him.

Not long after, The Close Associate asked Matz to prepare a chart listing how much money the engineers receiving county contracts could be expected to kick back. Matz calculated the likely profits on certain jobs, concluded that a 5-per-cent kickback was not unreasonable, gave a copy of the chart to The Close Associate, and took the original to Agnew. The county executive thanked him for his work.

The chart then became a manual by which kickbacks in Baltimore County and to Spiro Agnew were determined. When he turned over the copy of the chart to The Close Associate, Matz was told that he would be expected to pay 5 per cent on engineering contracts and 2½ per cent on surveying contracts. This arrangement, in which both parties would benefit, was soon implemented.

Whenever Matz learned which contracts the county was about to let, he would contact The Close Associate and tell him which ones he wanted. Matz usually delivered the money to The Close Associate in his office, handing him a plain white envelope containing the cash. He paid in installments, generally, making each payment when the county sent him an installment for the work performed. And when the size of the cash payments increased and Matz and Childs found themselves in a cash bind, they began to generate cash by having key employees kick back bonuses.

At mid-point in Agnew's Baltimore County administration, Matz complained to The Close Associate that he was not getting enough county work. They all met together at Agnew's home, and Agnew promised to contact the appropriate county officials and order them to step up the flow of contracts to Matz, Childs.

It was no surprise, then, that in 1966, Matz and Childs were enthusiastic supporters of Agnew's gubernatorial campaign. Their faith in the man's abilities—and his financial value to them—was undiminished. With Jerry Wolff as chairman of the state roads commission and Agnew in the governor's mansion, Matz, Childs and Associates soon began to enjoy a steady flow of state contracts. By then, however, circumstances had made Matz reluctant to continue paying through The Close Associate, for he suspected that the intermediary was skimming money off the top and taking all the credit for the cash he handed over. Matz went to Annapolis for a face-to-face talk with the new governor. In Agnew's ornate office with its majestic fireplace, Matz proceeded to denigrate The Close Associate, warning that he lacked discretion and would sooner or later get them in trouble.

Matz had a proposition. Instead of paying through The Close Associate, why not deliver the cash to Agnew directly? He would put the money in a savings account from which Agnew could draw after he returned to the practice of law. The savings-account money, Matz continued, could perhaps be accounted for later in the form of legal fees. Agnew liked that idea especially.

Subsequently, Matz reconsidered the savings-account scheme and decided that it involved keeping too many records. He did not, however, reconsider his determination to make his payments personally, and from that time forth he dealt directly with Agnew. The contracts kept coming, increasing substantially as the Agnew administration matured. On one occasion, Matz recalled, he was asked by Wolff if he was taking care of his "obligations." Matz replied he was taking care of them directly.

All through 1967, Matz, Childs and Associates continued to share in the largess of the Agnew administration. So large were the contracts that Matz and Childs had to defer their payments to Agnew until they received their fees from the state. The fees began to arrive in the summer of 1968, and Matz, now far behind in his obligations to Agnew, was determined quickly to catch up, lest he be suspected of welshing. By July 1968, his payments totaled about $20,000. With the fees that would soon be in the mail from the state, Matz figured he would owe $30,000 more. He showed his calculations to Childs, who agreed on the sum.

The firm, however, was in a fix. Matz and Childs felt they could not safely generate $30,000 in cash. So Matz turned to a former client who generally dealt in large sums of cash and arranged a "loan." In a complicated transaction, Matz, Childs and Associates loaned this former client $30,000, transferring the funds by corporate check; the client agreed to deliver $30,000 in cash to Matz. On the books of the client's firm the loan was recorded as being repaid in installments of $1700—a sum Matz and Childs thought they could safely manage in cash. When they received a "loan" installment, they simply transferred $1700 in cash to their "debtor."

The friend was able to produce $20,000 of the total almost immediately. Matz showed the cash to Childs, then he stuffed it in a manila envelope and drove to the State House in Annapolis. Taking the elevator to the second floor, he passed through the governor's reception room, with its oversized portraits of past Maryland governors going back to the Lords Baltimore, father and son, to the governor's office. There, Matz handed the envelope to Agnew, thanked him for the state contracts, and left. It was the last payment Matz made while Agnew was governor of Maryland. Within the month, Agnew was chosen by Richard M. Nixon to be his running mate.

(Matz's payments to Agnew were not always for his personal use. In 1967, Agnew asked Matz for a $5000 donation to Nelson Rockefeller's presidential campaign. Cash or check? Matz asked. A check would be fine, Agnew said, and Matz put one in the mail. When the campaign temporarily collapsed with Rockefeller's declaration that he would not be a candidate, Matz's check was returned to him. By the time Rockefeller changed his mind again and re-entered the race at the end of April 1968, Agnew was well on his way into Nixon's fold.)

By 1969, Agnew had been promoted by Richard Nixon and by the American people out of Maryland and down the Baltimore-Washington Parkway to the seat of national power. What he gained in stature, however, he lost in the authority to grant contracts. There were virtually none at his disposal. Nevertheless, Matz felt that he owed Agnew money for Maryland contracts received under the old Agnew administration. On a piece of yellow paper, he calculated the sum he thought was due Agnew and called the Vice President's office for an appointment. Matz took the yellow paper and an envelope containing $10,000 in cash and went to see Agnew in his office in the basement of the White House.[2] The engineer showed Agnew his calculations, reviewed them with him, and handed the Vice President the envelope. Agnew took it and put it in a desk drawer. Matz then told Agnew he might "owe" him more money as the contracts negotiated during Agnew's Maryland administration continued to generate fees. Agnew told Matz to call his secretary when the next payment

---

[2] Agnew received a White House office after Nixon proclaimed that his new Vice President would be a principal domestic adviser. Agnew coveted the office formerly occupied by one of Lyndon Johnson's domestic advisers, Joseph A. Califano, Jr.—it had a bathroom—but it was assigned to Bryce Harlow, and Agnew got a room in the basement. He later moved to the Old Executive Office Building, where the President himself later established a hideaway office.

was ready and tell her he had more "information" for the Vice President.

On his return to Towson, Matz told Childs about his White House transaction with Agnew. This was no longer something he could be casual about, and he admitted to Childs that he was shaken. He had just paid off the Vice President of the United States in the White House. Matz told one other person about the payoff—Jerry Wolff, then vice presidential assistant for science and technology.

From there on, Matz's common sense conflicted with his sense of obligation. Since Agnew was no longer in a position to award contracts, the pace of the payments diminished, though Matz did make one to him for $2500 in return for a federal contract awarded in 1971 to a subsidiary of Matz, Childs. Then about a year later, in the spring of 1972, Matz was contacted by The Close Associate, who pressed hard for a $10,000 contribution. Matz complained to Agnew himself.

"Say you gave at the office," the Vice President told him.

Arnold Weiner, having explained the meaning of "substantial federal crimes," took his leave of the U.S. attorney. It was already early evening, and the pleasantly warm early summer day still had some sun left to it. At their home in northwest Baltimore, George and Nancy Beall decided to take advantage of the weather and sit on the porch for a chat. For the first time in a long time, the prosecutor treated himself to a before-dinner drink. As he sipped his Bloody Mary, Beall told his wife about Weiner's disclosures. Nancy Beall reacted with the incredulity of one who knew the public Spiro Agnew.

Lester Matz, she said firmly, was a liar.

6 Ally
in Washington

On May 25, when Elliot L. Richardson took over from Richard
Kleindienst as Attorney General of the United States, he had no
real idea what his subordinates in Baltimore were up to, and his
mind was otherwise occupied. He inherited a deeply demoralized
Department of Justice. Kleindienst had stepped down amid the
mushrooming Watergate scandal with only the barest hint to
Richardson about the Baltimore County investigation. Although
Watergate had not implicated Kleindienst directly, it was tainting
many of his associates and particularly the man he had succeeded
and under whom he had served through the first Nixon administration—John N. Mitchell. And Kleindienst, ever the loyal sol-
dier, had suffered a final indignity on April 30 when President
Nixon rewarded his service by including the announcement of his
resignation with the forced departures of three of the central
Watergate figures, White House aides H. R. Haldeman, John D.
Ehrlichman, and John W. Dean III. There was not much credibility left in the administration, and whatever amount Kleindienst
contributed Nixon thus willfully spent in an obvious effort to
convey the impression of a wholesale house-cleaning. Kleindienst

was dismayed at the company he was forced to keep, but he went out with his mouth shut, publicly anyway.

While Kleindienst himself had escaped personal implication in Watergate, his Department of Justice had become a prime institutional casualty. When Nixon instructed the department in March 1973 to make a thorough investigation into any White House involvement in the scandal, Kleindienst had felt obliged to cut himself out of the inquiry, because of his close association with Mitchell and other principals. He turned the job over to his highly respected subordinate, Henry E. Petersen, assistant attorney general in charge of the criminal division, who had overseen the prosecution of the seven principals convicted in the actual break-in of the Democratic National Committee at the Watergate complex on June 17, 1972. When one of the seven, James W. McCord, Jr., had begun to talk and the scandal grew to involve many others, criticism of Petersen mounted for having pursued too narrow a case. On top of that, he was humiliated when an embarrassed and embattled President took the Watergate investigation away from him and gave it to a special prosecutor. The case was "snatched from us," he protested, at a time he and his Justice team had it 90 per cent in hand.

Such was the situation in the Justice Department when Richardson took over with his dual mission. The first he enunciated publicly—to restore credibility in the administration of justice. The second he did not have to enunciate, because it was obvious for a man of his experience and political ambition—to maintain and if possible enhance his personal integrity and credibility. An extremely proud and conscientious public figure, Richardson had endured since 1969 in one subcabinet and two cabinet posts (under secretary of State, secretary of Health, Education, and Welfare, and secretary of Defense) not only to serve the nation but to preserve his reputation as an independent voice within the Babel of conformity that was the Nixon administration.

Through these years, Richardson had been a sort of fireman for Richard Nixon, a man of keen administrative skills and diplomatic sensitivity who could be called on to pull chestnuts from fires. Thus, when Kleindienst's resignation was announced, the only surprise about the President's choice of Richardson to succeed him was the fact that he was doing so even though Richardson had been at the Pentagon only three months. This fifty-three-year-old proper Bostonian—who had been an honors graduate of Harvard Law School, law clerk to Judge Learned Hand and Justice Felix Frankfurter, a U.S. attorney and then attorney general of Massachusetts—was an obvious choice to head a badly shattered Department of Justice in this heretofore ostentatiously law-and-order administration.

Richardson had some definite ideas about the face his new department should show to the American people. "To a large extent," he said on moving from the Pentagon to Justice, "their respect for government is affected by the fairness and integrity of the law-enforcement process. I think there is an opportunity to restore confidence [by] finding ways in which the law-enforcement process can be made to be, and perceived to be, scrupulous in the ways in which it carries out its job."

Elliot Richardson was an impressive man, with the bearing and style to go with his background. There was a serenity and strength about his angular, handsome face, and although he was not particularly tall, he carried himself with an assurance that bespoke confidence rather than pomposity. He was an inveterate pipe-puffer, with an occasional excursion into cigar smoking, and he capped his aristocratic manner with a measured, halting way of speaking that suggested he was weighing each word on the scale of history before uttering it.

In his effort to restore public confidence in the department, Richardson brought with him three young men who had served with him before. They were labeled by one newsman "Richardson's Mafia"—an apt description to the career bureaucrats at Justice. J. T. Smith, executive assistant to Richardson, Jonathan Moore, associate attorney general, and Richard G. Darman, special assistant to the attorney general, constituted Richardson's brainstorming team on all major issues that came before him. In their earlier associations, the four men had worked out a system whereby they put their collective knowledge and wisdom together to anticipate problems, to map out various alternatives, and, after the fact, to assess their own performance and decide what to do next. In all these deliberations, the three aides were motivated by the same dual objective that Richardson himself sought—to restore the integrity of the department and, bluntly, to protect the new attorney general politically in the process.

Of the three Richardson mafiosi, J. T. Smith, a stocky, stolid, thirty-year-old Washington lawyer given to conservative pin-stripe suits and clipped sentences, was the closest in terms of daily access to the attorney general. He occupied a small office just off Richardson's own and in effect held the key to his boss's door. He maintained Richardson's schedule and controlled his time in and out of the office; if you wanted to see Elliot Richardson, you saw J. T. Smith first. Smith also had other jobs, including editing speeches, but primarily he was the gatekeeper and confidant. A graduate of the Yale School of Law in 1967, Smith had been a special assistant to the comptroller at HEW when he met Richardson and joined his inner circle. Before that, he had worked as a programs analyst in planning, programming, and budgeting at the Central Intelligence Agency. He was a man of precise speech and thought, which made him an ideal first lieutenant for Richardson, who was the same.

The second man in the triumvirate, Moore, was an intense, dynamic, yet personally gentle man of forty-one, also stocky, with a shock of brown hair that perpetually leaped over his temple and gave him a boyish look. Originally a foreign-policy scholar on the staff of Nelson Rockefeller, Moore played a brief but important role in the 1967–68 presidential aspirations of George Romney. When Romney was stumbling in his inability to cope with the critical issue of Vietnam, Moore helped him arrive at his eventual proposals for winding down the war by turning more responsibility over to the South Vietnamese. Romney and Moore called their plan "de-Americanization," and it got nowhere. A year later, the man who drove Romney out of the New Hampshire primary, Richard M. Nixon, trotted out a very similar approach with a better label on it—"Vietnamization." By that time, though, the name Romney had become a laugh word in the American vocabulary, like Brooklyn and, yes, Spiro T. Agnew.

After Romney's collapse, Moore signed on with the equally doomed Rockefeller campaign, then joined Richardson at the State Department at the outset of the Nixon administration. After that, their fortunes were wed. Moore moved with Richardson to HEW, to the Pentagon, and finally to Justice, where he served as personal troubleshooter and political adviser.

The youngest of the trio, thirty-year-old Dick Darman, was doing public-policy analysis for HEW on a consulting basis from the Harvard Center for Educational Policy Research when he was tapped by Richardson to be a deputy assistant secretary, managing Richardson's staff. A *cum laude* graduate of Harvard College who later received a master's degree from the Harvard Business School, Darman became special assistant to Richardson in all three of his cabinet posts. He was responsible for coordination of all top-level policy planning, management, and analysis going to Richardson, and in times of crisis was the third voice and opinion fed into Richardson's decision-making apparatus. Like the others, Darman was intent on putting Justice on its feet in the wake of Watergate and making sure that Elliot Richardson was not knocked off his in the process.

The new team at Justice had barely assembled in the last days of May when Richardson was asked to receive a visitor from nearby Maryland. George Beall was only one of the ninety-four U.S. attorneys in the department, and when he simply showed up at Richardson's office, asking how to get to see the new attorney general, J. T. Smith wasn't sure what to do. "What's the normal procedure?" he asked a secretary. "Does a U.S. attorney just wander in and see the attorney general?" The secretary told Smith that it was just not done. Beall was turned away, but before he left he got an appointment to discuss an important matter that, he said, former attorney general Kleindienst would have talked to Richardson about.

When Kleindienst was about to step down, Beall had asked him whether he ought to alert his successor to the Maryland kickback investigation and his status reports on Agnew's noninvolvement. Kleindienst said that he should and also promised that he would mention it to Richardson. The fact was, though, that Kleindienst had only told Richardson there was an investigation going on in Baltimore that he ought to discuss with Beall.

Had Beall seen Richardson that day, he could have told him only that the investigation might be moving Agnew's way. All he had to go on at this point were the periodic inquiries of Judah Best, and Joseph Kaplan's hints about what Lester Matz and John Childs could say in return for total immunity. They were tantalizing elements but clearly not enough to warrant informing the nation's chief law-enforcement officer that the Vice President of the United States was on the road to indictment as a crook.

But by the time Beall finally did see the attorney general, on June 12, there had been a significant development. William Fornoff's pleading guilty on June 4, which obviously triggered Matz and Jerome Wolff to say they were ready to involve Agnew, gave Beall something to make Richardson take notice. And so Beall decided (apparently without the knowledge of his assistants) to tell Richardson that much, at least. He could not go too hard with the story, because Matz and Wolff were still balking at signing the letters of negotiation that would clear the way to getting corroborating testimony against Agnew. And so he proceeded cautiously, telling Richardson at first essentially only what he had been telling Kleindienst through the late spring—that the prime target of the kickback investigation was Dale Anderson and that there was yet no hard evidence that Agnew was involved.

Through most of Beall's recitation about his Baltimore County investigation, the attorney general seemed preoccupied but cordial, sitting at his desk with his feet up, chair back, drawing on a pipe, and doodling with a blue felt pen on a notepad, taking notes occasionally. But when Beall told him that within recent weeks his team was starting to get second-hand information that indicated the Vice President might be involved, Richardson doodled less and took more notes. At one point he asked Beall for a personal appraisal of Agnew. Beall said he didn't know him very well but that he was represented by a member of the Colson and Shapiro firm—a fact that seemed to puzzle Richardson.

As Beall talked more about Agnew, Richardson lit up a huge

cigar that lasted him the rest of the meeting. He began to talk about his own experience as U.S. attorney in Massachusetts. He was pursuing a somewhat similar kickback case involving highway contractors in Worcester in 1961, he said, when John F. Kennedy became President. Richardson had asked the new attorney general, Robert F. Kennedy, for permission to stay on and complete the investigation, but Kennedy had refused. The story gave Beall heart; the man now running the Department of Justice understood what the Baltimoreans were about, and he was sympathetic. Beall emphasized that his team was still negotiating with Matz and Wolff for whatever they had to say, but there was no telling whether anything was really there. Richardson asked to be kept posted, and Beall promised to do so.

Baker later explained Beall's cautious presentation to Richardson this way: "Our conclusion here was that there wasn't anything to tell Richardson. In part we suspected that Matz and Wolff really didn't have very much on Agnew or anything else because of their unwillingness to sign the letter [of negotiation]. We also thought there would be a period of time now when we would press ahead toward an indictment and that they would be back. Our strategy always was to keep pushing to the indictment, even during the negotiations phase."

According to Richardson's aides, the attorney general didn't say much about what Beall had told him. He asked Kleindienst about Agnew's interest in the Baltimore investigation, and Kleindienst said he just hadn't had a chance to mention it—an indication of how lightly Kleindienst took the possibility of Agnew's involvement, or of how little interest he had in having it pursued.

In Baltimore, however, the prosecutors were now taking the possibility most seriously and were pursuing it with vigor. When Kaplan and Weiner finally came in on June 21 and laid out Matz's whole grisly case against Agnew, the scope and venality of it itself dictated a decision: they must tell Washington what they had.

Attorney General Richardson already was hearing from other sources that Beall and his team were hard at work. One day he received a call from J. Fred Buzhardt, Jr., President Nixon's chief troubleshooting lawyer, relaying a complaint—he did not say from whom—about the tactics being used by members of Beall's staff in connection with allegations involving Agnew. Richardson told Buzhardt that if anyone had any complaints about the conduct of anyone in the Department of Justice, he should make them to Richardson personally; otherwise he would ignore them. That was the last the attorney general heard of the matter.

During the week of June 18, Beall phoned Richardson's office with an urgent request for a meeting for himself and his three assistants. After at least two postponements, the team was scheduled for Tuesday, July 3. This was to be the first time that Skolnik, Baker, and Liebman would meet the attorney general. Skolnik, impressed, arrived at Beall's office at about nine o'clock that morning in a new blue suit. He had just bought two suits and was saving one for his wedding on July 14. But no sooner had he entered Beall's office than his boss told him the meeting with Richardson was off. The attorney general's secretary had called to say Richardson was too busy. The three assistants, primed for the big audience with Richardson, were outraged. Here they were sitting on perhaps the hottest case in the annals of American politics, and Beall was benignly accepting another postponement.

"God damn it," Skolnik said to him. "Call the secretary up and tell her that we must see the attorney general today. It's a matter of great urgency to the United States."

"Do you really think it's quite that urgent?" Beall asked.

"Yes," Skolnik said emphatically.

So Beall picked up the phone and called back Richardson's secretary, Concetta Leonardi, known as Chetta.

"I must see the attorney general today," he told her. This time he managed to convey the urgency of the matter, but without mentioning the subject and certainly not the name of Vice President Agnew. Baker, Liebman, and Skolnik stood anxiously as Beall listened for the secretary's response. Finally he hung up and said, "She's going to call me back." In a few minutes Beall's phone rang again.

"Yes, hello. . . . We're on our way." He put down the phone. "Let's go."

The four men rushed downstairs, piled into Beall's 1972 green Audi, and headed for Washington.

There was more to their urgency than simple natural eagerness to let their powerful superior know what a big catch they had made. The Baltimoreans also feared that he might find out about it from another source. "The thing had gotten to that point and the Attorney General of the United States still didn't know a thing about it," Skolnik said later. "That just instinctively struck me as a very bad situation. You know, there are all kinds of horribles. Matz could go talk to a newspaper reporter the next day and there'd be headlines about Matz telling the U.S. attorney all about Agnew. The attorney general could call up and say, 'What the hell is this? How come I don't know?'"

Now they were going to take care of that worry, and as they drove south to Washington—eighty to eighty-five miles an hour, well above the speed limit—the four men engaged in much the same planning for the meeting that marked the preparatory style of the Richardson Mafia. With Beall and the long-legged Liebman in the front seats and Skolnik and Baker in the rear, they went over every inch of the terrain they thought the attorney general might cover. Beall, to underline at the outset that these young colleagues were responsible citizens, would introduce each to Richardson at some length, stressing their Ivy League educations when they had them, their clerkships and experience. He would then recapitulate the whole investigation and turn the detailed briefing over to Baker, who, reading from notes, would give Richardson a comprehensive rundown of the case against Agnew.

Richardson was busy. For forty-five tense minutes the Baltimoreans cooled their heels; as they waited, Liebman the comedian, pointing to some medieval prints on the walls, conjectured that the Justice Department probably had a torture chamber in the basement for upstart U.S. attorneys. It was a lame line, but it cut the tension and the others laughed. Liebman, encouraged, conjured up the image of a new law firm in distant Frostburg, Maryland, specializing in workmen's compensation cases: Beall, Skolnik, Baker & Liebman. No, thought Beall, he would probably be reassigned instead—to be the next U.S. attorney in American Samoa.

At around noon, more relaxed now, they were told the attorney general would see them. They were admitted to the long conference room that adjoins Richardson's office, and they were impressed. To these men who toiled in the colorless federal bureaucracy in Baltimore, where everything in sight was low-cost government-issue, the rich-grained furniture and other appointments were another world. Elliot Richardson himself was an impressive sight to the three assistant U.S. attorneys from the boondocks. He invited them to sit around a conference table, and he sat at the head.

Beall proceeded with rather lengthy introductions of his young aides and the retelling of the general Maryland investigation, which he had already outlined to Richardson at the June 12 meeting. Skolnik, Baker, and Liebman grew restless, concerned that they were unduly imposing on the attorney general. But Beall eventually arrived at the part of the story where, as they all knew, he was going to say the name Agnew. Just then, Richardson's secretary came in and handed him a note. Richardson looked at it, got up quickly from his chair, excused himself, went into his private office, and closed the door behind him.

"Get to it, George," one of the aides said as soon as he was gone. "He's going to throw us out of here."

"I'm right there," Beall said. "I was just about to mention it."

Behind the closed door Richardson was hearing something that by itself was cause enough for apoplexy—and this was even before he heard Beall's revelations. Alexander Haig, the President's new chief of staff, was on the phone telling him that the President was livid over a story that morning in the *Los Angeles Times*. Archibald Cox, the special Watergate prosecutor, had started a preliminary inquiry into the President's real-estate transactions, the story said, centering on the $1.5 million paid for his home in San Clemente. The paper quoted one source as saying that a key aspect of the inquiry would be a check on whether any of the money used came from union funds, corporations, or Republican campaign resources.

There was good reason for Nixon to be concerned. The story

was published at what was already perhaps the most trying time for him in the Senate Watergate hearings. John W. Dean III, his discharged counsel, had just completed exhaustive testimony alleging an elaborate and deliberate cover-up of the Watergate burglary within the White House, with the President himself aware of it. And Nixon already had ample reason to regret his agreement with Richardson to accept Cox—Harvard lawyer, liberal Democrat, and former solicitor general under Presidents Kennedy and Johnson—as special prosecutor. Cox had plunged into his work with uncommon vigor and tenacity; he was taking his mandate of independence at face value, and he had the President squirming. So the report of a San Clemente investigation on top of everything else (a report that proved to be untrue) was intolerable to the President, Haig told the attorney general. Nixon always labored under a persecution complex, and that complex was now working overtime. Tell Richardson to find out exactly what Cox is up to, the President had instructed Haig. Richardson said he would do so, and then he headed back into the conference room to hear what the young eager beavers from Baltimore wanted from him.

It would help if they got to the point. The President on the warpath about Cox was quite enough for one day. Richardson was now understandably distracted. He had reservations himself about the nonpartisanship or lack thereof of Cox's prosecutorial staff; and when Beall resumed, he doodled on his ever-present pad. Beall at last mentioned the incriminating testimony against Agnew. Richardson, pipe in mouth, a look of deep consternation on his face, stopped doodling and feverishly started taking notes. Baker took over and filled in chapter and verse in a crisp summary of the story Kaplan and Weiner had laid out in Baltimore.

Richardson took it all in, grimly. Compared to this, Nixon's complaint about Cox was a mere temper tantrum. Carefully, he went over all the points that had been raised, asking questions, encouraging his visitors to discuss what collectively should be done next. But whenever they began to get into the matter, there would be another note under his nose about another White House phone call.

Richardson, getting up and striding out to mollify the White House, then returning to hear more about a development that might not only rock the administration but throw the Republic into political crisis, was being batted back and forth by events each more bizarre than the one before. What finally tore it for him was yet another call from Haig, during which Nixon himself broke in. He wanted, he told Richardson in no uncertain terms, a flat public denial from Cox that any San Clemente investigation was under way, and he wanted it at once. (Cox eventually made this denial, but he acknowledged at the same time that he had ordered a staff review of "relevant public knowledge"—newspaper stories—about the purchase and improvements on the President's property because he "did not have even the most elementary knowledge of the facts" in the matter.) This demonstration of presidential temper severely jolted Richardson, coming as it did when he had also to act responsibly on another shocking development of immense importance and immense potential harm to the President and his administration. According to Richardson insiders later, their boss in fact was so vexed at the President's conduct that he considered resigning that very day. Among the elements that persuaded him to stay on was his concern about the Agnew affair, and the governmental crisis it posed in the event of sudden succession to the Presidency.

When Richardson returned to the conference room, he told the Baltimoreans he owed them some explanation as to why he kept running out on them. Actually, the prosecutors already had some inkling as to what was going on. Skolnik had caught a glimpse of one of the notes Richardson's secretary had put before him, and he told the others he thought it read "The President." There were intakes of breath and raised eyebrows, and so they were not wholly taken aback when Richardson came back in and told them, "The President's a little upset about Mr. Cox today." To that bit of inside intelligence the prosecutors reacted coolly, as if they heard things like that every day. One of them gave Richardson a kind of knowing smile that said, "Yes, I'm sure the President can be a pain sometimes."

Richardson, for his part, seemed outwardly at least to take the interruptions and the irritations in stride. He grasped at once the dimensions of what the Baltimoreans were telling him, and he never challenged the authenticity of it. "I had a kind of instinctive confidence in what appeared to me both the decency and the professionalism of the way in which this whole thing was being handled by Beall and his staff," he said later. As an old prosecutor and investigator into similar kickback scandals in Massachusetts, he said, he knew they "were already in possession of what on its face was more complete and convincing testimony than I had ever been able to assemble in my own investigation."

Methodically, Richardson began to raise the big issues. What would the effect of the Agnew case be on the capacity of the administration to govern? Almost from the start, Richardson was appalled at the possibility that, if Agnew were guilty, fate could result in the ascendance of a felon to the Presidency. He wanted immediately to confront the Vice President with the evidence against him. Agnew would have to deny the charges and offer proof of his innocence, or he would have to resign. Richardson authorized Beall and the others to press forward with their investigation in the most thorough manner, and expressed the hope that Agnew would indeed resign if guilty and confronted.

From the very first, then, the resignation of Vice President Agnew was seen by the attorney general as the most direct, desirable way to serve the public interest. It was a judgment that was to be the cause of considerable debate and some heat before the whole matter was resolved.

There was some discussion about whether it would be constitutionally permissible for the Vice President to appear before a grand jury, and Beall told Richardson that he and Judah Best had explored the idea of questioning Agnew by deposition. The group also talked about Matz's pleas for total immunity, and Richardson said only that a grant of total immunity ought to depend on the extent of Matz's cooperation and the strength of his evidence—so a decision should be deferred until a better judgment could be made on these points. He made it clear that he expected such final decisions would be made by Beall, but he told Beall to check with him before making any binding commitments.

It was vital, he stressed, that a case of such magnitude be solid, and that it be proved that Agnew actually had received cash. On the basis of his own experience as a U. S. attorney in Massachusetts, he said, that would be the toughest part. All those present understood that to confirm this key fact, it would be necessary to conduct a sweeping "net worth" investigation of the Vice President—this meant a check on everything that he and his wife had bought and received during and after the alleged payoff periods. It would have to be what is called a third-party net worth, getting the information from the others in any transaction —shopkeepers, car salesmen, jewelers, even local haberdashers in this case, since Agnew was renowned as a meticulous and impressive dresser—and that, they knew, risked undesirable publicity. But eventually it would have to be done.

Finally, Richardson came to a question that had been on all their minds all along—and his particularly, given Nixon's agitation over the San Clemente story. He turned to one of the prosecutors and, without fanfare, asked simply: "Do you think I ought to tell the President yet?" That the Attorney General of the United States would pose such a question to three young underlings he had never met before both startled and pleased them. Asking the question, more than the question itself, set a tone of shared concern and responsibility that marked all their later meetings and brought the Baltimoreans quickly into Richardson's camp.

On the question itself, the prosecutors were not anxious to have Nixon told yet, because they were frankly concerned that, in the words of one of Richardson's men, "things told the President might get back to the Vice President. If you have two business partners, you don't tell one that the other is under investigation. And telling the President was telling Haig and Buzhardt. We kept quiet because we were terribly afraid." The prosecutors, also cool to Richardson's notion of confronting Agnew with the evidence already in hand, did not want Agnew to start building a defense after the fact, based on any inside knowledge of what the government knew. Nor did they want new pressure to remain quiet applied to their witnesses.

Richardson himself weighed the matter heavily, both then and later. The matter was, indisputably, of intense national importance, and it would be most embarrassing if the President were to learn about it from another source, including the press. At the same time, the President had plenty of trouble with Watergate; Agnew might be exonerated after all, and there was no reason to worry Nixon needlessly. "I did not want to disturb him prematurely," Richardson said later, "in the event that it should turn out that those people were not telling the truth or that the evidence might otherwise just not add up." So he agreed to sit on the story for the time being.

In making this decision, and in confiding to them about his tribulations with President Nixon over Cox, Richardson got off to a good start with the three assistant U.S. attorneys. They had gone to the meeting with general trepidation, but they were greatly encouraged by his open discussion of a key matter of high administrative policy that was entirely within his prerogative to dispose of as he saw fit. Indeed, they were impressed with Richardson in every way, and any thoughts that he was going to snatch up their gem and quickly pawn it to improve his own position—always uncertain—within the uptight administration were dispelled.

Tim Baker's reaction to his cool, aristocratic superior was particularly amusing. Describing the attorney general's demeanor later, the young prosecutor recalled: "Every once in a while, while somebody else was talking or while something was going on, he'd look at me and give me this little smile. Like, 'Isn't this fun, being here?' You know, a couple of guys from the Harvard Club." But Skolnik, as well, was vastly impressed by Richardson's coolness and magnanimity. "I had envisioned it very much as a private-to-general kind of report, with a salute at the beginning and the end of what we had been told. And then you say politely, 'What we would like to do, with your permission, sir, is to interview them,' and whatever. It wasn't that kind of thing at all."

Beall and his associates were with Richardson for about three hours, but because of the frequent interruptions, sometimes last-ing fifteen minutes or more, their actual time with him was prob-ably less than an hour. Richardson had presented an outline of the matters he hoped to cover, so each time he received a note from his secretary and ducked out, the Baltimoreans would hud-dle. Skolnik, who to the surprise and amusement of his team-mates had remained silent for the most part in the attorney gen-eral's presence, would take the lead, giving his reading of how the meeting was going, how Richardson was reacting, and what ought to be said to steer him down the road they wanted to take. But for all that, it was Richardson's meeting with subordinates, and he never let them forget it. All their future encounters were to be the same.

The Baltimore team left Washington satisfied and encouraged. They had feared they might encounter an obstructionist, and they had found instead a strong and impressive ally, with plenty of reasons of his own—dramatically demonstrated to them that very day—to keep a wary eye on the White House as the now-enlarged Justice Department investigation of Agnew went forward.

Richardson, for his part, came out of the meeting shaken, for all his surface composure. He called in J. T. Smith and told him what he had heard, "by way of reassuring myself that there really wasn't anything I could or should do." That night, when he went to his home overlooking the Potomac in McLean, Virginia, he told his wife, Anne, that "a bad scene was developing, and that it involved the Vice President. I expressed some worries about the fact that I might be perceived to have some personal interest or animus" in seeing Agnew go—since Richardson as well as the Vice President was being mentioned as a possible Republican presidential candidate in 1976. "It was a deeply disturbing pic-ture," Richardson said later. "I felt sick, almost. It was as bleak a day as I'd ever had." The satisfaction that the Baltimore team felt, knowing Richardson was there, was not present in the man himself, as he contemplated the crisis ahead for his embattled department, his beleaguered administration, and above all his country.

7 The Ring Closes

In the fantasy world of every criminal investigator is the discovery of the perfect witness—the man or woman with total recall and a personal diary to back it up. The Baltimoreans, returned from Washington with a mandate to build an airtight case against the Vice President of the United States, were greatly in need of such a witness. They already had Lester Matz, who several days after the meeting with Elliot Richardson came in, edgy and obsequious, and spilled out his story. It was substantially the same account that Joseph Kaplan and Arnold Weiner had conveyed earlier, including the payoff in the Vice President's office in the spring of 1971, and it was plenty damaging to Agnew. But what the prosecutors needed now was solid documentation.

Beyond their wildest expectations, they began to get it at the beginning of July, when Weiner presented the letter of negotiation signed by Jerry Wolff and told the outlines of Wolff's story. On July 10, Wolff himself provided the deeply incriminating details. Tense, agitated, punctuating his story with overly loud, nervous laughter at things that were not funny, he offered this account:

In April 1966, Wolff was approached by The Close Associate of Baltimore County Executive Agnew. The Close Associate asked Wolff for money in return for county contracts that Agnew had arranged for him to receive. Wolff paid The Close Associate $1250 in cash, another payment of indeterminate amount to another Agnew associate for "legal fees," and one or two other payments.

Later in the same year, when Agnew ran for governor, Wolff gave him a cash contribution of $1000 and also worked in the campaign. If he were elected, Agnew suggested, Wolff might be made chairman-director of the state roads commission. Governor Agnew made good on the promise and Wolff took office on March 1, 1967. One of his chief tasks was to monitor every consulting engineering and construction contract in the state. It was a commanding position; under state law, for all practical purposes he controlled the selection of engineers and architects on every roads commission contract, subject only to Agnew's approval.

Shortly afterward, Agnew's old friend Bud Hammerman approached Wolff. Agnew had instructed him to ask Wolff to join in an arrangement whereby Wolff would notify Hammerman which engineering firms were in line for state contracts, so that Hammerman could contact them for cash payoffs. Agnew had advised Hammerman that this conformed with a long-standing Maryland system under which engineers made large "cash contributions" in return for government contracts. Both he and Hammerman would be burdened with substantial financial demands from the political community, Agnew said, and it was only fair that those benefiting from the contracts bear their share of the burden. Wolff agreed to participate in the scheme and proposed that he, Agnew, and Hammerman split the proceeds in three even slices. Agnew balked; at first he told Hammerman he didn't see why Wolff should receive anything at all, but he agreed as long as he—Agnew—got his *half* of the pie. Hammerman went back to Wolff and they agreed to split the remaining half between them.

For the next eighteen to twenty months, Wolff told Hammerman which engineers were in line for state contracts, and Hammerman kept him informed of which engineers were paying off. In time, the contracting community came to know that Hammerman was the man to see, and in time there was no need for Hammerman to make a hard pitch. The engineers were expected to make "political contributions," almost always in cash, and even when there was no campaign to contribute to. Wolff told Hammerman the kickbacks should average 3 to 5 per cent of the contract, but Hammerman took any reasonable amount—sometimes at time of contract award, sometimes as contract payments were made by the state, sometimes in a lump sum, sometimes in installments. When Hammerman got the name of an engineer with a new contract, he would call, "congratulate" him, and arrange for a meeting at which the payoff was made. Hammerman would keep his 25 per cent, give Wolff his 25 per cent, and put Agnew's 50 per cent in a safe-deposit box until Agnew called for it.

At first Wolff kept his share at home, then he transferred it to two and later to three safe-deposit boxes, two in Baltimore and one in Washington. He spent most of the money on ordinary personal expenses over the next four years, but he used a small portion of it for kickbacks to other public officials in return for contracts given to two consulting firms in which he retained an interest—kickback money to pay kickbacks!

Wolff was a highly qualified engineer, and so it did not seem out of the ordinary that he would make recommendations to the governor on who should do government work, and that Agnew generally would concur in his selections. As a basic premise, Wolff insisted that the firm chosen be competent to do the job, and Agnew and Hammerman on occasion would suggest to Wolff that a particular company ought to receive special consideration. Sometimes Wolff was asked to "recommend" a firm that was not kicking in—in order to create a pattern of general fairness and to avoid large and transparent deviations from that pattern, such as giving any one company a disproportionate share of the available contracts. But Wolff was so clearly the czar in making contract awards that some of the engineers and architects who were not kicking in took to wearing buttons that said, "Who's Afraid of Jerry Wolff?" And in pressuring engineers, Hammerman was so heavy-handed that one of them once went to Agnew and complained. Agnew, apparently fearful that the engineer would make his complaint public, gave orders that the engineer's firm receive some work.

Sometime after Agnew's election as Vice President in November 1968, but before his inauguration, Agnew asked Wolff to draw up a list of the contracts awarded during his term as governor to Green Associates, Inc., a Maryland engineering company. Wolff discussed the list with the firm's president, Allen Green, revised it somewhat, and turned it over to Agnew. The clear inference to be drawn from this exercise was that Green had been paying off and Agnew planned to use the list to persuade him to continue.

The details of Wolff's story were damaging enough. But what made his willingness to cooperate with the government even more important was the supporting material he brought with him. He was, in the description of one of the prosecutors, "a pack rat, a guy whose nature is just to keep a lot of documents . . . who had kept an incredible amount of paper contemporaneous with events and had destroyed none of it." He also kept diaries, small pocket-sized day-timers in which he wrote painstakingly detailed notes in tiny script of what had gone on each day. (An example, in blue ink, read: "Paid to _____ _____, $9024, Bay Bridge.") He had, the prosecutors found out to their joy, a little book for almost every month of every one of the last ten years, with only a few gaps—none of them in the years 1966–68, when Agnew was governor. The inks in the small diaries were chemically tested and other tests of authenticity were made. A fifty-two page report by the Scientific Services Division of the Treasury Department's Bureau of Alcohol, Tobacco, and Firearms established that the inks Wolff used, of various colors, were on the market at the times the notations were said to have been made.

Wolff was able to produce the list he prepared of Green's business with Agnew and other documents that, in one of the prosecutor's words, "screamed authenticity because of the way they were. They were little handwritten pencil things on a piece

of notepad paper . . . some scruffy little thing which is all dog-
eared from its age." He also had lists prepared in the summer of
1968, in advance of Agnew's campaign for the Vice Presidency,
of all the engineers whom he understood to be paying Agnew,
on the assumption Agnew would want to have them to raise
campaign funds. One was a list of the top ten engineering firms
that had received government contracts under the Agnew administration, in order of how much they received. He even had a
code of pluses and circles by which he marked those who were
paying through Hammerman and those who were paying directly
to Agnew. It was from this list that the prosecutors first identified
the seven firms that were making kickbacks through Hammerman
and the two or three that were paying Agnew directly. Wolff's
detailed contemporaneous documents, with dates and amounts
of contracts and kickbacks he received through Hammerman,
were all turned over to Beall and retained as corroboration for
presentation to the grand jury and, eventually, for use in trial.

All this incriminating and detailed information clearly called
for another meeting with Richardson. And so did one other development. On the morning of July 9, Beall had gotten another
routine phone call from Judah Best, and he had had to tell him
that while there was nothing they could talk about on the telephone, things were indeed happening. He suggested that Best
phone for an appointment when he returned the next day from
his business trip to Florida.

But Skolnik thought that meeting, or even talking to, Agnew's
lawyer was a bad idea. The case against his client had become
too strong to maintain any casual relationship with Best. So when
Best phoned again—it was the same day Wolff told all—the three
assistants were in Beall's office with him. Best wanted to come in
the next afternoon, but Beall told him that on reflection it seemed
to him inappropriate to talk any more. If the need arose for the
U.S. attorney's office to get back in touch with Best, Beall said,
they certainly would do so. "I understand," Best replied, simply.
"Thank you." And he hung up.

Best did no doubt understand. His periodic calls to Beall,
they both knew, were fishing expeditions, to determine whether

the Maryland investigation was veering in Agnew's direction and, if so, how close it was coming. Beall's don't-call-us, we'll-call-you message to Best could have only one meaning: the Baltimore investigators now had the Vice President of the United States squarely in their sights.

Now Best had not made these periodic calls to Beall after simply raising a wet fingertip to the wind or perusing an astrological chart. The calls nearly always came right after some significant break in the case—the coming forward of some witness who contributed information, or the like. It was not hard to conjecture what was going on: some of the principals in the case, old Agnew friends like Matz and Wolff, had been sending out SOS signals through Hammerman, perhaps with the veiled or open threat that unless the Vice President bailed them out of their trouble, he would find himself in it with them.

From all this, it was clear that the time had come to give the attorney general another full-blown briefing. In the late afternoon of the next day, July 11, the team again drove to Washington in Beall's car and met with Richardson into the early evening, this time in his small inner office. Although their first meeting with the attorney general eight days before had gone a long way to quiet their fears that the Justice Department might somehow interfere with or compromise their work, that fear again welled up in them as they walked in. There sat somebody who Skolnik, Baker, and Liebman had never laid eyes on before. The old paranoia started working again: was he a White House type, on hand to throttle them or to find out what devious and disloyal business they had been up to? Or to infiltrate their circle and report back to the Vice President? (Actually, in their usual pre-meeting effort to consider all eventualities in advance, the quartet had weighed what they would do if there was someone present from the White House or from Agnew's office.) It was a few minutes into the discussion before Richardson in his casual way said: "Oh, by the way, this is J. T. Smith"—his executive assistant and member in good standing of his inner circle. The atmosphere eased somewhat but not entirely, for Beall's assistants were so accustomed to carrying their huge secret alone that they had difficulty comfortably discussing it with an individual they had never met before. Soon, though, the Baltimore group was functioning as a team with their counterparts on Richardson's staff, yet always with their own loyalties and interests guiding them.

The attorney general had an agenda this time. The items he wanted to talk about were:

1. When, if ever, and under what conditions should Agnew be confronted with the allegations against him and given an opportunity to answer questions under oath?

2. Should the attorney general advise the President that the investigation was going on?

3. Which potential witnesses in the investigation should be given complete immunity from prosecution?

4. Did the investigation come under the jurisdiction of special prosecutor Archibald Cox?

The first three questions were not new and they gave the Baltimoreans no pause. At the very thought of the possibility of Cox being brought in, though, Beall and company saw wings sprouting on their cherished Agnew investigation. But before getting to Richardson's own agenda, Beall and Baker briefed him on Matz's personal testimony, which they had just taken. Richardson, doodling as he listened, wanted to make certain that the connection could be made between Matz's payments and the contracts he received; the Baltimoreans assured him that Matz had so testified.

Richardson then launched into a long discussion of what could be expected from Agnew in defense. He might claim either that the payments were only campaign contributions, or that Matz's story was a total fabrication. Only the net-worth investigation would establish that Agnew had taken the money and used it for personal benefit. But you couldn't conduct the kind of investigation required, he said, without letting the story get out.

Richardson was a careful, methodical conversationalist who paused often in mid-sentence but didn't like to be interrupted. Baker listened to him for a long time, waiting for a chance to break in, while the attorney general played devil's advocate. Finally, Baker availed himself of a lull and told Richardson about the Agnew-Wolff-Hammerman arrangement and about Wolff's documentation supporting his story. That was all Richardson needed to hear. He never again raised the question of Agnew's possible lines of defense; he realized, as the Baltimoreans had when they bagged Wolff and his bonanza of notes, that they now had evidence on which the Vice President of the United States could be indicted.

But once again Richardson raised the idea of going to Agnew and telling him what they had, in the hope that he would resign. He feared that in the crisis atmosphere of Watergate and concern about the President's own durability, fate or circumstance would intervene to elevate Agnew to the Presidency, creating what he called "consequences for the ability to govern."

The logic that Agnew would step aside so easily perplexed the Baltimore investigators, whose experience told them public officials did not act that way. Of Richardson and this logic, one of them said later: "That guy was so straight that he could not even think corrupt. He really did genuinely and sincerely suggest to us the possibility that if what we were now being told by the witnesses were true, when we confronted the Vice President he would say, 'Gee, that's right. You've got me, and I resign from the office.' We were saying—politely, of course—'Gee, Mr. Richardson [always that, never "Elliot," as his own lieutenants called him], most public officials don't do that.' And he would say, 'That's what I would do.' Very straight fellow."

To Skolnik, the old pro at thirty-two whose foremost interest was in preserving the case, Richardson's approach was amusing but insane. The time had come for the education of the Attorney General of the United States on the subject of confronting the target of a criminal investigation with the evidence, and giving him an opportunity to respond. As his colleagues indicated to him with facial expressions that they expected him to make the case to Richardson, Skolnik pitched in with a brief discourse, couched in the necessary diplomatic language one uses when one instructs one's ultimate superior on how to do his job.

Yes, Skolnik said, it was certainly true that for several reasons— and before any final decision were made, certainly before any indictments were offered to the grand jury—the Justice Department would want to give the Vice President an opportunity to respond to the allegations. But in giving him this opportunity you certainly didn't want to give him all your evidence. It just was not done in criminal cases; it could set a bad precedent. For one thing, it would give a suspect the opportunity to manufacture and tailor evidence and documents to the evidence you had against him. So with that in mind, you gave him only the general nature of the charges. Second, there was the matter of equal justice, of even-handed treatment for all citizens under investigation by their government. A Vice President ought to be treated exactly the same way as anyone else—no better, no worse than the average Joe down the street. But the problem was that in a routine criminal case, there never was any formal investigation by the prosecutor. Usually the investigator and the prosecutor were two different people: the investigator put the case together, and the first time the prosecutor learned anything about it was when the investigator turned it over to him, ready for indictment. Thus it was very rare for the investigators also to be the prosecutors.

(Skolnik delivered his lecture to the patient Richardson with as much finesse as he could muster. His own, bare-knuckles version of how the target of an investigation should be given a chance to respond was more like this: you gave him the opportunity to hang himself. You told him if he had anything to say, to come right in and tell it to the grand jury under oath. If he refused, you proceeded with the case, with more reason to believe your case was solid. If he came in and talked, and he was guilty, you had him.)

In any event, Skolnik went on, it was premature to confront the Vice President now. It was not customary to invite a potential defendant to respond until the investigation was nearly completed. Before confronting Agnew, you had to track down all the other individuals whose names had been provided in Wolff's material and build the full, airtight case. This could be done without excessive fear of publicity because the individuals themselves would have no interest in seeing their roles laid out in the press.

Richardson took over now. He stressed that although an early resignation of Vice President Agnew was in the best interests of the country, he agreed that it still would be necessary to proceed with the investigation and possible prosecution. It was of the utmost importance that the case be handled in such a way that the public was satisfied that whatever the final disposition, justice had been done. As for Agnew's eventual interrogation, and the possible granting of immunity to witnesses, Richardson said he was inclined to leave both matters to the Baltimoreans, but he asked that recommendations be submitted to him for final decision. And as before, the attorney general expressed concern that he was sitting on this historic case while the President of the United States did not know of it. Nixon had a right to know, he said, but there were some considerations. Suppose, after all, Agnew could establish his innocence to their satisfaction? The President, he observed again, had plenty to worry about as it was. With John Dean's testimony that the President lied when he said he did not know of the cover-up of the Watergate affair, there were the first rumblings of the previously unthinkable: impeachment. Still, for all that, Richard Nixon was the President of the United States, and Spiro Agnew was his man, the man who would succeed him in event of death or removal from office. And what if the President found out from some other source? How would that make Richardson look?

By this time, none of the four Baltimoreans was opposed any longer to having Richardson tell the President. First of all, they were convinced Nixon already knew about the case. They could not conceive that Agnew had not gone to the White House already with his problem. And because they had already developed a strong feeling of support and admiration for Richardson, they "didn't want him to get his ass in a sling with the White House," as one of them put it later. At the same time, though, they didn't want the President told in any great detail. They feared that he might say: "That's very interesting. Give me a ninety-page memo on it." Also, they continued to fear that the story would be leaked out of the White House to Agnew or the press.

It was the impression of the Baltimore team that Richardson started out in this meeting favoring the idea of telling Nixon almost at once, and that he then backed off in the face of these arguments. At any rate, he ended by assuring his visitors that in any report to the President he would exercise discretion, and that he had no intention of disclosing more than the bare bones of the case. Tentatively at least, he said, he would not advise the President until it was time to inform Agnew.

There was, it developed, a specific personal reason for Richardson's concern about the President remaining in the dark, and about the possibility that publicity growing out of harder pursuit of the case might tip the story to the press. The next day he was leaving on a ten-day vacation, during which time he would be virtually inaccessible, since he and some of his family were going to go down the Little Fork of the Salmon River in Idaho by raft with the environmentalist Russell Train's family. "I worried a good deal about whether or not I should go," Richardson said later, "because I was afraid that some newspaper story might break without my having told the President about the general situation. If it did break, I ought to be on hand. I decided I'd run for luck on that and I went anyway."

According to one of Richardson's aides, the attorney general was well aware that Nixon suspected he had national political ambitions; if the story got out while he was sitting on it, Nixon could have accused him of engaging in some kind of high-risk political gambit. Richardson himself told the Baltimoreans that the fact he was being mentioned publicly as a possible Republican nominee for President in 1976 might create a "problem of appearances"—the whole investigation might be seen as a personal effort by him to knock off the man then regarded as the frontrunner for the 1976 nomination.

It was in the context of the "problem of appearances" that Richardson finally arrived, nearly two hours into the meeting, at the question about which Beall and his team were most apprehensive—whether the Agnew case called for the involvement of Archibald Cox. Richardson reminded them that in his confirmation hearings to be attorney general, in which the appointment of a special Watergate prosecutor had been a key element, certain senators had made the point that there might be the appearance of impropriety if an attorney general appointed by the President conducted the Watergate investigation himself. With a wry smile, Richardson mimicked one of the legislators: "Of course, you understand, Mr. Richardson, we have no question at all about your personal integrity. It's just a matter of appearances." Richardson hadn't appreciated the remark, but he acknowledged that it was valid to be concerned about how the public perceived the Watergate investigation. It had been not only justifiable but necessary that a special prosecutor be appointed for that case.

In the case of Agnew, he said, the same argument of appearances could be raised, and so it was necessary to consider whether Cox should play a role. He was inclined, Richardson said, as the Baltimoreans held their breath, to think not. He was reluctant to turn the matter over to Cox because of the partisan cast of the staff Cox had been assembling (an observation that later was to take on great pertinence in the light of Richardson's own fate at Justice). Besides, he had complete confidence in the professional way that Beall's team had handled the case. What did they think?

Beall seized the opportunity. One of the objectives they all knew was uppermost in the attorney general's mind, he said, was the restoration of public confidence in the Department of Justice in the wake of Watergate, the ITT case, and other scandals. The Agnew case offered a great opportunity to do just that: to demonstrate the department's ability and willingness to vigorously enforce the law, even if it involved the Vice President of the United States. They could do it, the department could do it, Beall said forcefully.

This was exactly what Richardson wanted to hear. He expressed his agreement; Cox would be kept out. (Shortly thereafter, Richardson advised the Baltimoreans that he had discussed the Agnew matter with Cox, and there were no problems. They had been worried not only about having their case taken away and given to Cox but also about the possibility that some of their witnesses, dissatisfied with the deals offered them to testify in Maryland, might go shopping for a better arrangement from Cox; Richardson instructed Cox to send anyone approaching him in any way about the Agnew case straight to Beall.) The matter of jurisdiction never came up again.

One of the Beall team noted that the press had been making pointed inquiries about Agnew in Baltimore, and the prosecutors until recently had truthfully been giving them a negative response about his implication in kickbacks. What were they to do now? Lie? The attorney general made clear that they would have to do whatever was necessary to keep the story out of the press.

Once again the Baltimoreans returned home with the firm support and encouragement of the attorney general, and with instructions to press on to strengthen the case. There were many bases to touch: all those names in the Wolff "library," the engineers like Allen Green he said had participated in the kickback scheme; and, above all, Hammerman.

It so happened that during this intensive period of nailing down the case against the Vice President of the United States, Skolnik had on his schedule the only conceivable event that for a criminal prosecutor could take precedence: he was getting married. The wedding was three days after the meeting with Richardson, and Skolnik and his bride would be off on their honeymoon for a week. So Skolnik planned with his colleagues the procedures to be followed in his absence in contacting the key witnesses and potential defendants. The usual approach was to call the individual, ask him if he had a lawyer "knowledgeable about federal criminal practices," and tell him to call the U.S. attorney's office. That, for openers, was pretty good psychology. Then, when the lawyer called, he would be asked to come in, whereupon he would be given "The Speech." Skolnik, who had perfected "The Speech," held a seminar for the others before he left town on how to bring it off to best effect. It went something like this: "Your guy is in a lot of trouble. We're investigating the Vice President, and your client's in it. He's going to get indicted unless you cooperate. If you want to cooperate, and you tell us you're interested in pursuing negotiations [on a plea] we'll give you a form letter. We want you to talk to your client and tell him he's got to make a decision, or else he'll go to prison."

Calls started going out on July 12, the day after the last meeting with Richardson, and two of the earliest were to Allen Green and Bud Hammerman. Green retained one of Washington's most prestigious law firms—Williams, Connolly & Califano; Hammerman turned to Sachs, Greenebaum & Tayler of Washington, seeking the talents of Sidney Sachs. At Williams, Connolly & Califano, Green was assigned to one of the firm's young lawyers, Brendan Sullivan, instead of a principal partner—Edward Bennett Williams, Paul Connolly, or Joseph A. Califano, Jr.—since from what he had said on the phone, there seemed no need for him to have one of the heavies. He had mentioned something about contracts in Maryland—"It wasn't much of a problem," was the impression Califano received at the time. Sullivan, considered one of the firm's brightest prospects, went off to confer with Green about this matter concerning Maryland contracts.

A night or two afterward, the phone rang at the Califano residence. It was Sullivan, agitated. He had to talk to Califano, but not over the phone. The two arranged a meeting for late the next afternoon on Califano's sailboat. As the boat sailed the Chesapeake Bay with Califano's two children, Mark and Joe, aboard, the two lawyers walked to the bow. Sullivan told Califano that Green admitted paying off Agnew. Califano was stunned. He went home and ruminated over what he had just learned. Like the other lawyers before him, he worried about the future of the country, the ability of the administration to continue governing. Joseph Califano was a man who had long been drawn to the center of political power in Washington. He had been general counsel for the Department of the Army, then President Lyndon B. Johnson's chief domestic aide. Later, he was counsel to the Democratic National Committee, working the Democratic side of the street during the many legal wrangles generated by the Watergate break-in. Whatever Califano might have thought of Agnew, he was not cheered to learn that the political system had taken another punch to the solar plexus. Califano kept the news to himself.

Within the week, both Sidney Sachs and Brendan Sullivan had paid visits to Baltimore for preliminary talks with the prosecutors.

There was a steady traffic in and out of the courthouse as lawyers for still more panicked Maryland contractors hastened to Beall's office for a better understanding of what Baker meant when he contacted their clients.

On the day Skolnik returned from his honeymoon, July 23, Sullivan presented the details of Green's involvement with Agnew—about the $50,000 in cash payoffs while Agnew was governor and Vice President—and Green himself came in shortly afterward. But Hammerman held out. From Green, the prosecutors were able to identify others who had kicked in, and to contact them and deliver "The Speech" to their lawyers. But in addition to corroborating Wolff's account of how Agnew had asked for a list of his state contracts, Green also told an entirely new and incriminating story about his personal dealings with Agnew, both as governor and as Vice President.

Long before Governor Agnew's tenure, Green had become accustomed to making cash payments to public officials in return for various state and local contracts. It was seldom necessary that an express agreement be talked out; everybody involved knew the system, which functioned on a tacit understanding that engineers who paid got contracts and those who didn't got none, or at least few, and not the most lucrative ones.

Green first knew Agnew in mid-1963, when Agnew was Baltimore County executive. When he ran for governor in 1966, Green gave him between $6000 and $10,000 for his campaign, and after his inauguration, Green met him several times in the governor's offices in Baltimore and Annapolis. At one of those meetings, Agnew began to complain about the heavy financial costs of being governor. As leader of the Maryland Republican Party, he said, he needed money for his own political organization as well as funds to help Republican candidates around the state. Not only that, but he had to adopt and maintain a life-style far beyond his means. As county executive, he had served at a financial sacrifice, given the low salary of $22,500. The governor's newly raised salary of $25,000 was only the barest improvement;

it still wasn't enough to handle the new load. Throughout Agnew's tenure, this theme recurred in his conversations with Green.

As one who had been around the state capitol for some time, Green did not need the message spelled out. He told Agnew he recognized that the governor had financial burdens and wasn't a wealthy man. His own firm had done well on public contracts and probably would continue to do so; there was no reason why he couldn't help with periodic cash payments. Agnew said he would appreciate such assistance very much.

In the past Green had paid public officials up to an average of 1 per cent of the fees he received on public engineering contracts, both in campaign contributions and in straight kickbacks. On this basis, he calculated that he could make six payments a year to Agnew in amounts of $2000, $2500, or $3000 each, depending on how much cash he had at the time—always cash, to prevent anyone tracing the payoffs on the company books. Six times a year he would ask for an appointment with the governor to deliver the money.

On the first occasion, Green handed Agnew an envelope containing between $2000 and $3000 in cash, saying as he did that he knew of the governor's financial bind and wanted to help. Agnew took the envelope and placed it either in his desk drawer or in his coat pocket, and thanked Green. Over the next two years, as Green made regular payoffs, they gradually said less and less about them to each other; Green would just hand over the envelope and Agnew would take it.

The two men usually discussed state business at such meetings, and Green nearly always would take the opportunity to bring up the subject of special interest to him—state road contracts. He would tell Governor Agnew which road and bridge contracts his company was interested in; sometimes Agnew would promise him a contract, sometimes tell him it had been committed to somebody else. In all this, the payoffs were never mentioned, but they continued on a regular basis.

In each of the two years Agnew was governor, 1967 and 1968, Green paid him $11,000. In the same period, his firm received about ten contracts from the state roads commission with fees of between $3 and $4 million. Occasionally, Wolff asked Green whether he was taking care of his "obligations" with respect to the state contracts he was getting. Green said that he was.

As Wolff had testified in his own account of his arrangement with Agnew, he came to Green shortly after Agnew was elected Vice President and showed him the list he had prepared at Agnew's request of the contracts Green had gotten from the state roads commission under Agnew. Green concluded that the purpose of the list was to assess what he owed Agnew. Wolff and Green discussed the matter and bargained it out, Green arguing that some of the contracts on the list had been awarded during the previous administration of Governor Tawes. True, Wolff said, but the Agnew administration could have canceled some of them or switched portions of them to other firms. Green prepared a revised list and gave it to Wolff.

Only once during the two years that Agnew was governor did he ever expressly mention any connection between the payments Green made and the state work he received. That occasion came just before Agnew's inauguration as Vice President, when Green made a payoff in Agnew's Baltimore office. Agnew, referring to the list, noted that Green's firm had received a lot of work from the state roads commission: he was glad matters had worked out that way, Agnew said. Then came the poverty plea again. During the two years in the governor's mansion, he still hadn't been able to improve his finances and although his salary as Vice President ($43,000 plus $10,000 for expenses, raised to $62,500 in 1970) would be much higher than his salary as governor, the social and other demands of lofty national office would put even greater pressure on his personal funds. So he hoped Green could continue the help he had been giving him, and he in turn hoped he could help Green get federal contracts. Green told the Vice President-elect he was willing to continue the payments, but he wasn't certain he could produce such large amounts as he had in 1967 and 1968. Contracts already awarded to his firm in Maryland would generate some income over the next several years, and so he could make the payments for a while; and he hoped his firm's federal contracts would indeed increase as a result of what the new Vice President could do for him. But there was one thing that did worry him, he told Agnew. The new state Democratic administration might take credit for and possibly demand payments on the basis of contracts that had been awarded to his firm by Agnew. The Vice President-elect told him he didn't believe that would happen.

Thus it was that Green continued to pay Agnew off personally, delivering $2000 three or four times a year either to the Office of the Vice President in the Old Executive Office Building, or to Agnew's apartment in the Sheraton Park Hotel. As in the past, cash was always in a plain envelope, and Green and Agnew were alone when it was handed over.

The first time he did it, Green felt particularly uncomfortable. Making a payoff in the very office of the second-ranking official in the government of the United States, with the Seal of the Vice President on the wall behind Agnew's desk, was bad enough; but Green was concerned that his conversation with the Vice President might be overheard or even taped. So when he handed over the envelope he told Agnew the money was part of a continuing and unfulfilled commitment in "political contributions." As he said it, he raised his eyes to the ceiling, silently conveying to Agnew the reason he was saying something the Vice President patently knew was not so.

The last payment Green made was during the Christmas season in 1972, after the U.S. attorney's office in Baltimore had begun to look into corruption in Baltimore County. All told, in addition to the $22,000 Green paid Agnew when he was governor, in 1969 and 1970 he paid the Vice President $8000 a year—four payments of $2000 each; and in 1971 and 1972, $6000 a year—three payments of $2000 each. That brought the total Agnew received from Green over the six years to $50,000.

The Green story was explosive in its detail, and in the portrait it painted of Agnew: a blatantly greedy public official who somehow justified his demands for graft on the social and political obligations placed on him as he climbed the political ladder.

Green himself had been matter-of-fact about the relationship he had enjoyed with Agnew. He told the prosecutors, as he had told others, that he long ago concluded that payoffs were an integral part of the engineering scene in Maryland and some other states. He had plunged into this with his eyes open, waiting for the day when his firm would reach the size at which it could no longer be ignored—payoffs or no payoffs. In his estimation, he had nearly reached that point when he received the phone call from Baker. He had closed his business in West Virginia, complaining that the politicians there were getting greedy, and he also refused to do any more business in Baltimore County. It was only a matter of time until the politicians there got caught, he told his staff.

Green's participation in the kickback scheme was particularly upsetting to Beall. Green was an old friend of the Beall family, a former race-track chum of Beall's father, the late senator. And one of his new employes was Richard Beall, a brother of the senator and of the U.S. attorney. George Beall from that day forth refused to handle any aspect of the investigation dealing with Green and prayed that his brother would remain simply an anonymous employee.

On July 27, the Baltimoreans went for a third time to see Richardson, who had managed to navigate the Salmon River without the interference of a national crisis. Almost miraculously, though reporters were heavily on the scent, not a word about Agnew had broken into print since May 18, when the first disclosures were made to the prosecutors concerning what Matz had to offer. It was too much to hope that this good fortune would continue much longer. In a meeting lasting about two and a half hours in the attorney general's office, Skolnik told Richardson that press discovery of the investigation had to be imminent, since the inquiry now involved more and more principals and their lawyers. It was time, he said, to take formal action against Agnew.

Richardson wanted to be absolutely sure there was a federal criminal case to be made against Agnew, in light of the fact that most of the evidence the team had gathered concerned payoffs when he had been governor of Maryland, not Vice President. The

Baltimoreans cited applicable federal statutes concerning tax evasion, conspiracy, and extortion. Richardson also asked them if they had researched whether a Vice President could be indicted, and they told him they were satisfied he could.

Next the attorney general reiterated his reluctance to grant immunity to potential anti-Agnew witnesses, out of fear such grants would weaken the case in the eyes of the grand jury and the public, and would give Agnew the opportunity (which he later took, though no immunity was granted) to say that others were talking to save their skins. The Beall team reminded Richardson they had not promised anyone immunity in return for cooperation, though they were considering it for the three key witnesses who did cooperate early—Matz, Childs, and Wolff—and hadn't ruled it out for Green.

In fact, the manner in which immunity was granted or withheld was a very important factor affecting the U.S. attorney's ability to do future business with criminal lawyers in Baltimore. It was vital that the office have credibility, that when a lawyer was encouraged to bring a client into a case early, he would have reason to know the government would reward such action—or conversely, that when a potential defendant waited he would not get so good a deal. The U.S. attorney's office did not live by the parable of the vineyard, in which the householder paid the laborer hired at the eleventh hour the same wage he gave those who had worked a full day. It was first come, best served.

In any event, Richardson continued to worry about the immunity problem, and he told the Baltimoreans he was considering consulting about it with Henry Petersen, assistant attorney general for the criminal division. Petersen, then on vacation but due back in about a week, knew nothing of the Agnew case, even at this late date. The Baltimoreans expressed no objection to consulting him.

Finally, Richardson told his visitors, he had decided it was time to inform the President. He turned to the four Baltimoreans and asked, "Do any of you have any moral doubt as to Agnew's guilt?" None of them did. Skolnik said he thought that while the President should be informed, one would have to reserve final

judgment on Agnew until the Vice President had made a statement—through the grand jury. But the group was unanimous in
seeing no tenable defense for Agnew in the face of the available
evidence. Agnew already had been in touch with the White
House, the attorney general said, and there was a good chance the
story would soon break in the press. Richardson had to tell the
President now.

Along with Richardson's notification of the President, it was
decided that Beall's team would prepare a formal letter to Agnew
advising him in general terms that he was under investigation
for possible violation of federal criminal statutes. Its main purpose
was to elicit cooperation without giving too much information
away, and specifically to request Agnew's financial records. This
step was routine but in this case would be a milestone. Once the
Vice President of the United States was formally notified he was
under criminal investigation, the burden of proof was on the
Department of Justice, and the reputation of a national leader
was at stake.

According to the prosecutors later, it was not expected that the
letter would become public, and hence it was not considered a
point of no return, only a serious and necessary next step. For
Agnew, after all, it would not come out of the blue. Judah Best
had been calling since April to find out what was cooking, and
when on July 10 Beall had told him he'd better not call any more,
he certainly got the picture. The letter was to be drafted in
Baltimore and given to Best. Richardson knew what would be in
it but didn't ask to see a draft before it went out. Washington-
Baltimore collaboration was principally centered on the timing:
it was agreed that the letter would not be sent until J. T. Smith
had advised Baltimore that Richardson had met with and informed the President.

Soon thereafter, Richardson made a call to General Alexander
Haig and went over to the White House to talk to him about
getting an appointment with the President. Richardson told Haig
in sketchy outline the reason for his request, and Haig agreed to
arrange an appointment. Agnew had already talked to Haig and
the President about his troubles, Richardson learned, and had

also asserted his complete innocence. "What I told Haig," Richardson said later, "put a much more serious light on it than anything Haig had learned up to that point."

That weekend, Richardson went off to his summer place at Eastham on Cape Cod, awaiting word about when he would be able to see the President. On Sunday, Jonathan Moore, who was staying in nearby Orleans, dropped over, and as Richardson clipped the small cedars outside his home, he brought his aide up to date. They "talked through the topography" of the planned meeting with the President, Moore recalled later, and tried to anticipate what Nixon's reaction might be.

One might have thought that by now President Nixon would be burning up the wires to reach his attorney general. But Monday and Tuesday came and went with no word from the White House. Richardson, back in Washington, authorized release of the letter to Agnew—without informing the President of that action. As one who had served Nixon for a long time in various positions, he knew by then that one did not see the President the moment one asked. He knew too that when you told the full story about anything to Bob Haldeman or Al Haig, you were telling it to the President. You had done your duty.

On Tuesday, July 31, the letter of notification to Agnew was ready. Beall phoned Best in Washington and asked him to come to his Baltimore office the next day. Best agreed. Needless to say, the letter had been drafted and redrafted—the prosecutors wanted it to be perfect—and earlier versions requested many more documents than were eventually sought. But it was decided finally that if they asked for too much, Agnew could reply that the request was unduly burdensome. Enough was requested—personal bank records and tax returns—to suck him in; when he complied, the prosecutors hoped, they could hit him with a second request for more incriminating material. In its final form the letter said:

Dear Mr. Best:

This office is now conducting an investigation of allegations concerning possible violations by your client and others of federal criminal statutes, including but not limited to Section 371 (conspiracy), Section 1951 (extortion), and Section 1952 (extortion and bribery) of Title 18, United States Code, and certain criminal provisions of the tax laws of the United States (Title 26, United States Code).

It is possible that your client may choose to cooperate with this investigation. It is, therefore, the purpose of this letter to invite your client, or his authorized representative, to produce and deliver to this office on either Tuesday, August 7, 1973, or Thursday, August 9, 1973, at 10:00 in the morning or 2:00 in the afternoon, whichever is more convenient for your client, the following materials, to the extent that such materials are now in or under his actual or constructive possession, dominion or control:

(a) All bank statements, cancelled checks, check vouchers, check stubs, check books, deposit tickets, and savings account books (a copy of any active savings account book will be sufficient), for any and all checking and savings bank accounts in the United States and elsewhere in which your client has or had any beneficial interest or over which he has or had any control for the period January 1, 1967, to the present;

(b) Any and all retained copies of federal and state income tax returns for the period January 1, 1967, to the present.

I would appreciate your notifying me personally, on or before Monday, August 6, 1973, as to whether or not your client chooses to accept the invitation tendered by this letter.

In view of the serious nature of the allegations now under investigation by this office, any production of materials by your client, or his authorized representative, pursuant to this invitation must be completely voluntary on his part. Your client should understand that under the Fifth Amendment to the United States Constitution, he has a right not to produce the requested materials if he believes that the materials might tend to incriminate him. He should also understand that, should he choose to produce materials, they could be used against him in a criminal case, should any charges be returned naming him as a defendant.

I await your reply.

> Very truly yours,
> George Beall
> UNITED STATES ATTORNEY

It now was five days since the attorney general had told Haig about the investigation and had asked to meet with Nixon. He had done his part. Beall was authorized to give the letter over. At three o'clock in the afternoon of August 1, Best came to Beall's office. There he found the U.S. attorney and his three assistants, all seated in chairs placed far apart around the room. Wherever Best might sit, he would be surrounded by the prosecutors.

Beall made light of the scene. "Would you like to sit with your back to the wall so you won't be surrounded?" he asked Best.

"If it's all the same to you," Best replied, "I would rather sit near the window." They all laughed and Best sat down on a chair in the middle of the room.

"Jud," Beall said, "I prepared a letter which I wish to hand you."

"I'd be happy to accept it," said Best, taking the letter in its unsealed envelope. "Do you mind if I read it?"

"No," Beall said. "I think you should."

When Best had read the letter he acknowledged that this was very serious business. Beall apologized for requiring him to come all the way to Baltimore, but he had not wanted to trust such an important matter to the mails. Best assured him he had done the right thing, and thanked him. Best said he would be in touch with his client and would have a reply. It was all very, very gracious.

With that, Judah Best drove back to Washington to tell Spiro T. Agnew that he was the first Vice President in American history to be formally placed under criminal investigation.

8 The Dam Bursts

When Spiro Agnew received formal notification that he was under investigation for possible conspiracy, extortion, bribery, and tax evasion, he appeared to be looking even at this very late date to the power and influence of the White House to bail him out.

In all those weeks when Richardson was debating whether to tell Nixon about the Baltimore investigation, Agnew had been reaching into the President's political circle for advice about his troubles. It was naïve in the extreme to assume that Nixon did not already know—except for one possible consideration, the one that had persuaded Richardson to hold off informing him: concern that the Watergate-beleaguered President already had more woe than he could handle. In the isolation-prone White House, the possibility that others were protecting Nixon from more bad news could not be ruled out.

But all the signs pointed to Nixon's knowing. In April, when Agnew had felt the Maryland kickback scandal moving his way, he had not relied primarily on his own legal and political counselor, George White. Instead, he had sought out the Washington lawyer who had been the most notorious political schemer in the first Nixon administration, Chuck Colson. That Colson, with easy entree to the Oval Office, could be privy to such a morsel of inside political news and not pass it on to the President did not have much credibility among those who knew how Colson operated. Sources in the White House acknowledged later that at least four key presidential aides—General Alexander Haig, the new White House chief of staff; Bryce Harlow, special presidential adviser and old Agnew friend; and the two Watergate troubleshooting lawyers, J. Fred Buzhardt, Jr., and Leonard Garment—knew about Agnew's troubles sometime in July. That they would know and the President would not, strained credibility too.

Although Colson, facing possible indictment in Watergate-related affairs, asked his law partner Judah Best to handle the Agnew case, he was not one to keep his nose or his advice out of such a delicious bit of high-powered political intrigue. As late as July, he was meeting with Best and Agnew in the Vice President's office. Colson's presence there perplexed some of Agnew's closest staff aides, who were still completely in the dark about the gathering storm. "We were wondering what the hell Chuck was in there for," one of them recalled later. "And we didn't even know who the hell Best was."

Anyone who knew how Agnew felt about the White House and about the President would not have been very surprised that he had looked in that direction for assistance. All Vice Presidents, though constitutionally independent, have in a real sense been subject to the pleasure or displeasure of the Presidents under whom they have served, and Agnew certainly was no exception. The role they have played has always been circumscribed by the President, and for all Nixon's insistence that Agnew would be a major policy man in his administration, Nixon did not in his first term seriously alter the traditional relationship. What Agnew got in the way of challenging assignments and rewarding travel, and it was not much, had come to him as largess dispensed from the White House. The Prussian authoritarianism that was revealed and underlined in the White

House cover-up of Watergate demonstrated that not only the king but also key members of his court held monarchical power, and none understood this better than Agnew. He regarded the White House—President Nixon and the principal figures around him, even after Watergate—with something approaching awe. "The Vice President always spoke of White House power—how powerful they were," one of his associates said later. "It was basic to his approach to the Vice Presidency. . . . This awe of White House power we saw last January [1973] when the White House came in there and stripped his staff. He should have told them to go screw themselves. What in the hell could they do to him? I told him, 'You don't have to take anything from those people. They didn't give you the Vice Presidency this time. You earned it this time. If you're going to run for President, then you've got to do it on your own. You can't do it with his [Nixon's] help because he's going to be the kiss of death in four years.' "

But Agnew would not do anything he thought would anger the President or his men. "It bothered him," the associate said, "but he was not as reckless as he appeared. He was not as independent as he appeared. I guess it may have been an authority complex, or maybe it was something else, but his priorities were such that he stood in awe of the White House. I could never understand why he should, on certain essential things. I didn't even think it was politically intelligent to defer to them. I told him, 'What's the worst thing they can do? Take your airplane away? Fly commercially. What do you think's going to happen when Haig and those people over there say, "Well, we don't like the way you're running around the country and making speeches. So we're going to take your airplane away." You say, "Fine, I'll fly Eastern." And then you're going to do that, and you know what the White House—Richard Milhous Nixon—is going to do? They're going to give you two airplanes. Because it will look socially embarrassing.' But there was always a vacillation on his part, not wanting to tear it in terms of his standing in awe of the White House and of the President."

For all his estate as one of the best-known men in America,

Agnew was not one to forget that the beneficence of one man—the President of the United States—had first brought him to that elevated position. While he often champed under the limitations placed on him as a functioning member of the Nixon team—especially by the autocratic John Ehrlichman, who took over the domestic domain in which Agnew had the most experience—he never lost his overpowering feeling of obligation to and respect for Nixon. Furthermore, he had seen the power of the Presidency at close range and how the man at the top got his way. So it was predictable that the Vice President would almost obediently turn to the White House in his trouble, particularly to Colson, who, in or out of the administration, was regarded as Richard Nixon's hatchet man.

In addition, there was one other reason for Agnew to look to the White House for help. If a Vice President could be indicted, then perhaps, in the climate of Watergate and the suspicions of Nixon's culpability, so could a President. Thus it seemed to be in the interest of the White House to support the defense that neither official could be indicted under the Constitution so long as he remained in office. For a number of weeks, Agnew was able to maintain that identity of legal interest with Nixon, and to use it to some degree as a crutch.

There were from this point on really two Agnew defenses, one political, the other legal. The political defense was the responsibility of Best, with Colson and his partner David Shapiro in the wings: finding out what the prosecutors were up to, then working through the White House to try to strike a deal. For the strictly legal, courtroom defense, Agnew looked elsewhere. On Thursday, August 2—the day after Beall gave his letter to Best—Shapiro, a Democrat and veteran of civil liberties and civil rights cases, phoned Jay H. Topkis, a New York lawyer who had championed these same causes with him.

"Would you be interested in representing somebody in a criminal investigation who is near the top in this administration?" Shapiro asked.

"All the way to the top?" Topkis inquired.

"No, not all the way to the top."

Topkis began to name names, but not the right one. Each time, Shapiro would say, "Higher, higher." Finally, Shapiro gave the New Yorker some help. "Maryland," he hinted.

"Who's from Maryland?" Topkis replied.

When Topkis finally got the picture, he told Shapiro he was interested but would have to bring the matter up with his firm's new-business committee. What made Shapiro's offer concerning Agnew so remarkable was the identity of that firm: Paul, Weiss, Rifkind, Wharton & Garrison, among the most prestigious Democratic legal powerhouses in the country. Partners in the firm included or had included Arthur Goldberg, Ramsey Clark, Theodore C. Sorensen, and Judge Simon Rifkind (who had handled the projected defense in the abortive impeachment proceedings against Associate Justice William O. Douglas in 1970 [1]). When one of the authors of this book phoned Topkis shortly afterward, a secretary asked: "Are you calling on the Agnew case? Isn't it just incredible? Imagine him picking this law firm!"

The new-business committee agreed that the firm would take the case. Topkis, a liberal Democrat who had voted for George McGovern in 1972 and had an anti-Nixon poster in his office, chose as his associate Martin London, also a liberal Democrat who had helped to represent Jacqueline Kennedy Onassis in her invasion-of-privacy suit against the photographer Ron Galella.

Topkis asked London, "Marty, is there any reason we can't represent the Vice President of the United States?"

"Are we going to be paid?" London inquired.

"Yes."

'Then there is no reason we can't represent the Vice President of the United States."

Shapiro wanted Topkis and London to come to Washington the very next day, a Friday, to confer with Best. Both New Yorkers were excited over the prospect of defending the Vice Presi-

---

1 Among those who urged that Douglas's record be examined at that time was Agnew. "It may be appropriate," he said in a CBS interview on April 11, 1970, "to look at some of his beliefs, among which, as I recall, is a statement that rebellion is justified in cases where the establishment has acted the way it's acting at the present time."

dent, but each had weekend plans, and Topkis played it cool: "Can't it wait until Monday?"

By now Agnew had conferred several times with General Haig, and at last the matter was deemed of sufficient importance to warrant Nixon's personal involvement. On Friday, August 3, Richardson's appointment with the President finally came through. Richardson was at the Cape again, and Haig phoned him there; the President would see him on this unprecedented, shattering dilemma—the next Monday! On Saturday, Haig called again to suggest Richardson meet with Buzhardt and Garment on Sunday so that the two White House lawyers could properly brief Nixon in advance of the Monday meeting.

Up in Baltimore, at long last, the story the prosecutors had been sitting on at least since May 18—the day Kaplan first hinted of Agnew's involvement—was about to surface. Jerry Landauer of *The Wall Street Journal,* a tenacious investigative reporter who had been looking into Agnew's past for several years and had heard of payoffs to him but could not prove enough to write the story, finally hit paydirt. On Sunday, he talked to Beall by phone and to the prosecutor's surprise and dismay recited the first paragraph of Beall's letter to Agnew nearly word for word. The reporter, according to Beall, later said he had a source inside Agnew's office and that *The Wall Street Journal* was about to print the story. Beall immediately phoned Richardson and told him. The paper, however, instead of running the story in its Monday editions, held off a day to get additional information and comment from Agnew. The *Journal* didn't yet know whether the investigation concerned the period when Agnew was county executive, governor, or Vice President, nor what the alleged payoffs had been made for. By early Monday afternoon, *The Washington Post,* which also had been pursuing the story, learned from sources outside Agnew's office that something was about to break, and a team of reporters was working Washington and the state of Maryland by phone and by foot to track the story down.

The Sunday meeting, at Richardson's house, marked the first time that anyone at the White House learned in any detail what the case against the Vice President was. In effect the President's lawyers were confronted, as the President himself was to be the next morning, with a *fait accompli*. By delivering Beall's letter to Agnew's lawyer, the prosecutors were now committed, and any possibility that the President might try to quash the whole enterprise was removed.

There was, however, no evidence at all that there was such presidential interest. Beall's case against Agnew was so strong that almost at once the consideration was not how the investigation could be derailed, but how Agnew could be compelled to resign. Once the evidence was known at the White House, one aide said later, "The charter [to Richardson] was, 'You do what you have to do.'" The fact that Richardson had proceeded with the formal notification of charges against Agnew was actually welcomed, because it obviated the President's making a painful but necessary decision. Nor was there any suggestion that Richardson had moved too fast. Some of Agnew's people, and Agnew himself, later charged that this sort of case never would have reached this stage had it not been brought to light "in the climate of Watergate," when new standards of political morality were being applied and cover-up was impossible. There may have been some truth to this, one White House aide conceded later, but if so that made Agnew "a guilty bystander."

Buzhardt and Garment did express some concern about the origins and quality of the investigation; about the possibility that these young unknowns—especially Skolnik, who had worked for Muskie—might have run wild in their eagerness to bag such a major prize. Richardson assured them that Skolnik was a professional prosecutor with no partisan motivation. What about self-serving witnesses, trying to save their own skins? Richardson noted that no immunity had yet been granted to anybody. What about impeachment of a Vice President? And in particular, was there any distinction between the President and the Vice President as to whether they could be indicted before impeachment? Richardson said he would have a brief prepared on this question. The President's lawyers pressed these and other questions because they wanted to be sure the President had a factual basis on which to make determinations. But so persuasive was the evidence that

Garment and Buzhardt both felt that Agnew ought to resign at once. They were in the center of the Watergate mess, laboring daily to keep the President a step ahead of all the scalp-seekers, and they felt there was enough tumult without having a man under serious criminal investigation on the very doorstep of the Presidency.

Even short of that, what if Agnew, instead of resigning, elected to "go public"—with a counteroffensive of press conferences and television talks and speeches? Public confidence in government officials would be completely shattered. There was, the White House well knew, an antipolitics mood sweeping across the country as a result of Watergate, and such an extravaganza would only fan it.

Garment, in a briefing paper for the President's meeting with Richardson, included his opinion that it would be best if Agnew resigned. He quoted Richardson as saying, "If half the evidence stands up, this case will be stronger than any kickback case I have ever seen." But Haig deleted this opinion and sent Nixon just the facts as Buzhardt and Garment had gathered them. The memo was on the President's desk Monday morning.

On Sunday night, Richardson did some preparing too. He had his aide J. T. Smith track down Robert Dixon, the Justice Department's legal counsel, who was off having dinner at the Chevy Chase Club; Smith asked him to call Richardson back on a phone from which he could not be overheard. Dixon finally found one in the club's empty bar—a particularly unfortunate circumstance, for he certainly could have used a drink when the attorney general out of the blue asked him to get to the office early the next morning to do a crash research job "on the indictability of a sitting Vice President." Richardson also had trouble reaching Beall; neither the White House switchboard nor the Justice Department had his unlisted phone number. (His brother the senator finally produced it.) Richardson asked Beall and Baker to be in Washington for a briefing and planning session in the morning.

There was, in short, more time being spent getting ready for meetings than was being spent in the meetings themselves. It was

sound legal and tactical practice, but at the same time it underlined the adversary atmosphere, or at the very least the climate
of wariness, that existed on all sides within the high-level bureaucracy of the Nixon administration.

All the men in the Justice Department who were privy to what
was going on had expected *The Wall Street Journal* to break the
Agnew story on Monday morning, August 6, and when it did not,
they knew that Monday would be Richardson's last chance to
put the situation to Nixon. Before Richardson went to the White
House, Beall and Baker reviewed for him the origins, early goals,
and present status of the investigation. They had testimony from
a "Mr. X" who had refused to make kickbacks, and they predicted
there would be two sets of indictments, probably in mid-September. They would be in a position to indict Agnew for violations
of federal acts dealing with bribery, conspiracy, and extortion,
but did not think they would be ready to indict for tax evasion.
The "net-worth investigation" on Agnew was not yet under way,
so it could not be proved that he had undeclared income. (Richardson at one point asked whether there was any truth to allegations that they had used abusive techniques. Beall bristled. The
very idea angered him, he told Richardson, because the investigation had been entirely proper—aggressive but proper—with hard
cross-examination of all witnesses who had appeared to be lying.
Richardson didn't seem to take the allegations very seriously, and
he alluded once again to his experience as U.S. attorney in Massachusetts: most potential defendants were critical of the prosecutors and the process.

Richardson also was armed by now with Dixon's briefing papers
on indictability. Among his conclusions were that as head of the
executive branch the President could direct his own prosecution
prior to removal from office and exercise his pardon power on
himself, whereas the Vice President could do neither and hence
could be indicted.

The briefing session lasted until ten minutes before Richardson was to see the President at the White House at 10:30, and he
rushed straight from it to 1600 Pennsylvania Avenue. In the Oval
Office, Haig and Buzhardt were there waiting with Nixon, a

President already groggy from the Watergate developments revealing further excesses of greed for political power in his administration. Now he was to hear details of a much more old-fashioned brand of greed, as practiced by a man he himself had plucked personally from obscurity and to whom he had given the chance for fame and, possibly, even greatness. The attorney general proceeded to provide an outline of the case against the Vice President. Nixon listened attentively, somberly. "The President appeared to be ready to believe it," Richardson said later. "His reaction was remarkably objective and deliberate. . . . He was disturbed and concerned with the correctness of any action or anything he did or did not do. At first he thought he ought to have an independent assessment of the evidence from Henry Petersen and me, on the basis of which he could then decide whether or not the situation called for Agnew's resignation. He later concluded that he ought not to try to be fully informed about the state of the evidence, and that his position ought to be more insulated. I was prepared to give him the assessment. Henry, who had been on a long vacation, had only got back the same day. At that point, the interests of the President, the Vice President and myself seemed to converge on the desirability of Henry's making his own review of the investigation." And so it was ordered that Petersen would assess the case and report to Richardson and Nixon.

Within the White House, one man who was an adviser and admirer of both the President and Vice President, Patrick J. Buchanan, picked up some early signals of bad blood between the White House and Agnew's staff loyalists. Friends on Agnew's staff were complaining that the Vice President was being cold-shouldered, so Buchanan went to Haig and inquired what was going on. Haig filled him in on the essentials of the Justice Department's case, and Buchanan was stunned. He couldn't believe it. It was this sort of reaction that made a review by Henry Petersen—who had the credibility in the White House that a Barney Skolnik lacked—so advisable. If Petersen said Agnew was a crook, Agnew's defense, and his support within the administration, would be seriously undercut. Although it was clear to

Richardson almost from the start that the President wanted Agnew out, there was always the matter of the Agnew constituency to be considered. Agnew's removal, in the White House view, had to be accomplished in a way that would not unduly alienate conservative voters and conservative Republican leaders, whose support Nixon in his own travail now needed desperately.

Hence Petersen's report was politically important. In the meantime, though, if Agnew could be persuaded to go quickly and quietly, without waiting for that report, then so much the better for everybody—and especially for Nixon. When Richardson got back to his office at Justice, Haig called and suggested that he go talk to the Vice President. Maybe a direct confrontation with the facts would push Agnew over the edge; then they all would be done with it. This, of course, was exactly what the prosecutors in Baltimore wanted to avoid, and what they thought they had averted with their formal letter to Best specifying the charges against Agnew. But when Haig made a "suggestion," he spoke for the President, and so Richardson in mid-afternoon went over to the Old Executive Office Building and called on the Vice President. Agnew's new legal team of Best, Topkis, and London was already there. The story was about to break in *The Wall Street Journal,* and they were considering what kind of statement he ought to put out in response, when Richardson came in.

Richardson arrived without preconceptions about how Agnew would react, but—unlike the prosecution-minded Baltimoreans— hopeful he might agree to resign. "I thought it was important that this result be achieved," he said later. "I didn't know what he was going to do but I got the impression from the President and his staff, Buzhardt and Haig, that they believed that this was a real possibility." The White House, along with Richardson, wanted that swift resolution, he said, as direct applications of White House pressure then and in the days to follow amply demonstrated. "There were certainly discussions between Haig and the Vice President about the possibility of resignation and the rather practical implications of this, and all the arrangements that would be involved. It looked for a while that this was a possible course being seriously contemplated by the Vice President himself." The suggestion that he and Petersen give Nixon an independent appraisal of the strength of the case, Richardson said, "looked toward a meeting between the President and the Vice President at which the Vice President would be told that he faced indictment and that he could best serve the public interest by resigning first." In other words, if Agnew wouldn't go quietly at once, Petersen's report could be the crusher that would persuade him.

But for now, Richardson had the assignment to try for a quick knockout blow. So anxious was the White House to achieve this end, he later reported, that in several conversations with Haig and Buzhardt they had even discussed the possibility of the President offering Agnew a pledge of executive clemency, so the Vice President could not argue that fear of jail was keeping him in office. Executive clemency, though, was recognized, Richardson said, "as a possibility but an exceedingly difficult step for the President to take." What made it more than exceedingly difficult, of course, was the allegation of the discharged White House counsel John Dean (an allegation denied by the White House) that Nixon had discussed executive clemency for the convicted Watergate conspirator E. Howard Hunt, Jr.

To begin, Richardson informed Agnew that he was there at the request of the President to provide a summary of the status of the investigation in Baltimore. This he proceeded to do in somewhat more detail than is usual in prosecutions because, he said later, there were considerations "transcending the situation that would apply to a person who was not in immediate line of succession to the Presidency itself." Reading from notes, he finally told the Vice President specifically that Matz and Green had said they could testify they had made direct payments to him; Matz alleged that some of his payments were made after Agnew took office as Vice President and involved work done for the federal government subsequent to January 1969; Green alleged periodic payments to Agnew both as governor and as Vice President, the most recent having been at a family Christmas gathering in December 1972. Other engineers said they made payments they believed were intended for Agnew through Hammerman and The Close Associate. Six or eight had said that they regarded their payoffs in cash not as gifts or political contributions but as necessary payments to obtain county or state business. Finally, the attorney general said, Wolff would testify that he regularly submitted to Governor Agnew a list of architects and engineers eligible for state jobs from which Agnew would select primarily the ones who had made payments; Wolff had copies of such lists.

The Vice President's reaction was aggressively defensive. He was a proud man, with a demonstrated capacity for moral indignation, and he gave it full rein now. As Richardson reeled off the allegations, Agnew interruped. The whole matter, he insisted irately, was a pack of lies. Matz was crazy. True, he had chosen the architects and engineers for state jobs, but that was the normal thing for any governor to do. Agnew, always a man who deftly and mercilessly sought out others' vulnerabilities and attacked as his best defense, adopted the tactic now—against the prosecutors. They lacked objectivity, he charged. If the investigation were being conducted by a more objective team, it would have turned out differently. "He said he didn't trust the U.S. attorney's office," Richardson reported later, "but if Henry Petersen were supporting these allegations, that would be different, because Henry was an experienced professional with an established reputation for fairness and courage—a somewhat ironical attitude by contrast with statements he later made. . . ." What Agnew seemed to be saying was that if "objective" prosecutors had come up with the same facts, he wouldn't mind. But it was clear that Agnew and his lawyers were intent on undermining the credibility of the investigation no matter who the personnel were.

Best complained to Richardson about the prosecutorial tactics used in Baltimore, the statements like "You'd better get into the boat or it will be leaving without you," the witnesses being threatened with indictment, the cocktail-party chatter about "breathing down Agnew's neck." And he was particularly in-

censed about another thing: the way the prosecutors kept referring to the Vice President as "Agnew." That was disrespectful. He
should have been called "Mister Agnew." Richardson was amused
by this punctilious protest in the midst of such a tremendously
serious case, and so were the Baltimore prosecutors when he told
them about it later. (Richardson's aides had their own term of
endearment for the Vice President: in their internal discussions,
they called him "Spiggy.")

Agnew asked whether all the allegations were restricted to him.
Richardson said county officials also were involved. There had
been some testimony, he said, that kickbacks by architects and
engineers were still being paid.

Once again, Agnew thrashed out at the prosecutors. Not only
were they not objective; they were arrogant! Beall had lost control of the investigation. He had been off attending bar-associa-
tion meetings while his zealous assistants pressed ahead on their
own. Agnew wanted the prosecution in the hands of a more experienced professional. Like Petersen. But Richardson defended
Beall on all counts.

Then Agnew, attempting desperately to punch holes in the
government's case, started in on Allen Green. He first met the
man, he said, through Glenn Beall, George Beall's brother. Green
was constantly seeking his help, and he had a thick file of requests from Green he had turned down. As for Lester Matz, he
had seen him only four times in the five years he had been Vice
President, though Matz had been thundering to get in and crying
that he had been unable to get help.

Now came the old poverty pitch. As for his own finances, he
was a man of very modest means, with the bulk of his assets
tied up in the house he had just bought. The letter handed to
him on August 1 asking for his financial records by August 7 had
been delivered without warning, he complained. He was shocked
by the prosecutors' tone of contempt toward him, and it left him
with no confidence in their investigation. He did not relish being
indicted by testimony from individuals who were under the gun,
trying to save their own skins by shunting the blame upstairs. It
was grossly unjust. Indictment alone would be tantamount to

destruction for him, the end of fifteen years of political struggle. He was a citizen and he had his rights. Was he receiving the same treatment afforded normal defendants?

Topkis observed that if there was ever a need for a special prosecutor, a prosecutor removed from any political role in the state where the case was being brought, it was surely in this situation. But Richardson quickly disagreed. Beall hadn't lost control of the case and his assistants hadn't been overzealous, and in any case, he intended to ask Henry Petersen to make an independent assessment of the evidence.

The lawyers tried to pry more facts loose. London asked for a chance to make a detailed response to the allegations but said he would need a more specific summary, and complained that the attorney general was being particularly stingy with information. More was usually made available by federal prosecutors in routine cases, he insisted. But Richardson was noncommittal. Out of concern for avoiding leaks, he said, potentially corroborative steps had not yet been taken, like checking whether a meeting had occurred at a place and time testified to, and he re-emphasized that the secrecy of the investigation had to be preserved. Once Petersen had completed his review of the entire case, he said, the Justice Department would be in touch with Agnew's lawyers as to what the next step should be.

It so happened that at this juncture Henry Petersen knew absolutely nothing about what was going on, not even that there *was* an Agnew investigation. He had been off on vacation; he was a great sailor, and he had been isolated on his boat on the Chesapeake Bay throughout most of July, relaxing from what had been a bad year for him and preparing for his appearance before the Senate Watergate Committee on the very next day, Tuesday, August 7. Now, back at Justice, Richardson called him. "Henry, am I glad to see you! But are you going to be sorry you're here! Sit down, I've got something to tell you." And then the attorney general gave him the whole Agnew story and asked him to conduct a complete review of the investigation, at the request of both the President and the Vice President.

Petersen was not eager to get involved. He asked Richardson

to consider two things. Did the attorney general really want him to continue at all as head of Justice's criminal division, in view of the widespread criticism he had received of his handling of the Watergate investigation? If so, he went on, should a man in his situation, already under fire, get involved in what promised to be an extremely controversial case? Richardson answered "yes" to both questions, and Petersen agreed to undertake the review.

Richardson also brought one other principal into the matter. He briefed his still-to-be confirmed deputy, William D. Ruckelshaus, and asked him to join the key meetings.

After Richardson left Agnew's office, Agnew and his lawyers continued to work on a statement for the press. They recognized that their client had to make some sort of response, but they wanted it as brief as possible. They got pretty much what they wanted—a short statement—and everybody just waited into the evening for the story to break. Topkis and London, who had failed to bring a change to clothes to Washington, returned to New York. London called his father on Long Island and told him to be sure to watch the eleven-o'clock news. Topkis phoned his daughter at camp and told her the same. But this was one night when television was caught napping. The late news shows had nothing on Agnew.

Agnew and his press secretary, J. Marsh Thomson, stayed behind in the Old Executive Office Building, waiting for the threatened *Wall Street Journal* story that had failed to materialize once before. But any chance that another day might pass without the investigation becoming public vanished. *The Washington Post* also had the story and, like the *Journal*, was pressing Agnew for a reply.

"Where's the Vice President?" Thomson was asked by a *Post* reporter.

"He's in his office," Thomson replied.

"What's he doing there at this hour?"

Thomson admitted Agnew was waiting for the *Journal* story to break. The *Post* gave Agnew a deadline for releasing a statement. At eleven o'clock, Thomson finally phoned it to the *Post*, the wire services, the television networks, and—lastly—the *Journal*. By then, the *Journal* story was already being reported by the wire services, with the *Post* story not far behind.

The *Journal* story, by Jerry Landauer, began:

Vice President Spiro T. Agnew was formally notified by the Justice Department last week that he is a target of a far-ranging criminal investigation by the U.S. attorney's office in Baltimore. The allegations against him include bribery, extortion and tax fraud.

The investigation is being carried on in strictest secrecy. On receiving the Justice Department notice, the Vice President sought a White House audience, presumably to inform President Nixon. . . .

The *Post* story, by Richard M. Cohen and Carl Bernstein, said:

Vice President Spiro T. Agnew and two of his Maryland political associates are under federal investigation for possible violation of bribery, conspiracy and tax laws in connection with an alleged kickback scheme, *The Washington Post* learned last night . . .

Agnew, sources said, was informed of the investigation last week in a hand-delivered letter from George Beall, the U.S. Attorney for Maryland. Other targets of the investigation, according to reliable sources, are two of Agnew's long-standing friends and important fundraisers.

Agnew's reply was categorical and remarkably terse:

"I have been informed that I am under investigation for possible violations of the criminal statutes. I will make no further comment until the investigation has been completed, other than to say that I am innocent of any wrongdoing, that I have confidence in the criminal justice system of the United States, and that I am equally confident my innocence will be affirmed."

In Baltimore after midnight, when the prosecutors had all gone to bed, their phones began to ring; reporters from everywhere, scrambling to catch up on the story, pleaded, threatened, and cajoled for more details. But the prosecutors had nothing to say.

The word spread to others too. In Palm Springs, Peter Malatesta, a nephew of comedian Bob Hope and one of Agnew's chief aides, took calls from two other Agnew friends in the East. He could not believe the news, but he quickly passed it on, incredulous, to his neighbor Frank Sinatra (to whom he had originally introduced the Vice President). Together, he, Sinatra, and Sinatra's lawyer, Mickey Rudin, flew to Washington that very night.

In the capital itself, the political community took the news like a punch-drunk fighter walking into yet another haymaker. Victor Gold, Agnew's recently resigned press secretary, learned of the development in a phone call from a reporter. For one of the very few times in his life, Gold was at a loss for words. What finally came out were expressions of total disbelief and disorientation; he knew the man, he said, and the man had to be innocent, it had to be a mistake.

By the next morning, Tuesday, August 7, the whole nation and the world knew: Spiro T. Agnew, Vice President of the United States, voice of Middle America, straight-shooting Mr. Candor, Mr. Integrity of the Republican Party and American conservatism, was accused of being a crook and a fraud. True enough, there had been no indictment yet or even any submission of evidence to a grand jury. But the news that an official letter had informed Agnew that he was under investigation—signed and sent by a Republican U.S. attorney—was compelling. Surely, considering the tremendous stakes involved, no Republican prosecutor, or any prosecutor for that matter, was going to go out on such a limb unless he already had a case.

Still, at the Justice Department, Richardson was being pressed by the White House for further assurances that the case was airtight, and, if so, for more of it to be laid out to Agnew in the hope he would resign. At 8:30 that morning, Richardson met with Beall, Petersen, Ruckelshaus, and Smith. He wanted to know, once again, how good the government's case was; bluntly, what were the probabilities of conviction? And second, did it make sense to give Agnew and his lawyers more details than one normally might, in order to speed resolution of a national crisis? It would be easy simply to forbid any deviation from the normal practice, the attorney general said, but this was no ordinary case or ordinary defendant. The task facing the Justice Department might not be limited to the administration of justice in a narrow sense, because there was the contingency that if the Vice President were confronted with more specific factual information about the government's case, he might be compelled to resign. He acknowledged the risks in spelling out the case, but would it really enhance Agnew's ability to assess his own position? He asked Beall to go over the whole case with Petersen and Ruckelshaus so that the two newcomers could render independent judgments on what course to take. Beall agreed, but he argued that it would be highly undesirable to make greater disclosure to Agnew because he might inflict serious economic hardship on individuals who were unwilling to cooperate with the prosecutors, thereby drying up potential testimony. The threat of impending indictment ought to be enough to compel his resignation if he were so inclined, and Beall and his team felt strongly that the case had to be played "by the book." Agnew's lawyers had all they needed to make a legal decision on what to do. What they were fishing for was more information to help Agnew make a political decision on how best to fight the charges.

Petersen, in the case less than a day, opposed the idea of Richardson's meeting again with Agnew, and he complained that the White House seemed once again to be damaging the Justice Department by interfering—a view that squared with the Baltimoreans'. But what Petersen said next did not. He proposed that instead of another personal visit, a letter be prepared to give Agnew in detail the allegations against him, including the period of time, the firms, and the manner of payment involved. This would provide a formal record and would put the ball in Agnew's court; he could not then claim he hadn't been given a fair chance to respond to the charges; also, it would keep Richardson out of it. Beall objected strongly for the same old reason: the place for the accused to have his "opportunity" to respond was before a grand jury, under oath.

Again, the question arose—how much more should the President be told? Nixon might want a full memo on the prosecution of the case, and the group at Justice felt he was entitled to it if he were to exercise his responsibility on the disposition of the matter. But the Baltimoreans, still operating on the premise that

Agnew would come to trial and still suspicious that information going to the President might be leaked to Agnew, firmly opposed giving Nixon a full report. Debate on this point continued intermittently for weeks, while Petersen worked away on his "independent assessment."

After the meeting in Richardson's office, Beall phoned Baltimore and told his assistants about Petersen's proposal for a letter to Agnew. (Ruckelshaus and Petersen had said they wanted to hear from the three assistants before making any final decisions.) Baker forcefully objected to another meeting between Richardson and Agnew, or to a letter as suggested by Petersen. He said he could see no reason why the President needed a memo or needed any greater detail; to provide either would merely be another instance of the White House damaging the Department of Justice. When Petersen himself told him about the White House pressure to give Agnew more information and suggested his letter as "a middle ground" (a favorite Petersen phrase), Baker was even more turned off, but he told Petersen that at least the letter was less inappropriate than another visit to Agnew. Could Baker prepare a draft? Petersen asked. It had to be sufficiently general so that Agnew could not concoct a defense from the information gleaned, yet could not say he had not been given an opportunity to reply. The attorney general, he said, should not be forced to disclose any more information without a formal record. Baker agreed only with the first part of this—no more information, with or without a formal record.

Then there was the matter of giving the President the full story. The President was the senior political officer in the government, Petersen said; he had to make decisions based on legitimate political considerations—such as whether to force the Vice President to resign or to take a hands-off attitude. Baker countered: to afford the Vice President special treatment would severely damage the integrity of the Justice Department at a time when it was already under attack and losing public confidence. But, said Petersen, the President's position was like Beall's would be if he received allegations against Baker and had to decide whether or not to fire him. The analogy was imperfect, Baker countered: the

President had no constitutional power to fire the Vice President.

Beall came on the phone again. Baker told him that he and the others were not raising a "red flag of rebellion" in Baltimore, but they felt they were members of a team and the team was making a very serious error. It was agreed that the three should come to Washington and Beall promised that no decisions would be made until they had a chance to express their opinions. But within an hour Beall called back and said the White House had eased off about another Richardson-Agnew meeting that day. No reason was given.

While this inner-circle debate was going on in Richardson's office about how to handle Agnew and Nixon, Agnew's startled friends were beginning to come out of the first shock that had afflicted nearly all of them. They proceeded to examine their man's response, particularly the weak comment that nothing more would be said about the case, and they found it wanting. This, they felt, was not smart; more than that, this was not Ted Agnew. Vic Gold and Peter Malatesta, who had talked late Monday night by phone, agreed that Agnew had to say more. An innocent man—and they had no doubt that's what he was—did not behave in this way. Gold, on his own now and working with his customary frenzy to establish himself as a commentator and columnist, had been trying to move out of the automatic identity with Agnew that his service as the Vice President's very visible and vocal press secretary had brought him. It was not out of any desire to dissociate himself from the man; for Gold continued to admire Agnew greatly and demonstrate personal loyalty to him at every turn. But in order to achieve success in the news business, Gold knew, he could not forever open doors with somebody else's name, nor could he function as a serious political analyst if he was always thought of as "Agnew's man." He had been reluctant to cast himself in the role as counselor, even unofficially, to the Vice President. But this was a crisis, and his friend needed to be set straight. Gold called the Old Executive Office Building across the street from his own office and told Arthur Sohmer, Agnew's gatekeeper, "I think the Vice President is making a very great mistake. His statement is idiotic and I want to see him. I don't care who drew it up, I want to see him." Sohmer checked and told Gold to come over. "I told him," Gold said later, " 'You're an innocent man. You can't stand on this. You go right ahead and have a news conference.' " Agnew was noncommittal, and Gold left under the impression there would be no press conference.

Other friends, including Malatesta, who was not often given to offering advice to Agnew, weighed in with similar pleas. Agnew's own staff aides, more politically than legally oriented, did not buy the argument, put forward to them in measured tones by their boss, that he was involved in a legal matter which had to be left to his lawyers to handle in the way they deemed best. "He kept saying that," one of his aides said later. "We told him, 'You've got more than just a legal battle to fight.' "

Not all the advice Agnew was getting was running this way, however. At the White House, standard operating procedure as a result of Watergate, as well as the natural disposition, was to hunker down in time of adversity. Any thought of Agnew "going public" was distasteful—particularly so because the hunkered-down President was under increasing pressure to speak out on Watergate. The press wolves were howling again for a news conference; Nixon had not held one for nearly five months, and a battle was raging over whether he would surrender the White House tapes—evidence critical to establishing his guilt or innocence in the Watergate cover-up. If Agnew were to step out on the firing line in his darkest hour of crisis, an invidious comparison would be made. No, Agnew had better keep his mouth shut.

Thus Agnew found himself, as he would more and more in the weeks ahead, caught between pressures from his closest personal advisers to go public and proclaim his innocence, and pressures from the awesome White House to quit or at least play it their cagey way. To Gold and the others who pressed him to speak out, Agnew simply listened and said little. Then, without consulting them again, he called the White House and asked to see the President late that Tuesday afternoon. He had advised Nixon months before that friends in Maryland had told him some young hot-shot prosecutors were snooping around and might try to embarrass him, though he had done nothing wrong. Now, in a somber meeting in the President's E.O.B. hideaway, he reported that his worst fears had been realized. He just wanted the President to know that he was innocent, and that he had decided to hold a press conference the next day to say so and to answer questions openly and freely.

The President, who took great and vocal pride in staring down nuclear holocausts and international confrontations, but who could not bring himself to restrain or fire a subordinate, gave the Vice President what had come to be known around the White House as "the Wally Hickel treatment." Walter Hickel, the outspoken Secretary of Interior in Nixon's first administration, had drawn the President's ire by suggesting in a letter (leaked to the press) that Nixon ought to improve his communications with the nation's youth; Nixon finally called Hickel in, and stood by in silence as his chief aide, H. R. Haldeman, fired him. On this occasion, the President told Agnew face-to-face that he had complete confidence in him, and the Vice President went back to his own office feeling much better. But within fifteen minutes, General Haig, accompanied by Bryce Harlow, went over to see him with a message. According to a key White House aide speaking later in pure White House gobbledygook, Haig informed Agnew "that if the allegations in respect to him were likely to be sustainable, and if out of those allegations he was likely to be indicted, in his own judgment as a lawyer he ought to consider the timing of his actions to deal with that. Because once indicted, then you're off into uncontrollable circumstances that are ordained, and his performance and activities as the Vice President would be obviously impaired in various unforeseeable and unprecedented ways." Translation: Haig was not there as an executioner; his job was merely to suggest hara-kiri. But Agnew was not buying. He was, he told Haig and Harlow as he had told Nixon, an innocent man beset by enemies. The White House aides left to report the failed mission to the President.

The next morning, August 8, the team of Baltimore prosecutors met with Ruckelshaus and Petersen to bring these two key Richardson lieutenants up to date on the case. At the conclusion of their briefing, Petersen asked each of them whether he was convinced "to a moral certainty" of Agnew's guilt—a legal phrase that is part of the standard charge to the jury in a criminal case. Each in turn indicated that he was convinced. Once again, the go-around over how much should be told Agnew and the President was played out, with the Baltimoreans forcefully arguing against any further disclosures at all. The Vice President was not going to resign, Baker insisted, and since that was clear, there was no point in giving him any more information. It would only suggest to the public that Agnew was getting special consideration in the pre-indictment phase.

But a Vice President, Ruckelshaus and Petersen replied, was not like any other individual under investigation, and he could not even be compared to other public officials in the same boat. The Baltimoreans might be concerned that the Justice Department was showing favoritism to Agnew, Petersen said, but in the atmosphere generated by Watergate the department had also to resist the temptation to overcompensate by treating Agnew more harshly than in ordinary circumstances.

On the idea of writing a memo for the President, Skolnik came down hard. The President had no legitimate need for detailed factual disclosures; all he needed to know was how his attorney general and assistant attorney general assessed the strength of the case, and what their judgment was as to whether the Vice President should be indicted. Actually, he argued, it was against the President's own interests to have any detailed factual knowledge, because that would only make it seem that he had improperly involved himself in the investigation. But, Ruckelshaus and Petersen both said, if they were President, each would want to satisfy himself that his attorney general was acting responsibly before permitting the Vice President to be indicted. Once again, the matter was left open.

That afternoon, Agnew's press conference was called, with only a few hours' notice, in a studio-auditorium on the fourth floor of the Old Executive Office Building. The television networks decided at once to cover the event live, and by three o'clock more than 200 reporters were there. Agnew came out, ramrod straight as always, tense but in control. In a sense, his whole political career, and his self-image as a righteous man unfairly put upon, had prepared him for this moment. When he had run for county judge against entrenched incumbents and lost, the system was against him; when he was dropped from the county zoning board of appeals, he was unjustly done in by partisans; when as Vice President he shared the invectives hurled at Richard Nixon by war protesters and the criticisms leveled by the news media, he cried that he was wronged, and he had flailed back with bombast and counteraccusation. Now finally he was called upon to cash in all the chips he had gathered since 1969 in building and cementing his reputation for blunt and honest talk. He was equal to the call.

"Because of defamatory statements that are being leaked to the news media by sources that the news reports refer to as close to the investigation," he began, "I cannot adhere to my original intention to remain silent following my initial statement a few days ago, which asserted my innocence and which indicated I would have nothing further to say until the investigation was completed.

"Under normal circumstances, the traditional safeguard of secrecy under such proceedings would protect the subject. But apparently this protection is not to be extended to the Vice President of the United States.

"Well, I have no intention to be skewered in this fashion. And since I have no intention to be so skewered, I called this press conference, to label as false and scurrilous and malicious these rumors, these assertions and accusations that are being circulated and to answer your questions regarding them, and any other questions that I might be able to answer concerning the general situation."

With some uneasiness at the start, but soon with firmness, even aggressiveness, as he stood straight and unsmiling before the microphone, Agnew proceeded to field every question asked of him.

One of the first questions was based on what later proved to be erroneous allegations, that Agnew had received $1000 a week in kickbacks. Did he deny these charges? Agnew knocked it out of the park: "I am denying them outright and I am labeling them, and I think a person in my position at a time like this might be permitted this departure from normal language, as damned lies."

Another question, broader but on the mark: "Mr. Vice President, have you ever received money for your personal use from any person, contractor, doing business with the state of Maryland or the federal government?" Agnew replied without a moment's hesitation: "Absolutely not."

To many television viewers, these categorical answers made the Vice President look like the same Ted Agnew they had known since Nixon had found him five years earlier—a man who could be counted on to call a spade a spade, and never mince words about it. He added to that impression with other responses: that he had been "thoroughly investigated" before when he had run for governor in 1966 and for Vice President in 1968, and had been exonerated. "I have absolutely nothing to hide in this respect." He had retained counsel in April, he said, because he had heard "rumors in the cocktail circuit" passed on by friends in February that his name was being mentioned in connection with the Maryland investigation. Some of the rumors indicated he was trying to apply pressure to impede the investigation, and rather than make a personal contact with a federal prosecutor, he said, he hired the lawyer, Judah Best, to assure the prosecutor "that I would in no way attempt to impede the investigation."

When he heard the rumors, Agnew said, he discussed the matter with General Haig, who brought it to the President's attention. Later, probably sometime in May, after hiring Best, he "may have" spoken to Nixon briefly about it in the course of other discussions; the U.S. attorney in Baltimore, Agnew said, had told Best he was not concerned about allegations against Agnew.

In meeting with the President the previous day, Agnew went on, Nixon had expressed confidence in him "directly to me." But when he was asked if the possibility that he might resign had come up, Agnew replied: "I'm not going to discuss my conversation with the President. I am sorry."

Why was all this trouble descending upon him? somebody asked. With the U.S. attorney a Republican, could there be political motivation? Agnew—who of course had been in communication directly or indirectly with Wolff, Matz, and Hammerman—replied unabashedly: "I have no knowledge of who is leaking this information. As you ladies and gentlemen know, one of the things the press does best is protect its sources. I could not comment in response to the motives of the individuals because I don't know who they are. I would say this, that the accusations that are being made, if they do come from people who are also under investigation, must be looked at as accusations that are coming from those who have found themselves in very deep trouble, and are looking to extricate themselves from this trouble, and are flirting with the idea that they can obtain immunity or reduced charges, perhaps, by doing so."

Agnew offered other answers to other questions that, in light of what the prosecutors knew, were particularly interesting to them.

Q. "Have you ever had a political slush fund financed by a Baltimore County contractor?"

A. "No."

Q. "Do [campaign contribution records] include gifts from contractors in the State of Maryland?"

A. "I would suspect that they do because anyone that's been around the political scene in the United States who would expect that campaign contributions don't come from contractors doing state and federal business is quite naïve."

Q. "How did you approach your dealings with the contractors? What kind of ethics did you have, did you feel that you had, when you dealt with them?"

A. "I did not deal with contractors at all. I had some people who were in the engineering business who were long-time friends and political supporters. I did not ever have any financial transactions with these people. I did consult with them. I did listen to their complaints. I did allow them access, as most political figures do, to persons who are supportive of their political campaigns."

Q. "Did any of these contractors ever offer anything approaching a bribe . . . ?"

A. "I don't know who 'these contractors' are, so I can't answer that question. But I will say that, and I can't remember the exact circumstances—it's a matter of news record. Way back in county records at one time, I was offered a bribe and I reported the bribe."

This reference was to Agnew's acknowledgment in the 1966 gubernatorial race, after his Democratic opponent had said he had been offered a "bribe," that he too had been approached by a representative of the state's slot machine interests.[2] He had mentioned nothing about it when it happened, he had said then, because he had been approached by "an innocent person" acting as an intermediary relaying the information "second or third hand."

But pressed now as to whether he had indeed reported it as a bribe at the time, Agnew admitted he hadn't. "I mentioned it and reported it later on," he told the press conference. "If you ask me why I didn't report it, I can only say that I was very inexperienced and quite uninformed about such matters at the time."

One other element in the press conference was worth noting. Although Haig, the President's chief aide who never acted on his own, already had suggested that he resign, the Vice President of the United States was still pledging undiminished fealty to his leader. Asked why he was having a press conference and Nixon wasn't, Agnew shot back: "The best answer I can give you to that is that President Nixon hasn't received a letter from the United States attorney telling him he's under investigation. . . . And I think the matter of how President Nixon is going to respond to the matters that are being discussed currently regarding him is a matter for his own determination, and I want to repeat I have absolutely total confidence in him, and the fact that his response is going to be entirely satisfactory."

---

[2] See Chapter 2, page 25.

All through the public and private trial of Spiro Agnew in the next weeks, the Vice President would maintain this posture of complete loyalty to the man he must have known was maneuvering to extricate him from national office. When his own staff aides began to charge that the White House was leaking damaging information, he told them to lay off—it was not in his best interests for them to be sniping at the President, or for himself and the President to be off on separate paths. He appreciated their loyalty and efforts to help him, but he'd better not find out that anybody was backbiting the President. For his own part, Agnew continued to genuflect toward Nixon whenever the public occasion offered. He had decided early to try to use the power and influence of the White House to save himself, and he was to cling to it to the very end.

This demonstration of loyalty was not, however, what most intrigued two separate groups of viewers that afternoon. Each was more interested, indeed was almost mesmerized, by the quality and technique of Agnew's press-conference performance.

The Vice President's lawyers, Topkis, London, and Best—who had huddled with Agnew that morning, lunched at The Palm restaurant, and then gathered at the Washington office of Paul, Weiss, Rifkind & Garrison to watch the press conference on television—were delighted at their client's straightforwardness. He would, they all agreed, make one hell of a witness.

Simultaneously, Skolnik, Baker, and Liebman gathered in Liebman's apartment, not far from their Baltimore office. Skolnik, who was looking forward to cross-examining the Vice President of the United States when he was brought to trial sometime in the spring of 1974, studied his quarry like a boxer watching old fight films of an opponent. He and the others were impressed and pleased, because they felt that although Agnew was a worthy adversary, cool and quick, he was giving answers with which they could hang him later. "We were always delighted when a defendant talked prior to trial," one of them commented. "Because he usually will lock himself into untenable defenses because he doesn't know what you can prove. . . . Agnew was locking himself in. . . ." Assuming that Agnew's defense would be that he had received money but simply as political contributions, one of the prosecutors envisaged this scene: "There's a wonderful line of cross-examination opened up. 'Okay, if that's true, how come you told the press on August 8 you'd never received any cash? Though you were lying to the press, I see you're not lying now.' You know, you can really get a guy going."

Particularly enticing to the prosecutors was Agnew's statement that he had retained Best because he felt it would be improper for him to contact the prosecutors himself, and that he had not done anything to interfere with the investigation. "That was something we all loved, because we knew we were going to have Kleindienst [testify about his phone calls from Agnew], who we all think would be a terrific witness for us."

Though they drew confidence from Agnew's press conference, the prosecutors acknowledged at the same time that it was likely to have a great positive effect for Agnew around the country. But, said one of them later, "I don't think we were at all worried about it because we knew what we had. We knew we were going to murder him. . . . I thought he was handling himself very well, that he was an impressive performer, that he would be a tough opponent. But I was also delighted at his willingness to speak out on the merits and answer questions. Because the more questions he answered, the more he would look great in August and terrible in April."

There was, of course, to be no April in the sense he meant it— a full-blown public trial of the Vice President of the United States. But neither the three prosecutors sitting around a television set in Baltimore nor the three criminal lawyers doing the same thing in Washington knew that at the time. Each group was poised to join legal battle with the other to decide the fate and the reputation of the Vice President—and, perhaps, the credibility of American politics in the eyes of so many millions who had come to see and accept Spiro T. Agnew as the embodiment of honesty, truth, and candor.

9 The Cruelest Month

For Spiro T. Agnew, August was the cruelest month.

Helplessly, the nation's second highest constitutional officer stood by as the government and the press sifted through his past, piecing together a picture of a Janus-like figure—one face of honesty toward the public, another of deceit toward those who knew his secret life. Drop by drop, leaked allegations against Agnew began to erode his public image and standing, until he stood exposed. Not once during August did the special federal grand jury in Baltimore hear from a witness about the Agnew investigation; not once did a Justice Department official in Baltimore or Washington issue a statement that in any way revealed the substance of the allegations against Agnew. No indictment was handed down; no trial was held. Yet by the end of the month Agnew's steep climb to the top of America's political world had been arrested and he was tumbling down even faster than he had risen. The Gallup Poll, as usual, recorded the damage. In April, Agnew had been selected by 35 per cent of the nation's Republicans as their first choice to be the GOP's presidential candidate in 1976, far outdistancing the field of prospects. At the end of

August, the figure had tumbled to 22 per cent, leaving him in a dead heat with Governor Ronald Reagan of California.

The grease under the slipping Agnew was the press. Still high from the heady experience of Watergate, American reporters were zealously determined to report the Agnew story in full and not to be sidetracked by his protestations of innocence. Even before Agnew's press conference, reporters began to flock to Baltimore. The Baltimore Hilton looked the way hotels do when they are caught in the maelstrom of a political convention. *The New York Times* gave Agnew a hint of rough days ahead when it dispatched five of its reporters, an editor, and a copyboy to Baltimore. Other news organizations followed suit. Daily, *The Washington Star-News* and *The Washington Post* sent contingents to Baltimore, with at least one *Post* reporter in the city around the clock. *The Baltimore Sun* mobilized its local troops. The New York *Daily News,* the nation's feistiest tabloid, established a two-man bureau in the Hilton. The news magazines and television networks covered the story, too, and like all the other news organizations also had their reporters combing the Justice Department for the slightest crumb of information. Every day in Washington, Baltimore, and Towson a small army of reporters searched to uncover the secret life of Spiro T. Agnew. It was as if the news media had declared war on his past.

At the same time, Agnew's ultimate security blanket—the White House—began to fray. Instead of fulsome endorsements of an embattled Vice President, President Nixon's spokesmen played word games, leaving the distinct impression that Nixon intended to say no more in Agnew's defense than common decency required. At first there were "no comments," tempered later on with support for Agnew—*as Vice President,* with no mention made of his tenure as governor of Maryland. He was being damned with faint praise, and to a Washington attuned to the near-silence of a high level purge, it was clear that Agnew was fast becoming a nonperson. The President who had introduced him to the world with fanfare would be silent at his passing. It was better not even to mention his name.

Still, in the early part of the month Agnew had some cause for hope. He was not, after all, without weapons. He was, to start, the Vice President of the United States. He was privileged, a member of the elected aristocracy, and therefore he enjoyed rights denied others. It was far from certain, for instance, that he could be indicted before he was impeached by the House of Representatives and removed from office by the Senate. To extend that argument a bit further, there were some who believed that the Vice President was immune from criminal investigation. If he could not be indicted, why investigate him?

Agnew could also make common cause with the President, who was himself claiming immunity from the criminal-justice system, while speculation continued about *his* impeachment over the Watergate mess. Nixon, as Agnew's lawyers were quick to note, had extended the frontiers of executive privilege, claiming that no tribunal but the Congress acting as one could try him. Surely, there was room under this mantle of executive privilege for America's only other nationally elected official. Surely, the President and his Justice Department would not choose this moment in history to draw fine distinctions between the occupant of the White House and his potential successor next door in the Old Executive Office Building. Surely, a President who stood in danger of impeachment would appreciate the utility of a now-suspect Vice President. And would Congress dare presidential impeachment when the heir apparent stood in jeopardy of criminal indictment?

Finally, Agnew had another weapon—his old adversary, the press. He could command from it the headlines and air time he needed to wage the kind of fight Ted Agnew had always fought best—brazening it out, making it so uncomfortable for his opposition that it would shrink from its duty, fading away like all those who had put up their dukes to him. He could rally his constituency, the Middle Americans who believed in him and now distrusted President Nixon, and turn the screws on a Washington already catatonic from scandal. Whom would the people believe? Spiro T. Agnew, talking to them in their living rooms with the vice-presidential seal in full view, or a collection of corrupt engineers intent on survival?

Already the signs were propitious, the initial response to the press conference heartwarming. In the first forty-eight hours, of the 1500 telegrams to reach Agnew's office, only six were said to be critical. (At one point Western Union reported that the telegrams were arriving at the rate of one a minute.) In the Vice President's office, aides reported that telephones were swamped with calls encouraging Agnew to fight on. The boss, they said, was "feeling a sense of relief" after his press conference, and they stretched the new mood of euphoria into fantasy: Agnew, they insisted, might just possibly convert his present predicament into a long-term political triumph.

One aide, in a private memorandum to his boss, underlined the prevailing view among the staff that Agnew would have to take his case to the people if he was going to have a chance to survive. "During the next few days it will become increasingly obvious that we are involved in two overlapping but separate battles," he wrote. "The first of these is, of course, the legal battle, and it is in winning this one that strictly legal advice can prove most helpful. But we shouldn't forget for a moment that you can win the legal battle while losing the equally important political struggle, and if you lose that one you have indeed lost the whole war. The advice you might follow as a private citizen involved in legal difficulties and that you should heed as a public figure who must win both before a grand jury and the more fickle court of public opinion may differ significantly—or even conflict."

Even at the risk of putting the President in a bad light by comparison, the aide wrote, Agnew had to provide whatever documents were requested of him. "Under ideal circumstances I know that it would be best to avoid any action that might embarrass or irritate the President," he said, "but we are not faced with such circumstances. If you waive your rights and turn the requested material over to the grand jury, you may irritate the President; if you don't, you could be committing political suicide. Your political life is on the line and I firmly believe that you should take whatever honorable steps you must to save yourself."

Agnew, being the man he was, had no choice but to tell all, his loyal lieutenant said. "Millions of Americans see you as a symbol of candor and integrity," he concluded. "This is your great political strength and must help shape your response to this entire affair. Anything short of a direct and open refutation of the original charges would have been 'out of character' and particularly suspicious. I am personally convinced that if you continue to hit back at your accusers, while at the same time demonstrating to the satisfaction of the public that you have nothing to hide, we will witness a significant backlash that could leave you stronger than you were when this whole thing first broke."

Armed with this kind of bold advice, Agnew left Washington the day after the press conference for a four-day holiday at the Palm Springs home of Frank Sinatra. Sinatra, once a liberal Democrat and admirer of John F. Kennedy, was a frequent Agnew host—and one of his closest friends. As he always did when he visited Sinatra, Agnew dropped out of sight, appearing only for the stereotyped picture of himself on the golf course or tennis court, otherwise retreating into a well-guarded sanctuary away from the pressures of Washington. Whatever Agnew's mood was that weekend, the nation saw nothing more than a confident Vice President on the golf links. It was summer in the desert community, well above 100 degrees every day, but somehow it seemed cooler than Washington.

While Agnew played, his lawyers went to work. At 11:15 on the morning of Thursday, August 9, Topkis and London met with Henry Petersen and Philip T. White, his deputy. The meeting was most unusual—a portent that Agnew's lawyers were going to receive unprecedented VIP treatment. For this meeting at least, the Baltimore prosecutors—the Justice Department employees with direct responsibility for the investigation—were excluded. Topkis and London had already managed to end-run them, to go directly to their superiors and question the propriety of the investigation conducted in the field. This was a natural response to an extraordinary situation. For the first time in American history, the President might have to ask a Vice President to resign. He simply could not do so on the word of four prosecutors from Baltimore, who were all under the age of thirty-six. He would obviously have to rely on the first-hand judgment of the most senior officials in the Justice Department. Of these, Petersen was certainly one. Ever since he had temporarily taken over supervision of the Watergate investigation, the President had repeatedly expressed confidence in him. Because of the unique circumstances, Petersen had been allowed to pierce the White House veil and report directly to the remote President, and, from all reports, Nixon liked what he saw and heard.

So Agnew's lawyers had the chance to question at the top the manner in which the case had been investigated in the field. If they could convince Petersen of the validity of their client's grievances—that the investigation had been developed in a bungling fashion by prosecutors seeking headlines rather than justice—then they would have performed a valuable service for their client.

This, essentially, was their objective in meeting with Petersen. They attacked the credibility of the prosecutors and of the witnesses against Agnew: the witnesses had contacted the Vice President early in the spring and asked him to have the investigation aborted; when Agnew refused, they had intimated that they would incriminate him. Still, Agnew refused to obstruct justice, and he was always prepared to cooperate with the government. The Justice Department would not find him hostile. In fact, Agnew would be glad to offer explanations for all the allegations against him—if only he knew what they were. He would be willing to submit to an interview. He might even consider a grand jury appearance. As for the documents Beall had asked for in his August 1 letter, they would be provided in due course— after the lawyers had reviewed them, and after they had made certain that turning them over did not compromise the executive-privilege position the President had asserted on the Watergate tapes, or prejudice a position Agnew might later assert: that he, too, was immune from prosecution. Topkis remarked casually that he would be meeting the next week with Professor Charles Alan Wright of the University of Texas, the President's chief adviser on the question of executive privilege. Regardless, the lawyers added, the Department of Justice could rest assured that the Vice President had no intention of invoking his Fifth Amendment right to withhold the documents.

Petersen sat and listened as White took notes. This was his initiation to the Agnew case, and one could not blame him if he had a sudden yearning for his boat and the quiet of the Chesapeake Bay. Already things looked hopelessly complicated. The lawyers were charging that the prosecutors were clumsy zealots. Agnew would cooperate, but there were all these constitutional problems, not to mention President Nixon's own position on executive privilege.

But Petersen was a sagacious and poised prosecutor, and he did not blink. First he defended the Baltimore prosecutors. Both he and the attorney general had every confidence in them. As for the witnesses, Topkis and London had a good point; he, too, was concerned about their credibility, although there was substantial corroborative evidence. He would definitely review the case, and would even consider interviewing the witnesses himself. He would not, however, interview Agnew. If the Vice President had any explanations to offer, he could make them to the prosecutors in Baltimore, although under no circumstances could an interview or even a deposition take the place of a grand jury appearance.[1] (As a man who had been roundly criticized for allowing former Secretary of Commerce Maurice Stans to substitute a deposition for an appearance before the Watergate grand jury, Petersen was not about to fall into that trap again.)

Petersen had one additional caveat. This meeting would be the last without the Baltimore prosecutors. Whatever the lawyers had to say could be said in front of Beall, Skolnik, Liebman, and Baker, who were running the investigation. Topkis and London offered no protest. Later, however, they resolved never to conduct their business with Beall and his staff. If Petersen—or even Richardson—would not hear them, then the White House would. From that time, Judah Best—already designated liaison with the White House and Capitol Hill—would deal first with the office of

[1] The Justice Department's policy left Agnew two choices: he could submit a signed statement to the prosecutors, or he could make an oral statement to them with a court reporter present. As the target of the investigation, however, Agnew would not be accorded the privilege of a question-and-answer session with his lawyers present.

the President, usually Buzhardt, then with Richardson or Petersen, and never, if he could help it, with their minions in Baltimore.

In contrast to what they had to say about the Baltimore prosecutors, Topkis and London waxed eloquent about Petersen. The
veteran civil servant had their trust, they told him, and their
client's as well. They knew him by reputation, and it was sterling.
They and their client felt better just knowing that Petersen would
be reviewing the case and advising the attorney general.

If Petersen was affected by this flattery, his actions certainly
did not reflect it. He made plans at once to close all the doors
opened by Agnew's lawyers. If they were concerned about the
credibility of the witnesses (as, in fact, *he* was) then something
would be done. By late afternoon, Petersen had arranged for an
FBI technician to administer lie-detector tests to both Matz and
Wolff. (Petersen chose the same technician who earlier in the
year had given tests to the former White House aides and Watergate witnesses Jeb Stuart Magruder and Gordon C. Strachan.)
Moreover, Petersen concluded that he would personally interview
the witnesses—cross-examine them and look them in the eye. He
was no slouch at that sort of thing; what he could see for himself was worth a fistful of reports from Baltimore.

By 6:10 that evening, the busy Petersen was in Richardson's
conference room, prepared to report on his meeting with Vice
President Agnew's lawyers. The four Baltimore prosecutors were
there, as well as Richardson, Ruckelshaus, and J. T. Smith. Before Petersen could speak, Richardson pulled rank, asked a series
of routine questions, and then launched into the sort of profes-
sorial soliloquy that seemed to come as easily to him as pro-
fanity to a master sergeant.

First, the attorney general wanted to know, had there been
any new developments in the case? None, Beall reported. Next,
what was the status of the net-worth investigation of Agnew?
Progressing, Beall said, but it would take time to complete. Richardson nodded. The net-worth investigation, he told Beall, should
not divert the prosecutors from the principal investigation of
Agnew, nor alter the timetable that called for a mid-September

indictment. If need be, Agnew could be indicted first for bribery, conspiracy, and extortion and sometime later for tax evasion.

Agnew was, of course, a citizen like any other, Richardson said, slipping into his lecture. But he was also the Vice President, and his indictment was likely to precipitate foreign and domestic consequences of considerable importance to the nation. Richardson assumed that if an indictment were returned there was a 50-50 chance Agnew would either resign voluntarily or the President would demand that he quit. The resignation of a Vice President was at issue here, not the indictment of an ordinary citizen. In historic terms, therefore, the group assembled there that day had grave responsibilities. Richardson understood that everyone in the room was convinced by now that there was sufficient evidence to seek an indictment, but they had better be damned sure. This was not a decision to be left to the grand jury. The prosecutors in Baltimore and the attorney general in Washington had better be certain of their evidence before they took such a momentous step. They must be sure that the witnesses would testify both before the grand jury and in open court exactly as they had when questioned by the prosecutors, and they had to be sure the testimony was truthful.

Richardson paused. By now it was clear that his lecture was directed at the four Baltimore prosecutors. They did not know it, but he was preparing them for Petersen's announcement that he would personally interview the witnesses and submit them to lie-detector tests—decisions that undercut their authority and had not been foreseen in their dealings with the lawyers for Matz and Wolff. But they sat in rapt attention, listening to this Boston Brahmin with the chiseled profile giving them a crash course in Richardson I—the workings of his mind and the pressures upon him.

Richardson continued. Both he as attorney general and Petersen as head of the criminal division had great—and graver—responsibilities than did the prosecutors. He therefore wanted Petersen and himself to be in the best possible position to assess the case before an indictment was sought. Richardson did not spell out what he meant by this, but it was fairly clear to everyone that he was referring to his special responsibility to report to the President.

Now, stepping outside his role as attorney general, member of the President's cabinet, and Atlas shouldering the burdens of the government, Richardson suddenly turned prosecutor. Agnew, he said as if he were passing on a state secret, had made certain admissions at the Monday meeting that might later prove useful. He had said that he had selected the engineers for state work; that he had met frequently with Matz, Green, and Wolff; and that Green was an incessant favor-seeker whose requests filled a file—here Richardson stretched out his hands—"this big." The prosecutors, who knew Agnew could never deny selecting the engineers or knowing these three men, sat respectfully silent and looked impressed.

Richardson, going on to explain why he had met with Agnew, made no mention of the White House pressure on him to do so. He returned instead to his theme that anything that encouraged the Vice President to resign—including supplying him with information about the government's case—was beneficial to the nation, and he recounted the information he had passed on to Agnew.

The Baltimoreans were aghast. Richardson had done the unspeakable—turned over an outline of the case to the target of the investigation. All kinds of "horribles," using Skolnik's word, could result. Potential evidence could be destroyed, pressure could be brought to bear on the witnesses to have them change their stories—the list was virtually endless. Richardson had blundered, they thought, his eyes clouded by the naïve belief that Agnew would resign. Elliot Richardson would resign under such circumstances, but not Spiro Agnew. He was just another politician, no different, really, from the others they had dealt with over the years. They never resigned. Moreover, the attorney general had failed to write a memorandum about the talk with Agnew and his lawyers—had even failed to take notes for a portion of the meeting. At Skolnik's urging, Richardson agreed to prepare a memorandum.

Richardson went on with his description of the meeting with

Agnew. The "moral indignation" Agnew had shown in his press conference was completely missing, he said, and when Topkis had suggested that a special prosecutor should handle the Agnew case, Richardson had had to "bite his tongue." He doubted that Agnew would prefer to be investigated by Archibald Cox, of all people. But how in fact would Agnew be interviewed by the prosecutors, if the time ever came for that? They all agreed that the Vice President would either go to the grand jury or be allowed to offer the prosecutors an oral or written statement.

The President would be returning to Washington from Camp David on August 16, Richardson said, and might want a briefing from him and Petersen on the investigation and on whether an indictment was likely: the President was entitled to this information to guide his own actions, for under no circumstances did he want to issue a resounding endorsement of Agnew only to be caught later in a "McGovern-Eagleton situation." The presidential campaign had not been totally uninstructive. Nixon, at least, would hesitate before supporting his number-two man "one thousand per cent." Richardson also advised the prosecutors and his own aides not to be taken in by Agnew's claims of presidential support. Nixon already believed that the case against Agnew was strong, and that Agnew's assertions of White House support were without foundation.

Petersen was the man on the spot, Richardson continued, the man the President would turn to for a personal assessment of the case. Nixon believed that Petersen was the only person involved in Watergate who had been thoroughly honest with him; he perceived Petersen as a man of honesty to the point of bluntness; he liked Petersen's style.

At that point, Richardson left the room for a telephone call. Baker took the opportunity to admit to Petersen that he and his team had not the slightest idea how to get the White House to supply the logs that would show who had visited Agnew's office in the Old Executive Office Building. Petersen volunteered to handle that chore, and was given the names of Matz, Hammerman, Green, and Jones. (Wolff was not included because he had worked in the Old Executive Office Building and would have been in and out too frequently.)

Petersen moved quickly on the Baltimore prosecutors' request. On August 10, he called Leonard Garment at the White House and asked him for the logs. Garment not only promised cooperation but also volunteered to find out whether Agnew's office, like the President's, had been outfitted with recording devices, and whether tapes of conversations between Agnew and any of the witnesses were available. Garment called back later to tell Petersen it would take twelve men a whole week to review the logs, but the job would be done. The President, it appeared, would be unstinting in his support of the Justice Department. (Garment said later he had no knowledge that the Vice President's office had been bugged.)

That same day, Petersen met with Plato Cacheris, the lawyer for J. Walter Jones, Jr., the real-estate developer from Towson. It was the first of several meetings Petersen had with lawyers for principal witnesses in the case. Jones, too, had been notified that he was under investigation, had issued a statement asserting his innocence, and was sticking firmly to his position—a position Cacheris now echoed in Petersen's office. The two were friends. Cacheris had worked under Petersen in the criminal division of the Justice Department and his law partner, William Hundley, was one of Petersen's closest friends. But this was no social call: Cacheris was there to tell Petersen what he had earlier told Beall and Skolnik: Jones was asserting his innocence and would not be a government witness.

The news was a setback. Certainly the government had the evidence to indict Agnew: Jerry Wolff's notes alone were sufficient to convince a grand jury that Spiro T. Agnew had probably committed a crime. An indictment was one thing, though, a conviction was something else again. Any prosecutor straight out of law school could lead a grand jury around by the nose. A grand jury, after all, heard the witnesses the government chose to bring before it. There was no cross-examination, no opportunity for a defense counsel to impeach the credibility of a witness.

Indictments, when requested, were almost never denied. The purpose of a grand jury was not to determine guilt or innocence but merely to determine whether there was reasonable cause for trial.

Conviction after trial, though, was a different matter entirely. Here the government's case might turn out to be less formidable than it looked on paper. Agnew—poised, articulate, and still Vice President—could make a wonderful witness in his own behalf. Aligned against him—and presumably character witnesses galore testifying on his behalf—would be a trio of engineers, all of whom had confessed to personal corruption and had come on their knees seeking whatever mercy the government might see fit to offer. The case against a Vice President should be overwhelming. One juror unable to bring himself to the judgment that the Vice President of the United States was a common criminal could deadlock the jury.

No, what the government needed was a man like Jones: a respected bank president and former fund-raiser for both Agnew and Nixon. He was a nonengineer whose difficulties did not originate with the investigation of corruption in Baltimore County and who could not be accused of serving up Agnew as an offering to the government. But Jones would not or could not cooperate.

The only other alternative was Hammerman. Here, even more than Jones, was a man of stature in the community: former president of the prestigious Advertising Club of Baltimore, mortgage banker whose wealth was estimated in millions of dollars, real-estate developer, civic leader, and philanthropist. If Hammerman could be persuaded to turn against his old friend Ted Agnew, the government would have a compelling case that any jury would buy. Moreover, the government's case might be strong enough to convince Agnew that a jury trial was sheer folly. Faced with that kind of evidence, he might resign and strike a deal. It was unlikely, but certainly worth the effort. "Turning Hammerman" became the order of the day.

Of all the men who eventually were to cooperate with the government, Bud Hammerman was indisputably the odd man out. Unlike Matz, Green, or Wolff, Hammerman was neither an engineer nor had he been extorted. He was personally close to Agnew—a true and warm friend who seemed to cherish the company of the man whom he had known since childhood and whom he got to know a lot better once Agnew became county executive. Beginning then, Hammerman joined a select circle of Agnew's friends that included Jones and George White, the former Towson lawyer who had become a successful Baltimore attorney. But more even than Jones and White, Hammerman became Agnew's benefactor—a sugar daddy of seemingly limitless means who took Agnew on shopping trips to New York and vacation trips to Hawaii. From the suits in Agnew's closet to the new kitchen in Agnew's apartment at the Sheraton Park Hotel, Bud Hammerman was the proud donor. There were other gifts, too—cash on the occasions when Agnew complained of his financial plight, even a new car and jewelry for Agnew to give to a long-time secretary.

The gifts, Agnew later told others, were pressed on him by Hammerman, who insisted in the manner of a proud father that Agnew had to comport himself in a vice-presidential manner. Hammerman was using his friendship for his own benefit, Agnew was later to complain, dropping the name of the Vice President for business purposes. Once, when Hammerman had accompanied him to a New York affair, he took advantage of the occasion to approach a vice president of the Ford Foundation about a business deal involving a commercial project in downtown Baltimore. Later, when Agnew summoned the same Ford Foundation vice president to Washington to chastise him about the grants the foundation had been awarding, he was amazed to discover that the executive thought the topic of the meeting would be Hammerman's project.

Still, Hammerman was hardly a unique Agnew friend. For years, Agnew and his associates had enjoyed symbiotic relationships in which Agnew's name with his title of the moment— county executive, governor, or Vice President—was exchanged for more practical considerations. Jones, who steered Agnew into business deals, had Agnew's name listed on his bank's letterhead. Hammerman, too, benefited from his close association with Agnew

despite the constant flow of gifts. Matz also was an Agnew benefactor; aside from the kickback money, he boasted that he occasionally gave Agnew cash—no strings attached—just because the
man needed the money. Harry Dundore, Sr., another Baltimore
County chum who appeared smitten with Agnew, also reportedly
gave his friend cash gifts. Agnew received some of his household
food from Joseph Rash, an executive of Food Fair Stores, Inc.,
who made sure that periodic shipments were delivered to the
Agnew household in Montgomery County from a nearby Pantry
Pride store. Even in the Sheraton Park Hotel (owned by International Telephone and Telegraph) Agnew as Vice President
received a so-called celebrity discount of at least one third of
the $1900 monthly rent.[2]

In this respect, Agnew was not much different from many
other politicians. Governors at governors' conferences, as Agnew
well knew, were routinely showered with gifts from local man-
ufacturers—anything and everything from nameplates to motor-
ized golf carts. Congressmen hitched rides on the corporate
airplanes of firms doing business with the government, and governmental officials leased cars at a discount from corporations
seeking government contracts. Presidents, too, had shown the
same weakness. Richard M. Nixon, as it later turned out, had
taken advantage of loopholes in the tax code to accumulate a
real-estate fortune touching both the Pacific and Atlantic oceans.

As a Marylander, Agnew at least had a ready explanation for
his conduct—the perennial squawk that he was the underpaid,
overworked guardian of the political system. To an extent, he had
a point. For years, the state's voters had assumed that politics
was a calling and had awarded those who entered it with the
wages of a monk. Until 1967, the governor's salary was only
$15,000 annually (a marked increase from the $4500 a year
awarded Theodore Roosevelt McKeldin when he first became
governor in 1951 and had to supplement his income through

---

[2] The Sheraton Park Hotel had offered celebrity discounts to, among others,
former Treasury Secretary John Connally, former Chief Justice Earl Warren, the hostess Perle Mesta, former Democratic National Chairman Lawrence O'Brien, and the producer of *Meet the Press*, Lawrence Spivak.

speaking engagements). Even in 1974, the constitutionally man-dated salary was only $25,000, hardly a princely sum for an official who annually prepared a budget of nearly $3 billion and super-vised the performances of 40,000 employees. The governor, in fact, earned less than any of his cabinet secretaries or even his press secretary, and only slightly more than some of the reporters who covered his weekly press conferences. And while the state provided living quarters (the mansion), transportation (the limousines), and an expense account, it provided no funds for the constant political obligations of a governor—trips to partisan governors' conferences, a political convention, or meetings held in a Baltimore restaurant where the governor felt obliged to pick up the tab.[3]

As a result, a man either had to be rich or a scoundrel to hold high public office. If he held a no-show city hall job through the good graces of a political organization, he suffered not at all. If he was a rising lawyer seeking state business or the business of others seeking state business, he could weather the sacrifice until it became remunerative. But if he simply wanted to enter politics for the joy of the thing, he was going to take a financial drubbing. Those of modest means who zoomed to the top or inched their way to a committee chairmanship soon found that like the rock-and-roll stars of the 1960s, they had their own camp followers or groupies, men like Matz or Hammerman, who were willing to pick up a restaurant tab or slip an envelope—bar-mitzvah style—into the hand of a politician. The envelope somehow enhanced the importance of both parties; it was nice to receive and it was nice to give. Maryland politicians, like the classical composers and artists of Europe, had to have patrons. If Agnew was dif-

---

[3] State legislators long suffered the same sort of disregard. In the era when the General Assembly was a biennial convocation of slave-owning planters and Baltimore merchants, salaries were hardly a consideration. By 1970, however, the legislature was nearly a full-time job. What with a ninety-day annual session, out-of-session committee meetings, night meetings back home in the county, and casework for constituents, many a delegate or senator felt that $2400 a year was not just compensation. In 1971, the General Assembly recognized this and increased legislative salaries to $11,000 a year.

Richard M. Nixon on October 31, 1968, with the man he had recently chosen as his running mate, Spiro T. Agnew.

President Nixon confers with his Vice President before leaving on a trip to Europe, September 1970.

George Beall, U.S. attorney for Baltimore, at a press conference at the Justice Department on October 11, 1973, the day after his investigation of Spiro T. Agnew ended with the Vice President's resignation.

Russell T. Baker, Jr., assistant U.S. attorney and the first of the prosecutors to argue that Agnew was "acting like a guilty man."

Barnet D. Skolnik (*left*) and Ronald S. Liebman (*right*), assistant U.S. attorneys, are fatigued from a sleepless night preparing the government's exposition of evidence against Agnew. They mount the steps of the courthouse in Baltimore on October 10 to attend the hearing at which Agnew pleads *nolo contendere*.

Attorney General Elliot L. Richardson at the press conference on October 11, 1973. In ten days Richardson himself was out of office, having refused to follow President Nixon's order to fire special Watergate prosecutor Archibald Cox.

Doug Chevalier, *The Washington Post*

Henry E. Petersen testifying at the Watergate hearings, summer 1973. He had something else on his mind.

James K. W. Atherton, *The Washington Post*

Federal Judge Walter E. Hoffman leaves the Baltimore courthouse after issuing a supplemental charge to the grand jury and granting Agnew's lawyers the authority to subpoena reporters and high Justice Department officials. This was a week before the end.

UPI Photo

UPI Photo

Lester Matz. He was mortified when he paid off his old friend Agnew in the White House.

Associated Press

William E. Fornoff, the Baltimore County bureaucrat whose testimony led directly to Agnew.

Attorney Arnold Weiner (*left*) accompanies Jerome B. Wolff (*right*) for yet another meeting with George Beall and his assistants at the Baltimore courthouse. Wolff was the prosecutors' dream witness.

UPI Photo

Above: Two Agnew chums from Maryland—J. Walter Jones (*left*), who told the prosecutors he had nothing to say; and I. H. Hammerman II (*right*), who told all he knew. *Below*: Dale Anderson, Agnew's successor as Baltimore County executive and the original target of Beall's investigation. He is arriving at court for his arraignment, September 14, 1973, on thirty-nine counts of conspiracy, extortion, and bribery. Four days later, he announced for reelection.

J. Fred Buzhardt, Jr.,
for a while the
President's lawyer,
and the matchmaker in
Nixon's efforts to get
the Justice Department
and Agnew to agree on a
deal that would assure
Agnew's resignation.

Charles Del Vecchio, *The Washington Post*

Alexander Haig, a major general when he served on Henry A. Kissinger's staff, as he received the Distinguished Service Medal at a White House ceremony in 1972.

Agnew's lawyers, Jay H. Topkis (*left*), Martin London (*center*), and Judah H. Best (*right*), arrive at the Baltimore courthouse for the hearing at which the Vice President pleads *nolo contendere*.

UPI Photo

Associated Press

Late in September 1973, Vice President Agnew accepts a poster and a card from Congressmen William L. Dickinson of Alabama (*left*) and Samuel Devine of Ohio (*right*), both Republicans. The poster, captioned "Hang In There, Baby," shows a cat hanging on to a rope, and the card bears the signatures of a hundred congressmen who were supporting Agnew.

October 11, 1973, the day after the resignation. Once more Mr. and Mrs. Agnew.

Doug Chevalier, *The Washington Post*

ferent, it was only because he was greedier than most—and because he got caught.

In this environment, Bud Hammerman felt at home. He moved easily among politicians and gave them frequent donations. He shared with others a certain awe of those who wielded power, and he relished his association with the county executive *cum* governor *cum* Vice President *cum*—knock on wood—President. From the available evidence, it seemed also that Hammerman cherished his role as an intermediary in the kickback scheme. It added a dash of excitement to a very secure life. Taking his cut strengthened his bonds with Agnew and enhanced his own position: he was *the* man to see on contracts in Maryland—a combination patron/bag man. Sam Hammerman's kid, with his Wharton Business School education, his impeccable civic credentials, and a fortune that came to him at birth, was one of the boys.

And, ironically, Hammerman could use his cut of the take. The philanthropies established by his father were becoming a burden to him. In addition, the Hammermans had long been known in Baltimore as political contributors, and while hardly a politician could ignore the Hammerman wealth, neither could the Hammermans ignore the men who made zoning or other decisions crucial to the success of their business empire. Hammerman's desk, more than most others in Maryland, contained its quota of bull roast tickets or requests for funds—preferably cash. By his own estimate, Hammerman was spending $1000 a week, much of it for political donations. The cash from the kickback scheme, which probably could not have earned Hammerman more than $100,000, came in very handy indeed.

By August 1973, however, Hammerman's silver spoon had become tarnished. Wolff and his omnipresent notebooks had incriminated him in a dozen shades of ink. The documents, coupled with Wolff's own testimony, had led the prosecutors to still other engineers who had confessed making payments to him. The evidence was damning. Hammerman faced certain indictment—or would have to make a deal. He chose the latter course—and it was a decision that sewed the case against Agnew into an airtight package that could probably withstand the inspection of any jury.

Hammerman, though, would not come cheaply. His value to the government was not lost on his principal attorney, Sidney Sachs, whose Washington firm, Sachs, Greenebaum & Tayler, had represented E. Howard Hunt before both the Senate Watergate Committee and the Watergate grand jury.

To his fellow lawyers, Sachs was somewhat of a mystery. Seemingly as much in the dark as they and apparently equally dependent on the newspapers for his information, he nevertheless refused all telephone calls from other lawyers in the case, some of whom were scratching for any information that could help in the defense of their client. Sachs was the very model of discretion—as discreet a lawyer as there was in Washington. That reputation earned him some of the area's most prominent clients (including Barbara Mandel, whose settlement with her governor-husband he negotiated). Discretion aside, Sachs was known as a talented, even brilliant negotiator. More than any other lawyer involved in the investigation, Sachs impressed Skolnik, the prosecutor detailed to deal with him, with his candor and professional demeanor. The man meant to do business—but on his terms.

It was clear to Sachs that his client's only recourse was to strike a deal. He entered the case in early July, and by the beginning of August, he was engaged in negotiations with Beall's staff, while refusing to confirm to reporters that he represented Hammerman.

And by the second week of the month, Skolnik was prepared to move. Choosing carefully among the engineers who had admitted to paying off Hammerman, Skolnik selected two of solid reputation: in his letter of negotiation, he advised Hammerman and Sachs that he did not want any information concerning these two engineers—thereby suggesting they were prepared to testify against Hammerman and giving an impression of great strength in the government's case.

The strategy apparently worked. On Friday, August 17, Hammerman, Sachs, his associate Hal Witt, and the four prosecutors converged on the Holiday Inn North, in the working-class Baltimore suburb of Glen Burnie. There, in Room 240—miles from the carefully watched courthouse—I. H. Hammerman II, surrounded by stock plastic furniture, turned informer. His face flushed, his hands shaking, Hammerman talked through the day, spelling out ten years of a corrupt relationship with Agnew.

Hammerman had known Agnew for years, but what brought the two men close together was Agnew's election as Baltimore County executive in 1962. Significantly, their first conversation after the election concerned Hammerman's offer of an illegal campaign contribution. The day after the election, Hammerman met with Agnew and congratulated him on his victory. Hammerman, repentant for having supported Agnew's opponent, told the county executive-elect that he knew all campaigns had deficits. He offered Agnew a post-election contribution of $10,000.[4] Agnew rejected the offer but added that he would expect a $30,000 contribution the next time he ran for office.

From then on, the two were close personal friends. Hammerman brought Agnew into his social set, introducing him to men who would later be substantial financial contributors to Agnew campaigns. Agnew, as usual, was in a financial bind, and he gave Hammerman the story that was to become so standard with him: that his salary was not commensurate with his title, his lofty responsibilities, or the demands being made on him; that his public position required a certain standard of living; that he was a man who had been unable to accumulate wealth before going into public life and had no inheritance. Hammerman got the point, and the Hammerman treasure chest opened for Agnew.

In 1966, when Agnew ran for governor, he gave Hammerman an ultimatum—to choose between himself and his Democratic opponent. Hammerman was clearly in a fix. Whenever an election looked like a tossup, major Maryland fat cats—as their counterparts in presidential campaigns—would generally contribute to both candidates. But Hammerman would not be permitted to lay off his bets on both candidates. He chose Agnew,

---

[4] The legal limit for campaign contributions then was $5000.

the underdog, contributing $25,000 to the campaign. Hammerman also stepped out front in Agnew's campaign, becoming a financial chairman. By inauguration day, Marylanders had no doubt that Bud Hammerman was Ted Agnew's boy.

It was not generally known, however, that Hammerman was an intermediary in Agnew's massive kickback scheme, customarily the man who usually retained Agnew's 50 per cent of the graft and squirreled it away in a safe-deposit box. Between the two men, every $1000 was called a "paper." From time to time Agnew called Hammerman and would ask how many "papers" he had and, if Agnew desired, Hammerman would bring them over.

Hammerman's role in the kickback scheme was not strictly limited to engineering firms. At one point, Hammerman discussed with Agnew whether a certain Baltimore bond house should be chosen to float a state bond issue. Agnew was against it unless the officers of the bond house made a substantial cash "contribution." The governor, who apparently did not want the state's largess to be taken for granted, called the bond-house partners—members in good standing of Baltimore's aristocracy—"a cheap bunch" who "don't give you any money."

Hammerman talked on and on, corroborating in detail the arrangement about which Wolff had testified earlier. So extensive was his knowledge that a second meeting had to be scheduled for Saturday.

Spiro T. Agnew, oblivious of what was happening in the motel room in Glen Burnie, was in Centreville on the other side of the Chesapeake Bay that Saturday, addressing a rally for Robert E. Bauman, a Republican state senator seeking the congressional seat left vacant by the suicide of Republican congressman William O. Mills.[5] Looking tanned and relaxed after his Palm Springs holiday, the Vice President worked the sympathetic crowd like an evangelist at a tent meeting. Agnew, after all, was the home-state boy; this was heartland Agnew country—conservative to its core. (In 1966, when Agnew ran for governor, the Eastern Shore

---

[5] Bauman won the election, defeating Democratic state senator Frederick C. Malkus.

might have misjudged the man, for it chose instead the conservative George Mahoney. But Agnew had since changed—or so it seemed—and he was now the spokesman for conservative voters everywhere.) Even with Agnew's image soiled by the investigation, Bauman insisted that he fulfill his obligation, and from the reaction of the crowd it appeared that Bauman had correctly read the sentiments of his constituency. It was no accident that Agnew, who had spoken only to a Boilermakers Union convention in Denver since his August 8 press conference, had accepted a speaking engagement in Centreville.

As he had done in Denver, Agnew anointed himself defender of the President, and proceeded to lump both Nixon's critics and his own investigators into a single enemy camp. There was no room for any distinction between the investigation of Agnew for bribery and the assaults on the President for the Watergate affair. He denounced both as if they were one, attacking what he called "voices of gloom and despair in America. . . . What we need is hope and faith in America," he went on. "Forget the masochistic persons [who are] looking for all that is wrong."

When it came to his own investigation, the Vice President inveighed not against the accusations, but against those newspaper reports that had by then given the American public a detailed and generally accurate picture of the allegations against him. "They call themselves informed sources close to the investigation . . . and they don't have any hesitancy about violating my civil rights. . . . I intend to fight to establish my innocence of any wrongdoing. Today, much of official Washington reminds me of a morbid crowd gathering around a fire-gutted building watching to see who will be the next corpse carried out." Agnew promised he would have more to say later. The Vice President then uncharacteristically waded into the crowd, shaking hands for a campaign that would never come.

"Hang in there!" one man shouted as he shook Agnew's hand.

"I'll be there," Agnew said. "Don't you worry."

"We're going to see you in the White House yet," cheered another bystander.

Later, when *Washington Post* reporter Philip A. McCombs

sampled sentiment in the crowd, he reported overwhelming support for Agnew. "I feel that he's innocent," said George Fuller, a seventy-five-year-old retired timekeeper. "When it all comes out, they'll find it's a lot of talk." (Fuller's comments were representative of a wide segment of the American people. Gallup had found that while Agnew's stock as a future presidential candidate was quickly sinking, his supporters remained unshaken in their faith in him.)

Across the bay in Glen Burnie, though, Bud Hammerman was undoing everything Agnew was accomplishing in Centreville. Hammerman had slept little in the past few weeks. He was washed out, virtually in hiding. Now he was being asked to remember events that had occurred years before. He could remember, he said in a weak voice, that he had once gone to Pennsylvania to pick up bribe money from an engineer. The prosecutors made a mental note as they carefully jotted down Hammerman's words. Good, they thought, that's an interstate violation—another count in the growing indictment they were even then framing against Agnew in their minds. Hammerman's memory was not good—he could not recall details—but he was excellent on the highlights of the kickback scheme. He could recall the engineering firms from which he received money, although unlike Wolff he kept no detailed accounts. What documents he retained, he produced: for instance, the safe-deposit records that tended to corroborate his contention that he kept Agnew's share of the money, and where. He also told the prosecutors about his attempts to discourage Matz and Wolff from cooperating with the government, and his recent conversations with Agnew.

Sachs, wanting to enhance his client's importance to the government, suggested that Hammerman be "wired" and sent to see Agnew, so the conversation would be recorded. The prosecutors rejected the suggestion. By now they believed they had more than enough evidence to indict Agnew on about fifty counts of bribery, extortion, conspiracy, and tax evasion. There was no need to gamble with the public's abhorrence for electronic eavesdropping devices. Skolnik, for one, blanched at the thought of bugging the Vice President of the United States. Enough was

enough. Besides, two very practical arguments were raised—
Agnew might contradict every one of Hammerman's leading
statements and, God forbid, the Secret Service might frisk Hammerman and find the device. Under the circumstances, it was a
risk distinctly not worth taking.

The next day, Sunday, August 19, George Beall made two calls.
The first was placed through the White House switchboard to
Elliot Richardson. Hammerman was in hand, Beall told the
attorney general. The second was to Sidney Sachs. The government, Beall said, thought the time had come for Hammerman
to sever his relationship with Agnew. What prompted the second
call was one placed to Hammerman's home the day before while
he was in the Glen Burnie motel. His wife, Lois, had taken the
message.

"Where's Bud?" the Vice President asked.

"He's out until six-thirty," Lois Hammerman said.

"I've got to talk to him," Agnew said. "I'm going to launch a
new attack. It looks encouraging. I wanted to give him a good
weekend. I'll tell him all about it on Monday."

Whether Hammerman ever returned that call or not mattered
little. He had done all the talking that counted to the prosecutors,
and the long and mutually rewarding friendship of Bud Hammerman and Ted Agnew was at an end.

10 My Friend the Press

If Spiro Agnew had a Greek ancestor with whom he could empathize in the late summer of 1973, it could surely have been Sisyphus—condemned in Hades forever to roll a heavy stone up a steep hill, only to have it roll down again as he approached the top. Like the mythical king of Corinth, Agnew seemed doomed to have his every effort turn futile. Every move he made to repair his image was countered by a new, damaging revelation in the press. No matter how he struggled, despite every twist and turn in his broken-field run from the prosecutors closing in on him, there lay another rebuff.

The situation was ironic. Agnew, after all, had been a master of the news media; indeed, the press had been both his servant and his scapegoat. Back when he was executive of Baltimore County, he had been labeled a reformer. When he ran for governor of Maryland, he was proclaimed a liberal. As Vice President, he was the spokesman for the media-battered proletariat that persistently had its values questioned, scorned, or worse yet mocked by spokesmen for alien ideas—ideas that someone in

New York or Washington had determined were important. In every role Agnew was lavishly publicized. Even his attacks on the press were dutifully reported by the very newspapers and television networks he criticized. The press did not seem to know how to cope with Agnew. He was an irritant, but he was also good copy. For all his protestations and invectives, the press had been Agnew's best friend, had helped make him who he was. Though what he did was virtually ignored, what he said got maximum attention.

Agnew thus was a major benefactor of the media baronies he deplored. With their growth, especially in television, hometown news was neglected. There was no way for the national television networks to report the actions and speeches of 100 senators and 435 congressmen. Almost by definition, the coast-to-coast coaxial cable required that the networks concentrate on national personalities. The office of the Vice Presidency no longer fit Alben Barkley's story about the two brothers: "One of them ran off to sea. The other was elected Vice President of the United States. Nothing more was ever heard of either of them." Ted Agnew was frequently heard from.

By August 1973, however, Agnew had had enough. What he wanted now was obscurity. In the few public appearances he made that month, he pleaded for his investigation to be handled like any other—routinely and secretly. It was, though, a tardy request for the man who had long adhered to the speaking schedule of a Chautauqua orator and who through dint of self-promotion had made his name into a household word across the land. The press paid him no heed. Almost daily during the month, one publication after another printed an exclusive story on the Agnew investigation. *The Wall Street Journal*, which had broken the story in the first place, reported on August 10 that Agnew stood a 50-50 chance of being indicted. Three days later *Time* magazine named Wolff and Matz as the government's key witnesses, and *The Washington Star-News* contributed a story that four Baltimore contractors had told the prosecution they made cash payments to Agnew. On August 15, *The Washington Post* reported that several Maryland engineers had testified they made cash payments personally to Agnew "to receive choice state contracts." The government was also investigating allegations, the *Post* said, that Agnew had received payments while he was Vice President, in exchange for his influence in the award of a General Services Administration contract.

Thus, by the middle of the month the revved-up American press, working in the superheated atmosphere generated by two major political scandals, had managed to give the nation a fair idea of the case against the Vice President. Agnew and his lawyers were beginning to do a slow burn. What they believed at first was nothing more than the indiscretions of a few well-placed persons with friends in the press corps seemed to them to be taking on a sinister cast. Some of the newspaper and magazine articles had cited Justice Department or government sources, and the lawyers were now willing to take the articles at their word. The government, they concluded, was purposely leaking the allegations against the Vice President, destroying him through the press even before a jury got a crack at him.

The leaks were undoing Agnew, canceling out the persuasive performance he had mounted in his press conference and rebutting his public insistence that he was the victim of a horrendous frame-up. Moreover, they were causing internal dissension within Agnew's staff, making it all the more difficult for the Vice President to present a united front to the world. The boss's constant assurances that he was innocent—though persecuted—were being controverted by newspapers and were ringing hollow. The staff itself, a group of very bewildered individuals, was willing to rally around the Vice President but apprehensive that the ship they were clinging to was taking on water faster than it could be pumped out. Most of the staff knew no more about the case— and Agnew's legal and/or political strategy—than careful readers of the daily newspapers. The boss had never been chummy, and the office functioned like a defense plant making highly secret weapons: compartmentalized, with one section ignorant of what another was doing. Like the President, Agnew worked in seclusion, relying on his closest aide, Arthur Sohmer, to run the staff. Later, General John (Mike) Dunn also became a trusted assistant.

Agnew, in a sense, was doubly cursed. He held an exalted, even unapproachable office. By virtue of his very position it was difficult for well-meaning persons to offer unsolicited advice. And by virtue of his cold, aloof personality Agnew made it even more difficult for the sympathetic to get his ear. As a result, the good intentions of his staff hardened into resentment, and for a time some of Agnew's aides considered confronting their boss and demanding an explanation. That course was shelved, however, and the staff drifted off into melancholy isolation.

As for the leaks themselves, canny Washingtonians had plenty of sources for them. It could be, some thought, that Justice Department officials and/or the Baltimore prosecutors were leaking information to the press to prevent any silent abortion of the investigation within the confines of the White House. Others took a different view, laying the blame for the leaks on the White House itself. President Nixon was notoriously unable to demand a resignation. To steadily erode a man's position by leaking the allegations against him was a pure Nixonian tactic, and it had been used by the White House in the past. Agnew's staff, if not the Vice President himself, subscribed to that theory. The double-dealing White House, in their eyes, was the devil and the President's henchmen no more than traffickers in vicious gossip. As for Agnew's lawyers, they had their own prime suspect: William Ruckelshaus was a Justice Department official with friends in both the press corps and the White House. And on the other side of the table, the Baltimore prosecutors had a suspect: Judah Best, who after all was an associate of Chuck Colson. But no side could offer any proof, and people formed their judgments on little more than the cryptic comments of reporters.

Speculation about the prosecutors as the source of press stories focused on Skolnik, the most flamboyant and outspoken of Beall's assistants and the one with the closest relationships with the national press. As a Harvard undergraduate, Skolnik had made no secret that his career choice was politics, and there were some who suspected that he had never abandoned that goal, indeed, that he was trumpeting the investigation to further his old ambition. Skolnik's critics would cite his service in the Muskie campaign to emphasize his partisan politicking—a story Agnew's staff repeatedly tried to get reporters to write about.

Regardless of their source, the leaks were downright destructive to a man clinging for all he was worth to the claim that the investigation was a horrible concoction of perjury and fantasy. Nothing Agnew could say or do could compensate for the steady dribble of incriminating information. How many times could a man protest his innocence? And who would expect him to say otherwise?

On August 15, Agnew mounted a mild public-relations counterattack. The innocuous personal financial documents that Beall had requested in his letter of August 1 would be turned over to the prosecutors. In keeping with the dignity of his office, though, Agnew refused to have the documents delivered to Baltimore. Beall was forced to send for them, and for the covering letter, which Agnew made public.

"I have done nothing wrong, I have nothing to hide," the Vice President wrote to Beall. "And I have no desire save that justice be done speedily and efficiently." By making the records available, "I do not acknowledge that you or the grand jury have any right to the records of the Vice President. Nor do I acknowledge the propriety of any grand jury investigation of possible wrongdoing on the part of the Vice President so long as he occupies that office. There are constitutional questions which need not at this moment be confronted." In addition, Agnew volunteered to submit to an interview, writing, "I am eager to be of any help I can. Specifically, should you wish, I shall be glad to meet with you and your colleagues for a personal interview so that I may answer any questions you may have."

What, to the unsophisticated, could appear more straightforward than voluntarily turning over potentially incriminating material that was protected by the Fifth Amendment? Agnew was telling Beall that while the prosecutor had no call to trifle with the Vice President, he would not stand on ceremony. He had done nothing wrong and would turn over the documents. Surely, this was not a man with something to hide.[1]

But whatever triumph Agnew scored with the letter was eradicated the same day. Coupled on the front page of *The Washington Post* with the story of the letter was still another Agnew story —a report that engineers had testified they personally made payments to Agnew. The very next day, *The New York Times'* Nicholas Gage disclosed Richardson's meeting with Agnew on August 6, providing even more details of the allegations against the Vice President. Agnew, who just the day before had seemed the most cooperative and innocent of men, took another public-relations pie in the face. The *Times'* story was particularly galling to Agnew since the meeting with Richardson involved just five persons—the two principals and Agnew's three lawyers. Unlike stories about the investigation itself, this one could not have been leaked by potential witnesses or their lawyers.

The Vice President seethed—and finally exploded—when on Sunday, August 19, *Time* magazine released to the news services an advance version of a story in the edition dated August 27, entitled "Heading Toward Indictment?" " 'The Department [of Justice] has no choice,' " the magazine quoted a "Justice official in Washington" as saying. " 'At least three witnesses have told of delivering cash payments to Agnew. The evidence is so strong that the case must be taken to trial.' " The article gave the reader an outline of the case against Agnew and mentioned that some Justice Department officials were puzzled about "the comparatively paltry amounts of money involved."

" 'It's less than you think,' " *Time* quoted one Justice official as saying. " 'Agnew wasn't greedy; he was quite cheap.' " Aside from the information and the explosive quotes contained in the article, the *Time* piece was noteworthy in one other respect: it cited Justice Department officials *in Washington* as its source. The

---

[1] The personal financial records requested by Beall were expected to be of almost no value to the prosecution. No one expected that Agnew would deposit bribe money in a bank account or declare it on his taxes. The documents—especially the canceled checks—did provide, however, the nucleus for the net-worth investigation by offering the IRS an idea of how and where Agnew spent his money.

news-starved Sunday radio and television newscasts that reported the *Time* piece must have sounded to Agnew like chalk squeaking on a blackboard.

Elliot Richardson did little to assuage Agnew's ire. He, too, condemned the leaks, saying they had caused him "considerable distress." His concern, however, was couched in Richardsonian terms. The viewers watching the ABC television program *Issues and Answers* did not see an attorney general who seemed visibly upset at the injustice of the leaks. He was satisfied, Richardson said, that the leaks did not stem from Beall and his staff. As for the investigation, Richardson said he would make the ultimate decision whether the evidence gathered by the prosecutors should be submitted to the grand jury.[2]

Richardson's *sotto voce* commiserations were clearly not enough. Agnew, steaming, called his second news conference of the month on August 21. Reporters alerted just shortly before the event assembled in the auditorium in the Old Executive Office Building, expecting a question-and-answer session. Instead, Agnew read a statement and allowed no questions. Looking fit if a bit thin, he strode onto the stage and—before a national television audience and hundreds of members of the Washington press corps—proceeded to attack the Justice Department of his own administration.

Agnew began by recounting that he had been informed of the investigation through Beall's August 1 letter and had made every effort to keep that information secret. "I had every right to expect that a similar effort to prevent publicity would be made by the attorney general and Mr. Beall and their respective staffs in Washington and Baltimore," Agnew said. "That, of course, was their legal duty. Therefore, I was shocked during the course of the next thirty-six hours to discover that the news media were reporting numerous detailed allegations that had to be coming

---

[2] Although Richardson's pronouncement seemed self-evident (who else could make such a decision?) his aides were vexed with their boss for stepping out front on the investigation. Until the *New York Times* story appeared, Richardson's role had been a matter for conjecture. Now, he was making himself a target for Agnew and his followers—something that could seriously limit his effectiveness in resolving the crisis.

from people who were actually participating in the investigation. I therefore called a press conference on Wednesday, August 8, 1973, to set the record straight.

"Since then the leaks have continued unabated. I regret to say that it has become clear that the 'sources close to the investigation' so frequently quoted were indeed just that—persons involved in the investigatory process. A national news magazine account entitled 'Heading Toward an Indictment?' published yesterday and picked up by the wire services freely quotes unnamed Justice Department officials. I can only assume from this account that some Justice Department officials have decided to indict me in the press whether or not the evidence supports their position. This is a clear and outrageous effort to influence the outcome of possible grand jury deliberations."

As a politician, Agnew said, he had long ago become accustomed to "unsubstantiated charges, rumors, innuendo, and speculation. I have been subjected to these before, and I am accustomed to fighting this kind of battle." What he found intolerable was the effect this kind of publicity might have on the rights of others—particularly private citizens involved in the investigation.

Therefore, Agnew continued, he had written a letter to Attorney General Richardson asking him to honor his obligations and conduct an investigation of the source of the leaks. What he wanted was not a limp going-through-the-motions investigation, but a full-scale inquiry that would use "all available investigatory tools to compel sworn testimony to reveal the identity of unnamed Justice Department officials and 'sources close to the investigation.'"

Agnew made sure the press and the public understood that his anger was directed not at the media but at his enemies in government who were daily sticking barbs into his hide. The press, he said, was not to blame for "publishing information given you by informants within the Department of Justice. The blame must rest with those who give this information to the press and who do so with an obvious motive of interfering with the independent investigative process of the grand jury."

One almost had to check the transcript to verify that Agnew had indeed spared the press another tirade. Suddenly, Agnew was an understanding and sophisticated critic of journalism—the press was merely doing its job in printing the leaks! This, after all, was the Carry Nation of American journalism. For years he had wielded his verbal ax at the news media. He had been in office only ten months when in November 1969 he inaugurated his self-proclaimed secular jihad against the major media powers, especially the Eastern press. From that time forth, Agnew had been an unrelenting—and uninformed—press critic. His scorn was aimed primarily at the television networks and *The Washington Post* and *The New York Times,* all of which had poured more effort, manpower, and financial resources into the gathering and reporting of news than any of those lethargic journalistic house organs of Middle America to which Agnew paid constant court and which indiscriminately parroted his self-serving line. Now all that had changed. Where the press had been wrong in printing the Pentagon Papers, it was now correct in printing the allegations against him. Agnew, who was to humble himself even more in the near future, was finally courting the press. Why? Because, obviously, now he needed it on his side.

Agnew concluded by once again asserting his innocence and declaring he had nothing to hide. "I have made all requested records available to the prosecutors and have offered to meet with them and answer any questions they may have." The Vice President made a sharp right turn and exited through a side doorway.

It was a moment before the press corps reacted. Then there was an explosion of chatter. In a Washington gone stale on innuendo, *double-entendres,* and "on-the-other-hand" statements, Agnew had issued a broadside. Once again, the Vice President had not minced his words. Here was a frontal attack on his own administration's Department of Justice, a bald accusation that it was seeking an indictment and conviction of him not in the courts, but in the newspapers. Although Agnew had limited his attacks to the department—and had not attacked Richardson by name—he had by implication come perilously close to attacking both the attorney general and the President. Not since the halcyon days of the Truman administration had Washington seen such a division within the ranks. In the Nixon administration, where the independence of Wally Hickel had been an instructive lesson to his colleagues in the cabinet, it was unheard of for one member of the "team" to have a public tantrum.

Beall, who had been listening to Agnew's statement on the desk radio in his office, responded quickly. He would stand by his statement of August 8 denying that the prosecutors were in any way "the source of the information reported by the media concerning this investigation." He, too, was "gravely concerned" about the leaks and would "continue to preserve the secrecy of the proceedings until such time as public disclosure can be properly made."

Richardson also denounced the leaks. "I fully share the Vice President's concern about unfair and inaccurate publicity," he said. ". . . Every reasonable step is being taken to assure that the Justice Department has not been and will not be the source of such disclosures. By observing restraint in what they report, the media themselves can help to assure fairness. I would like to point out, moreover, that we do not have any firm basis for the assumption that the information which has appeared in the press has come from law-enforcement officials. In any case, any plausible leads implicating the Department of Justice will be pursued vigorously, and appropriate disciplinary action will be taken against any department employee found to be responsible."

Suddenly, the world had turned upside down. It was not Spiro T. Agnew, arch enemy of the press and the victim of the leaks, calling for "restraint"—self-censorship—on the part of the media, but Elliot Richardson. And the attorney general was bitter. The Justice Department he was striving to rehabilitate was taking a public-relations pounding for allegedly leaking like a sieve. Worse, Agnew had suggested that a conspiracy was afoot to deprive him of his civil rights—his right to a secret investigation. Richardson understood, of course, that some leaks were inevitable. In the massive Department of Justice, there always could be someone with a loose tongue—a secretary who had typed a memo, a courier who had peeked into an envelope, an official who had a drinking buddy in the press corps. An occasional leak was part of the Washington landscape. Agnew certainly knew that. And he knew that there was just as great a chance that the leaks stemmed from his own office, his lawyers, or their secretaries. The attorney general had already been informed by his aides and the Baltimore prosecutors that they suspected this likelihood. In addition, Baker, ever the archivist, had carefully compared all the accurate newspaper stories with the information he thought Justice had given the White House. The conclusion was inescapable: the Executive Mansion was the culprit.

The President was now clearly in a fix. Regardless of his ultimate aim—the removal of Agnew—he could not sit by after his Vice President had publicly complained that he was the victim of what amounted to a conspiracy. Nixon called Agnew and told him he would support his request for an investigation. Nixon's deputy press secretary, Gerald L. Warren, announced to the White House press corps, "The President feels that the leaks in a situation such as this are certainly alien to our due process of law and the rights of individuals, and certainly do not assist the proper authorities in investigating certain matters."

The next morning's *Washington Post* lined up squarely in Agnew's corner. The Vice President, a *Post* editorial said, "is well within his rights to be powerfully annoyed if those charged with the responsibility for the investigation are acting in a way careless of the protections that are due him." The *Post* said it would honor its obligation to report the story of the investigation, but it expected the government to honor its obligation to protect its own "legitimate secrets." It was one of the few occasions when *The Washington Post* agreed editorially with Vice President Agnew. And it was not alone. *The Washington Star-News*, which had earlier contributed some important exclusive stories about the investigation, now said: "The Vice President is entirely correct in insisting that the Justice Department . . . find and stop the many sources of leaked information." Similarly, *The New York Times*, which had also significantly contributed to the public's fund of knowledge about the Agnew investigation, editorialized:

"Vice President Agnew had every right to complain that his constitutional rights are being violated by leaks attributed to 'Justice Department sources. . . .' "

The press, obviously was in a quandary. There were reporters in Washington who believed that their colleagues should practice extreme caution. They argued that since there had been no attempt to cover up the investigation—as there had been in Watergate—the press was under no compulsion to get and print the facts prematurely. The facts, they argued, would surface in the indictment or at the trial. One of those who argued that the press was speaking with a forked tongue—editorializing against the leaks while simultaneously pursuing the story—was David S. Broder of *The Washington Post*. Broder, the nation's most respected political writer, wrote: "There hasn't been such a suspiciously conspicuous display of civic virtue since a San Francisco madam led her string of girls to the Red Cross blood bank during World War II." Broder warned the press against relying exclusively on "informed sources" for its information. If the government's case was all that good, he reasoned, why would Justice Department officials leak parts of it? And if the leaks were not coming from Justice, but rather from witnesses or their lawyers, shouldn't the public be told that the stories were based on information imparted by persons who had a vested interest in seeing the Vice President indicted and convicted?

Broder had a point. But many others in the Washington journalistic community argued that the Nixon administration's sorry record on enforcing justice was reason enough for the press to go all-out to enlighten the public about the case against Agnew. Even Richardson had not yet proved that his Justice Department would be markedly different from that of his Nixon administration predecessors. In any case, Agnew was not an ordinary citizen. The public was entitled to learn everything the press could discover about the nature of the case against him. Certainly, one had to concede that here was an example of rights in conflict. Agnew was entitled to a secret investigation, and the press was entitled to pry the secrets loose. Besides, strictly speaking, the investigation had not yet gone to the grand jury. Even if it had, Agnew would not have been the first grand jury target to see the case against him surface in the press.

Moreover, reporters at this point had managed to rehabilitate the term "informed sources." It was the citation for almost every story about the Watergate burglary and cover-up reported by Carl Bernstein and Bob Woodward in *The Washington Post.* Defenders of the administration, from press secretary Ronald L. Ziegler down to Republican Party hacks at the precinct level, had railed against this reportage, juxtaposing the claims of anonymous "informed sources" against the word of the President and some of the nation's most trusted officials. In the end, of course, the "informed sources" won out, and Ziegler's circumlocuted denials became "inoperative." As a result, by the summer of 1973 the press was speaking with added authority. What it meant by the term "informed sources" was not simply some anonymous person who had provided some information, but that the newspaper itself was satisfied with the accuracy of the information and that it was staking its reputation on the veracity of the story.

Still, the pressure was building. Agnew had struck a responsive chord in America and the President was quick to react. In a televised press conference held on the lawn of his San Clemente home the day after Agnew's attack, Nixon announced that he had ordered Richardson to conduct a full investigation into the sources of the leaks. Any Justice Department employee found to be responsible for leaking information to the press would be "summarily dismissed from government service." The President was less emphatic, however, when it came to expressing confidence in the man he had twice chosen as his running mate. Aware that the gist of the case against Agnew involved his two years as governor of Maryland, Nixon carefully limited his endorsement to Agnew's term as Vice President. It was as neat a high-wire act as the nation had seen in some time.

"My confidence in his integrity has not been shaken and in fact has been strengthened by his courageous conduct and his ability even though he's controversial at times, as I am, over the past four and a half years," Nixon said. "And so I am confident in the integrity of the Vice President and particularly in the performance of the duties that he has had as Vice President, and as a candidate for Vice President."

Was the President confident in Agnew's integrity while executive of Baltimore County or governor of Maryland? "Now obviously the question arises as to charges that have been made about activities before he became Vice President," Nixon said. "He would consider it improper, I would consider it improper, for me to comment on these charges and I would not do so." As for any possible resignation, Nixon said, "The Vice President has not been indicted. Charges have been thrown out by innuendo and otherwise which he has denied to me personally and which he has denied publicly. And the talk about resignation even now . . . would be inappropriate."

Quite obviously, the President was being less than candid with the public. The charges against Agnew, as Nixon was well aware, amounted to a great deal more than "innuendo." Alexander Haig had already met with the Vice President and suggested strongly that he resign. White House lieutenants like Melvin R. Laird, the former defense secretary, had been flagging down Agnew loyalists in both the House and the Senate before they publicly committed themselves to the Vice President. Privately, Laird had told at least one key Republican, Representative John B. Anderson, chairman of the House Republican Conference, that the case against Agnew was substantial and that a strong endorsement of the Vice President would inevitably redound to Anderson's embarrassment. The net effect of the President's statement was to further obscure the White House's position. It had been less than a ringing endorsement, yet far from a call for Agnew's head.

Elliot Richardson, though, had little doubt where the President stood. Indeed, the real meaning of Nixon's tepid endorsement was not lost on any of official Washington, least of all Agnew's staff. What Nixon said about his Vice President was compared with his earlier affirmation of confidence in Ehrlichman and Haldeman, both of whom had been implicated in the Watergate scandal: he had flatly predicted their eventual exoneration. Moreover, the White House chose the next day to reveal in an interview with *The New York Times* that the attempts of Agnew's lawyers to formulate a joint legal strategy with the President had been re-buffed. On the dual issues of executive privilege and indictability, the President's lawyers saw no common interests with the Vice President. They had no intention of meeting with Agnew's attorneys and, as a matter of fact, were even going out of their way to avoid social contact with them. The President was not going to let Agnew share the legal shelter he had constructed for himself. Agnew could manufacture any legal defense he wished, but not in common cause with Nixon. In the words of Samuel Goldwyn, Nixon was saying, "Include me out."

Still, for all of Agnew's growing isolation from the White House and the antipathy with which he was viewed in the inner sanctums of the Justice Department, Richardson had no choice but to launch the investigation publicly ordered by Nixon. He designated Glen E. Pommerening, the acting assistant attorney general for administration, to undertake a "systematic inquiry" into the source of the leaks, with the help of Clarence M. Kelley, the newly named director of the FBI. Even agents of the Internal Revenue Service were detailed to find out whether the leaks had stemmed from fellow IRS agents working on the Agnew case. In the end, the department reported that 134 employees had signed affidavits denying they were the source of information provided the press. Some of the interviews, especially those with persons whose knowledge of the case was extensive, consumed hours. (In Baltimore, for instance, the interview of Baker and preparation of his affidavit took about six hours.) During these interviews, Justice employees were asked, among other things, where they thought the leaks came from. Some, like Skolnik, pieced together information provided by reporters and suggested that perhaps some of the information had come from Agnew's own camp.

The issue of the leaks was for a time to overshadow all others. Agnew's lawyers would contend in a motion filed September 28 that the Justice Department had deprived their client of his civil rights by leaking information to the press. For the moment, though, the matter was simply a major annoyance, resented by the prosecutors because it deflected them from the task at hand and by Richardson because it put his department on the defensive. The result was that the Justice Department withdrew into a shell, its staff refusing to answer any press questions about Agnew's investigation. It was a perilous tactic, for it left reporters with virtually no way to check the accuracy of information gleaned elsewhere. Richardson, though, had proclaimed total silence, and his aides followed that dictum to the letter—refusing, for instance, to confirm that George Beall was in the building, although both he and his car had been spotted.

So concerned was Richardson that Skolnik was later instructed to ask reporters to publicly state—either in their papers or in letters to Richardson—that they had not received all their information from Justice sources. Skolnik made this request of Landauer of *The Wall Street Journal* and Cohen of *The Washington Post;* both papers rejected the overtures.

By the end of the third week in August, one thing the Vice President and the attorney general had in common was their impatience with the leaks. On Friday, August 24, a visibly upset Richardson assembled nearly everyone who had substantial knowledge of the investigation—about forty persons, including Richardson's own staff, Petersen, the Baltimore prosecutors, Pommerening, and a collection of revenue and intelligence agents from the IRS—and warned them not to talk to the press. The normally placid Richardson delivered a tirade, attacking the newspapers that editorialized against the leaks but printed accounts of the investigation anyway. In language that few had ever heard the attorney general use, Richardson said that such hypocrisy was "burning my ass. We've got to be goddamn sure that we're not contributing to the leaks," he yelled.

While Richardson was excoriating the group, Pommerening took the Baltimore prosecutors aside and made a confession: he had not the slightest idea of how to conduct the investigation Richardson had announced to the press. The Baltimoreans gave him some pointers.

With most of the others dismissed, Richardson, Petersen, the Baltimore prosecutors, and Richardson's aides—the Justice Ten—went to the attorney general's private office. The talk turned to framing an answer to a letter Topkis had written to Richardson on August 21, after the attorney general's appearance on ABC's *Issues and Answers*:

Dear Mr. Attorney General,

We write as counsel to the Vice President. We understand that on a television program on Sunday, you said that you personally will make the decision as to what personal information concerning the Vice President will be presented to the Baltimore grand jury. According to the press, you said that the decision would involve two issues: the sufficiency of the evidence and the question of whether the Vice President could be indicted. We would like to be heard by you in connection with the matter. We have no wish to rush you, of course. May we have your early assurance that at a time you deem appropriate and before any final action, we may call upon you for this purpose?

Skolnik reacted to the letter as if it were a personal affront. Topkis's request, he recommended to Richardson, should be denied. The "sufficiency of the evidence" was just another way of saying "allegations against Agnew," Skolnik said; here was the Vice President again asking for the evidence against him. Richardson seemed convinced and asked Skolnik to draft the reply letter. For once, Skolnik's debating prowess had landed him in trouble: somewhat nonplused, he was forced to admit that he was about to leave on a one-week camping vacation with his children.[3] Couldn't someone else do it? Richardson said nothing, but his expression led Skolnik to fear he had just lost points for having the nerve to go on vacation while the investigation was in progress. The letter was eventually written by Beall.

Instead of inviting Agnew's lawyers to a meeting, the letter to Topkis again offered Agnew a chance to provide a statement and appear before the grand jury. In addition, the letter dropped the other shoe. It asked Agnew to supply the documents that the prosecutors wanted in the first place but had not requested in their letter of August—just about every personal financial record a man would be expected to maintain from "1 January 1962 to the present." The records the government asked for included: all cash payments of $100 or more to Agnew by either Hammerman

---

[3] These were children of his first marriage.

or The Close Associate; political contributions received; gifts of more than $100; savings accounts; savings certificates; securities; bonds; real-estate transactions; loans; mortgages; inheritances; interest; safe-deposit boxes; personal property in excess of $500; gifts of value in excess of $500 made by or in behalf of Agnew to others; insurance policies; and similar information. The government, in effect, was asking Agnew to do his own net-worth examination—it was asking him to dig his own grave.

Around the room in Richardson's office, not a man there thought Agnew would comply with this request. There was not a lawyer present who would have allowed a client to incriminate himself in such a fashion. Still, for the Justice Department the idea of his noncompliance was nearly as attractive as compliance. No longer would Agnew be able to strut about declaring that he was doing everything the government was asking of him. In fact, he would be hard put to explain why he had complied with the first request and not with the second. And at this point, anything that made Agnew uncomfortable cheered the men in the Justice Department. He had made them exceedingly uncomfortable in recent weeks, and some of the prosecutors had picked up rumors (apparently unfounded) that they were being followed. They, instead of Agnew, had been momentarily on the defense. The man's constant posing, his sanctimonious statements, were downright vexing.

Moreover, Agnew was still the Vice President, next in line of succession. This above all continued to trouble Elliot Richardson and the men around him. The President in the White House was weak and emotionally shredded. Just that week, he had shoved Ronald Ziegler, his press secretary, in full view of the White House press corps and then snapped an order at him. Moments later, giving a speech, Nixon had slurred his words. There was speculation that the President was tipsy or that the strain of the last several months had unhinged him. Official Washington was clearly concerned about the President's health, and Richardson had not been alone in suspecting that Nixon's mid-summer bout of pneumonia might have been something much worse. Rumors swept the city that the President was behaving irrationally, that White House staff members were calling General Haig "the nurse." Even Richardson, a member of the President's cabinet and an extraordinarily well-connected Washingtonian, could not be sure. Nixon was a secluded President, seen by a few people of unswerving loyalty and dubious credibility. While Washington worried, Richardson brooded. This man Agnew should resign. It was, after all, the honorable and decent thing to do. It was what Elliot Richardson would do under similar circumstances.

But Richardson was also the nation's first prosecutor and like his subordinates in the department's office over in Baltimore, he was beginning to enjoy the chase, the thrill of closing in on a man and bringing him to terms. History and its demands aside, the investigation of Agnew was a damned exciting chapter in one's life. One moment the self-perceived guardian of the political system, the next moment the attacking Mr. District Attorney, Richardson bounced back and forth between the roles like Spencer Tracy in *Dr. Jekyll and Mr. Hyde.* He seemed to enjoy the moments when he could lay aside his Olympian concerns, take up his badge, and join gut fighters like Skolnik in this most momentous of chases—the investigation of a sitting Vice President of the United States. More and more he led in the planning of prosecuting strategy, offering illustrations from his experience in Massachusetts—"war stories," his colleagues called them. No longer was there a strict dichotomy between Washington and Baltimore. Richardson's pre-eminence and Agnew's attacks had taken care of that. The entire case was now being handled from the Justice Department in Washington; Richardson's office was the war room. "You know," the attorney general said to the group at one point, "I can feel the old prosecutorial instincts coming out in myself as we get deeper and deeper into this. My first instincts were to worry about the ability to govern, to function. But now I'm getting the feeling—'Get the bastard!'"

It was an elated group of prosecutors who left the Justice Department that day. Traveling back to Baltimore, Liebman, who was generally silent in the presence of the attorney general, gave Beall some mock advice on how to handle Richardson. "Look," he said to Beall with a perfectly straight face, "tell Richardson to keep his hands off the case. Tell him we're going to do it ourselves.

If he comes anywhere near us, he's going to regret it." The three laughed and Beall gunned his car northward on the parkway, exceeding the speed limit as usual.

When the prosecutors returned to the courthouse, Skolnik dictated a memorandum—"Miscellaneous Thoughts for the Team to Ponder While I'm on Vacation"—that quickly brought them all back to earth. One of the things Skolnik suggested was a sweep of the prosecutors' home and office telephones for possible taps.[4] Secondly, he reminded his colleagues of the work still to be done: Green still had to be personally interviewed; a formal deal had yet to be negotiated with Hammerman; the response to Topkis's letter had to be drafted; and, finally, the press should be chased from the waiting room outside Beall's office. Skolnik had encountered one witness in the Baltimore County investigation, Joel Kline, stammering before the receptionist, reluctant to give his name while surrounded by reporters. The memo completed, Skolnik set off for Brandywine Meadows, Pennsylvania, and a week in the woods with his children.

It had been a busy week for the prosecutors. On Thursday, the grand jury had indicted Dale Anderson, Agnew's successor as Baltimore County executive, on thirty-nine counts of bribery, conspiracy, and extortion.[5]

Dale Anderson, who just a few months before had been only a minor political figure from a border state, became a national celebrity of sorts, his indictment front-page news in both *The New York Times* and *The Washington Post*. To the prosecutors, though, the indictment was anticlimactic at best. Long the target of the investigation, the Democratic political boss had become a distinctly secondary figure. There were bigger fish to fry. (Ron Liebman was detailed to handle aspects of the continuing Balti-

---

[4] None were found.

[5] Five additional counts of tax evasion were later added. To those familiar with the Agnew investigation, the Anderson indictment read like a family reunion. Among the firms that had bribed Anderson through Fornoff, the government charged, were Matz, Childs and Associates, and Greiner Environmental Systems, whose president, Jerry Wolff, was named in the indictment as the company official who had passed money to Fornoff. Another name to surface was Gaudreau, whose firm, the government alleged, kicked back almost $24,000 to Anderson in the years 1968–72.

more County investigation that did not involve Agnew, while continuing as a member of the Agnew investigation team. By late August he had received the ultimate accolade from Beall and Skolnik—he was allowed to interrogate witnesses on his own.)

With the Labor Day weekend approaching, the investigation of Spiro T. Agnew slowed down. Skolnik was off in Pennsylvania, Baker on Martha's Vineyard, Beall at Ocean City, and Richardson on Cape Cod where, the press reported, he was deciding in isolation whether to allow the case against Agnew to proceed to the grand jury. Actually, Richardson had already decided and was waiting only for the signed statements of the witnesses and their agreement to testify for the government. Neither he nor the Baltimore prosecutors envisioned protracted grand jury sessions. The grand jury would be used as an investigatory tool; recalcitrant witnesses had the choice of telling the truth, committing perjury, or invoking the Fifth Amendment. The indictment of Agnew, the prosecutors believed, would take no more than two days of the grand jury's time. The four chief witnesses—Matz, Green, Wolff, and Hammerman—would read their signed statements and be followed to the witness stand by IRS agents who would report on other aspects of the case.

As for the twenty-three grand jurors, theirs was a frustrating lot. Despite Agnew's frequent references to a "grand jury investigation" directed at himself, it was nothing of the sort. The jurors had yet to hear from a single Agnew witness, and what they knew of his case could only come from the newspapers. Several times, Skolnik and Baker had warned them to read the newspapers with skepticism and withhold judgment until all the Agnew evidence was finally presented to them. That day would never come.

During the Labor Day lull, the press reported that Agnew's attorneys were conducting interviews in Baltimore County in an attempt to demonstrate that the case against Agnew had no merit and that the prosecutors had been overzealous in interrogating witnesses. The reports only fueled the suspicion with which Agnew's lawyers and the prosecutors viewed each other. In fact, the counterinvestigation had amounted to nothing more than a one-day excursion into Baltimore County by Best and Topkis—two lawyers with time on their hands—in the course of which they had interviewed Alice Fringer, Agnew's former secretary in Annapolis, Scott Moore, an aide to Agnew when he was Baltimore County executive, and Alfred B. Kaltenbach, the director of Baltimore County's department of public works contracts.[6] The lawyers hired a credit investigating firm, Proudfoot Reports, Inc., of New York, to prepare a report on Matz and Wolff. For $250, Proudfoot reported among other things that its investigators had picked up rumors that Matz was a friend of Vice President Agnew!

For a brief period, it seemed that the lawyers had actually found something significant in their meanderings around Baltimore County. Suddenly, rumors swept Washington that Nixon was cutting short his stay in San Clemente and flying back to Washington for a meeting with Agnew—rumors confirmed first on network radio and then later by White House deputy press secretary Gerald Warren. Almost simultaneously, Agnew's press secretary, J. Marsh Thomson, was denying that a meeting was planned. Thomson, who through no fault of his own was quickly becoming one of Washington's least reliable sources, said he had checked with Agnew, but later in the day, he had to acknowledge that a meeting was planned.

Warren, in San Clemente, was having problems of a different nature. He was having to deny the scenario that seemed to be in everyone's mind: Agnew being summoned to the Oval Office so that the President could demand his resignation. The meeting was being held at the Vice President's request, Warren said, and had been scheduled since Tuesday. Still, the reporters persisted, wasn't this the first time in years that Nixon would spend the Labor Day weekend in Washington? Yes, Warren said, that was right. What in the world could compel him to forsake the balmy weather of southern California for the muggy heat of the nation's capital? The White House had no answers, and it provided even

---

[6] Although the exact nature of Agnew's disclosures to his lawyers remain veiled, it appears that he told them as little as possible and that they learned more from the newspapers than they did from their client.

less explanation the next day when Nixon and Agnew finally met for what was believed to be a showdown.

Nothing of the sort, was the report after the meeting. Nearly two hours had been spent in a "thorough discussion" of the investigation, a White House aide explained, but the President had not requested, nor had the Vice President offered, his resignation. The subject, the White House said, was not even mentioned. The Vice President, Warren said, "simply wanted to bring the President up to date on the investigation."

White House aides went out of their way to discourage speculation that the meeting between Nixon and Agnew was held in a crisis atmosphere. All the adjectives normally reserved for summit conferences with heads of state were employed for the occasion—"amicable," "thorough," "good." (As for the hapless Thomson, he reported that Agnew's lawyers had been pursuing their own investigation and that the Vice President had given Nixon information from "the lawyers he talks to regularly.") But these efforts to characterize the meeting as routine strained credulity. The White House reported that Nixon and Agnew had found time to discuss "domestic priorities and the legislative session coming up. . . ." If so, it was a strange time for the President to choose for such a discussion. The Vice President had virtually no responsibilities in that area, and his future in the administration was, to say the least, clouded.

After the meeting, Nixon and Agnew went to their respective helicopters—the President to Camp David, and Agnew to Ocean City and a seaside weekend at the home of his old Baltimore County chum, Harry Dundore, Sr. Both men were at their holiday retreats by the afternoon, almost at the same time that George Beall was trying frantically to find an airplane to take him *out* of Ocean City. He was fuming. It was hardly fun to have his cherished vacation with his wife and daughter interrupted by a summons from Ruckelshaus to a meeting at Ruckelshaus's home in the Washington suburb of Rockville, Maryland.

When Beall and his assistants—also summoned from their vacations—arrived, Ruckelshaus was in his flower garden watering the plants. Soon Petersen pulled up and they all went into the den, where Ruckelshaus' wife, Jill (a special assistant to Anne Armstrong, counselor to the President), served them beer. Richardson had been grounded in Boston, Ruckelshaus announced regretfully, and could not make the meeting. Beall sagged in his chair. The entire meeting, he thought, would be a waste of time.

But Ruckelshaus had an agenda. Al Haig had called him after Agnew's meeting with the President and had intimated that Nixon would soon want to confer again with Richardson. Their task, Ruckelshaus explained, was to prepare for Richardson's meeting with the President.[7]

In addition, Haig had revealed some of what Agnew and Nixon had discussed—although, the presidential aide had to admit, his boss had not told him much. Agnew had once again complained about the prosecutors—this time singling out Skolnik by name and calling him an "antiwar activist." Ruckelshaus smiled as if he, too, found it hard to believe that Agnew in extremis would cling to such a frail reed. Beall, catching Ruckelshaus's mood, added facetiously that the Vice President was ill-informed: he obviously was not aware that Skolnik had prosecuted the Catonsville Nine.

"Once you get involved with the Berrigans," Petersen observed dryly, "you get tarred with their brush."

There was more, Ruckelshaus said. Agnew had also complained that the prosecutors were measuring his old apartment at the Sheraton Park Hotel in Washington to compare its cubic footage with the apartment Lyndon Johnson briefly maintained in the same hotel. The men in the room exploded in laughter. Skolnik explained that he had once suggested that the government investigate whether Agnew's celebrity discount at the hotel was related to some illegal deal, but nothing had ever been done about the matter.

Just then Richardson called from Boston and Ruckelshaus left the room to talk to him. He came back to ask how long it

---

[7] These presidential audiences were a constant source of wonder to the Baltimore prosecutors. Richardson seemed perpetually to be getting ready for a summons from the White House, although he never knew for sure when the moment would come.

would take to finish the investigation—Richardson wanted to know. Sixty days more, was the consensus. The attorney general, Ruckelshaus eventually reported without fanfare, now authorized the prosecutors to bring the evidence against Agnew before the grand jury as soon as possible. It was the green light the Baltimoreans had awaited for so long. It had not been a bad summer's work.

The discussion then turned to Richardson's expected meeting with the President. Should Richardson simply report that he, Petersen, and the prosecutors were certain of Agnew's guilt, and leave it at that? Should he give the President an oral outline of the case? A detailed memo? Once again the room split into opposing camps, and as Richardson was absent, Petersen stood alone in arguing that the President should be told whatever he asked. The Baltimore team, and to some extent Ruckelshaus maintained that the President needed to know no more than that his attorney general and the head of the criminal division of the Justice Department were certain of the Vice President's guilt and were proceeding toward indictment. It was a simple enough matter for the prosecutors to take this tack. They, after all, were not the ones who would meet with Nixon and have to say to his face, "Sir, I think I have told you all I can." It just was not done. Nixon was the President, and the man who had appointed Richardson.

Still, everyone was agreed on one thing: telling the President anything at all ran the risk of more leaks. There would be a memo of the meeting, and aides would read and relate it to others. The more people who knew details of the case, the greater the chance of leaks. So the group struck a compromise: Richardson would offer the President an advance copy of Agnew's indictment.

Petersen then announced himself as certain of Agnew's guilt. He had completed his interviews with the major witnesses and had subjected Matz and Wolff to lie-detector tests. (Matz and Wolff had passed them, although Matz had to be retested when he answered "yes" to the question whether he had told the prosecutors all he knew about the kickback scheme and the needle nearly went off the graph. The polygraph was disconnected, Matz admitted he had withheld information to protect some friends, furnished the information, and was retested. Wolff, who presumably learned of this experience from their attorney Arnold Weiner, had paused before undergoing the test and had furnished information he had previously withheld. Then he, too, was tested and passed. Both men were incensed at the whole procedure and complained bitterly at what they considered to be a humiliating and unnecessary experience.) The government, Petersen said, had no choice but to prosecute Agnew and prosecute him quickly. If the Justice Department flinched and the detailed allegations of the witnesses became public, it would result in "a scandal of Gargantuan proportions." They had to speed the evidence to the grand jury and seek an indictment.

In fact, the Agnew investigation was all but completed, for within a week, details of an agreement with Hammerman would be worked out. The net-worth investigation was still in progress and would take months to finish.[8] On September 15, reports of Richardson's decision to bring the case to the grand jury reached the press. Less than two weeks later, on September 27, the grand jury summoned its first Agnew witness—a former Agnew fundraiser turned public-relations man named William J. Muth. He took the Fifth Amendment. Two weeks later, he was brought back, given "use immunity," and compelled to testify.

The grand jury never heard from any of the major witnesses. Instead, the prosecutors began by calling minor figures from Agnew's Baltimore County days. Some of these provided tantalizing allegations. Agnew, one witness charged, had demanded—and received—a nickel-a-pack kickback from cigarette vending machine firms that operated machines in Baltimore County's public buildings. Another said that Agnew had attempted to extort payments from the area's utility companies.

Some of the witnesses, both major and minor, attempted to offer information dealing with Agnew's personal life. The prosecutors, as was their custom, ruled such information out of bounds. Some of these unverified allegations were later pumped into the Washington rumor mill, adding to the story that the Agnew investigation had uncovered what one magazine said would be a "moral

---

[8] It was still under way when Agnew resigned.

bombshell." At the request of Agnew's lawyers, none of these unsubstantiated allegations made either in the grand jury room or in the interrogation room were included in the forty-page exposition of the evidence against Agnew that the government made public in October.

When the meeting at Ruckelshaus's home concluded, Petersen and the Baltimore prosecutors climbed into their cars and headed off into the muggy Maryland night. The investigation of Spiro T. Agnew was going to a grand jury composed of twenty-three of his fellow Marylanders.

Agnew, however, had other plans.

11 Plea Bargaining

As the Baltimore prosecutors readied their case against Spiro Agnew for presentation to the grand jury, Elliot Richardson found himself in an old-fashioned political squeeze play. Word came to him privately from the White House that the Vice President, in a daring effort to avert criminal indictment, was threatening to "go to the House."

That meant, of course, voluntarily setting in motion the impeachment mechanism, making a conscious decision to put his fortunes in the hands not of twelve ordinary citizens of the Republic—the faceless silent majority of forgotten Americans whom he had championed for so long—but of his political peers. The logic for any politician was obvious: it would be infinitely easier to persuade a majority of 435 men and women, who themselves had lived with the corrosive influence of campaign costs, that the allegations against Agnew amounted to little more than their own accommodations to the financial realities of seeking public office.

Beyond that, as Agnew knew, Capitol Hill was the grazing land of political sloths. If you wanted to have anything at all talked

217

to death, or ignored to death, or just consigned to limbo, Congress customarily was the place to take it. By placing his case before the legislators—particularly the Republicans for whom he had campaigned and raised money in his four years as Vice President—Agnew could hope to buy time, and possibly even exoneration. In the climate of Watergate especially, the Hill was a place of even more milling and hand-wringing than usual, and of less serious and sustained legislating than normally.

The gambit had arithmetic as well as logic in its favor. The House of Representatives impeaches; that is, it acts as the grand jury in the case, considering the allegations and deciding whether the man should be formally charged. If that step is taken, the trial then takes place in the Senate, where a two-thirds majority is required for conviction and removal from office. Another, more pertinent way to put it is this: 34 of the 100 members of the Senate can acquit. In the fall of 1973, there were 43 Republicans in the Senate and, equally significant, many Democrats who for one reason or another might prefer to keep Spiro Agnew in office. Not the least of these reasons would be to continue the Republican embarrassment and avoid building up a new 1976 Republican presidential prospect—as almost any Agnew replacement would have to be regarded. Even before any impeachment move in the House had been taken, there was widespread speculation that the President would use a vice-presidential vacancy to elevate former Democratic Governor of Texas John B. Connally and thus position him to run for President in 1976. Nixon continued to regard Connally, despite a falling out between them that persuaded Connally to leave his ill-defined post as a presidential adviser, with the awe of a schoolboy toward his favorite teacher. A Connally-for-Agnew switch would not set well with many Democrats, nor for that matter with some Republicans who regarded the recently converted Connally with considerable suspicion.

The White House, for its part, was at the outset dead against Agnew's going to the House. "The impeachment track," as this option for the Vice President came to be called, was fraught with ominous parallel for the President himself. If Agnew could be impeached and convicted, then perhaps it would not be so difficult for the now-reluctant congressmen to place Nixon on the same track and ride him out of office. Also, an Agnew impeachment trial would raise in unavoidable terms the basic constitutional question vexing the Watergate-plagued President: was impeachment the mandatory first step for a President or Vice President accused of crime, or could he be indicted first in a court of law? Finally, once committed to the impeachment track, Agnew would be much less likely to agree to the swift, surgical solution that the President wanted—his resignation.

Agnew's threat to go to the House so concerned the White House that on September 8 it asked Elliot Richardson to postpone submitting evidence to the grand jury in the hope that with more time the Vice President could be talked out of it. But the Justice Department wanted to keep the heat on Agnew, letting him know that with each passing day indictment drew closer. "We're dealing with power plays on both sides," Richardson told his aides as they considered whether to accede to the White House request.

Although Agnew was the man in trouble, his capacity for making mischief for the President by rallying his constituency against him was prominent in the minds of presidential aides General Haig and J. Fred Buzhardt. They urged Richardson, if he did go ahead and present Justice's case against Agnew to the grand jury, to do so as unobtrusively as possible. Richardson conferred at length with his aides about the possibility of merely taking depositions from key witnesses and having them ready to submit to the grand jury. This procedure would not run the risk of discovery by the press as witnesses trooped in and out of the grand jury room, or of leaks from the grand jury itself, both of which might provoke Agnew. The case could be advanced while granting the White House more time to persuade Agnew to abandon the impeachment track and quit. Nor was there any constitutional prohibition against going this far, even if indictment of a sitting Vice President was open to question.

But any kind of postponement troubled the Baltimoreans, and they remained suspicious of the motives of the White House.

They continued to argue that sooner or later Agnew would have to resign. "Sooner or later" was not good enough, Richardson insisted: Agnew had to be removed as soon as possible.

Richardson, for once, was in step with the current White House thinking. Whatever the President might be saying for public consumption, it was now apparent that he wanted his Vice President out. The White House, despairing that Agnew would ever take the hint, resorted to direct action. For the second time since the beginning of the investigation, the President's men on September 10 approached Agnew and in no uncertain terms suggested that he vacate the office. As usual, Haig carried the message. He and Buzhardt called on Agnew and Best in the Old Executive Office Building. Buzhardt, in a scholarly and dispassionate fashion, reviewed the case against Agnew. It was as bleak a prognostication as the Vice President had yet heard. When Buzhardt concluded, Haig moved in. Abandoning the White House's addiction for circumlocution and subtlety, the keeper of the President's gate let Agnew have it. The Vice President had to resign. It was a simple, straightforward demand, and Haig kept hammering away at it. Finally, Judah Best protested. His client did not have to listen to such a harangue, he suggested; perhaps he and the presidential aides should leave the room and continue the discussion out of Agnew's hearing. No, Agnew said, *he* would go. He did, leaving Best to deal with Haig and Buzhardt, and giving no indication that he had any intention of following Haig's advice.

The next day, however, Richardson received a call from the White House. Agnew's lawyers wanted to talk, to discuss the "procedural options" open to the Vice President. Although no one suggested that this was plea bargaining, the Justice team regarded the overture as a possible signal that, for all his proclamations of innocence and his affirmations that he would stand and fight, Agnew might be exploring the chances of a deal. (One of his lawyers, Jay Topkis, also called the attorney general directly.)

Elliot Richardson gathered his personal aides together, along with George Beall and Henry Petersen, to consider what options they would lay out. Richardson listed four considerations that would have to be satisfied in any negotiated settlement. First, he insisted, there must be prompt resolution of the matter—resignation—in the national interest. Second, justice must be done. Third, any agreed solution had to be publicly understandable and perceived by the public as just. Fourth, full disclosure of the facts against Agnew had to be made, preferably as part of the court record, so that the public would have a basis on which to conclude that justice had indeed been done and that the solution was equitable. These four points made it clear that Justice would not buy the kind of deal the Baltimore team feared Agnew would seek and the White House would support—resignation in return for no prosecution at all. Richardson, too, wanted Agnew out in a hurry, but not at that price.

On Wednesday morning, September 12, after still another planning session, the attorney general, Petersen, and Beall met with Agnew's three lawyers for an hour in Richardson's office. "It was just like preparing for the SALT talks," one of Richardson's men observed later. But in this first meeting it turned out that the cautious Justice team had overprepared. Agnew's lawyers were not pressing hard for anything, merely trying once again to find out where Justice was going and how fast, and how much time Agnew had to launch his own strategy.

Jay Topkis did most of the talking—from a prepared statement. On the basis of much research, he said, he and his legal colleagues were prepared to advise the Vice President that he was immune to indictment under the Constitution. Richardson said his own legal research was approaching the opposite conclusion. Topkis suggested that they might share research on the point, but Richardson said he didn't have much interest in pooling his knowledge with his adversary on such an important legal question. Agnew's lawyers then asked at least to be heard on the issue, and Richardson said he would be happy to look at any memorandum they cared to prepare. (The memo was never furnished.)

Then Agnew's lawyers said they were considering going to the House of Representatives for an investigation. The grand jury was going to be a circus, Topkis said, what with all the leaks in the case. Richardson seemed amused: how, he asked, could Topkis consider even a leaky grand jury more of a circus than a proceeding on Capitol Hill, possibly televised? Topkis argued that whereas a grand jury was one-sided, the individual under investigation having no chance "to get his licks in," in the House he could give his side.

Richardson, after listening to all this, decided it was time to end the fencing. He told the Agnew lawyers that the Justice Department, under the circumstances, was prepared to press on for indictment. And that concluded the meeting. "It was," one of the Justice aides recalled, "just like dogs sniffing each other." Later, though, Richardson told his colleagues it would be a "tragedy" if either of the two long roads of indictment or impeachment were to be traveled in this sad affair.

That Richardson preferred to make a deal was sensed at once by Agnew's lawyers. Best went back to Agnew and reported that although the Justice Department was prepared to press for an indictment, the time might have come to negotiate. The Vice President, personally torn apart by the investigation, finally agreed to have Best explore the possibility. Buzhardt and Haig were notified, and both called Richardson and arranged another meeting for Best with the attorney general. For all the later protestations, it was clear that Agnew's side, working through the willing White House, wanted to get the plea bargaining in motion. None were more surprised than the men at the Justice Department who had accepted with chagrin the prospect that Agnew did indeed intend to carry his fight to Congress and the people.

Best wanted to deal directly and only with Richardson. Late on the same day, September 12, the White House conveyed this message to the attorney general, and Richardson agreed to see Best alone, but only for about five minutes. In their short time together, the two men quickly exchanged pleasantries and banter, then got down to business. Richardson called the lawyer "Judah," which Best asked him to shorten to "Jud," and Best called the attorney general "Elliot." Best noticed a framed Latin inscription over the desk of one of Richardson's secretaries that said, "*Orchides Forum Trahite Cordes Et Mentes Veniant.*" "Do you know what that means?" Richardson asked. "Grab them by the balls; the hearts and minds will follow," Best replied. "I see you're a Latinist," Richardson said. Then Best came out with it. They had, he said, a mutual problem that had to be resolved consistent with the best interests of the Republic. He wanted to make a deal.

Before the discussion continued, Richardson insisted that Henry Petersen join them. He was not going to be put in a disadvantageous or vulnerable position on so sensitive a matter. Petersen was, after all, the man whom the Vice President had wanted to review the case. And Richardson knew that some of his lieutenants were still wary about Best and his connection with Chuck Colson—wary that Best, while representing Agnew, might also be representing the President's interests. (Petersen, in fact, had once referred to Best as a possible "double agent.") It was not clear, either, why Best had come without Topkis and London. But at any rate, all Best apparently had wanted to do in this meeting was to get the talks started, and that he did.

The plea-bargaining talks began in earnest at 9:30 Thursday morning, September 13, in Richardson's office. Before they started, Richardson—without yet informing Beall of what had happened—phoned him in Baltimore and told him to ask the grand jury to vote to accept evidence in the case; the prosecutors were to start presenting it that same day. Beall did so. The screws were turning on the Vice President even as his lawyer came in to cut a deal. Left open for the moment was the question whether the major witnesses would testify in person before the grand jury or submit depositions.

Despite the prosecutors' fears, it was evident from the start that Agnew was not going to demand that prosecution be dropped altogether in return for his resignation. Best made a quick pass at that notion, but Richardson said no, and the idea was not brought up again. That the price of any settlement would be Agnew's resignation was assumed by all. Best reported that the Vice President would consider making a plea of *nolo contendere* to a single count, resigning his office in return for a recommendation to the judge from the Department of Justice that no jail sentence be imposed. Staying out of jail was vital to Agnew in any deal. The plea would achieve that prime objective and minimize the stigma, technically at least, of his removal from office. He could then contend outside the courtroom, if he chose, that he still had done nothing wrong. *Nolo contendere* is defined in The American College Dictionary as "a defendant's pleading which does not admit guilt but subjects him to punishment as though he had pleaded guilty, the determination of guilt remaining open in other proceedings."

Richardson was noncommittal, except to say he would discuss the offer with his prosecutorial team. When he called the Baltimoreans and asked them to come to Washington late that afternoon, he still did not let them in on the break in the case. But Petersen had tipped off Beall, and none of the four Baltimore prosecutors greeted the news of plea bargaining with unrestrained glee. They had made it clear all along that under any circumstances they would prefer getting an indictment against Agnew, bringing him to trial, and, if convicted, sending him to jail. That would have been the normal way a similar case involving some lesser-known citizen would have been handled. Once again, on the way to Washington, they plotted furiously to formulate their positions.

For two hours in Richardson's office, the Justice Ten reviewed and assessed the morning meeting with Best. Out of the session came no firm consensus, only food for thought. Richardson said two points had to be recognized by all: that the government had a valid case and had behaved properly, and the only reason Agnew was considering resigning was that he realized the government had enough evidence to convict him; at the same time, the government would have to pay a price to get Agnew out quickly, and no one should think otherwise. This last was obviously aimed at the eager beavers from Baltimore. The overriding requirements, he reiterated, were that there be swift resolution of the matter, that the outcome be just, and that it be so perceived. He cited the adverse public reactions in the Dreyfus affair and the Sacco-Vanzetti case as illustrations of what had to be avoided at all cost.

There were four basic components in any deal: the "information"—i.e., the charge against Agnew—and his plea to it; what the Justice Department would say—i.e., its full disclosure of the facts; what Agnew would say in response; and the disposition—i.e., the sentencing, and what position Justice would take on it. Of these four, the one that Richardson thought likely to be the most troublesome was the third—what the Vice President would be permitted to say in response to the government's statement. To be acceptable, he said, Agnew's statement would have to acknowledge in some way the force and validity of the government's position. It would not do, in terms of public understanding and acceptance of the outcome, for Agnew to say it was all a pack of lies and that he had been railroaded out of office. Jonathan Moore made the point that all the components had to be taken as a package; if one were weakened, another had to be strengthened. The total settlement had to seem fair and just.

Tim Baker contributed his own six points as essential to any settlement. They were: 1) get Agnew out of office; 2) avoid a protracted national constitutional debate and crisis; 3) end the system of public corruption in Maryland; 4) provide deterrence against repetition of the practices; 5) restore confidence in the administration of justice; and 6) assure public belief in Agnew's guilt. Again Moore stressed the need that all goals be considered together as a package.

A basic difference between the Baltimore prosecutors and the Washingtonians remained. The former seemed to think that resignation was virtually automatic, that Agnew had no other choice. If he elected to go to the House, they indicated, he would be impeached and convicted anyway. But the Washingtonians did not see resignation or impeachment as automatic. Agnew could very well fight both in the courts and on Capitol Hill, they noted, a circumstance that would assure public chaos. Or the court might give way in the face of impeachment proceedings, at least until Congress acted. And again they pointed to the political realities: there were good reasons to believe that one third plus one of the senators might *not* vote to convict the Vice President. Rather than securing a conviction against Agnew, the impeachment route might produce "vindication," leaving the government's strong case against him high and dry, at least before the court of public opinion.

"We had done a much better analysis [than the Baltimoreans] of the chances for Spiro getting let off up on the Hill," one of Richardson's lieutenants said later. It was possible, he said, that Agnew could get one third of the Senate plus one from among "conservatives who believed in him and thought he was getting railroaded by either Nixon or Richardson or the anti-ethnic people, from Democrats who wanted Agnew to stay because he would be a continuing embarrassment to the administration, and from guys who didn't want to see him convicted because they didn't want it to happen to them." The Beall team didn't seem adequately to appreciate this point.

Also, the last thing the Washingtonians wanted was to make of Agnew what one of them called "a cornered tiger" who, seeing no avenue open to him, would try to fight his way out in public, swinging wildly at all comers. That would be pure disaster. Richardson, knowing that staying out of jail was Agnew's prime objective, saw insistence on imprisonment as the kind of thing that would back Agnew into a corner. So the attorney general wanted to remain neutral on the point, making a recommendation on the matter only if the judge insisted on one. To advocate no jail would compromise the department, but if it came to that he was ready to yield as the price for Agnew's resignation.

In a vigorous debate, he and Baker parted company over this question of a jail sentence. Richardson saw it not as a necessary element but as a key bargaining tool with which to force Agnew out of office under conditions of full disclosure. Baker, on the other hand, argued that Agnew was guilty of venal crimes and the government could prove it. In such cases, he said, public officials usually go to jail—it would be a deterrent for others in public office if Agnew were imprisoned. As a man at the top of the pyramid in public service, Agnew should get the stiffest penalty. After all, the government had already dealt sternly with others, and Agnew could not justly be let off with less. Baker said he didn't want people to get the impression they could get away with such crimes.

Richardson listened patiently. When Baker had finished, the attorney general, with a trace of sarcasm, observed: "Yes. Well, every little boy will know that if he gets to be Vice President of the United States and is forced to resign, his name will go down in the history books in disgrace." Baker replied that humiliation and disgrace were not enough; every minor character in the scandal had been disgraced and humiliated. But Richardson was firm, and Baker did not press. Through all this, Richardson played the role of the temperate Olympian—the one man with the public-interest, national-interest overview. If he seemed at times to be pressuring the Baltimoreans to relax their hard-line posture, he was merely, in a euphemism of diplomacy used by one of his aides, trying to "enlarge their perspective" or, in another, to "broaden their horizons" on the matter of compromise for the general good.

Though the discussion was provocative and at times heated, it was, this aide said, "a very respectful dynamic" that served to get the Baltimoreans and the Washingtonians onto the same general track. This was only the second time all ten men from the Justice Department had gathered to consider the case. Out of the meeting came not only ideas but a sense of working together toward a single purpose, and this carried through and strengthened in the plea bargaining ahead. This was not to say that there were no strong clashes of wills and opinions; there definitely were. But the Justice Ten were beginning to measure and know each other. In subsequent sessions, Richardson drew on the electricity surging out of this combination to make his eventual decision in a most sensitive exercise in human relations. Even in the first meetings, there were Baltimoreans who agreed with their associates from Washington, and vice versa. Before long, ten individual voices contributed to the Justice Department position, and if the alliances usually followed the expected lines, there were also frequent exceptions. It was part of Richardson's system of sorting out all the possibilities beforehand, of enhancing one's ability to act in negotiation by anticipating the opposition's moves, of charting responses, and hence seldom being caught unprepared.

J. T. Smith, Jonathan Moore, and Richard Darman usually met prior to the Justice Ten meetings and tried to outline what department policy should be. Having done so, they would sit back in the larger meetings and mostly listen, especially to the group from Baltimore. They wanted to hear the Baltimoreans' views, but more than that they tried to gauge what it would take to bring them around, and to focus on which of them would take the most persuasion or deft handling. In that first meeting, they got the distinct impression that Baker was the "hawk" on dealing with Agnew. He said things like, "Agnew is a bad man. He must go to jail." It was a remark that Skolnik often made, but at this meeting Baker said it, and it led one of Richardson's aides to conclude that Baker was the least mature and most emotional of the prosecutors. Skolnik meanwhile said little and seemed to go along with Richardson's concerns about "the national interest."

Because the next plea-bargaining session was not to take place until the next Monday, September 17, Richardson asked all participants to take thirty-six hours to consider what Justice's position ought to be, what they might expect from Agnew's side, and to meet again on Saturday. So the prosecutors returned to Baltimore and tried out their positions on plea bargaining on each other, Skolnik taking the lead. In one long discourse in Beall's office on Friday, he argued that it was inappropriate to bargain a plea in the Agnew case. Generally the government bargained when its evidence was weak, and the case here was very strong. Also, bargaining was a device often resorted to because the judicial system was overloaded. If ever there was a case for which the courts would make room on their dockets, this certainly was it. And surely, Skolnik said, this was one case that should be aired. Daily newspaper coverage of a trial, with all the allegations made public and witnesses examined and cross-examined, would insure the kind of microscopic public scrutiny the case warranted. Instead, if it were bargained away, there would be one day of splashy front-page headlines, a short speech by the prosecutor, and a short response by Agnew admitting as little as he could get away with. The public would be left with only a very bare outline of the government's evidence, and with Agnew acknowledging involvement in practically none of it. No one would know just what the truth was.

The argument reflected valid concerns on Skolnik's part. Although he did not say so, it also reflected an obvious disappointment for any young assistant U.S. attorney who had been looking forward to playing a starring role in what would have been one of the great courtroom dramas in American history. Skolnik was a prosecutor, and neither he nor the others needed any great flight of imagination to see themselves before the bench confronting the Vice President of the United States with the evidence that would reduce him to political and personal disgrace.

There was also, as always, the prosecutors' deep-seated suspicion of the Vice President and the men around him. What evidence was there that Best had been acting with Agnew's authorization? What if the government said it would accept the *nolo* plea, and then Agnew called a press conference and said the Justice Department was trying to railroad him out of office on a weak tax-evasion rap? These and other possibilities were discussed. But what course *should* be taken? Baker disagreed with Skolnik that a trial was always the best way to disclose all the facts. Important details were often lost in a barrage of wordiness, legal wrangles, and tangential cross-examination that only the best reporters could decipher and translate for the public. If instead a bargain were struck, Baker said, the prosecutors could be sure that detailed books would be written afterward laying out the whole case. Yes, Skolnik replied, but how many people read such books compared to the millions who depend on newspaper and television accounts of a trial?

It was not that Baker didn't want to go into court. He did, but he also saw the virtues in Richardson's arguments about getting Agnew out of office as quickly as possible. Why couldn't Justice make a counterproposal, he suggested, that Agnew resign at once and then fight his case out all the way in the courts? This would be an appropriate reaction for a Vice President facing criminal indictment, he argued, and it would resolve Richardson's prime concern. Yet the trial would still be dynamite. The constitutional issue about indictability would no longer be relevant, but there still would be tremendous public interest. Baker resolved to put these arguments before Richardson on Saturday.

While the Baltimoreans were conducting their skull session, Richardson's aides were doing the same in Washington. Friday was to have been "a day off from Agnewistics" to attend to department matters that had been shunted aside, they had been told. But they spent considerable time assessing what Agnew's lawyers wanted—a single tax count that was not a felony. Smith and Darman thought a tax count was all right, but they felt it had to be one of sufficient degree to be a felony, and there had to be full disclosure of the rest of the case. This insistence on some felony count became a bedrock of the Justice position. In some ways, Darman and Smith argued, a single tax count would be a better vehicle for airing the evidence against Agnew than a single bribery or extortion count. All the evidence and damaging testimony about Agnew's activities over a long period could be laid out in court as a supportive of tax evasion, whereas only small portions of it could be related to a single incident of a bribe taken or sought and could be ruled not pertinent by the judge. The Richardson camp was also concerned about the possibility that in accepting a *nolo* plea, the judge might ditch the rest of the deal, including the full disclosure of evidence they considered so vital.

The approaching weekend was marked by one other notable incident. In searching for a resolution to his dilemma, Agnew had been conferring with some older Republican leaders, among them his party's 1964 standard-bearer and the pillar of its right wing, Senator Barry Goldwater. Agnew had told Goldwater, as apparently he was telling everyone else, that he was innocent but that there were great pressures on him to resign. Goldwater told him to hang in and fight. The advice carried with it at least implied support, and Goldwater, with a reputation for integrity to match his reputation for candor, was a force to be reckoned with among conservatives everywhere. He was bound to have a telling influence on the beleaguered Vice President.

After his conversation with Agnew, Goldwater phoned Bryce

Harlow, one of Agnew's most trusted friends in the White House, and protested about the pressure being put on the Vice President. Then he set off for Arizona. Concerned about Goldwater's unhappiness, Harlow and Buzhardt flew west after him, to the senator's home in Scottsdale, in order to acquaint him with the realities. They gave Goldwater some of the basic evidence that Richardson had supplied, but the senator was not buying. He didn't "give a damn if Agnew was as guilty as John Dillinger," said Goldwater, he was entitled to be presumed innocent until proved guilty. Instead of telling *him* about evidence against the man, he said, they should have been giving it to a grand jury. Harlow and Buzhardt were wasting their time.

On Saturday morning, September 15, at ten, the Justice Ten met again in the conference room off Richardson's office. The meeting, which lasted about seven hours with Richardson attending for the first five, was described by one participant as the single most fascinating session in the whole Agnew case—which was not surprising, for in its course, the government's position on plea bargaining was orchestrated, again with Richardson as maestro.

Baker opened with his proposition that they first force Agnew's resignation and then prosecute him as a private citizen. Richardson, with a look of disdain, dismissed this out of hand, saying, "That's a total nonstarter." Then he took over, restating the deal Best had offered and inviting comment—not on whether there should be plea bargaining but on what the terms of the plea bargaining would be.

At the outset, Skolnik listened as the others expressed general acquiescence in Best's suggestion. There was some discussion about whether the plea they accepted from Agnew should be *nolo contendere* or guilty, and whether Justice should recommend no jail. But satisfaction was expressed on two counts: that the Vice President actually was offering to quit, and that in so doing a constitutional crisis would be averted. As the discussion went smoothly on, with a consensus apparently building to accept Best's offer, Skolnik sat and seethed. After about an hour and a half, the tiger of the Baltimore prosecutorial team could contain himself no longer. Nearly everybody else had spoken, and it looked as if the consensus might already have formed. Like an anxious schoolboy, he raised his hand slightly to catch Richardson's eye, then gave him a please-call-on-me look. Richardson nodded. "I would like to hear from Barney."

Skolnik was in total disagreement with what had been said over the last hour. First of all, he said, the Vice President's resignation was inevitable. When indicted he would have to resign, plea bargain or not. If Agnew didn't realize it, then his aides certainly would impress upon him that he would otherwise go down as the greatest scoundrel in American history. And for him to remain in office, especially with the President already under such a cloud, would subject the country to an agony that not even Agnew could insist on.

Skolnik pressed on. The Department of Justice was being blackmailed, he protested, and the public would never consider the deal being offered as a just one if the department accepted it while maintaining the position that Agnew was really guilty of bribery and extortion. He had always believed that it was a mistake for public officials to talk as some of the people in that room were talking, to assume that they knew what was in the public interest better than the public did. It was a very undemocratic and very dangerous way for public officials to think. If the public perceived something to be in the public interest, then almost by definition it became the public interest.

The prosecutor spoke with emotion but with his voice under control. He believed very strongly that the department must insist that Agnew admit his crime of bribery; not necessarily formally plead guilty to a bribery count, but at least admit certain facts that would be recognized as bribery and would constitute admission to the crime. What he meant by the department being blackmailed was that despite the fact that it had the evidence and the power to indict Agnew on numerous counts of bribery and extortion, it was being obliged to let him off with nothing more than an admission of a "tax peccadillo." He could not go along with it. "I dissent," Skolnik said grandly, in the simple but classic legal phrase.

There was a long pause. Then Attorney General Richardson spoke. The only thing he really disagreed with, he said, was Skolnik's first premise. He was not at all sure that Agnew's resignation was inevitable. Indeed, he was not at all sure Agnew would be the scoundrel Skolnik had said history would paint him if he did not resign. No one could be sure. Yet it was so important that he do so, that even probable inevitability was not enough.

As Richardson spoke, he doodled on the customary white notepad. He liked to rip the sheets off when he was finished, crumple them into a ball, and try to toss them into a wastebasket. When he was secretary of defense, the Vietnam group—a logistics and supply task force—had bought him a miniature backboard and basket that attached over the rim of his wastebasket, and he had brought it with him to his inner office at Justice. He would stand up, take aim, and let fire, no matter who was in the room with him, and he could sometimes sink five in a row from a fair distance. Now, in the conference room, he crumpled up another doodle, one of his geometric specialties, and looked around. He spied a large bowl in the center of the table and, with a mischievous look, let go. He missed, and the paper ball nearly landed in Petersen's lap. Such were the preoccupations of great men in moments of crisis. Then Richardson asked the others in the room for their views.

Most everyone agreed that Agnew must not be let off too leniently. To Skolnik, this meant that his impassioned harangue had saved the day by swinging everyone to his side. But Richardson's young aides did not see it that way at all. Skolnik, in their view, was beating a dead horse. They insisted later that there never had been any intent to permit Agnew to plead to anything short of a tax felony, never to allow him to get away with a "tax peccadillo." The Richardson men saw Skolnik as a lively and impassioned voice, perhaps the real leader of the Baltimoreans, but to them he was hardly the champion of harsh justice he pictured himself to be. He seemed to them as much concerned about having a voice in the plea bargaining as in what was decided.

Richardson, ever the diplomat, handled all of the Baltimoreans with finesse, and he accentuated the positive when assessing them later. "They were a well-balanced group," he said. "Liebman was clearly the junior member and tended to defer in the discussions to the other three. Baker was highly intelligent and deeply immersed in the facts of the investigation. The most experienced prosecutor and tactician was Skolnik, who also carried a lot of weight in discussions, but George Beall was at all times the team captain. He was the ballast; he was in my view a highly decent, honorable, sensible person, and these qualities were recognized and respected by the others. I thought they were dedicated, intelligent, and I thought they behaved with restraint and good judgment. I was very impressed with them individually and as a team." Richardson also knew the value of keeping them happy, and how to go about it. "I thought it was important," he said later, "that anything that was done be done on the basis not only of communication with them but full opportunity of every one of them to be heard, and we spent long hours together for that purpose. . . . We had long sessions at which every aspect of the situation was discussed. Theirs was the perception of a prosecuting team pursuing a criminal investigation. Mine embraced that perspective but included a greater relative concern with the problems that would arise if the Vice President were under indictment while clinging to the office."

This particular meeting exemplified well the Richardson approach and diplomacy. By the time all had been heard from, only one man at the table still seemed to want to bargain on the terms put forward by the Vice President—Henry Petersen. Petersen, who had been and continued to be tough in his discussions with Agnew's lawyers, in this gathering appeared to place the highest priority on getting Agnew out of office quickly. Far from the stereotype of the bland, faceless bureaucrat, Petersen struck others in meetings of the Justice Ten as extremely volatile, emotional, and changeable. The high regard in which the President held him was not universally shared by his Justice colleagues, especially those who thought they saw the problems and solutions in the Agnew affair in other than black-and-white terms. At one point in the heated discussion, Petersen got up and began pacing behind the long table, as was his custom, his hands thrust through his belt. Suddenly, he wheeled, faced Skolnik, and, as some in the room recalled it later, shouted at him: "The man is the goddamn Vice President of the United States! What are you trying to do? Get him to crawl on his belly?" [1]

Skolnik, the young subordinate, shouted back: "It isn't a question of making him crawl on his belly. It's a question of the public perception of whether or not what we're doing is honorable."

The debate continued, in somewhat less emotional tones. Out of it came a general agreement that at the very least the government should insist on Agnew admitting bribery or facts that amounted to bribery, perhaps in the context of a guilty or *nolo* plea to a count of income-tax evasion.

Once this was agreed to, the team discussed procedure. Moore, wary of Agnew's motives, proposed a devil theory: suppose Agnew was simply trying to trap the Justice Department into a weak deal, with the idea of then "exposing" it—in a televised press conference, say—to undermine the department's whole case? He could say that the Attorney General of the United States was perfectly willing to let him plead *nolo* to one little tax charge and drop all the rest, in spite of all the talk about extortion and bribery. What then? Skolnik suggested that to guard against such a development, Best should be asked to sign a letter indicating that he understood the department would make no deal unless Agnew admitted to bribery or to the facts that evidenced bribery. Richardson balked at this notion: he liked to deal with lawyers in good faith and not oblige them to sign papers. But Skolnik pointed out that it was routine procedure in other Baltimore investigations, not out of lack of good faith, but out of an awareness that plea bargaining could break down.

Richardson finally agreed: a letter setting forth the department's terms for negotiation should be drafted. Petersen still disagreed, but Richardson overruled him. Skolnik said he thought not only Best but also Agnew ought to be asked to sign the letter.

---

[1] Petersen later recalled his words as being somewhat milder: "Barney, we can bring him to his knees. But should we?"

Petersen again objected, and this time Richardson sided with him.

By now the meeting had gone on for about five hours. It was three in the afternoon and nobody had eaten. Richardson got up. Others too started walking around. Skolnik was standing at the far end of the room, away from the door, and Richardson walked down to the end of the table right next to him, and looked at him. He said he was leaving and asked that the others stay to draft the letter and have it ready for his signature. He thanked them all, in very flowery, patriotic phrases, again with his eyes on Skolnik. Then he turned and walked the length of the room back to the door. He took the doorknob, turned around, and waved to Skolnik. "Shalom," he said. He turned again and walked out.

For the remaining two hours, the Justice team ate dry ham and cheese sandwiches and drafted the letter to Best. Petersen was in charge (Ruckelshaus also having left). The final version read:

September 15, 1973

Dear Mr. Best:

On Thursday, September 13, 1973, at your request a meeting was held in my office to discuss options presently available to your client, the Vice President, with regard to the investigation of the Vice President and others now under way in the office of the United States Attorney for the District of Maryland. Present at the meeting were you, me and Assistant Attorney General Henry E. Petersen. At that time you indicated that one of the options available to the Vice President was resignation of his constitutional office and a plea supporting conviction of a criminal charge arising out of the foregoing investigation, and you suggested that negotiations be instituted on this matter. It is the purpose of this letter to state the terms and conditions under which the Department of Justice will enter into such negotiations with your client. A final agreement between the Department of Justice and your client which does not contain the following terms and conditions will not be acceptable to the Department of Justice:

1. The Vice President will resign from his constitutional office on or before the date upon which one or more judgments of conviction are entered upon him in open court.

2. Your client will enter a plea supporting conviction of a criminal charge arising out of the foregoing investigation.

3. At the time of such a plea, representatives of the Department of Justice will in open court make a full disclosure of the facts ultimately developed by the present investigation.

4. At the time of such plea your client will in open court acknowledge as true the fact that while as Governor of the State of Maryland he did receive and accept cash monies which he knew to be given by engineers knowing as he did so that said monies were given by these engineers with intent on their part to influence the performance of his official duties with regard to the selection of engineers for consulting contract with the State of Maryland. Or as an alternative,

5. At the time of his plea your client will in open court acknowledge as true the fact that he did receive and accept cash monies which he knew to be given by engineers seeking contracts from the State of Maryland, knowing as he did so that said monies were given by said engineers pursuant to an illegal scheme entered into by your client and others in regard to the selection of engineers for such contracts.

During the contemplated negotiations, the Department of Justice intends to continue the present investigation of the Vice President and others to present evidence to the special grand jury now sitting in Baltimore.

The Department of Justice is willing to participate in the contemplated negotiations only if and when you sign this letter with the full knowledge and authorization of the Vice President. The Department of Justice understands that your signature to this letter does not constitute an admission by your client of any fact at issue, but constitutes only an acknowledgment by your client that you are authorized to proceed to negotiate with the Department of Justice in accordance with the terms and conditions set forth above.

Sincerely,
Elliot L. Richardson
ATTORNEY GENERAL

I acknowledge and agree to the terms and conditions set forth in this letter with the full knowledge and authorization of my client, the Vice President of the United States.

Judah Best
ATTORNEY FOR THE VICE PRESIDENT

After the meeting broke up, Darman repaired to Richardson's home and filled him in on the last part of the session. Talking of Skolnik's speech, Richardson remarked with some dismay that it was too bad the Baltimoreans had to be so heavy-handed about so sensitive a matter. Skolnik may have looked back on the meeting as the one at which he had single-handedly saved the reputation of justice, but Richardson's men remembered it rather as the one in which Skolnik was targeted as the man who had to be brought aboard to assure that the prosecutors stayed in line during the critical days ahead.

On Monday morning, September 17, when the Justice team was to meet with Agnew's lawyers again, word came to Richardson by way of the White House that Agnew was balking at the idea of full disclosure of the evidence the government had accumulated to support its case for his indictment. The attorney general continued to insist that full disclosure was a nonnegotiable item: the fair administration of justice was as much at stake as Agnew's career.

On Tuesday, September 18, they did meet again, and Richardson handed Best the letter. After checking with his client, Best reported that the Vice President did not want him to sign, that acceptance of it should be enough. Richardson didn't press him, and they started talking about a deal—precisely what the Baltimore prosecutors had hoped to avoid, concerned as they were with Moore's devil theory of an irate Agnew later telling the world he was being railroaded on a minor charge. The *nolo* plea did not seem to disturb anyone greatly, and everyone seemed to agree that it could be made to some kind of tax count. But the matter of full disclosure remained a sticking point. After ninety minutes, the meeting broke up and Beall returned to Baltimore.

Later that same afternoon, Petersen called Beall. What Petersen had in mind as "full disclosure," he said, was a summary of the evidence in about two pages. Beall objected even to this. Any real summary would have to be much longer; all that Agnew's lawyers should be given now was a two-page *example* of the sort of information the eventual summary would contain, and Petersen agreed to consider such a paper and asked him to draw one up. The example Beall chose to use was an arrangement between Hammerman and one of the Maryland engineers who had kicked back to him, and he used the names Smith and Carter—a precaution taken to keep the specific information about the government case from Agnew, lest he be tempted to manufacture a defense against it. Though the two-page example itself was not critical, it did signal a significant turning point in the bargaining. Agnew in principle at least had accepted the idea that the government would make a full disclosure of the facts it had.

Another development that day jolted Washington. *The Washington Post*, under a banner headline that read "Agnew Discussing Resignation," ran a story by David S. Broder quoting a senior Republican Party leader as saying he had spent two hours trying to argue Agnew out of quitting. The source said he was "99½ per cent certain" that Agnew would resign, probably that week. To the nervous and even paranoid members of Agnew's staff, the story smacked of White House authorship, and could only be considered a blatant attempt to push Agnew out the door. Some pointed the finger—incorrectly—at Bryce Harlow, Agnew's friend who was also a presidential adviser. In politics-wise Washington, the story—and the clout of Broder's by-line—convinced many readers that the die already had been cast for Agnew. The impression grew the next day when the White House declined to comment on the story or even say whether the President still supported his Vice President. Washington waited for the other shoe to drop; Agnew's aides and friends seethed. Vic Gold, for one, was irate. "This is calculated by the White House to keep the Agnew story alive," he said of the official "no comment" from Gerald Warren. "Let's have the President and his people stand up. They can wipe this out overnight. Why don't they say, 'We support the Vice President,' like they supported Haldeman and Ehrlichman?" Agnew himself, though, outwardly at least remained the President's most trusting follower. He had enough trouble without taking on Nixon; his lawyers had a job to do; and they needed time and a favorable public climate.

On Wednesday, September 19, Richardson, Petersen, and Beall met once again with Best, Topkis, and London. Beall was armed with a memo from his three nervous and somewhat put-out assistants cooling their heels back in Baltimore, urging him to impress their basic views on Richardson: that Agnew's plea, whether to income-tax evasion or bribery, should carry a penalty more severe than that of pleas allowed from other principals like Hammerman; it should be to a felony, not a simple misdemeanor; Agnew should plead guilty, not *nolo,* which was obscure to the public; the government should not let Agnew off more easily than key witnesses who were providing testimony since he was offering nothing; Richardson should hold firm to all the points in his letter to Best; no recommendation *against* a jail sentence should be made except as a major trade-off; the grand jury investigation should proceed during the negotiations.

Again, Best said he would not sign the plea-bargaining letter, and again Richardson did not insist. But he informed Agnew's lawyers that the government therefore intended to go forward with its full-disclosure statement. All that was to be negotiated now was what Agnew would be permitted to say in reply to it in court. As for Agnew's desire to escape imprisonment, Richardson reiterated that he would prefer to make no recommendation, leaving the decision to the judge unless the court insisted he give his view. So this key element remained open. The Vice President was ready, his lawyers said, to admit to one payment received in 1967 on which he had paid no taxes, but that was all.

That evening, all the Baltimore prosecutors were asked to come secretly to Washington the next morning to discuss strategy. But that posed a dilemma: there was to be a grand jury session in Baltimore on Thursday, and to call it off would alert the press that something important was in the works. So Skolnik called Paul Kramer, the deputy U.S. attorney, and asked him to go to the grand jury and hold its members in session for an hour, then release them, instructing them to tell no one that testimony had not been heard. It was done, but not without *The New York Times* reporting "Crucial negotiations" had halted the investigation.

Thursday, September 20, was a day of frenzied meetings, mounting pressures, and counterpressures that engaged all the principals including the President himself, as Agnew stiffened against the Justice Department's efforts to impose a deal on him and finally went to the Oval Office for relief. In Richardson's conference room that morning, everyone except Petersen thought the attorney general should hold firm on the need for substantive admissions from Agnew. It was Petersen's position that the government could never foreclose a defendant from saying what he chose, and that even if he said what the prosecution wanted him to say in court, later he could retract as much of it as he wanted to. The fact that the focal point of the discussion already had become what Agnew would be permitted to say in court was itself significant, a clear reflection of the strength of the government's position.

Two hours had been scheduled for this meeting, from ten o'clock until noon, at which time Agnew's lawyers were to come in again for more plea bargaining. But the pep talk to Richardson about holding firm consumed nearly all the time, eventually wearing down the patience of even this constitutionally placid man. Finally, just before noon, he abruptly cut off a lecture by Skolnik on how important it was that the Attorney General of the United States not appear to be yielding in the negotiations, and Skolnik, Liebman, and Baker were shunted off into Moore's office nearby.

For more than four hours that afternoon, the arguments with Topkis, Best, and London over the fate of the Vice President went on. Although Best had been the initial contact and appeared to be the lawyer in charge of the politics of Agnew's situation, including liaison with the White House, Topkis emerged as the legal and intellectual heavy of the trio, putting forward the most telling points over what Agnew should or should not say to warrant one plea or another. The relationship between the partners Topkis and London on the one hand, and Best on the other, mystified the Justice team. They were not sure the three were really communicating among themselves; Best seemed off on his own. Petersen continued to warn that he might be a double agent working for two clients, Agnew and Nixon, and that whatever was told him might wind up in the Oval Office in short order. Richardson, for his part, did not appear to be particularly bothered about this possibility, since he himself was conferring with the President's men.

Although Richardson had insisted that resignation, a plea to a criminal charge, full disclosure, and some admission of guilt were nonnegotiable terms, Topkis nevertheless came in with a counterproposal—a significantly scaled-down version in which Agnew would admit some facts that would justify a plea of *nolo* to a misdemeanor, skirting any acknowledgment that he knew he was being bribed. The key word was in paragraph 4 of the letter: Agnew fought the inclusion of "knowing"—"knowing as he did so [accepted cash from engineers receiving contracts] that said monies were given" to influence him. Although the specter of jail hung ominously over him, and for all his awe of White House power pressuring him to make a deal, he hung tough. And Richardson, though he kept the door open to further counter-proposals, which chagrined the prosecutors, did the same.

Two hours after the meeting broke up, Haig phoned Richardson—there was no attempt to hide the close White House liaison now—to say that Agnew and his lawyers would be conferring too late that night for the lawyers to return that day. And once again Richardson post-mortemed with his lieutenants and Beall's three assistants. Of equal interest, or at least equal amusement, to them all was an opening gambit that Topkis had made and Richardson immediately rejected, but that he now relayed to his colleagues: It was a statement Topkis had handed him that, he said, the Vice President was willing to make rather than admit a lot of charges.

Of all the chutzpah displayed by Spiro T. Agnew in the course of the investigation against him, this was the prizewinner—a cloying, transparently patronizing paean to his accusers and to the President in the incredible hope that they would not insist that he admit he was a crook:

There have been some suggestions in the media that this investigation was politically inspired; that the prosecutor or even the Attorney General sought to gain political advantage at my expense. I will have no part in any such suggestions. I do not believe them. Having served with Attorney General Richardson for five years in this administration, I know him to be a straight-shooting and devoted public servant. So far as the United States Attorney is concerned, I endorsed his appointment when it was made, and I would do so again today. [He had, in fact, tried to block Beall's appointment.]

Nor do I believe that the President had any role in this matter. I have been honored to serve in this administration. I have always held him in the highest regard as my President and my friend. I hold him in that regard today. Mr. Richardson and Mr. Beall are of course responsible for this prosecution of me, but I believe that they are only doing their jobs. I have no reason to believe that they act out of any political or personal motivation. When a prosecutor learns of evidence, it is his job to investigate, and if the evidence seems to support a charge, it is his duty to prosecute. That is what they have done here, no more and no less. I have no reason to complain of anything they have done.

This remarkable document, in addition to providing some comic relief, offered the tense prosecutorial team a new measure of the man they were jousting with: a desperate man, a cold, pragmatic, unprincipled man who, for all his pride, was willing to abandon it publicly to stay out of jail. Richardson's concern that a cornered Ted Agnew would be extremely dangerous was ironically borne out by this fawning statement; nothing, it seemed, was beyond possibility for him to say.

While his lawyers were busy trying to float this and other proposals past the Justice Department, Agnew himself was going to the top. Secretly, he asked for and received a one-on-one appointment with the President. (That, obviously, was why Haig had to call Richardson and tell him Agnew's lawyers wouldn't be getting back to him until the next morning.) The meeting ran on so long that Agnew had to cancel a tennis date; meanwhile the White House put a firm clamp-down on any acknowledgment of the meeting. (Even on the next day, when a reporter asked at the regular White House briefing whether the two had met, deputy press secretary Warren would provide no inkling of what was said.) It was very rapidly clear from developments, however, that Agnew was there to complain to the President that Richardson and the Justice Department were making it too tough for him to strike a deal, asking too much, especially in wanting him to plead to a felony and admit he had accepted payoffs made for the purpose of influencing him.

At the close of this whirlwind day, Richardson was summoned to the White House to discuss the whole matter with Haig and Buzhardt. This was a stormy and aggressive session, in which the two White House men made clear in no uncertain terms that Agnew had to go, and go quickly—that was what mattered—and Richardson must not be allowed to stand in the way with his overly tough terms. But Richardson held firm to his nonnegotiable conditions. Night had fallen when he left the meeting—feeling, he told aides later, very much like Sir Thomas More, who alone aligned himself against the divorce of Henry the Eighth from Catherine of Aragon to marry Anne Boleyn, and eventually lost his head for it.

The stumbling block, Richardson said later, had been "my insistence on a statement by the Vice President which explicitly acknowledged guilt not only of the specific one count of a felony with which he would be charged, but that he should in addition in open court make a statement which acknowledged complicity in acts that amounted to bribery and extortion." In the wake of the meeting at the White House, he said, "I had—prayerfully is not too strong a word—considered whether to stand on this requirement, and decided that I should stand on it. . . . I anticipated that there might be pressure to move me off that position, and the thought I gave it overnight was focused on the question whether I was sticking on a real issue of principle or whether I was being unduly formalistic. I concluded overnight I should stick on it."

Nevertheless, the next morning Richardson called in his lieutenants to discuss it once again. He told them Agnew had been in to see the President and had said he wasn't going to quit under the terms offered. Obviously, they would never accept language in an Agnew statement that simply said the government was presenting a case but he wasn't guilty. But was there some give in the Justice position, Richardson asked each of them? Moore said they should hold fast. There was a point at which the Justice Department had to be willing to rely on the traditional steps to solve a case, and to say so. Tactically as well, it was a time to be firm and tough. Public confidence would not survive any further compromise. Petersen agreed, and so did the others.

When Richardson called Buzhardt to tell him he was standing pat, he was braced for resistance, in light of the scene the night before. Instead, Haig called back and told him the President thought he was doing the right thing, and then Haig and Buzhardt said they now thought so too. Apparently Nixon had reconsidered, and decided that rather than precipitate a blowup with Richardson, he'd better go along. After all, it was no time to lose an attorney general. Not only was the Agnew matter in a critical stage; Nixon's lawyers were in stiff and unyielding negotiations with Watergate prosecutor Cox over release of the White House tapes in *that* stormy, unpredictable case.

Richardson later would not acknowledge that there had been strong White House pressure on the Justice Department to soften its position, but the prosecutors knew, and were greatly disturbed by it—none more than Petersen, who for all his dutiful bureaucratic background and style was a staunch defender of the integrity of the Justice Department. He and the others continued to harbor their suspicion of the White House men, who, behind a façade of neutrality, were playing go-between with Agnew while assuring the Justice team they shared its zest to get Agnew out.

A political man as well as a diplomatic one, Richardson sought always to keep before him the diverse political interests of the parties involved. To this end, he had asked Moore to appraise the political ramifications of the Agnew case in terms of the White House's interests as opposed to his own, and Moore complied. The President, he warned Richardson, might well be concerned about losing Agnew's Middle American constituency, and this would inhibit him from any overt support of the Justice Department, at least for some time. Nixon might maintain his public pose of neutrality, or, in fact, he might even support Agnew if he took his case to the people; continued leaks and a wave of public sympathy for the man who suffered from them would give Nixon an additional reason to side with Agnew. For all these reasons it was vital that the public record be made full and clear. It was essential, Moore said, that the importance of immediate resignation be articulated; that it be made clear that the initiative for plea-bargaining talks had been taken by the Vice President with the approval of the President; that the guilt of the Vice President be unequivocally established; that punishment be meted out. Such counsel once again underlined the uneasy climate in which the various interest groups functioned within a single, troubled administration.

There followed through the course of Friday a series of phone calls—between Richardson and Buzhardt, between Richardson and Best (who was in Buzhardt's office much of the day), and between Beall and his jumpy associates back in Baltimore. The interplay was predictable—the White House and Best leaning on Richardson to soften, the Baltimoreans imploring Beall to lean on him to hold fast. It was a time of tremendous stress and great confusion. Somebody in Baltimore got nervous that Agnew might try to cop what is called an "Alford plea"—so called after a defendant who had pleaded guilty to second-degree murder to make sure he avoided a first-degree conviction and a life sentence, and never admitted he was guilty; in 1970 the Supreme Court upheld the plea. Richardson was not familiar with the Alford plea and ordered a department brief on it. Then he notified Agnew's lawyers that if they were talking about such a plea, not admitting tax evasion on the tax charge, the Vice President would have to make bribery admissions elsewhere in the settlement statement in court. More draft statements were exchanged and points bartered back and forth—while the Baltimoreans, in their own words later, "were dying."

Buzhardt, a relentless broker, pressured for some significant concession. The Agnew side continued to be particularly hung up on the word "knowing" in the plea-bargaining letter's fourth paragraph, and finally Richardson agreed that it could be dropped if a few minor adjustments were made elsewhere in the statement. Petersen came up with a section that then became the focal point of all further debate. Known to all the participants as H.E.P. No. 3, it said:

Mr. Agnew's decision to resign and enter a plea of *nolo contendere* rests on the belief that the public interest requires a swift resolution of the problems generated by the investigation of his actions. Mr. Agnew acknowledges that, pursuant to a long-standing practice in the State of Maryland, he, directly and through agents, upon assuming the office of Governor, made arrangements for the payment of money to himself and his representatives by contractors who sought consulting contracts with the State of Maryland.

Mr. Agnew further acknowledges that contracts were awarded to those who paid such monies and that he was aware that contracts were awarded by state agencies to those companies. Government witnesses will testify that preferential treatment was accorded the paying companies, pursuant to an understanding with the Governor. Mr. Agnew stresses, however, that no contract was awarded to contractors who were not competent to perform the work, and he further states that there were, of course, many instances where State contracts were awarded without any arrangement for the payment of money by the contractor. He is confident that testimony presented on his own behalf would make this inescapably clear.

In all the circumstances, Mr. Agnew has concluded that a protracted investigation and trial, with the controversy surrounding them, would seriously prejudice the national interest. These, briefly stated, are the reasons why he is entering a plea of *nolo contendere* to the charge that he did receive payments which he failed to report for purposes of income taxation, and that such failure constitutes a wilful evasion of Federal tax liability.

This Petersen draft was very close to what Agnew eventually did agree to. But in Baltimore, the reaction to the offer was as might have been expected—anguish. To Petersen, it may have been a mild softening, giving away nothing vital, but to the Baltimoreans it was a clear retreat. It was one thing for Agnew's lawyers to propose a compromise that weakened what the government had said were its nonnegotiable terms. It was quite another for the government itself to come back with a weaker position. Beall, in Washington, got a telephone earful from his colleagues, but the prosecutors offered a few suggestions after they had simmered down, all the while complaining of having to argue over the phone when they ought to have been sitting around a table in Washington. Best finally came over to the Justice Department at 8:45 that night and Richardson handed him H.E.P. No. 3. He took it, read it, and said he would be back in touch. The Vice President would want to consider it over the weekend.

The Baltimoreans waited, and hoped that what they considered a major mistake would not be seized by Agnew, and that in further talks the damage wrought to the government position could be repaired. Late that night, however, something happened that provided at least a rationale for Agnew to break off negotiations entirely. *The Washington Post* was on the streets with a story by Richard M. Cohen and Lou Cannon that blew the cover on the plea bargaining:

Vice President Agnew's lawyers and Justice Department officials have been engaged in what was described yesterday as delicate negotiations concerning a possible Agnew resignation to be coupled with a guilty plea to a relatively minor offense, according to informed sources.

The negotiations, according to two sources, could be described as plea bargaining. One informed source refused to say whether the negotiations were close to a conclusion or to reveal the details of what has been discussed at the Justice Department. A Capitol Hill source said: "We've got it on good authority that Agnew is engaged in plea bargaining—that Agnew's resignation is part of it."

This news brought to public attention for the first time the reality that Agnew might indeed step down. None were more jolted by the story than Agnew's faithful staff and old friends, who had been told nothing about their man's willingness to cop a plea. He had been telling everybody that he was innocent and would fight, and, as always in the past, they had believed him. The solidarity that had existed within the Agnew inner circle began to show some cracks, though it yet held together.

On Saturday, September 22, the phones buzzed again. Marsh Thomson, Agnew's press secretary and one of those who had been enlightened about the plea bargaining only by the *Post* story, did not believe it and tried to get permission to put out a flat denial. To Thomson, it was inconceivable that a man who had been proclaiming his innocence—and charging that the prosecutors had entrapped others under investigation into accusing him—could be entering into negotiations with those same prosecutors. The press secretary received a swift education. The most he could get was a delayed statement that neither the Vice President nor his lawyers had initiated—not taken part in—any plea bargaining. Best was more categorical. He called the *Post*'s story "without foundation," and said Agnew "is not contemplating resignation."

As time passed, Agnew clung to this artful dodge—a tactic that rankled the Justice Department men. One of Richardson's aides recalled later: "There never was any question that it was plea bargaining, and that they came to us. They even referred to an article by Judge Walter E. Hoffman who eventually approved the deal on plea bargaining called 'Negotiating with Regard to a Plea.' Would you call that plea bargaining?"

Richardson, in Richmond that day, phoned Best when he learned of the developments. Best told him he had a client to protect and that in spite of the furor the attorney general should not conclude that the negotiations were ended. Later, he called back to say that Agnew would consider the latest offer. The Justice men concluded from this response that the plea bargaining was still alive and moving toward resolution.

The weekend was one of soul-searching and waiting all around. Richardson's team, in its fashion of preparing for all eventualities, began to draft a position for Justice in the event the negotiations broke down. They knew that if that happened, there would be a wild scramble to place blame. Richardson himself felt that if Agnew balked, it would be because he could not bring himself to go along with their insistence that he make admission beyond mere tax avoidance. He talked again with Haig and Buzhardt; Agnew deliberated. It was possible that a move to Judge Hoffman to obtain his approval of the deal might be at hand, and Richardson did not want the settlement to get away. The prospect of Agnew's taking his case to the public in a dirty, brawling spectacle dismayed him, but no more so than the idea of destiny suddenly elevating the man to the national leadership. In arguing his case to Ruckelshaus for compromise in the interest of speedy resolution, Richardson had conjured up a picture for his associate: suppose, he said, Agnew is on the witness stand being cross-examined when a messenger rushes in and hands him a note that says, "The President is dead. You are now the President." What then? It was a persuasive homily.

Up in Baltimore, the young prosecutors were running other pictures through their minds, such as one of the biggest fishes in American prosecutorial history getting off the hook with little more than a rip in his gill. On Monday, Skolnik, Baker, and Liebman in their despair prepared a memo to Beall saying they did not want to have anything to do with the plea bargaining any more. The three men most directly responsible for bringing Agnew to book suggested that in the event agreement were reached on the basis of H.E.P. No. 3, they might be obliged to do whatever in conscience they thought necessary—a hint they might publicly disavow the settlement. In the meantime, they would proceed as authorized to start presenting evidence to the grand jury, and they asked that their decision be communicated to the attorney general. This dramatic memo of dissent, had it become public, would have jabbed a gaping hole in Elliot Richardson's boat. The downcast trio eventually realized that, reconsidered, and never gave the memo to Beall.

In Washington, on Monday, September 24, Richardson and his chief aides waited all day to hear from Best, who was across town at the Old Executive Office Building with his client. Agnew was livid. As far as he was concerned, the *Post* story about the negotiations had been leaked by the Justice Department for the dual purpose of embarrassing him and eroding his bargaining position. The Vice President, in the words of one associate, said he was "being screwed to the wall." He was innocent, he said, "and the public must believe I'm innocent. This makes it impossible to have a fair trial." Elliot Richardson and his young punks with Harvard degrees could wait until hell froze over before the Vice President of the United States would authorize his representatives to return to the bargaining table.

As in wartime when there is a deadlock in truce talks, Agnew decided to return to the battlefield to improve his bargaining position. But the group at the Justice Department did not know that. All day they waited and heard nothing from Agnew.

What they, especially Richardson, heard instead was the heart-beat of Richard Milhous Nixon. This alone, they knew, kept Spiro T. Agnew, a man they were convinced to a moral certainty stood on the brink of indictment as a felon, from the Presidency of the United States.

12 Going on the Offensive

On the morning of Tuesday, September 25, convinced that the plea bargaining had failed, Attorney General Elliot Richardson, accompanied by Henry Petersen, went to see President Nixon. For two hours, they reviewed the facts in Agnew's case, including the negotiations with the Vice President's lawyers. Richardson told Nixon the Justice Department had all the evidence it needed to indict Agnew and the time had come to turn it over to the Baltimore grand jury and seek an indictment against him.

This judgment did not set well at the White House, where the President's lawyers in the Watergate case were busy building the legal position that a President could not be indicted. They wanted Justice to proceed before the grand jury without addressing the issue of whether a Vice President could be indicted or tried. "The President was concerned about the political implications of asserting the right to indict the Vice President while his lawyers were taking the position that the President himself was not subject to indictment," Richardson said later. "But we had arrived at the conclusion that irrespective of the political overtones of the situation the President is not subject to indictment but all other officers are."

Richardson argued to the President that the Justice Department could not present the government's case against Agnew in court without taking a clear stand that the Vice President could be indicted and tried *before* first having been impeached and convicted in Congress. But, he said, it was Justice's plan, after any indictment, to offer to defer to the House of Representatives, so that it could launch impeachment proceedings if it chose before a criminal trial was begun. In fact, some consideration was given to seeking only a presentment from the grand jury—a report of findings, without an indictment—and then turning over the whole package to the House. The Justice Department would contend that if the House acted, then Justice had no authority to go to trial until after the impeachment proceedings had been carried out against him.

The idea of giving way to the House was more to the White House's liking—short of a swift and clean resignation, which now seemed out of the question. In fact, in contrast to their earlier horror at the idea of Agnew taking "the impeachment track," White House aides had been lobbying on Capitol Hill to have the House open an inquiry into the Agnew charges. The reason for such interest was, obviously, the same as in their concern about Richardson going too far and too fast on the indictment track: Nixon's own legal dilemma on Watergate. If the House started an impeachment inquiry on Agnew, the action could obviate a court struggle on the whole question of the indictability of a Vice President—or President—while he was still in office.

Richardson and Petersen had not been gone long from the Oval Office when Agnew arrived to see Nixon. The tortured Vice President told the President—did not ask him, the White House emphasized later—that he had decided to go to the House of Representatives for a hearing and, he hoped, a "vindication." The news was not, of course, a surprise to Nixon. Agnew and his lawyers had passed the word as early as the Labor Day weekend that they were contemplating this course, since the leaks to the press about his situation had so poisoned the climate that he could no longer expect a fair hearing in court. Besides, the Constitution clearly indicated the House was the proper forum. Just as the President's own lawyers did in the Watergate affair, Agnew clung to the contention that he could not be tried in a criminal proceeding so long as he was in office; that the only recourse to those who wanted to remove him was impeachment.

The tactic was a shrewd one. It sought to substitute for the grand jury a jury of Agnew's political peers, to whom the matter of campaign "contributions" was a familiar one. It sought to neutralize the Justice Department and, in raising the matter of the leaks, mobilize public opinion in Agnew's favor, a development that could influence the judgment of the congressmen. In addition, it occurred to some skeptics, the move toward the House could put some new pressure on Richardson to yield ground.

The fact that the tactic at the same time put Agnew publicly in direct conflict with the official prosecutorial arm of the administration in which he served did not seem to disturb Nixon. In effect, he stood back and gave his blessing to the collision course on which each side was now embarked. This seeming neutrality was a bizarre demonstration of presidential decisiveness and leadership in crisis, and it showed well that the surmise had been correct that he feared alienating Agnew's Middle American constituency. The President contented himself with a mild reminder to the public that "the Vice President is entitled to the same presumption of innocence which is the right of any citizen, and which lies at the heart of our system of justice." He praised Agnew for having "served his country with dedication and distinction" as Vice President (but said nothing of his previous public service). At Agnew's meeting with Nixon, the White House reported later, no resignation was asked and none offered, although it was admitted the subject was mentioned in the general discussion of options. Marsh Thomson, asked by reporters whether his boss planned to resign, said, "No, unequivocally. He's not that kind of guy. No chance."

Over at Justice, Richardson was in the midst of preparing a statement that the evidence against Agnew would begin to go to the grand jury, when a presidential aide phoned to ask that no news be released until 4 p.m. He did not say why, nor did he say that Agnew had been in to tell the President that he was going to go to the Hill. Richardson complied with the request for a delay. But, ever suspicious of the White House, some of his team later concluded that the President wanted to give Agnew a jump on the news break, to make sure it would not look as if the Vice President had run for cover to the House after learning that Justice was definitely going after him. In any case, by the time the Justice Department's press release came out, Agnew had been to Capitol Hill and had called on the Speaker of the House of Representatives, Carl Albert—the man who would be next in line to succeed to the President if the Vice President were removed from office or resigned. He presented Albert with a letter that cast in its most positive terms the end run his lawyers had worked out. He was requesting "a full inquiry" (he did not ask to be impeached but that's what it amounted to) "in the dual interests of preserving the Constitutional stature of my office and accomplishing my personal vindication." His lawyers had advised him, he wrote, "that the Constitution bars a criminal proceeding of any kind—federal or state, county or town—against a President or Vice President while he holds office," and therefore he could neither "acquiesce" in any such criminal proceeding nor look to it for vindication.

Agnew cited as a precedent for a House investigation the similar request made by Vice President John C. Calhoun in 1826, when faced with charges that he had profited from an Army contract while he was secretary of war. Although he was aware that "the conduct of public servants is a fair subject of the closest scrutiny and the freest remarks," Calhoun wrote, "when such attacks assume the character of impeachable offense and become, in some degree, official by being placed among the public records, an officer thus assailed, however base the instrument used, if conscious of innocence can look for refuge only to the hall of the immediate Representatives of the People." The House in Calhoun's case appointed a select committee, subpoenaed witnesses and documents, held hearings, and about a month later issued a report exonerating him. Like Calhoun, Agnew said, he would cooperate fully and, like Calhoun, "I am confident that . . . I shall be vindicated by the House."

Agnew's confidence was based more on hope than on substance. In advance of making the formal request to Albert, he had conferred with a number of conservative Republican members of the House, including Leslie C. Arends of Illinois, Samuel L. Devine of Ohio, William L. Dickinson of Alabama, and House minority leader Gerald R. Ford of Michigan—the man eventually selected to succeed him. The consensus of these discussions was that Albert would respond in a partisan fashion—that is, reject the request or at least let it simmer, rather than give a besieged Republican Vice President an alternative to prosecution. Some of the Republicans suggested, however, that it was just possible that Albert, vulnerable under these circumstances, might go along with Agnew to demonstrate his fairness in a matter that might place *him* a heartbeat from the Presidency.

From Albert's office, Agnew returned to the Old Executive Office Building and called a meeting of his full staff—a most unusual occurrence. Speaker Albert had only said that he would consider the Vice President's request, but even that much was greeted with optimism by the Agnew staff, because the Vice President's willingness to testify soothed some of their gnawing doubts about his innocence. "There was a euphoria around here after that thing on the Hill," one key Agnew aide said later, "because he made his presentation. Everyone felt that if the Vice President had anything to hide or if there was anything to all these leaks and if there was any guilt, then obviously he wouldn't want to lay this whole thing out in front of television cameras and the world. He felt the water had been poisoned in terms of getting a fair trial in Baltimore, and he felt this was a very legitimate request. . . . I think to this day he resents the fact that that offer [to present his side] hasn't been focused on. . . . He felt he had some good friends up there [on the Hill]."

In short order, however, one of those good friends—Arends— told him it wasn't going to happen. Albert decided the next day, September 26—at the strong urging, the Agnew staff believed, of House majority leader Thomas P. (Tip) O'Neill, Jr. of Massachusetts—to let Agnew stew in his own juice. Of the three options open to Agnew—resignation, possible indictment, or impeachment—the third was swiftly cut off, at least until after indictment. Albert said it would not be proper for the House to act on a matter before the courts. A subsequent resolution by fourteen Republicans on the House Judiciary Committee, calling on that committee to investigate the charges against Agnew, got nowhere. The abrupt termination of the plea bargaining had seemingly ruled out the possibility of resignation, and so there was only the court test. Agnew told his key aides he was determined to fight it.

There were two means by which to accomplish this. The first was a legal effort to block the grand jury action on grounds that the leaks to the press about the investigation had been prejudicial to a fair trial, and also on the more sensitive grounds that the Constitution forbade the indictment of a Vice President—as well as a President—prior to removal from office. Agnew's lawyers indicated their intention to pursue this course, but on September 27, before they had a chance to begin, the prosecutors began calling witnesses before the grand jury in Baltimore. It was another day before Agnew's lawyers filed their motion.

This motion asked the court to "enter a protective order prohibiting the grand jury from conducting any investigation looking to possible indictment of applicant [Agnew] and from issuing any indictment, presentment or other charge or statement pertaining to applicant." It asked the court to prohibit the Justice Department from presenting any evidence at all, orally or by documents, to the grand jury.

These requests were based on two grounds. The first became known as the "constitutional issue," and it was straightforward: "The Constitution forbids that the Vice President be indicted or convicted in any criminal court." The second, however, was more subtle, possibly unprecedented. Agnew's lawyers maintained that the news leaks had deprived Agnew of "all hope of a fair hearing on the merits." But, not stopping there, they laid the blame for the leaks squarely on the government itself and contended that the prosecution had poisoned its own case. "Since this matter came to public attention on August 6, 1973, officials of the prosecutorial arm have engaged in a steady campaign of statements to the press which could have no purpose and effect other than to prejudice any grand or petit [trial] jury hearing evidence relating to applicant. . . ." In case anyone missed the point, Topkis, London, and Best attached a ten-page affidavit in which they accused the Justice Department of mounting a "deliberate campaign" to leak information on the case to major newspapers and magazines.

"One or two [leaks] might be forgiven as the products of deplorable but perhaps inevitable inadvertence," Topkis wrote. "But this case has seen leaks in such numbers and with such constancy as to rule out any explanation by accident. It is clear, I submit, that the Vice President is the victim of a deliberate campaign, calculated and intended to deprive him of his basic rights to due process and a fair hearing." Attached to the affidavit were copies of stories that had appeared in *The New York Times, The Washington Post, The Baltimore Sun, Time,* and *Newsweek.* Three in particular seemed to rankle the lawyers: the *New York Times* story that reported on Agnew's meeting with Richardson; a CBS report in which Petersen was quoted as saying, "We've got the evidence; we've got it cold"; [1] and the *Washington Post* story about the plea bargaining.

Agnew's motion had the prosecutors and Richardson livid. They had no quarrel with the constitutional brief—it constituted a legitimate legal argument, and while Richardson was confident that Agnew *could* be indicted, and therefore investigated, he was a lawyer who recognized there were two sides to the question—but asking the court to abort the investigation because of the leaks was a different matter entirely. To a man, the prosecutorial side felt that Agnew had moved prematurely; that he had no call to raise the specter of pretrial publicity even before he was indicted. A grand jury, after all, is not sequestered as a trial jury may be. Grand jurors are allowed to read newspapers about the

---

[1] Petersen could not recall making such a statement. It was reported by Fred Graham, who apparently was told of Petersen's comment by someone who had overheard it.

subject under investigation. Their role is not to convict but merely to find if there is sufficient reason for trial.

Moreover, the strident tone in Topkis's affidavit, the prosecutors felt, was an unwarranted attack on the Justice Department. Topkis had not offered any evidence that the information had come from the government other than to cite stories that quoted "Justice Department sources." That was hardly proof positive.

Topkis, for one, agreed. He had no intention of laying out his proof in an affidavit. His strategy called for Agnew's side to subpoena the reporters who had written the stories (and some Justice Department officials) and ask the newsmen two questions: did they actually write the story, and, if so, were they being truthful when they cited "Justice Department sources"? There, Topkis would stop. If the reporters answered "yes" to both questions, the lawyer envisioned telling the judge a *prima facie* case existed to indicate that the government was the culprit. He would not ask reporters to actually divulge their sources. Topkis was a civil libertarian, and he did not want to turn this investigation into a witch hunt of the press, a tactic that in any case would make no sense for his client.

But Topkis miscalculated. The news organizations whose reporters were subpoenaed—*The New York Times, The Washington Star-News, The Washington Post, Time, Newsweek,* the New York *Daily News,* CBS, and NBC—were some of the wealthiest in the land and prepared to bear the expense of protracted litigation. Most of them also were the most zealous in defending the rights of their reporters to keep their sources confidential. The *Post* and the *Times* had already been to the Supreme Court in the Pentagon Papers case, and they were not about to have Agnew diminish that signal legal victory. None of them was ready to answer any of Topkis's questions, regardless of how innocuous they might be. At that point, a judge might hold the newsmen in contempt of court and order them jailed. It would all depend on the judge, and the man chosen to preside over the Agnew case turned out to be a most unpredictable wild card.

Walter Edward Hoffman had been selected by Chief Judge Clement F. Haynsworth, Jr., of the U.S. Court of Appeals for the Fourth District, which included Maryland and Virginia. Hoff-man, who normally presided in Norfolk, Virginia, was selected on August 12 after all nine of the federal judges in Baltimore had disqualified themselves, citing some past association with Agnew. In Baltimore, Hoffman was an unknown commodity. Ap-pointed to the federal bench by Eisenhower in 1954, the judge was quickly classified as a liberal, an appraisal based almost en-tirely on his rulings during the 1950s when Virginia had con-structed its so-called "massive resistance" response to school in-tegration; Hoffman's most publicized decision was to reopen Norfolk's public schools after the state had closed them to avoid integration. (Hoffman's decision led Senator James O. Eastland of Mississippi to comment that his judiciary committee had "made a mistake" when it confirmed Hoffman's appointment.)

On other issues, though, Judge Hoffman defied categorization. If the man had a judicial characteristic it was steadfastness. After he had been criticized by friends for his Norfolk decision, he commented, "I have a duty to perform and I'm going to perform that duty if I lose every last friend I have." (One other charac-teristic also stood out: his love of food. It had earned him the nickname "Beef" and on his six-foot frame he carried at least two hundred pounds, well over his weight when he played football for the University of Pennsylvania or later when he officiated at local college games.) He was a judge who instinctively questioned positions of the government. Indeed, he appeared almost to have an antigovernment streak in him, much as some judges are initially suspect of anyone sitting at the defendant's table. And, most notably, he had a pronounced hostility to the press, which he treated as an unnecessary nuisance. When presiding over some of Virginia's most publicized desegregation cases, he had become wary and distrustful of newspapermen. This became clear early in the Agnew case when a reporter approaching Hoffman's car was nearly sideswiped. The press quickly got the message.

Judge Hoffman had jurisdiction over not only the Agnew criminal investigation but also the corollary civil suits. Richard-son already had a preliminary brief on the indictability of a Vice President and felt he was on firm ground there. On the issue of leaks, the Justice Department felt confident—but apprehensive. Some of the news stories undoubtedly came from the Justice Department, but not all of them. In fact, Skolnik, among others, had told the attorney general the suspected stories originated in the Vice President's office. (And, Beall said, he had been told as much by Jerry Landauer, when the *Wall Street Journal* reporter first said he would write the story revealing that Agnew was under investigation.) But how would the government prove that? Richardson had no wish to call reporters to the stand and ask them who their sources had been. The approach was anathema to him. As an alternative, the Justice Department resolved that it would call Agnew's own lawyers, possibly even the Vice President himself, and ask *them* about the leaks. The confrontation promised to be a bruising one.

With the filing of Agnew's motion to block indictment, the White House began to take even more enthusiastically to the idea of the impeachment track. White House aides were quietly lobbying on the Hill again to have the congressmen reconsider the possibility. Meanwhile, Richardson assigned his solicitor general, Robert H. Bork, to prepare Justice's position combating the Agnew brief. It was a position in which the White House, not surprisingly, shared a great deal of interest, and Buzhardt, concerned about the President's own indictability, was in repeated contact with Bork over what Justice's brief would say. Richardson and Bork were in firm agreement that a Vice President could be indicted while in office; the removal or incapacitation of a Vice President, ran their argument, unlike the removal or incapacitation of a President, would not immobilize the executive branch of the government. But Buzhardt explicitly pointed out to Bork that Agnew's situation vis-à-vis the Baltimore investigation and the President's situation in Watergate were hand in glove on the constitutional issue. Eventually, Bork's brief made a strong and clear distinction: the President could not be indicted while still in office; the Vice President could. Suddenly, Agnew had one less argument to use with the White House. His and the President's legal fortunes were no longer intertwined.

In addition to the legal track open to Agnew, he had another that he had used often in his career as Vice President and as ambassador to Middle America—taking his case to the people. The objective of his legal moves was obvious and direct; what was sought in his "going public" was less so. There was perhaps the hope of mobilizing public pressure on the House of Representatives to agree to undertake an inquiry into his case. Also, Agnew needed money. A lengthy court case would have to be financed. (Two days before his meeting with Nixon repeating his decision to go to the Hill, Agnew had established his own legal defense fund, and Chicago multimillionaire and Nixon benefactor W. Clement Stone soon volunteered to head it.)

But those cast as Agnew's adversaries also suspected that he was determined to demonstrate, by rallying the "great silent majority" and the "forgotten Americans" whose special hero he had become, that he could guarantee the Nixon administration even greater headaches than it already had—in other words, that Agnew's "going public" was also an unsubtle variety of public plea bargaining: make me a better deal, or I'll turn your country upside down for you.

One of Richardson's lieutenants said later, "They had indicated indirectly through Buzhardt and others in the White House that if they were going to fight publicly, they were going to make it one hell of a dirty fight. I believe the Vice President said something to the effect that it would be the dirtiest fight that the President had ever seen. What he was after with that, obviously, was to get the President to pressure the Justice Department to tone down. He was trying to put leverage on the White House by threatening them with one hell of a mess, the implication being that they might themselves be victims of the mess. And we believed that. Now, maybe he thought we didn't believe that, and so he decided to go public to give us a little taste of it. But we never thought so well of him as to think that he wouldn't do it."

Among those who were incredulous that Agnew would try this street-fighting tactic was, ironically, the man eventually to be most bloodied in the effort, Henry Petersen. Aware that several witnesses had volunteered very damaging information about aspects of Agnew's personal life, Petersen told other Justice aides it was inconceivable to him that the man would launch a dirty fight, knowing as he must have what the prosecutors had been told about him. (The reports of Agnew's personal foibles were never used in any way by the Justice Department.)

Agnew's first volley in the attempt to mobilize public opinion was fired on Thursday, September 27, when he held a thinly veiled background interview with James B. Reston, the *New York Times'* prestigious columnist. The lead on the story, which ran the next day, did not quote Agnew directly as the source but left no doubt that he was: "Vice President Agnew has made up his mind about the next phase of what he calls his 'nightmare.' He does not intend to resign, even if he is indicted by the Baltimore grand jury, but to fight for exoneration through the courts, and keep appealing to the House of Representatives for a full and open hearing, no matter how long it takes."

Reston then recited the chapter and verse of Agnew's public argument: that the news stories about his case had convinced him he could not get a fair hearing before the grand jury; that the criminal justice system about which he previously had expressed confidence had been poisoned by the leaks "from men close to the top of the Justice Department"; that he still hoped the House of Representatives would conduct the inquiry he had requested because the House would be more "sophisticated" about the charges. Agnew said the plea bargaining had been initiated by the Justice Department, not by him, Reston wrote, and he had rejected an offer to plead guilty to lesser charges because it was "a copout that would make him look guilty in the eyes of the public, and on this, he felt, there could be 'no compromise.'" All these remarkable statements were made, of course, after the first unsuccessful round of plea bargaining—with its tentative agreement on a *nolo contendere* plea.

Reston's article also fingered Petersen as Agnew's primary target. "Mr. Agnew is obviously angry about Mr. Petersen and the criminal division of the Justice Department," Reston wrote. "He feels that they are on the defensive because, as he suspects, they did not turn up much evidence in the Watergate case that came out later in the Senate hearings, that they mishandled an important case about organized crime, that they resented the appointment of Archibald Cox as special prosecutor . . . and were now trying to make up for their losses at his expense." The Vice President was not criticizing the President's handling of the case "but is less sure about members of the President's staff." The President "has never pressed him to resign or even to take a single step he did not want to take."

Reston's article concluded: "[Agnew] guesses that despite many doubts, he really would have tried for the Presidency in 1976 but this is obviously 'all over' now. But the fight is not all over, he insists, but just beginning, for he has to clear himself, and this is what he says he is determined to do."

The interview with Reston was, in effect, Agnew's declaration of war. The next thing was to select a proper battleground for his first personal assault.[2] He was to go to California that weekend to address the National Federation of Republican Women; David Keene, his political adviser, was asked to review a routine speech drafted by another aide. Keene sent it to Agnew with a memo saying if Agnew did indeed intend to speak out, this was the ideal occasion. The women would assure him a favorable audience for what would be a major television event. Art Sohmer transmitted Keene's recommendation to Agnew and came back with the answer: No. The Vice President was sure he could get television audiences anytime, Sohmer told Keene. But the young political adviser pressed his case. This was an especially friendly audience, he said, and in three weeks, the way things were going, Agnew wouldn't have that anywhere. Agnew sent word back again that he was considering the recommendation. But still there was only the bland speech.

En route to Los Angeles, Agnew, his military aide General Mike Dunn, and Peter Malatesta stopped off in Palm Springs on

---

[2] The night of the Reston interview, Agnew was the President's guest at a formal White House dinner for Prime Minister Norman E. Kirk of New Zealand. Introduced over the public address system to one hundred ten other dinner guests, he was roundly applauded.

Friday as the guests of Frank Sinatra. Agnew and Sinatra played golf in the afternoon, and later they gathered with the others, including Mrs. Agnew and their daughter Susan, in the living room of Sinatra's place. "We sat around that afternoon and he was in a terribly pensive mood, he was low," one of those present said later. Before dinner, three or four of the insiders—including Sinatra—discussed Topic A over drinks, unanimous that Agnew had to fight back in the way he best knew: going to the people with his side of the story. "There was no one there that didn't want to" have Agnew take that approach, one of the insiders said. Still, no new speech had been written. But one of the participants recalled, "There was no doubt in my mind, late that afternoon, that he was about to let loose the next day in the direction some of us had urged—that was, an all-out offensive to fight this thing."

In making this recommendation, this same insider acknowledged, the major ingredient was not his conviction of Agnew's innocence on the basis of any facts or evidence offered, but on the basis of personal belief in the man and in his protestations of innocence. "I never addressed myself during the whole time to the legal facts of the case," the friend said. "I am not a lawyer. I never asked for legal facts. I didn't want to know them because I figured in this particular case, a little bit of information could have been dangerous. I didn't have the facts; all I had was the word of the man that he was innocent of these charges, and that they were a damn pack of lies. My total blueprint in this thing was as a politician; if that be the case, then I almost tended to reduce it to its simplistics: that if he was innocent, if he was totally innocent as he said he was and as I believed he was and still do, then let's go get 'em . . . let's go out and defend ourselves . . . by taking it right into the courtroom."

The next morning, after breakfast at Sinatra's, the party—the Vice President and Mrs. Agnew, Sinatra, General Dunn, Malatesta, Dr. William Voss, Agnew's physician, and two Secret Service agents—boarded the Vice President's Jetstar for Los Angeles. En route, Agnew took a piece of white paper and a felt-tip pen from his pocket and began quietly to jot down notes for an addendum to the speech. In Los Angeles, the party went by car to the Republican women's convention, where about 2000 loyalists—and alerted network television cameras—were waiting to hear the embattled Vice President. Signs proclaimed the overwhelmingly prevalent sentiment: "Spiro My Hero" and "Agnew for President." Agnew, Dunn, and Malatesta went to a holding room, and Sinatra and the others slipped virtually unnoticed into the rear of the hall.

Agnew strode calmly to the speaker's platform amid a tumultuous greeting that told him emphatically: We don't believe it. He read through his formal text—in which his only reference to his troubles was a broad discussion of the need for grand jury secrecy to avoid his own "cruel form of kangaroo trial in the media"—then, taking the folded white sheet from his pocket but looking directly into the television cameras, he began what doubtless was one of the most scathing attacks ever made against members of a national administration by a ranking figure in that same administration. Henry Petersen again was the prime target.

"In the past several months I have been living in purgatory," Agnew began extemporaneously. "I have found myself the recipient of undefined, unclear, and unattributed accusations that have surfaced in the largest and most widely circulated organs of our communications media. I want to say at this point—clearly and unequivocally—I am innocent of the charges against me."

The declaration ignited the attentive women to wild cheering and applause. Even as Agnew resumed it continued, but he pressed on above the din: "I have not used my office, nor abused my public trust as county executive, as governor, or as Vice President to enrich myself at the expense of my fellow Americans."

Then the onslaught really started. Though he had heard rumors from Baltimore earlier, he said, "[I] had no idea that I was the target of an investigation" until receiving Beall's letter. That letter came to him, he insisted, after *The Wall Street Journal* got it (denied by the *Journal*); "it was not through my fault that this became a nonsecret procedure, but through deliberately contrived actions of individuals in the prosecutorial system of the

United States, and I regard that as outrageous and malicious." This statement was obviously intended as a denial that someone in his camp had first given the contents of the letter to Landauer. What he was dealing with, rather, was a conspiracy in the Justice Department to get him. "I say this to you," he declared firmly, "that conduct of high individuals in the Department of Justice, particularly the conduct of the chief of the criminal investiga- tion division of that department [Petersen], is unprofessional and malicious and outrageous, if I am to believe what has been printed in the news magazines and said on the television net- works of this country, and I have had no denial that this is the case."

Referring to his motion before Judge Hoffman about the leaks, Agnew said that if he could examine the Justice Depart- ment officials under oath and were to find that they "have abused their sacred trust and forsaken their professional standards, then I will ask the President of the United States to summarily dis- charge those individuals." It was the classic competitive posture: the best defense is a good offense. He tried to convince the sym- pathetic women and the millions watching on television that the charges were merely a convenient diversion for those at Justice —again he meant Petersen but did not use his name—who had bungled the Watergate case.

"Now people will say to me: 'Why? You don't make sense. Why should a Republican Department of Justice and Republican prosecutors attempt to get you?' Well, I don't know all the an- swers, but I will say this—that individuals in the upper profes- sional echelons of the Department of Justice have been severely stung by their ineptness in the prosecution of the Watergate case. They have been severely stung that the President and the attorney general have found it necessary to appoint a special prosecutor and they are trying to recoup their reputation at my expense. I'm a big trophy.

"And one of those individuals [again no name] has made some very severe mistakes, serious mistakes. In handling his job he con- siders himself a career professional, in a class by himself, but a recent examination of his record will show not only that he failed to get any of the information about the true dimensions of the Watergate matter but that he also through ineptness and blunder prevented the successful prosecution of high crime figures because of wiretapping error.[3] Those are the reasons why he needs me to reinstate his reputation as a tough and courageous and hard-nosed prosecutor. Well, I'm not going to fall down and be his victim, I assure you."

Agnew reiterated his basic argument that he was the scapecoat for others under criminal investigation who were trying to save their own necks by buying immunity. That was why he felt he had to turn to the House, he said—because "the well has been most successfully poisoned" in the courts by the Justice Department. The notion that "[I am] attempting to hide behind a constitutional shield and suppress the facts [his brief that a Vice President cannot be indicted, filed just the previous day] . . . amazes me, because what I want is not a suppression of the facts, but the fullest possible hearing of them widely publicized before the people of the American nation, so that everyone knows exactly what is going on in this nation. I'm not trying to hide anything."

And then, finally, was the categorical no-surrender declaration: "I want to make another thing so clear that it cannot be mistaken in the future. Because of these tactics which have been employed against me, because small and fearful men have been frightened into furnishing evidence against me—they have perjured themselves in many cases, it's my understanding—I will not resign if indicted. I will not resign if indicted. [Cheers and wild applause.]

"Our Constitution says that every man is entitled to a fair trial and a presumption of innocence. I intend to rely on the spirit as well as the letter of those guarantees. I would forsake the principles of the Founding Fathers if I abandoned this fight. And I do not intend to abandon it. . . ."

---

[3] Agnew was apparently referring here to a practice in the Justice Department in the first Nixon administration followed by Petersen and some others, of signing authorization for legal wiretaps upon delegation from then Attorney General John N. Mitchell. Numerous cases were filed in the Supreme Court charging that wiretaps were illegal because such delegations by Mitchell were violations under the Omnibus Crime and Safe Streets Act of 1968.

It was clear enough. The consensus at Sinatra's place in Palm Springs the night before had been converted unequivocally into the firm public posture of Spiro Agnew: he would fight to the end. There could be no turning back now, or so it seemed to the Agnew insiders. "That's a hell of a shot," Malatesta told his boss when he left the platform.

Immediately after the speech, Agnew went to a private room and met with California Republican Party leaders. He told them it would not be realistic to consider himself a 1976 presidential possibility any longer, but he gave them a GOP pep talk looking to the 1974 congressional elections. Then he and his party returned to Palm Springs, and for the better part of the next two days Agnew relaxed, like a man who had put a major decision behind him. "He was up, very relieved and very relaxed, and he continued that for the entire rest of the stay there," one of the party said later. "He played good golf, he played good tennis, he was delightful company, and there was never a doubt in my mind, never a moment's doubt in my mind. . . . I didn't detect anything but a relieved, elated state by all the people who were there that the die had been cast and we were on our way to go with this thing to the end, to its conclusion . . . whatever the legal approaches would be."

Back at the Justice Department in Washington, however, there was little relaxation or elation. There was only chagrin and bewilderment at the tactic. Petersen had been working at the department and was driving home in his car when Agnew's speech came over the radio. He heard most of the formal, impersonal part of it before arriving at his house. He was eating his lunch in another room, with the television set on in the living room, when Agnew concluded his text and launched into his attack of the Justice Department and its anti-crime chief.

"I ran into the living room to watch him attack me," Petersen recalled. "And I commented to my wife, I said, 'Jean, he just made a terrible mistake.' That's so commonplace in this business —for the prosecutor to be attacked when he's got a very, very strong case." At the same time, though, Petersen was aware that this was no commonplace investigation and that he could not counterattack. "I told her also, 'I'm not going to be able to say anything. This is going to be a tough week, and we're just going to have to grin and bear it, and it will all resolve itself when the evidence comes out.'

"But it's one thing to say that to your wife. It really is difficult to walk around and take it."

The attack was not a complete surprise. "When the negotiations broke down," Petersen said, "maybe I was regarded as a hard-liner [a self-characterization that certainly would have tickled many of the Justice Ten]. Buzhardt indicated to me that there would probably be a dirty fight and, if there was, it wouldn't be the President who was attacked, or Richardson. It would probably be me. My response was: 'God damn it, that's precisely the kind of thing we understand, and if that's done, his blood will be all over the place.' That's what defendants do when the law and the facts are against them. So I was not really taken by surprise at the bitterness and nature of the attack."

When Agnew concluded the speech and the Republican women were still in the throes of partisan ecstasy, Petersen reached for the phone and called Richardson at the Justice Department.

"If you haven't heard this," Petersen told Richardson, "you had better get a transcript of it because not only has he attacked me, but the rest of the department looks like a dumb ass." With that, Petersen told his boss that he was skipping town to avoid what he knew would be a deluge of calls from reporters. He retreated to southern Maryland.

Richardson, who was in his office with Smith, Moore, and Darman and had not seen or heard the speech, dispatched an aide to one of the networks for a tape and a transcript. The transcript came first.

"I was outraged by his accusations against Petersen," Richardson said later. "It seemed to me a highly dubious tactical move on his part." Richardson and his aides, after three hours of painstaking deliberation and several drafts, fashioned a brief response in Petersen's defense, calling him "a distinguished lawyer . . . greatly respected by his colleagues" who was "constrained from defending himself by the ethical standards governing a criminal investigation."

It took so long to write, Richardson said, "because we wanted it pitched right, in terms of the right note of indignation and confidence, without seeming to reply in kind. I think what we came up with had the right mix, but earlier versions were tougher and longer. We were determined not to get sidetracked into a debate with him, which is why we did not want in our response to seem to be joining a pissing contest with him."

It was not Petersen but himself, Richardson noted in the statement, who was in over-all charge of the Agnew investigation. Agnew had spared Richardson, but the Justice Department team believed it would be only a matter of time before the counterattacking Vice President got to him.

In Baltimore, the prosecutors were shocked at Agnew's Los Angeles harangue. They had been bracing themselves for an attack from Agnew, but they had thought the target would be Skolnik, whom Agnew had repeatedly denigrated in private. Baker, who caught only the last part of the speech, was flabbergasted. Agnew had committed an enormous tactical error, he thought. It was one thing to attack someone like Skolnik—a virtual nobody—but Petersen? Petersen was the man the Vice President himself had requested be brought into his own case! The prosecutors couldn't understand the strategy. Nevertheless, they concluded that Skolnik had merely received a stay of execution. His time would come soon.

The theory ran somewhat differently among Richardson's men. "We had been led to believe that Agnew had a phased escalation strategy," one of them said later. "First, he was going to attack Henry Petersen. Then, he was going to attack Beall and the Baltimoreans—ad hominem arguments. Next Richardson. Next the President. A four-stage shot." This incredible bit of cold-blooded intelligence actually came from the White House, "from what bits and pieces we could piece together in our de-briefs of conversations that were going on in the White House" (presumably those involving Richardson, Petersen, Haig, Buzhardt, and possibly the President), the Justice aide said. Haig had been in daily conversation with Agnew, Justice had been told.

That the White House had a theory that Agnew was undertaking an escalatory strategy that would ultimately put the President himself under fire, and yet did not openly move to derail him, strained credence. The Richardson insider acknowledged that in assessing what his group was told by the White House, "we didn't know what they were up to. They're professional negotiators. Haig worked on the Vietnam settlement. So when you get information from them you have to always quality-rate it. . . . They would have us believe that there was likely this four-stage strategy. And as they would represent themselves to us, they wanted a settlement as promptly as possible all along. They wanted the guy out of there. They wanted resignation without anything. They just wanted him out." But the White House couched its eagerness to let Agnew off more easily in terms so guarded that it could say there had been none. "To say that Haig told Richardson and Petersen their position was too tough is not the fair way of putting it," this insider observed. "They're smarter than that. You'll never find the words on a tape that say, 'Hey, Elliot, your position's much too tough on that.' They would go at it this way: 'Well, let's look at the national interest in avoiding that. And let's look at what we can realistically expect to get here.'"

On the day before Agnew's speech, Richardson had gotten a message directly from the President himself that was most revealing. When the attorney general had been at the White House to tell Nixon that he had determined the Vice President was indictable under the Constitution, and that he was going forward with presentation of a brief to that effect, the President had made no response to that. But, according to the notes of one of those de-briefed by Richardson immediately thereafter, he told Richardson that he was "looking forward to getting the Agnew thing over with, at which point he would fire Cox" or get rid of him some other way. Richardson apparently did not take this remark seriously, this insider said later, adding with a grin, "Not as seriously as he should have." Ten days after Agnew's resignation, Cox was indeed fired, at the cost of Richardson's own resignation in protest.

This presidential comment dovetailed with what the attorney general and his close aides were in fact actively discussing as "the hat-trick hypothesis." A hat trick in hockey—which is king in Richardson's Boston—is three goals scored by a single player in one game. "We thought possibly the President wanted to get rid of Richardson, Agnew, and Cox," one Richardson associate said, "but that he would get rid of them in some combination deal that would begin with Agnew." Such was the climate of deep distrust of the White House and the President within the inner sanctum of his own attorney general's office as the twin debacles of Watergate and the Agnew scandal unfolded.

It was a time, in other words, of unimaginable and rampant paranoia on all three fronts—among the prosecutors in Washington and in Baltimore, at the White House, and in the Agnew camp. Among the Vice President's men especially, where only two aides—Sohmer and Dunn—were privy to the Vice President's daily strategy and thinking, devils were seen or imagined lurking behind every public statement, behind every leak, or even behind the silences, as the speculation about Agnew's resigning refused to die.

The idea that Agnew might have a strategy of "phased escalation," aimed first at Petersen and eventually targeting the President himself as the cause of Agnew's woes, would have been incredible to the men around the Vice President. Repeatedly and to a man, those who would allow themselves any criticism of him at all would focus on only one shortcoming—that he held the President, and the power of the Presidency, and the influence of the men around it, in too much awe. This was the only factor, they would argue, that might immobilize or intimidate Agnew —and indeed, they acknowledged, he bowed to the White House at every turn, sought to curry its favor, and listened beyond prudence to its advice when his own political life was in the balance.

The Los Angeles speech, however, while not attacking the President or even Richardson, left no doubt in any quarter that there would be no resignation by Spiro Agnew, no matter what signals might be flashed from the White House. The explicitness, even viciousness of his speech seemed to seal that conclusion. The Justice Department accordingly pressed on with its case against him, the White House braced itself for the worst, and the Agnew loyalists looked forward with the faith of true believers to their boss's two-fisted counterattack.

All through these last weeks, Agnew had kept his own staff in the dark as to the real developments in his case, never acknowledging even to them that his lawyers had been engaged in plea bargaining. For counsel, all along he had turned not to them but to outsiders, men like Barry Goldwater and Bryce Harlow. But now the whole affair was out in the open and everyone knew—Spiro Agnew's fiercest defenders and antagonists. The battle at last had been joined in public, and it was, all seemed to agree, a fight to the finish.

13 A Candle Is Only So Long

In the golden days of Spiro Agnew's divisive oratory, in his days of alliterative anarchy when such ·perversions of the English language as "nattering nabobs of negativism" and "hopeless, hysterical hypochondriacs of history" tripped tastelessly from his tongue, he had been widely applauded for talking straight. When Ted Agnew spoke, everybody—friend and foe—got the message. And so it had been with his Los Angeles tirade against the Justice Department and Henry Petersen.

Among those who got the message most clearly was the President of the United States, and he was outraged. The brutish rhetoric of Ted Agnew was fine when it was directed at an "effete corps of impudent snobs," at "pusillanimous pussyfooters" or at "rotten apples" to be discarded lest they spoil the whole barrel—Agnew's more infamous characterizations of Nixon's critics in 1969. But when that rhetoric attacked the President's own official family, by inference it attacked him. Richard Nixon already was under criticism for seeming to stand blithely aside as his attorney general pressed for an indictment against his Vice President while the latter ran off to the Hill for relief. This was a strange sort of leadership. And now, remaining silent in the face of Agnew's public slap at his Justice Department and at his favorite, Petersen, Nixon looked like a marshmallow, and he knew it. Going after Petersen as Agnew did was Agnew's fatal mistake—as Petersen himself judged—and he was about to find that out in unmistakable terms.

Richard Nixon was not a man who liked to be perceived as a weakling, a pushover. As a youth, he had sought with little success to demonstrate what he considered manliness on the football field, and he carried that yearning through life. Later, in politics, he talked tougher than his introverted personality might have dictated, and as President he seemed to equate bold action, even brutal action, with masculinity. While he still found it near-impossible to be tough with anybody in a face-to-face situation, he had learned to use others to cut down those who crossed him. And that was, often, how he saw it: being crossed by somebody, being taken advantage of, because his true toughness was misread. So he would have to "show him." Ted Agnew, of all people, student of Richard Nixon, should have known better.

The President's first step was to determine whether Agnew knew what he was talking about when he accused Petersen. Nixon, after all, had said in his August 22 press conference that any official who leaked information about the case would be "summarily dismissed," and Agnew in effect was calling his bluff. Richardson was asked for, and swiftly provided, assurances that Petersen had not leaked to the press, nor had he told Fred Graham of CBS that the department had Agnew "cold." Next, the President phoned Elliot Richardson at home. While Nixon believed he must maintain a posture of neutrality for as long as possible, in order not to alienate the Agnew constituency unduly, he "wanted me to know that he was supporting me. . . . I didn't expect and I didn't think it was good for him or for us," Richardson said afterward, "for him to do any more than indicate his support for the integrity of what the Department of Justice was doing."

Agnew's blunder on Petersen was compounded in the eyes of the White House on Tuesday, October 2, when Marsh Thomson predicted to reporters that more of the same bombast dished out in Los Angeles was in the offing for the Vice President's next speech. Newsmen and the television networks had been pressing Thomson to determine whether the speech—at a $125-a-plate dinner of the United Republican Fund in Chicago on Thursday night—warranted the full treatment of a major news event. Thomson, who had seen a first draft of the speech, replied that "this kind of audience should lead us to anticipate a sequel [to Los Angeles]. The Vice President's in a fighting mood." Thomson knew that each outspoken performance by the Vice President sharply contrasted with President Nixon's relative reticence concerning his own Watergate troubles—and this to the displeasure of the White House. But as far as he knew, Agnew was set on his course, and his forecast was no more than the collective wisdom in and out of the Agnew camp.

At the White House, Thomson's remarks, printed on page one of *The Washington Post* the next morning, were a red flag of defiance. Alexander Haig called Art Sohmer, Agnew's right-hand man, and told him point blank: the President wanted no more public attacks on Petersen, the Justice Department, or the Nixon administration, or there would never be a deal. And without a deal, Agnew should know where the trail would certainly end—behind bars. For openers, this fellow Thomson had to be throttled, as evidence to the White House that Agnew got the message. It was getting down to what Richard Nixon, public moralist, liked privately to call "the nut-cutting."

Sohmer called in the unsuspecting sacrificial lamb, Thomson. A former foreign service officer in Southeast Asia with little public-relations and no press experience, Thomson had followed a tough act—the Don Quixote of press secretaries, Victor Gold. He had neither the drive nor the quick if frenzied political mind of his predecessor. He did not attempt to out-Gold Gold—that would have been like running a footrace with a rabbit—and Agnew didn't want his new press secretary to do that. He wanted a low-key technician to process handouts and inquiries by mostly saying he didn't know—which in Thomson's case was true. From all the evidence, Marsh Thomson filled the bill exactly. So when Sohmer began to tell him that the Vice President was generally dissatisfied with his work, the press secretary was totally befuddled. Sohmer finally got around to what really was on his mind—the statement Thomson had made about the forthcoming speech in Chicago. That was what had so upset Agnew. (No mention was made of White House displeasure.) Thomson was going to be relieved for a while as press spokesman. He was instructed to have his secretaries take press inquiries for him and to call back his answers to the reporters. He was not simply to adopt a low profile; he was, until further notice, to become a nonperson. Agnew was going to take no chances that the White House would not get his reply.

That same day, October 3, President Nixon delivered another message to Agnew—more publicly. He called a rare informal press conference in his office, and, while telling the reporters that he regarded Agnew's decision not to resign even if indicted "an altogether proper one," Nixon characterized the charges against Agnew as "serious and not frivolous." Also, most significantly, he defended Henry Petersen. Asked if he was still supporting Petersen's handling of the investigation, Nixon said if he were not, "[Petersen] would have been removed at this time. But it would be a disservice to an individual who has served both administrations with distinction for many, many years to remove him from handling the investigation, unless there was clear evidence that he had been guilty of an indiscretion." Richardson had assured him, Nixon reported, that there was no such evidence to support Agnew's charges, especially on the matter of leaks.

That issue—the leaks and their potential or real damage to the Vice President's chances for a fair hearing and trial in the courts or Congress—now emerged as a basic defense in Agnew's desperate legal fight to avert disaster. Jay Topkis, having filed the brief seeking to halt the grand jury investigation, had begun to try to build his case with personal testimony from reporters. He phoned Richard Cohen of *The Washington Post* and asked him to identify his sources on the Agnew story. Cohen, on the instruction of his superiors, told Topkis to contact Joseph Califano, who was the

Post's lawyer. Others who received similar calls were Fred Graham of CBS News, and Ben A. Franklin of *The New York Times.* They also declined to identify their sources.

On October 3, the same day as Nixon's press conference, Judge Hoffman in Baltimore took steps that threatened to move the focus of the case off Agnew's guilt or innocence and turn it into a freedom-of-the-press debate. He assembled members of the grand jury in open court for a lecture about their responsibility to ignore news reports and decide their course solely on the evidence presented to them in secrecy. Before doing so, he summoned Agnew's three lawyers and three of the prosecutors—Beall, Skolnik, and Liebman [1]—to Room 630 in the courthouse. It was 9:30 in the morning, and already Beall saw that it was going to be a rough day. The judge distributed to each of them a copy of the supplemental charge he was about to make to the grand jury and asked them if they had any comments. "Unfortunately, in the present-day grab for priority in getting news items, the news media frequently overlook the rights of others, especially where criminal matters are involved," the charge warned. "We are rapidly approaching the day when the perpetual conflict between the news media, operating as they do under freedom of speech and freedom of the press, and the judicial system, charged with protecting the rights of persons under investigation for criminal acts, must be resolved." In other words, Hoffman would not mind making this a landmark case on the press—the last thing the Justice Department wanted.

Beall could hardly believe what was happening. Raising this basic press question in an already historic case was dismaying enough; but cutting the defendant's lawyers in on the decision on how to instruct the grand jury was just too much.

The grand jury, he objected to the judge, was within the exclusive province of the prosecutors and the judges of the court—not lawyers for possible defendants; Agnew's lawyers had no standing and therefore should not be asked their opinion. Judge Hoffman noted Beall's objection but said that the Agnew case was different by definition and he, for one, was going to treat

---

[1] Baker was busy in a different courtroom having witnesses immunized.

it differently. Beall retreated and braced himself for further blows.

Judge Hoffman said he had written Jay Topkis a letter just two days before and sent a copy to Henry Petersen. Neither man had yet received his letter, and so the judge read it aloud. "Gentlemen: Relating solely to the publicity question raised by the applicant [Agnew], unless the brief of the Department of Justice persuades me to the contrary, I am presently inclined to the belief that the applicant would at least be entitled to an evidentiary hearing on his charges that the . . . prosecution was responsible for the allegedly prejudicial [leaks]."

Again the prosecutors were stunned. Firmly convinced that Agnew's civil suit on the leaks was premature, they were now being told that Judge Hoffman was already disposed to grant a hearing on the motion even before reading the government's response. Hoffman scheduled a hearing, closed to the public, for Friday, October 12.

Again Beall was on his feet. How could the judge discuss the mechanics of an evidentiary hearing when the government would contend the civil motion on the leaks was premature? Any hearing in advance of an indictment would be unprecedented.

Judge Hoffman brushed aside Beall's objection. Petersen had told him that the statute of limitations was a factor in the case, so he was setting up a tight schedule. He had already conferred with Clement Haynsworth, who was prepared to establish a panel in Richmond to handle any appeals on an expeditious basis. He had told Haynsworth that he would rule on the civil suits by October 19. He meant to adhere to that schedule.

Then the judge said something that made Beall feel better: he doubted that he could stop the grand jury or dismiss any possible indictment even if everything Agnew had contended was true. Hoffman cited a case in the Eastern District of Virginia in which he had reviewed a grand jury transcript and found that the U.S. attorney had "browbeaten witnesses" and accused other witnesses of "lying"—it had been a "disgraceful performance," but there had been nothing he could do about it. At any rate, Judge Hoffman said, he already had a commitment from Petersen that the government would not attempt to indict Agnew until the civil suits were disposed of.

Topkis, who was thus far doing quite well, volunteered that Agnew would waive his rights under the statute of limitations if it would help the judge.

Again Beall objected. Too tricky and too complicated, he said, citing a case in which the waiver had been overruled by the courts. Judge Hoffman agreed, for once, but Beall kept driving the point home. The government ran the risk of letting the grand jury's term expire; the statute of limitations relevant to others involved in the investigation might also expire; and any delay would bolster Agnew's attempts to have Congress take jurisdiction. Minor as it was, this was Beall's last victory of the day.

Martin London then got to the crux of the matter. His client would like to begin taking depositions on the leaks issue as soon as possible. They need not wait until October 12 but could be undertaken immediately.

This time Beall and Skolnik rose in unison. If the judge allowed Agnew's lawyers to begin taking depositions, he was presupposing the merits of their claim—namely that the leaks had come from the government. Moreover, Beall argued, taking the depositions seemed to be a transparent attempt to tie up the prosecutors in the civil action at the expense of the criminal case they were building. Beall, of course, assumed that he would be among those Agnew's lawyers wanted to question. That would be fine with him. But he wanted a crack at the other side— including Agnew.

Judge Hoffman, however, was not yet willing to have the government have its way. He would have to think about whether the government had the right to call Agnew's lawyers and Agnew himself as witnesses in the civil case. As for London's request to start taking depositions, Hoffman signed it on the spot. Hoffman added that he wanted to be present when the witnesses were deposed, since he wanted to be able to judge their demeanor when answering questions, even ask some questions himself, possibly. Now Topkis had gotten more than he bargained for. What Hoffman was saying, the lawyer knew well, was that he wanted to be able to hold in contempt immediately any reporter who would not answer a question. The last thing Agnew or his lawyers wanted at that point was to see reporters from some of the most powerful news-gathering organizations in the country thrown into the ancient Baltimore City jail on contempt-of-court charges.

Topkis, however, raised no objections to Hoffman's request. He told the judge he wanted to depose Richardson, Petersen, and Beall and would submit more names later that morning. When the list arrived in Hoffman's temporary chambers it read: "Witnesses: Elliot L. Richardson, Henry E. Petersen, George Beall, Glen E. Pommerening, Jonathan Moore, *Time* magazine authors of 8/27 and 9/3 stories, Fred Graham, Nicholas Gage, Robert Walters and Ronald Sarro, *Newsweek* author of 8/20 article, [and] Richard Cohen." [2]

The whole episode had been so casual—Topkis handing Hoffman the list and the judge accepting it—that it was possible to lose sight of what had just happened. The Attorney General of the United States, for one, would be commanded to appear in court to deny that he was a common gossipmonger. Judge Hoffman, peering down from the bench, would be there, and Topkis, a whiz of a litigator, would be asking the questions. Next would come the other Justice Department officials, one-by-one, all the way down to Skolnik (later added to the list). Topkis and Skolnik had taken an immediate dislike to each other: it would be a wonderful confrontation.

Beall and Skolnik, dismayed by the carte blanche Hoffman had given Agnew's lawyers, returned angrily to their offices, where Beall fired off a memo to his superiors in Justice suggesting that Justice bring in a lawyer to defend Justice officials and the prosecutors in the motion. Within a day, the department named the U.S. attorney for Chicago, James Thompson, to handle this

---

[2] Walters and Sarro were reporters with *The Washington Star-News*. Topkis and London, obviously unfamiliar with the Washington bureaus of the national news magazines, did not know which reporters had furnished the information for the offending stories. Later, they refined the list, adding more names: Stephan Lesher of *Newsweek*, Ronald Nessen of NBC, William Sherman of the New York *Daily News*, and Sandy Smith of *Time*.

aspect of the case. Next, Beall suggested, the government brief should argue "that the defendant [Agnew] has no standing to interfere with, or question, a grand jury proceeding. On the assumption that the Court will not accept this argument, but will insist that he should hold an evidentiary hearing, the Government should insist that the most he can do and should do is test the narrow allegations in the Topkis affidavit that 'officials of the prosecutorial arm have engaged in the steady campaign of statements to the press.'" Finally, Beall wrote, the government should countersue and charge that "the Vice President, his staff, and his attorneys are just as likely sources of news media stories, and request that counter-depositions be ordered by the Court to explore that assertion." The generally mild-mannered Beall was in the mood for a fight.

By Friday, Thompson was in Baltimore interviewing his new clients—Beall and Skolnik. For the two, it was a most uncomfortable—and unique—experience. Skolnik, who had been served with his subpoena that morning, spent until noon briefing Thompson on whatever information he had on the source of the leaks.

For Vice President Agnew, the civil suit about the news leaks was not so pressing as the President's clear message conveyed in his press conference and in the instructions to deflate Marsh Thomson: lay off, or else. When Agnew left for his Chicago speech on Thursday, October 4, he no doubt felt as much like Sir Thomas More as Richardson had a few days earlier. No wonder, then, that he seemed particularly preoccupied during the trip.

Yet, as if he were no more than the old fund-raising champion of the GOP, sallying forth on another quest for dollars to fire up the party machinery, Agnew had invited all the members of the Illinois Republican congressional delegation to fly with him. Aboard the plane, he chatted with the congressmen and for a time conferred with Arends, Paul Findley, and a few others about the dim prospects of a House inquiry into his affairs in the face of Carl Albert's refusal.

Although the Vice President was still publicly committed to

fight in the courts for his political life, privately his lawyers had continued to pursue the impeachment route as a way to move the fight into a friendlier arena. Earlier in the week, Judah Best and another lawyer in the Colson and Shapiro firm, George Kaufmann, had phoned Agnew's political aide, David Keene, and asked him how they could breathe life into the dormant House inquiry. Keene told them to go to Capitol Hill and explain to anyone who would listen the constitutional case against the indictability of a Vice President and Agnew's right to be tried first by his political peers in the House and the Senate. Best and London did so, adhering to a strategy that had been worked out with Keene. First, they would approach hard-core Agnew loyalists in the House, then all conservative Republicans, then Republicans of every political stripe, and, finally, Southern Democrats. When they had the necessary votes, Agnew's lawyers intended to present House majority leader Tip O'Neill with a *fait accompli.*

Best and London spoke to such disparate Republicans as Findley, Edward Hutchinson of Michigan, and Paul N. (Pete) McCloskey, Jr., of California. (McCloskey was the man who ran against Richard Nixon in the 1972 New Hampshire Republican primary on an antiwar platform, and who according to Agnew financed the campaign by selling his favorite painting: "Benedict Arnold Crossing the Delaware.") Findley agreed to introduce a resolution calling for a House investigation: "Resolved by the House of Representatives that the Committee on the Judiciary is directed to conduct a full and complete investigation of the charges of impeachable offences alleged to have been committed by Spiro T. Agnew." McCloskey, after telling Agnew's lawyers that their man was "either crazy or innocent" to ask for a full-scale inquiry in the House, took the floor on October 2 in support of the resolution. "By all means," he said, "let us grant to the Vice President the speedy, definitive hearing and determination which the House granted to Vice President Calhoun nearly a century and a half ago. The Vice President's courage and candor deserve the same on the part of the world's greatest deliberative

body." The Democratic majority remained unmoved, and Mc-
Closkey's speech was to no avail.

So it was in an atmosphere of general pessimism and despera-
tion that Agnew's plane arrived in Chicago for what Thomson had
billed in advance as another Agnew bombshell. (Thomson's
failure to make the trip stirred the curiosity of the reporters who
went independently to Chicago to cover the speech. This was
not an occasion at which the Vice President would be expected
to be without his press aide. But one of his advance men, John
Damgard, distributed the texts of the speech to anxious reporters
waiting at the Drake Hotel—he himself had only realized Thomson was not aboard a few moments earlier, when told the press
secretary was home taking care of "personal business.") The
Agnew party arrived in early afternoon, and for an hour in his
suite at the Drake the Vice President conferred with W. Clement
Stone. Stone, who had acknowledged contributions of $2.1 million
to the Nixon-Agnew ticket in 1972 and who was not a bashful
man about hard-money figures, would only say afterward that
he was getting "a response in volume" for the Agnew legal-de-
fense fund from all parts of the country. Actually, Justice Department sources learned later that a phone bank to receive
pledges had generated only $310 in a week! (Later, individuals
close to the defense fund said about $40,000 eventually had been
raised.)

Presumably this gloomy result was conveyed to Agnew, who
by now doubtless was toting up the pluses and minuses of his
fight to stay in office and finding himself in the red in nearly
every column: the government had the goods on him; the impeachment route appeared to be shut off; the public plea bargaining in Los Angeles had created neither a groundswell of support nor a whipped attorney general coming to him with a softer
deal; and money to fight in the courts—money was always a
factor in Ted Agnew's mind—wasn't coming in, either. Internal
Revenue agents were all over the countryside, tracking down his
spending habits practically to the last nickel. His attempts in
court to fight indictability were about to be undercut by strong

Justice Department briefs already in preparation. And there was the national interest to be considered, and the peace of mind of his family. Agnew made these points himself in conversation with his lawyers. And, finally, there was the threatening pressure from the President: that he must lay off scapegoating and demagoguing administration officials or take the consequences.

Agnew spoke that night in the Imperial Ballroom of the Conrad Hilton to a full house of party faithful, who were expecting a ringing defense of himself and a renewed attack on his adversaries. The theory of "phased escalation" held in the Justice Department suggested that Beall, Skolnik, and Company might be next, but, instead, the Vice President suddenly went bland. Usually all business on the speaking platform, uttering some of the most incendiary rhetoric in the annals of political oratory in a flat, unemotional style, Agnew this time seemed to some of the reporters to be downright gloomy, worn-out, and distracted. He opened with some personal references to individuals in the crowd who had befriended him in the past—a most unusual gesture for this studiously aloof man. Then he began to read a text whose words only contrasted his depression. "Visiting Chicago is always invigorating," he said with no appreciable enthusiasm. "There is a hum, a dynamism here, a vitality in the coming together of commerce, agriculture, and industry. . . . Add to that natural Chicago vitality the political excitement of a United Republican fall dinner, and you have a real energizer for any visitor." He knew it was so, Agnew said, because he had had his "battery charged" at the same dinner the two previous years, and it was "a real pleasure to be back to hook up my cables to this group of diehard Republicans again."

Many in the audience who had seen Agnew in less troubled days concluded at once that Agnew's battery was now in need of much more than a quick charge. Lou Cannon of *The Washington Post* later said that Agnew looked "white" to him, and he and his colleague David Broder both used the same word—spooky—to describe the atmosphere created by Agnew with his unexpectedly mild words and an even more understated style than usual.

At the outset, the Vice President turned his gaze to the national reporters who had gathered for the anticipated fireworks. "Tonight is not going to be an X-rated political show," he told them. "It's just going to be PG. So if you have to go someplace, go.

"A candle is only so long before it burns out."

Nothing Agnew said after that—in a weary Republican lecture against "social engineering," capped with an endorsement of the President as a man who had been serving under the "most unbelievable pressures"—erased that one phrase from the minds of those who had come to Chicago to see and hear him continue his war of political survival. It seemed to many of the reporters to make explicit the surrender that the rest of the speech conveyed implicitly. This was an astonishing turnabout from Los Angeles. Broder later said Agnew looked like a man who had received some terrible news or had been kicked in the groin; but the Vice President's aides, like Peter Malatesta, though disappointed that Agnew had not continued his offensive strategy, did not think their man had suffered any notable change, and they wrote off the softer speech as perhaps in keeping with the occasion. It was customary at such fund-raising dinners to blast the Democrats—Agnew had undertaken that mission with uncommon zest many times—but attacking fellow members of one's own administration was another matter. Or so the Agnew faithful reasoned. Also, most of the Republican Illinois delegation in the House was there, and Agnew's request for a House investigation was still pending. "It wouldn't be too suitable or proper for him to take up his own cause," an aide said later. "It would have embarrassed some members of the House."

But that one cryptic remark—"a candle is only so long before it burns out"—was pregnant with suggestion. The reporters who heard it, and who considered it in the context of the rest of the speech and Agnew's gloomy demeanor, thought they were onto something. After the speech, when Agnew and his party went back to the Drake Hotel for dinner, James Naughton of *The New York Times* and Pat Sloyan of the Hearst papers followed, camping outside the private club off the lobby and waiting for a chance to ask the Vice President about the "candle" reference.

According to one of Agnew's party, the Vice President saw the two—both of whom had traveled often with him—and proposed they be asked to the table for dessert. This gesture certainly did not hint at any dark secret being kept. (Others in the party said he was relaxed and bantering during dinner. At one point, Agnew had turned to John Damgard and expressed pleasure at his accommodations at the Drake. The next time the vice presidential party came to Chicago, he said, arrangements should be made to stay at the Drake. This observation did not suggest imminent disaster either.) Art Sohmer was about to be dispatched to get Naughton and Sloyan when a few more reporters came along, and the idea was dropped. Malatesta joined the reporters for a drink later, and there was more speculation about what the Vice President had meant in his cryptic line, but Malatesta, who had been with Agnew all day and evening, didn't put much significance in it. "I don't believe that when he went to Chicago he knew he was going to resign," he said later. "I didn't lose any sleep over it that night."

On Friday afternoon, October 5, Agnew returned to Washington. By that time, the subpoenas sought by Agnew's lawyers had been served on nine reporters, and the Justice Department had filed its brief (written by Bork) denying Agnew's contention that the Constitution protected him from being indicted in office. The serving of the subpoenas once again cast Agnew in his old role as tormentor of the press. To a reporter, there is no greater sin than turning on the law to force him to testify about his sources. So this new development was not likely to help Agnew in the long run. Within three days, Justice had submitted a persuasive brief opposing the subpoenaing of newsmen and denying Agnew's charge of a "conspiracy" to release information about his case. This action further isolated Agnew.

Bork's brief on the constitutional question, taking the Vice President out of the boat in which the President hoped to sail past possible indictment himself in the Watergate affair, also left Agnew more exposed than he had been only a few days before. It is conceivable that this fact was particularly persuasive to Agnew and his lawyers in determining whether to continue the fight; Richardson's team was inclined to think in retrospect that it was. In any event, a series of developments now began that finally culminated in the first resignation in disgrace of a Vice President of the United States.

Judah Best had another conference with his client Spiro Agnew on Friday. It must have been obvious to both of them that there simply was not much left for Agnew to go on. If it had not been clear before, it was clear now that the power of the White House, for which Spiro Agnew had such awe, was solidly arrayed against him. He told Best to contact Fred Buzhardt and get the plea bargaining going again. Best walked into Sohmer's adjacent office and tried to reach Buzhardt at the White House. Told the President's lawyer was in Key Biscayne with Nixon, Best had the call transferred on the White House switchboard. When Buzhardt got on the line, Best said to him, "Let's see if we can do something."

Buzhardt didn't want to return to Washington, for fear the press would see him and realize what was happening, so he asked Agnew's lawyer to meet him at the Miami International Airport that night. Best went home, changed into sports clothes, donned sun glasses, and boarded an Eastern Airlines night flight. Buzhardt met him at the gate at about 1:30 a.m., and they drove to the nearby Marriott Motor Hotel. The visitor registered as "Jud Best" and gave the New York address of his firm. He paid in cash so there would be no credit-card record. The two men went to Best's room and sat down. Best told Buzhardt that Agnew was ready to make a deal on the same basis as offered when the talks had broken down two weeks earlier. The only difference, he said, was that Agnew wanted to make a statement in court denying the allegations—exactly what Richardson and Company were determined not to permit him to do.

Buzhardt was conciliatory. He said the Vice President should feel he was under no pressure to do anything, that if he wanted to fight, if he wanted to keep trying the impeachment route, he was free to do so. Best said he had already made another stab on Capitol Hill, and that his instructions from Agnew were to see what could be done concerning a deal. He then produced a draft of the statement Agnew wanted to make. Buzhardt studied it; he thought something could be worked out, he said. He advised Best to get some sleep; he would do some checking and call him later in the morning. When he left, it was almost four o'clock.

About five hours later, the phone rang in Elliot Richardson's home in McLean. It was Buzhardt. They spoke for a few minutes, and then Richardson called Darman, who lived nearby, and asked him to come over right away. "When I got there," Darman said later, "I discovered we were back in the plea-bargaining business."

What had brought Agnew back to the bargaining table, Richardson was told by the White House, was the exhaustive net-worth investigation that the small army of IRS agents had undertaken—probably one of the most sweeping such inquiries in the history of the agency.

With the wraps off the Agnew investigation, the IRS had opened a full-court press on the Vice President's spending habits. The task under the best of circumstances was a difficult one—an attempt to reconstruct how much was spent by tracing every last nickel. In Agnew's case, the difficulties were compounded by his frequent travels and by the insulation provided by the Secret Service.

Using Agnew's own records as a starting point, the IRS was by now in hot pursuit of the Agnew dollars. In Arizona, agents asked about a painting bought in behalf of the Agnews by Peggy Goldwater, the wife of the Arizona senator. Inquiries were made about purchases Mrs. Agnew had made at a fashionable boutique. Washington and Baltimore stockbrokers received subpoenas for accounts, if any, maintained by Agnew and his wife. In Towson, agents called on Oliver's Men's Shop and, producing one of Agnew's canceled checks, asked the owner, Oliver H. Swick, to verify that Agnew had indeed purchased two ties there in 1968 for a total price of $6.18. That same week, the agents asked Edward Shannon, the president of Agnew's old Loch Raven Kiwanis, to produce the organization's records. Agnew, they confirmed, had maintained his $100 annual dues.

It was an intimidating example of governmental power—as intimidating, possibly, as the phone call from Haig. Had it continued, it might have resulted in an airtight tax case against Agnew that would have made his plea bargaining all the more difficult. Moreover, the spicy insights into Agnew's personal life that the prosecutors had already ruled out of bounds might well have surfaced here. (Skolnik, to the chagrin of some of his colleagues, ruled all such evidence inappropriate and at one point interrupted a witness in mid-point, ordering him to proceed to another topic.) If Agnew had spent money in ways that could prove personally embarrassing, only a gentlemen's agreement between the two sides could keep the information from the public eye at a trial. But by now, as Agnew knew well, he had drawn too much blood at the Justice Department to rely on its good graces. He had chosen to fight dirty, and there was no reason for him to believe that the other side would give him any help.

The net-worth investigation, the reports that the legal defense fund was bringing in very little money, and Agnew's awareness that Hammerman, Green, Matz, and Wolff had talked—these were enough, in Richardson's view, to bring Agnew back to the table. And although Richardson later said he knew nothing about direct pressure put on Agnew by Nixon, there were above all the signals flashed to Agnew after his attack on Petersen. If a candle could only burn so far, that point had clearly been reached.

So about 10:30 on Saturday morning, October 6, Buzhardt phoned Best at the Miami motel and suggested that they talk again in a little while—Best might as well go back to Washington and call him when he arrived there. Best did so, and Buzhardt then told him he could inform his client that it looked as if there were a deal. Best called Richardson and they discussed where the talks stood. When the negotiations had broken off fifteen days earlier, the parties had been debating the relatively minor matter of what Agnew would be permitted to say in a formal statement of reply to the charges. Best told Richardson Agnew required a further softening, and he dictated to Chetta Leonardi, the attorney general's secretary, the same statement he had handed to Buzhardt in the Miami motel the night before.

"The issue was would we allow some dilution of the statement we got hung up on last time," Richardson recalled later. The attorney general was willing to give in on minor points, but he still held firm that there would have to be some admission, and that the accused could not be free to engage in Agnewisms against the prosecutors in this final official act of his public career. As a last sop, Richardson agreed to the inclusion of a statement by Agnew that said—rather ridiculously, Richardson thought—that Agnew was not guilty of anything he hadn't admitted to.

To counter this concession, Richardson insisted on two things: Justice would say the offense took place not only in 1967, as Agnew wanted, but in other years as well, and the Agnew camp would have nothing to say about what went into Justice's full-disclosure statement of evidence against him. This latter point had long been considered nonnegotiable by everyone in the Justice Department, and Best finally agreed to go along in return for Justice reducing its requirements about what Agnew would say. (Agnew's statement in court was eventually negotiated line by line and word by word.) These amendments enabled Richardson's men to argue with the Baltimore prosecutors later that the final version of the settlement was actually stronger than the one they had had when the first round of plea bargaining had ended.

The time for niggling over the fine print was approaching an end. All that was left was to work out the details and the scenario of the actual resignation and settlement, and then to obtain Judge Hoffman's approval. Topkis and London were summoned to Washington, and the three Agnew lawyers awaited word about that final step.

In Key Biscayne, Fred Buzhardt by now had passed the word on developments to Haig and President Nixon. Among the handful of presidential aides in Florida that weekend was Pat Buchanan, the media monitor and occasional speechwriter, who shortly before had made a brilliant appearance before the Senate Watergate Committee, catching the senators ill-prepared for him and turning a weak interrogation on campaign "dirty tricks" to White House advantage. It was one of the few bright spots for Nixon in the long torment of the Watergate hearings, and Buchanan found himself in especially good favor as a result. The President had asked him to make the Florida trip and to work on a speech about Watergate. On Friday morning, after Agnew's startlingly submissive performance in Chicago, a *Post* reporter, knowing Buchanan was one of the few White House aides who had the friendship and was an admirer of both the President and the Vice President, phoned him to inquire about it. What had happened to make Agnew back off that way? Was he throwing in the towel? Buchanan said he knew nothing, but would check around. Later that same day he called the reporter back. There was no explanation; as far as he could tell, nothing had changed, and Agnew was still planning to stay in office and fight.

On Saturday, though, Haig called Buchanan in. About the Watergate speech he was drafting—the President wanted a new tentative ending for it, in which the President would announce that the Vice President was resigning! Buchanan, who had been kept out of all the Agnew talks because of his loyalties to both men, was again stunned. Not only was he to write that Agnew was resigning but Haig told him that the new ending should indicate a possible recommendation for the new Vice President, and he gave Buchanan a name—not Gerald R. Ford, the man ultimately selected, not John B. Connally of Texas or Nelson A. Rockefeller of New York or Ronald Reagan of California. (Buchanan later declined to say whose name it was, and would only suggest that it would have been a surprise.) Later, Ray Price, the White House aide in charge of all speechwriting, told Buchanan to write draft endings for several others, including Connally, Rockefeller, and Reagan. On Sunday, Haig told Buchanan that Agnew's resignation might come the next day.

Back in Washington, others were getting signals too. David Keene had been laboring hard with Judah Best to rally support on the Hill. Two Republican congressmen, Dickinson of Alabama and Devine of Ohio, had agreed to bring about a hundred of their colleagues together for a special breakfast on Wednesday morning, October 10, to consider the proposal for a House inquiry on Agnew. A Democrat, Joe D. Waggoner, Jr., of Louisiana, would try to round up some friendly Democrats, and Barry Goldwater, Sr., would make some introductory remarks. Keene was supposed to meet with Dickinson on Monday to work out the final details, but on Friday afternoon he suddenly was instructed not to do so. He called Best several times to inquire why, but Best did not return any of the calls. Something, clearly, was happening.

On the government side, Richardson had one critical task to handle—bringing aboard the hard-nosed young Baltimoreans, still intent on indictment. First he called the others in his own circle— Smith, Darman, Moore, and Ruckelshaus—to join him in McLean, and for five hours they engaged in their customary preparations. Petersen and Beall were notified by phone. As soon as Richardson had heard from Buzhardt on Saturday morning, he had called Beall, who was visiting his mother in Frostburg, in northwest Maryland, for the weekend. Beall was just having breakfast and was supposed to play golf with his brother, Senator Glenn Beall— it was one of the few free days he had had in weeks. Richardson told him only that things were happening fast and that there might be some new developments; he wanted Beall to be available because they might have to meet with Judge Hoffman later in the day. Beall reminded Richardson that the judge was at a family wedding in Pennsylvania and might not be reachable. He himself would need three hours to drive to Washington, but Richardson told Beall to go ahead with his golf date and if necessary he would send a helicopter to fetch him.

Beall drove out with his brother to the Cumberland Country Club. It was then shortly after ten o'clock. The club's golf pro, an old friend, Carroll Boggs, was standing in the driveway as they drove up. Boggs was determined that George Beall was going to play golf that day. Beall had received a call, Boggs said, but he was going to get Beall's bags out of the car first and then would tell him who called. Reluctantly, Boggs said it was the White House. He urged the Baltimore prosecutor to play his round first and then call. Beall phoned at once and was transferred over the White House switchboard to Richardson, who told him that the plea bargaining was on again. No time had yet been set, so the attorney general told Beall again to go ahead with his game. Beall did not argue. It was a beautiful fall day, with the temperature in the mid-seventies, perfect for golf. He arranged for Boggs to come for him in a car if Richardson called again.

Then the two brothers went off to play, and—according to George Beall—his brother deferentially never inquired what was going on. He could guess.

When they returned to the Beall home, there was another message from Richardson. Sunday afternoon at three o'clock at the Justice Department would be soon enough. Judge Hoffman could not make it before Monday. Arrangements were made to see him in a motel in Alexandria, Virginia, where he would stop on his way back to Norfolk. Beall called his men and told them to get to the Justice Department by Sunday afternoon too. Psychologically, the Baltimore prosecutors had been conditioned by now to the idea that plea bargaining was over and they were moving on toward indictment, their preference. Richardson was going to have to bring them around once more, and Skolnik, Baker, and Liebman were not in the mood for it.

The Sunday meeting was held in the conference room off Richardson's office, with all the Justice Ten present. The attorney general reviewed the events of the weekend, reiterated his reasons for pressing for a speedy settlement, and tried hard to reassure the Baltimoreans. As to their concern that Agnew might privately agree to an apparent deal and then blow the whistle publicly, both Richardson and Petersen said it was implausible. But if that happened, Richardson said, the department was reserving the right to answer publicly that Agnew had been plea bargaining again. As for feelings that Agnew ought to be made to admit to more, the attorney general suggested it was always possible that Judge Hoffman himself might extract more admissions from him at the arraignment. But the important thing was the department's own full-disclosure statement. That would make or break the issue of the justice of the government's actions, and Agnew's lawyers had abandoned any claim to have a say about what was to be included in it.

This was the weekend when the Middle East crisis between the Arabs and Israelis was boiling over. The Justice Ten were so preoccupied with the Agnew crisis that they scarcely had time to give it a thought. At this Sunday meeting, Petersen at one point asked, "Hey, does anybody know how the war's going?"

"If I were still Secretary of Defense," Richardson remarked pensively, "I'd be worrying about it right now." But, instead, he faced a domestic miasma—legal, political, and constitutional.

"Golda Meir can't be any tougher than Skolnik," Petersen mused.

"She's not any prettier, either," Baker added.

But even this moment of comic relief was used to focus Richardson's relentless argument that a swift resolution of the matter before them was essential. The Middle East war, he observed, was a good illustration of why it was bad business to have a Vice President hanging on under a cloud, perhaps for years, as the backup for a beleaguered President. He now felt even more strongly than he had two weeks earlier, when the first round of plea bargaining had broken up, that a settlement had to be struck and Agnew moved out of the line of succession forthwith.

Skolnik, who had been brooding throughout about the resumption of plea bargaining and about the fact that a no-trial, no-jail deal was apparently emerging as a *fait accompli,* launched into a forceful and at times heated demurrer. Nothing really had changed since mid-September when the plea bargaining had begun, he said, and he would find it personally difficult to be involved in a disposition that he felt was wrong on principle. Therefore, he warned, there was a possibility that he would find himself unable to participate in the arraignment.

The letter drafted on September 15, giving the government's supposedly nonnegotiable position, could become public, and if it did, the public would demand to know why the government had retreated. The press might speculate either that the White House had effectively applied pressure or that the department itself was so embarrassed about the leaks that it might have yielded. Both Skolnik and Baker kept referring to the nonnegotiable position set out in the September 15 letter—not without a trace of sarcasm.

Baker took a shot at the Petersen draft of H.E.P. No. 3, and argued that the government should go back to the original wording on what Agnew would and would not admit. Of Agnew's three cards to play—resignation, going to the House, and a civil suit—

he had played the last two ineffectively, Baker said, so the government was in a stronger position now than before and should be tougher. Petersen interrupted: weren't Baker and Skolnik "frightened," he asked, at the prospect of Agnew remaining Vice President, considering all they knew about him? Skolnik admitted he was, but Agnew would have to resign anyway, he said. It was back to that basic difference of opinion.

Richardson defended H.E.P. No. 3 as actually involving more admissions of venal conduct than the earlier drafts. In any event, he didn't think they should be "playing Russian roulette with the United States over a few words." Baker and Skolnik were failing to take into account that in the first round of plea bargaining, the government had failed to strike a deal, he reminded them. He agreed that the government's position was stronger now, but that didn't lead him to conclude that they ought to get tougher. Rather, it suggested that where they had failed last time, not having been strong enough, they could now succeed. He was just not willing to gamble that Baker and Skolnik were right on the inevitability of Agnew's resignation. The key task was to convey to the country the fact of Agnew's guilt of bribery, and the question was the extent to which Agnew's admissions in court would accomplish that purpose in any event. The plea would help convey the message, he said. So would the full disclosure of the government's evidence. And the government would have a further opportunity later to affect the public perception if the message did not get through.

Agnew himself, Richardson said, was distraught and in no psychological condition to start a crusade to vindicate himself. He was a beaten man, but he also was "a wounded animal" who wanted the best deal he could get so he could later earn a living and rationalize his conduct to his own family. Richardson added he didn't think Agnew would make any further admissions, and he didn't think he could force him to do so. What was going on, he said, was a game of chicken between the government and Agnew over Agnew's statement in court. For him to be allowed to make some self-serving remarks was not a sufficient reason to refuse to make a deal with him.

Ruckelshaus, who had been sympathetic to the position of the Baltimoreans, reminded them that especially in terms of public acceptability, any deal between the government and Agnew had to be considered as a whole, not issue by issue. While the public might be relieved at the outset that a prolonged crisis had been avoided by a resignation, that wouldn't last forever. Before long, the public would examine the agreement on its merits, and it was vital that the disposition square with the evidence. The government's full disclosure of the facts would spotlight any weakness in any arrangement by showing that Agnew was guilty of much more than the government had settled for.

But Richardson was determined. There was, however, one last hurdle: Agnew's lawyers, as a last-minute concession, wanted to see in advance the full disclosure that the government would make. The strongest objections to this came from Petersen, who was—as he had been all along—deeply suspicious of them. He feared that once they saw the full facts they would back out of the bargain and then use the information to construct a better defense. Richardson didn't want to let them see it either, but, more important, he didn't want any snags to develop. He suggested that rather than the full disclosure of facts (which eventually took forty pages but which they were then estimating would be sixty), a summary could be prepared to satisfy Agnew's lawyers yet essentially not tell them anything they didn't already know.

Petersen in fact had prepared a ten-page summary, and this he showed to the Baltimoreans. They felt it gave too much away, so Richardson asked them to do one of their own and have it ready for him the next day. The seven pages they readied for him overnight later became the summary introduction of the full-disclosure paper that was made part of the court record. Included in their draft were also these accusations against Agnew: that he had received money through still another associate, that he had received some vending-machine and other payoffs, and that he was guilty of obstruction of justice in February through July by virtue of his two phone calls to Kleindienst and other incidents. But when Richardson got the draft on Monday morning, he deleted nearly all these points on grounds that they were too petty or could not be proved and solidly documented.

Before the Sunday meeting adjourned, Richardson made one final effort to persuade the Baltimore team of the justice and wisdom of his position. He told them he did not believe they really had taken the full measure of the damage that would be done to the country if the Agnew litigation was allowed to run its course through the courts. It would be a divisive, prolonged contest that would impair the administration's capacity to govern. Also, while he thought the President would comply with the Supreme Court's order to turn over the White House tapes on Watergate, there was always the possibility that he might not. Richardson didn't want a situation in which the President was defying the Supreme Court, while the man next in line of succession was under indictment or facing impeachment proceedings.

There was also the question of Nixon's health. While Richardson was on vacation on the Salmon River in August, Nixon had been rushed to the hospital with viral pneumonia. When he first heard about it, Richardson said, he hadn't believed it; Nixon, he thought, must have had a stroke, and he was frightened, knowing what he did about Agnew. Remembering that, Richardson told the others, he wanted the man out. He wanted the Justice Department coming out of the Agnew investigation looking as clean as possible, and he was confident that if all the evidence were placed on the public record the American people would accept his solution. But the main thing was that Agnew be moved from the succession, and quickly.

On the question of disposition of the case—the sentencing—Richardson said he would make no recommendation unless it was clear Judge Hoffman required it. He wanted none of his Justice Department subordinates to take a public position on jail or no jail. But if any of the Baltimoreans disagreed with the eventual disposition, he would not hold it against him if he felt it necessary to publicly dissociate himself from the disposition or the court arraignment—as Skolnik had indicated he might feel compelled to do. He only hoped that if anyone were so compelled, he would not act in a way that questioned Richardson's "honesty of purpose."

This invitation to the others to act in conscience, and his last remark about their assessment of his motives, both surprised and touched the prosecutorial team. "I really didn't know why he said that," one of them observed later. "My God, he probably never met four people who were more impressed with his honesty of purpose than the four of us."

He hadn't come to the Department of Justice with the idea that he would enhance his own personal popularity, Richardson went on. He realized when he took the job, in the context of Watergate, that he was going to make a lot of enemies and not come out with a lot of friends. But in this confrontation with Agnew, there was so much at stake for the country that he didn't mind it being said that he was the one who "blinked"—if it had to come to that. He appreciated the candor, he said, and—pausing—it would not be inappropriate to say the courage, with which his subordinates had expressed their views.

All of this was by way of informing the four prosecutors from Baltimore that whether they liked it or not, the plea bargain was going to be struck on terms he, not they, wanted. A complaint by Skolnik that they had been shut out of the critical last talks was gently shunted aside by Richardson, who noted that he had solicited their views but decided contrary to their wishes on the Petersen statement, and that was that. They had not been involved in the plea-bargaining talks directly, he said, because there were three Agnew lawyers, and he thought it fair that there be only three government men—himself, Petersen, and Beall.

The attorney general was not without a keen awareness, however, that the dissociation of one or all of the Baltimore prosecutors from the terms of the final settlement would be an embarrassment at best and a public-relations disaster at worst. And he knew, too, that Skolnik was the key man—an experienced and forceful prosecutor, clearly the one the others looked to for direction. But his vulnerability, the Richardson team thought, was his personal desire to be part of the action and, in this case, part of history. Always the diplomat and handler of men, Richardson waited for the right moment and then dealt swiftly, deftly, and effectively with "the Skolnik problem." In the discussion about the final plea-bargaining talks before Judge Hoffman, Richardson suddenly turned to Skolnik and said, "It wouldn't be right to have all the Baltimore team there, Barney, but would you be willing to join the negotiating team?"

In the words of one of Richardson's admittedly partisan lieutenants later, "It was a stroke of genuis on Elliot's part. From that moment on, Barney Skolnik was more Catholic than the Pope. Nothing changed substantially. The final settlement was little more than what was being considered when Barney said he couldn't participate any more, but Barney bought it."

Richardson's gesture was the kind of flattery that Skolnik appreciated, but it was more than that. Skolnik's presence took Richardson out of the direct line of fire in the final talks and thus gave the government a valid excuse for delay if some element came up in the discussion to which the government might object: without Richardson present, his subordinates would have to ask for time to check with him—always a prudent negotiating gambit. What Richardson particularly hoped to avoid was having to make a no-jail recommendation until he was assured it would be required by the judge, and this way his representatives—Petersen, Beall, and Skolnik—would be in a position to take soundings for him. And of course with Skolnik in the talks, Richardson went a long way toward committing not only Skolnik to the outcome but also his two Baltimore colleagues. When Baker and Liebman heard Skolnik had been asked to go, they tried to talk him out of it, but he clearly wanted to be in on the climax, and he found sufficient reasons, including the virtue of having their collective voice represented. The crafty, independent Barney Skolnik was enlisted by Richardson, whether he realized it or not.

14 Sealing the Deal

The opening scene for the final act in the plea bargaining that cost Spiro Agnew the Vice Presidency took place in Room 208 of the Olde Colony Motor Lodge in Alexandria, Virginia, just across the Potomac River from the capital, on the historic road to Mount Vernon. There, Judge Walter Hoffman had agreed to meet representatives of the Justice Department and the Vice President on Monday, October 8, in one of the two suites he had taken on his trip back home to Norfolk. The line-up for Agnew was Jay Topkis, Martin London, and Judah Best; for the government Henry Petersen, George Beall, and Barney Skolnik. The Justice team met with Elliot Richardson before going over to Alexandria and received its instructions: to present the agreed-on package to Judge Hoffman—the *nolo contendere* plea to one count of tax evasion, coupled with the government's full-disclosure statement and Agnew's statement, which would be a slightly revised version of H.E.P. No. 3. Plus, importantly, they were to advise the judge that Justice had no recommendation on Agnew's request for a sentence of no jail. It was their job to find out whether Hoffman would go along with this arrangement and whether he would agree to no jail, preferably without a recommendation from Justice, or whether he would insist on such a recommendation.

A two-hour delay in the meeting had been caused by a prolonged session between Agnew and his lawyers, who frequently called the Justice Department to request postponements. Finally, when the Justice team was about to leave the building, Judge Hoffman himself called. He was furious because somehow the press had discovered his motel hideaway and cameramen were camped outside. (Predictably, he blamed the discovery on the Justice Department, assuming that Agnew's side would have no reason to let anyone know that plea bargaining was about to resume.) Outside Richardson's office itself, the press had been massed most of the day awaiting the government's brief on the leaks issue. Skolnik suggested that he, Beall, and Petersen go to the motel overtly, telling reporters at either end that their mission was simply to discuss "procedural matters." Richardson bought this idea, but emphasized that they should give a terse "no comment" to *any* question. With that settled, the three negotiators piled into a black government limousine and were chauffered to the motel.

As they pulled up, they momentarily forgot their strategy. Unsettled by the television crews spread all over the place in front of the entrance, they ordered the driver to pull down the street a bit. Suddenly, a man jumped in front of the car and flagged it down.

"Are you looking for the judge?" he asked.

"Who are you?" Skolnik responded.

"I'm the manager. I'll take you up to the judge's room through the laundry room."

They were about to accept that suggestion when Skolnik reminded them of the strategy they had agreed on in Richardson's office not ten minutes before.

Meanwhile, Topkis, London, and Best were arriving by cab. Like the Justice men, they approached the motel as a patrol would, setting out behind enemy lines in wartime. Dismissing their cab, they walked along the motel wall until they, too, spotted the camera crew. Panicked, they immediately decided to retrieve their cab and return to Washington. But the cab was nowhere to be found. Then they noticed the Justice men braving the camera's lights and somewhat sheepishly the lawyers followed the prosecutors. When they closed the door of Hoffman's motel room behind them, they were still muttering about their encounter with the press.

Judge Hoffman had two suites—one for himself and his wife and the other for Horace Weiss, his court reporter. For the meeting, the judge banished his wife to Weiss's room, and, as presiding officer, took a commanding position at the head of a coffee table. Agnew's lawyers sat on individual chairs on one side of the table, the government lawyers faced them on a sofa. By then, all six had done their required reading—"Plea Bargaining and the Role of the Judge," by Walter E. Hoffman, a speech delivered at the Ninth Circuit Judicial Conference in Portland, Oregon, in June 1971 that had been published as a nine-page article. In it, Hoffman set out his views on plea bargaining, views that the lawyers in the room could probably have recited by heart. If there was one passage that struck the Justice Department team as noteworthy, it surely must have been where Hoffman observed that plea bargaining "will initially impose on the prosecutor the responsibility of making a recommendation which is neither too lenient nor too excessive." Justice intended to do nothing of the sort. It would make no recommendation at all unless it had to.

After some introductory remarks by Judge Hoffman, Topkis asked that they be allowed to go off the record. He said he could indicate off the record to Hoffman that an understanding had been worked out and he hoped the judge would approve it. Hoffman reminded him that in court everything would be taken down by the court reporter and that Agnew would be asked questions. Petersen insisted that the discussions be on the record, and when Topkis—ever vigilant in his client's behalf—objected on the grounds that he wanted no record if the judge did not approve the terms of the arrangement, Petersen suggested that the transcript be sealed and not become part of the public record. Hoffman said that unless both sides had agreed otherwise, he wanted the meeting conducted on the record.

Topkis was clearly worried. Would the court reporter's notes be subject to subpoena by Congress? Yes, Judge Hoffman said. Well, Topkis asked, how about an agreement to destroy the notes if there was no agreement? The judge refused. The meeting would go forward on the record, but the stenographer's notes would not be typed up, simply sealed in the form taken down. Everybody finally agreed to that.[1]

Topkis then outlined what Agnew was willing to do: waive indictment and plead *nolo contendere* to one count of tax evasion for 1967, a felony, with the government submitting a statement of all the facts in the case, broader than just the facts to support the tax charge. The Vice President would respond with his "right of allocution"—the right to give his side before sentencing. Judge Hoffman broke in. He hoped that by allocution Topkis was not suggesting that Agnew in spite of his *nolo* plea was thinking of coming in and saying he had no intent to do what he did. If so, he said, the plea bargaining would be "at a crossroads" and there could be no deal. Topkis said that would be no problem, but he reminded Hoffman that this was a *nolo* plea, not a guilty plea.

The remark was pivotal. It showed the Justice team at the outset that Topkis was doing all he could to take the curse off the *nolo* plea, a maneuver that did not surprise them too much. But, more important, it elicited a response from Judge Hoffman that reassured them that the judge would be no pushover for Agnew's lawyers. Wait a minute, Hoffman said to Topkis. The only difference between a guilty plea and a *nolo* plea as far as he was concerned was that in a *nolo* plea the government didn't have to show it could prove the case. It didn't give the defendant the right to assert he was innocent. If that was what Topkis had in mind, they could all go home.

Topkis in response read the agreed-to Agnew statement—with one important exception. He left out the phrase that said

---

[1] The notes remained sealed as this was written.

Agnew knew that the payments he received were required to be reported for income-tax purposes.

Well, Judge Hoffman said, much of what Topkis had just read was obviously for the consumption of others than himself—meaning the public. But even though the plea was *nolo*, he had to advise the defendant through his lawyers that *nolo contendere* was the same as a guilty plea and the statement, while admitting Agnew received payments that were taxable, failed to say he knew he was required to report them on his tax return. If Agnew were to read that statement in court, Hoffman said, he would have to ask him if he had intentionally omitted this income for the purpose of defrauding the government. Topkis lamely said he thought what he had read was enough, but Hoffman insisted it was not. The statement as it stood left open the suggestion that Agnew didn't know there were legal consequences to his failure to report the money. Hoffman recalled a case he once heard in Beckley, West Virginia, in which two lawyers pleaded *nolo contendere* and said they didn't intend to defraud the government. Hoffman had rejected the plea, and they came in later and admitted they did act with intent to defraud. Eventually, the lawyers were disbarred because the *nolo* plea was the same as a guilty plea. In other words, as far as Hoffman was concerned, with a *nolo* plea, Agnew was admitting guilt; he could say what he wished in court, but the judge would ask him if he realized he had to have had intent to defraud to make the *nolo* plea. Topkis professed to be perplexed. He told the judge he had represented other tax clients who had pleaded *nolo* and never were asked anything like that. Well, if the defendant were to stand mute, Hoffman said, that would be one thing. But the elements of a *nolo* plea were identical to those of a guilty plea, except that a *nolo* plea could not be used as an admission of guilt in a collateral (civil) proceeding, such as in a tax-collection action.

Best spoke up. Did the judge mean that he would actually ask Agnew in court whether he had an intent to defraud? That's what he meant, Judge Hoffman said. Topkis said he wasn't sure Agnew would agree to make such an admission. Petersen, who didn't want to see the whole thing go up in smoke at the eleventh hour, came up with an idea. How about if the Vice President simply said he knew that the payments he received were required to be reported? Hoffman said that would be fine. Topkis grandly said he thought Petersen had made a very constructive suggestion, but he was not at liberty to say how Agnew or for that matter Richardson would respond. This was a good device to buy time, whether that was Topkis's intent or not, so the matter was passed over for the time being.

Judge Hoffman, after looking over the rest of the statement, raised no further questions. He would have to advise Agnew that he had no authority over Maryland officials and could not say whether they would prosecute him or that any bar associations would take action against him, but he could see to it that there would be no other federal prosecution.

At this point, with Petersen, Skolnik, and Beall sitting attentively, Topkis made his big move. Without fanfare, he proceeded to tell the judge what had been alleged concerning the sentence: it was their "common belief," he said, that no commitment to jail was needed. Petersen, Skolnik, and Beall could not believe their ears, but for the moment said nothing, just listened to see how far their adversary would go. Finally, Judge Hoffman asked for the government's view about sentencing. Skolnik whispered frantically to Petersen about Topkis's "common belief" statement, but Petersen said nothing about that at first. Instead, following Richardson's orders exactly, he told Hoffman that the government preferred to leave the matter of sentencing to the court, it being fully advised of the facts and the circumstances surrounding the investigation.

Topkis interjected. He was not authorized by his client to go into court with a deal unless the court indicated in advance its agreement—presumably including no jail. Judge Hoffman told him that he couldn't be a party to a plea-bargaining agreement in the absence of the defendant in court, and so could not give him a definite answer then. He was willing to hold court at any time they wanted, he said, but would authorize no deal before then, because he could not be sure the defendant and the government both approved. Well, Topkis said to the astonishment of the

Justice team, it was his understanding that it was the agreement of both parties that Agnew would not go to jail, and it was a "startlement" to him that the government now was saying it took no position on sentencing.

Petersen ignored this remark and handed Judge Hoffman the government's seven-page summary of evidence. Topkis had tried to make some changes in it but Richardson had said only that he'd discuss them with his staff. Now Topkis told Hoffman he thought it was to be amended, and Petersen said he had no such understanding. Hoffman took the summary and returned to the key question of sentencing.

The fact that the government was not recommending a sentence, he said, did not destroy the agreement, though there usually was a recommendation by the government in true plea bargaining. In other words, he was willing to go into court with the deal, but he was not going to tell the parties in advance what sentence he would impose, especially without a government recommendation. The maximum sentence would be five years in prison and a $10,000 fine. He said that in tax-evasion cases he had given jail sentences sometimes, sometimes not. He was aware that Agnew was a lawyer and he said another judge had told him that it was part of life in Maryland that people in government enjoy the fruits of state contracts. He would also remember that Agnew already had gone through suffering in his dilemma and would go through more for years to come.

Judge Hoffman seemed to be indicating strongly he would not send Agnew to jail. But he told Topkis specifically that under the circumstances he could only say now that he could not commit himself—the same would be true even if the government recommended no jail. Of course, if Agnew did not accept what was agreed to in court, he would have the right to enter a not guilty plea—but by that time the damage would be done; that is, if it was learned that he had sought a bargain that included resignation, he would be severely wounded in the court of public opinion. By saying he would hold court at any time, even in the wee hours of the morning, Hoffman was indicating he would do all he could to avoid press coverage, but Agnew would have to present the plea in public, and, considering who he was, it was not likely that they could escape press coverage at whatever hour.

Petersen then took the floor. While the government was not prepared to recommend anything concerning the sentence, there were several things the court should know, he said. Some co-conspirators in the case had agreed to plead guilty and would be coming before it for sentencing, and there were other investigations still to be completed that would involve other public officials. Also, there were large public concerns involved—the integrity of the investigation and of the judicial process, the stability of the government, and the public interest in succession if a tragedy were to strike the President. All of these things, he said, were proper concerns for the court.

Then, aware of Judge Hoffman's near-paranoia about the press and about leaking court business to reporters, Petersen said everyone of importance in the Justice Department was ready to swear under oath that they had never done so. The department's interest in plea bargaining, he wanted to assure the judge, was not because it wanted to avoid submitting depositions on the leaks matter. But Petersen had hit a raw nerve, and Hoffman interjected quickly. Perhaps Petersen was right, but somebody sure had leaked—the newsmen outside the motel were clear evidence of that. He didn't know where the leak had come from, but if a press story appeared next morning stating what the purpose of the meeting had been, it would be obvious that the government was the culprit, since the story would certainly not be in Agnew's interest. If there were a newspaper story on the motel meeting, Hoffman warned, the Justice Department was going to need a house-cleaning.

This was a slightly unsettling threat. The Justice team from that moment until the following morning lived in dread of a newspaper story on the negotiations. Early the next morning, all around Washington and especially in McLean, there were early risers who anxiously awaited delivery of *The Washington Post* at their doorsteps. To their great relief, no one had learned or divined that the motel meeting was anything other than a gathering over court procedure concerning the leaks briefs.

Once again Judge Hoffman returned to the final disposition. He inquired whether Petersen agreed there would be no other federal criminal proceeding against Agnew. Petersen said that was so—assuming Agnew resigned from the Vice Presidency first. Hoffman said he had no power over that; that is, this was an element to be worked out between the two parties and consummated before Agnew entered the court. It was what everybody wanted—Agnew appearing before Hoffman as a private citizen, not as Vice President of the United States copping a plea while still in office.

Topkis, whose performance so far had rankled the Justice trio no end, then contributed a new ingredient that further endeared him to them. As they talked about the resignation of Vice President Agnew, Topkis remarked that he hadn't conducted the prior negotiations on that point; Best had. Best asked for a recess; and the Agnew lawyers huddled for twenty minutes in Hoffman's other room (the judge had to ask his wife to leave for a while). From all signs, this recess was required so that Topkis could let London and Best know he wanted to back off in the absence of a commitment from Hoffman that Agnew would not be sent to jail. When they returned, Topkis told Hoffman that they had agreed that the talks had reached a point where further conversation would not be productive. Could they all meet again the next day, Tuesday? Hoffman said he already had told his wife he had to be in Baltimore Wednesday for hearings and so he would be available to all of them on Tuesday in Alexandria, Washington, or Baltimore. Petersen balked at first—the department needed time to prepare the depositions on the leaks issue that were due Wednesday—but Hoffman said wryly he thought they could handle it and still attend another meeting. They agreed to meet (subject to Agnew's approval) at the Justice Department, in the conference room of Ruckelshaus's office, and to enter the building through the basement to avoid the press.

Before adjourning, Petersen took one last stab at the sentencing issue. He knew how critical it was and how important Richardson regarded Judge Hoffman's feelings on whether he would have to make a recommendation. For purposes of clarity, Petersen asked Hoffman, what exactly was the court's position? That there would be no commitment from him in advance, even if there were a concerted action by all parties? Well, the judge replied, if all the parties were to agree, that would make it a lot easier for the court to use common sense. That seemed to be pretty clear: if Richardson would go along with no jail, so would Hoffman. He added for the record that this was a case in which the government in his view ought to take a definite position, since it knew much more about the facts than he did.

As they talked, the lawyers began to gather up their papers, piled on a hassock in front of the judge. But even if the government takes a position, Petersen pressed on, you won't commit yourself in advance? No, but the minute an agreement was made in court, Judge Hoffman said, he would indicate his approval or disapproval. Topkis looked up. Would you do it if they all came to you in your chambers? Hoffman would only remind Topkis that he had a record in favor of plea bargaining; but he noted also that he once refused to let a plea be bargained in a case involving auto theft by the son of a big politician in Norfolk, because he saw political favoritism in the way the charge was being made. In other words, he too was wary lest there be criticism that a Vice President was receiving special treatment. He agreed with Agnew that there should be a swift disposition of the case, and if Agnew were ever indicted, Hoffman said, he would insist that Beall give him a speedy trial. But it was customary for the judge to indicate agreement or disagreement on a plea bargain only in open court.

Topkis was not satisfied. This was not a normal case. If Agnew were to proceed normally to hear the judge's decision in open court, and then backed away because the judge was going to impose a jail sentence, his case would be forever compromised. You would never be able to put together a jury whose members did not know that the Vice President had tried to tender a *nolo* plea. Why couldn't Judge Hoffman, under these unusual circumstances, indicate his decision ahead of time *"in camera"*? Hoffman hedged. To do so, he said, would be to act contrary to what he always had advocated: that plea bargaining should always be consummated in public. If he established a precedent of agreeing in advance to a definite sentence, wouldn't he have to do the same for all defendants? No, Topkis replied, the circumstances were unique here. But Hoffman would not commit himself.

Topkis promised to let everyone know by 11 o'clock next morning whether they would meet in Ruckelshaus's conference room. The parties left Hoffman's room separately—it was about 7:15— and had their pictures taken again by the waiting cameramen. A television reporter asked Skolnik: "Will you tell us whether or not there was plea bargaining going on in there?" Skolnik replied: "No comment." Petersen, Beall, and Skolnik climbed into the waiting limousine and drove back to the department, where they went immediately to Richardson's office to report.

They told the attorney general that Judge Hoffman had been extremely ambiguous on how a no-jail recommendation would affect his decision, but that he seemed very close to agreeing to let them know in advance in chambers what his decision was. Petersen asked Skolnik to read his notes on the sentencing portion of the meeting, so that Richardson would have as accurate a picture of the judge's position as possible. Richardson listened. Then he said what he had never said right out before in the presence of the Baltimore prosecutors—that he *was* ready to recommend no jail, but only if without it the deal would fall through. Richardson doodled as he spoke, paced, picked up pieces of paper, crumpled them, and tried to toss them into his basketball wastebasket. It was clear that he was struggling with himself over taking that final, critical step. An Attorney General of the United States who actively participated in a decision that set a felonious Vice President free would not contribute to the restoration of public confidence in the equal application of the law. He just had to know beyond any doubt that the step was necessary.

Elliot L. Richardson then proceeded to do something no small-town lawyer would even consider—he announced he was going to phone the judge and just ask him. The other lawyers in the room were appalled. Skolnik spoke up: the attorney general could not do that! It would be an *ex parte* communication with the court! He could make a conference call with one of Agnew's lawyers on an extension, but he couldn't call the judge himself. Skolnik's remonstrance came out in a tone of mild disbelief that Richardson would seriously consider the idea—and Petersen shared it. But Richardson had made up his mind. He wasn't trying to influence the judge about anything—he just needed clarification. So he picked up the phone, while Skolnik, Petersen, and Beall stood by looking shocked, and J. T. Smith, who knew Richardson better than any of them and knew he could not be stopped, gazed into the middle distance, looking bemused. They all listened, waiting to hear the case blow up in their faces as a result of one elementary legal *faux pas*. Instead, what they heard, to their great relief, was the attorney general, even before he could say what he was going to say and should not have said, being bawled out by Hoffman like a schoolboy—not for making an *ex parte* call, but for leaking the motel meeting!

Richardson's side of the conversation, according to some of those in the room, went something like this: "Good evening, your honor. I'm sorry to bother you, but there's a matter I wish to discuss with you. . . . Yes, I'm disturbed about that also. . . . No, I don't know how the press found out about the meeting. . . . Well, your honor, I don't believe it was anybody in the Department of Justice. . . ." The others, standing some distance from the phone, could hear Hoffman's rising voice coming through the receiver, berating Richardson. This went on for several minutes, with the aristocratic Richardson listening patiently and injecting comments like ". . . Well, your honor, even if it is in the paper tomorrow, I don't think it's necessarily true that it had to come from someone in the Department of Justice. . . . There were reporters over there, you know. Right outside my office, they might have seen my men leave. . . ." Finally, Richardson said something like ". . . Well, your honor, under the circumstances, I don't suppose it's appropriate for me to discuss with you what I called about." And he hung up, never having asked Hoffman the question that might have gotten him deeper into the soup. Richardson was angry, and he paced some more, clutching himself around the waist as if he had a stomach-ache, griping about Hoffman's accusations, trying to shoot a few more baskets with crumpled paper. Well, he finally said, calming down, there wasn't anything else anybody could do now, and he sent them all home. Before the final good nights, the attorney general asked Beall and Skolnik what the other Baltimoreans' reaction to the deal was likely to be. Skolnik quickly replied that he would talk to Baker and Liebman and see that they went along.

Beall and Skolnik returned to Baltimore and filled in Baker and Liebman, who once again tried to talk Skolnik out of going back the next day. But Skolnik was convinced he was doing honest work and serving the general good by being there. He still didn't agree with Richardson on what they were getting from Agnew, but the attorney general had a way of bringing people along, soliciting their help even if they disagreed with what was being done.

Even Petersen, who was not the diplomat his superior was, had his moments. That night, driving home, he heard on his car radio an excerpt of a speech that Secretary of State Henry Kissinger had made to a conference on world peace. Petersen was so impressed that the next morning he had his secretary type the pertinent sentences and then gave copies to the Baltimoreans. "A presumed monopoly on truth," Kissinger had said, "obstructs negotiation and accommodation. Good results may be given up in the quest for ever-elusive ideal solutions." One had to "understand," he went on, "the crucial importance of timing. Opportunities cannot be hoarded; once past, they are usually irretrievable."

In all, it was a momentous and dramatic evening for the lawyers on both sides. For others, including Spiro T. Agnew, it seemed to be a night like many others. Earlier that day, the Vice President and a small personal party had flown to New York, where he was to make a speech before a builders' group at a lunch in the Waldorf-Astoria Tuesday. Agnew spent an hour or so with an old friend and political true believer, William Rusher, publisher of *The National Review*, during which he again declared his innocence and hinted that White House pressures were forcing his hand and making a scapegoat of him. Then, like any visitor to Fun City, he and his party—Art Sohmer, John Damgard, Mary Ellen Warner, and George Gowen (an advance man)—went to dinner at one of his favorite restaurants, Christ Cella. A drunk spied him as he entered and called out, "Hey, there's Agnew!" But the Vice President just walked through into a private room, where the door closed behind him and his group. During dinner, according to one of those present, Agnew seemed relaxed and affable. His troubles were not mentioned, certainly not the fact that earlier that day his lawyers had been in a motel room laboring to have Judge Hoffman approve his plea with an assurance that the Vice President would not be forced in the near future to dine at a federal penitentiary.

The next morning in Washington, Richardson discussed several points again with Petersen, Beall, and Skolnik while they waited to hear whether there would be another meeting with the judge. Agnew's lawyers called Richardson to say that they wanted no mention in the summary statement of The Close Associate by name. Skolnik thought that would be no problem. But more important, was it in the Justice Department's interests to join with Agnew's lawyers in asking Judge Hoffman to indicate in advance whether he would go for no jail? Richardson saw no reason why not, but Skolnik said it was important that Hoffman see the seven-page summary before he decided. There was always the danger that if Hoffman agreed to no jail first and *then* saw how much evidence of offenses other than tax evasion there was, he would scrub the arrangement as being too soft. Richardson agreed, and it was decided too that Hoffman should be asked to read the summary if he pressed again for the department's recommendation on sentencing.

Soon Topkis, London, and Best joined the group to discuss outstanding questions before meeting with Judge Hoffman. The major item was again the no-jail recommendation. Before he would even consider it, Richardson said, he again had to have the Agnew side's agreement to a full disclosure of the facts as drawn up by the Justice Department. Topkis said that he and his colleagues wanted to see it before they went into court; Richardson said they would be shown it when a bargain was struck, but it was to be absolutely nonnegotiable. The Justice Department was going to put whatever it wanted into that report, so that the government's full case provable at that time would be on the public record.

Skolnik didn't want the full case shown to the Agnew lawyers until they got to court, but Best assured him they just wanted to "check it for typos." What would happen when the Agnew lawyers saw the finished product was a source of some uneasiness until the last moment. The Baltimore prosecutors feared that it might cause Agnew to say no deal. But Richardson gave the Agnew men his word that the longer statement would merely expand on the seven-page summary and would introduce no new allegations.

As for a no-jail recommendation, Richardson said he had informed the Agnew lawyers at the time the first round of plea bargaining broke off that if a government recommendation were crucial, he would make it, but he had to be satisfied that the judge really required it. Hoffman had been ambiguous, so this time he would attend the meeting with Hoffman himself that afternoon. Although there was disagreement within the department about such a recommendation, Richardson said, he would make it if the judge demanded it, on grounds that the public interest was best served by avoiding a constitutional crisis through a drawn-out trial or impeachment proceedings. This statement was met by a large sigh of relief from the Agnew lawyers, who had been on the edge of their chairs waiting for it.

It turned out that Agnew wanted to avoid not only jail itself, but also a suspended jail sentence or a humiliating probation. Topkis asked Richardson also to recommend against these, but Richardson said that would be up to the court to decide. But, protested Topkis, these points were so important to Agnew that failure to receive assurance on them could wreck the whole deal. Richardson would not budge, and the Agnew team finally let it go at that.

London next urged Richardson to lend his weight to persuading Hoffman to indicate in advance what his decision on no jail was. Richardson said he was willing to do that, for he agreed that Agnew could hardly be expected to appear in court and offer a plea unless he had a clear indication of the outcome.

Topkis also urged Richardson to appear personally in court at the arraignment, obviously to add weight to the no-jail recommendation. His appearance, Topkis said, would lend dignity, help the court, and help demonstrate the settlement was fair. Richardson took the idea under consideration.

Finally, there were a number of other concessions the Agnew lawyers wanted. They wanted dropped from the full disclosure any reference to Matz's payment of $2500 in cash to Agnew when he was Vice President in return for the award of a General Services Administration contract to the small engineering firm in which Matz had an interest—a payment that, though small, showed Agnew taking payoffs not only for contracts granted when he was governor but also as Vice President. Topkis argued that it was not in the national interest to trot out accusations of improper behavior in the Vice Presidency, and besides, it might be ruled inadmissable since the rest of the case concerned payments based on contracts granted when Agnew was governor. Richardson refused to delete this reference; he did not want the government later charged with suppressing evidence in order to justify a lenient outcome. There were bound to be people who still would not believe Agnew was guilty, and a charge of suppressing evidence or covering it up could lead to a congressional inquiry, and nobody wanted that.

Topkis also asked that specific amounts of income Agnew received in the various payoffs not be mentioned because there would be trouble with the Internal Revenue Service on collection of back taxes. Petersen said the tax division would insist on it. The figures stayed in. But Richardson did agree to cut out some less important charges in the short summary (including the one about Agnew receiving vending-machine payola) and to drop specific identification of The Close Associate.

That was the deal. Topkis asked for a complete scenario in advance of what would occur at the arraignment; also, he wanted the requirement of mug shots and fingerprints of the defendant waived. Best asked whether the summary could be ready by midnight. Skolnik said he doubted it. The arraignment was set for two o'clock the next afternoon.

At lunch, Beall and Skolnik phoned Baker and Liebman in Baltimore and told them about the last-minute adjustments. For Skolnik particularly, this was a sticky task. He himself had been against making any more concessions, and he knew that his two colleagues in Baltimore felt the same way, but having been brought into the final negotiations he found himself cast in a different role. Now, he was more an agent of Richardson's, a loyal lieutenant who had had an opportunity to have his say and was enlisted in the task of implementing a decision. He could not in conscience argue with Baker and Liebman on the substance of their objections, because he shared them. But he could try to get them to go along, as he was doing, without making a public disavowal.

As expected, Baker and Liebman balked, but two facts were persuasive with them—Richardson's assurances that they would be free to express disagreement if they felt it necessary, and Richardson's decision to *personally* recommend no jail—either in person or by letter to the court. Baker also objected to showing the full-disclosure statement to Agnew's lawyers, and he forecast, correctly, that the Baltimoreans would have to stay up all night writing it. He urged Beall and Skolnik to return as soon as they could to help. The Baltimore office already had its hands full: Richardson had also been pressing for complete signed statements under oath from the four key witnesses in the case—Hammerman, Wolff, Matz, and Green. So that night, all four witnesses were brought into the Baltimore office, without knowledge of the press, and their depositions taken.

After their talk with Baker and Liebman, Beall and Skolnik went to the attorney general's dining room for lunch. This was an eating spot reserved for the highest-ranking Justice officials, and there was some concern that the appearance of the two prosecutors from Baltimore would tip off everyone there to plea bargaining on the Agnew case being under way again. But it also was known that government briefs in the case were being discussed, and Petersen told them it was nonsense to worry. For Skolnik, the middle-class kid from New York, the whole thing was very impressive—fancy silverware and glassware, good linen, white-jacketed men serving—and he told his colleagues all about it later.

At two o'clock, the same group that had met with Judge Hoffman in the motel the previous evening, plus Richardson, now gathered with him in Ruckelshaus's conference room. (The judge had come in unnoticed through the basement.) All parties shook hands with the judge and with each other. Hoffman sat at the head of the conference table. Again Agnew's lawyers and the Justice team lined up facing each other. The attorney general waited until everyone was settled and then he began.

He told Hoffman that he had met with Agnew's lawyers again and had reached more complete agreement on points previously unresolved. He asked Agnew's lawyers if they agreed that he give Judge Hoffman the seven-page summary of evidence, and they said yes. Hoffman said he knew nothing about the evidence except that he had read in the newspapers that it concerned kickbacks. He said he also didn't know whether the government would be making a specific recommendation on sentencing, but in any case it was his responsibility. He had written articles urging harsh treatment of public officials guilty of tax evasion as an example and a deterrent, and he knew they could be thrown back at him if he broke with past practice. But he also was aware that a more important question of the national interest was involved.

Richardson, as Topkis had suggested he do, then asked the judge whether he might infer that a recommendation from the government would be not only appropriate but would be given substantial weight. A true plea bargain, Hoffman replied, should include an agreement on sentencing. Richardson took up the invitation. The issue of disposition, he said, was peculiarly difficult for the government. There were co-defendants who had cooperated, and the government's evidence against Agnew was very compelling. Also, the government lawyers were split on whether Agnew should be sent to jail or not. In these circumstances, he said, the department felt that if not called upon to help the judge decide, it would not do so. But he inferred a recommendation would be helpful to the court and so he was prepared to make one.

Judge Hoffman said it would indeed be helpful. If Agnew were just another Norfolk lawyer, all things being equal, he would probably give him a split sentence—some time in jail and some time on probation, because he had a strong feeling that lawyers and other professional people convicted should serve some time as a deterrent to others. Income-tax payment worked on an honor system, Hoffman observed, and he could not recall having let any experienced lawyers, accountants, or other sophisticated tax-preparers off with only probation and a fine.

This was his attitude, Judge Hoffman said, without having looked at the summary of evidence, which he imagined would not be too complimentary to Agnew. It might show some nontax evidence, he guessed, but he could not take that into account because this was solely a tax case. By the same token, he had read Agnew's statement, and the defendant could say whatever he liked, but his denial of the other charges carried no more weight in the tax case than did the government's nontax charges; it was all for public consumption. Clearly, Hoffman said, a long-term sentence would be inappropriate. He wanted neither to punish nor to favor Agnew because he was Vice President. He was trying to look at the case as if the defendant were an ordinary citizen—but Agnew was also a governor at the time in question and a qualified lawyer. As a judge, Hoffman had written an important article for the instruction of new judges on the subject of equal treatment, and it was going to be very difficult for him to depart from his prior stated principles unless a great national interest required it. If the parties were going into a public courtroom, he said, he would certainly ask if the government had a position on sentencing.

Richardson was satisfied. In light of that, he said, and the overriding national interest involved, he would make a recommendation. His own reasons for his position would become clearer after the judge had seen the substance of the government's evidence, a summary of which both sides had agreed that it was essential the judge see. The document was handed to Hoffman, who recessed the session while he read it.

Having done so, Judge Hoffman resumed the meeting. He said the summary obliged him to reiterate that he was trying an income-tax evasion case only. In his sentence, he would have to prepare some statement explaining why he was literally disregarding the factual government summary and Agnew's response, and acting solely on the one tax count. What he seemed to be saying here was that the overwhelming government case of bribery, extortion, and conspiracy as presented in the summary supporting the single tax-evasion charge was going to make it awfully difficult for him to let Agnew off without a jail term. He could take mitigating factors into consideration, Judge Hoffman said, such as Agnew's character. He assumed the government knew nothing adverse about Agnew's character other than what was in the statement; except for the summary and the further details to be added in the full-disclosure statement, he assumed that Agnew enjoyed a high reputation. Richardson said he would agree to that; the purpose of the full disclosure was not to influence the judge in sentencing but to satisfy public opinion and scrutiny about the performance of the Department of Justice in a case of such importance.

Judge Hoffman was being moved close to a decision on no jail, and Richardson deftly eased him closer. It had been suggested by Agnew's lawyers that the judge might be willing to indicate in advance, *in camera*, what his decision would be, and the government agreed this was important to do. The Vice President, Richardson said, should not have to be brought to a public court proceeding and obliged to enter a plea under circumstances that might later persuade him to withdraw it. In this situation, the Vice President did not stand in the shoes of a normal citizen. If the course negotiated by the parties were to be pursued into open court, he said, they should know in advance that the course could be run to completion.

Well, Judge Hoffman replied, he had indicated what he would do without a recommendation. He was doing a little pushing himself, evidently, and Richardson was willing to waltz. Yes, he said, the government's evidence pointed to acts by the Vice President in previous capacities that constituted serious wrongdoings, and there even had been a carryover of the payoffs into his tenure as Vice President. He himself, said Richardson, as a former U.S. attorney and state attorney general, would normally recommend a jail sentence. But he felt it necessary to keep in view that the Vice President stood in immediate succession to the President and could be called on to assume the Presidency at any moment.

Hoffman interrupted. He understood that Agnew was going to resign. Yes, Richardson said, but only as part of the deal now under discussion. Agnew had the right to go to trial, or if Congress acted there would be an impeachment. The government believed that under the Constitution Agnew could subsequently be tried on an indictment, and if Agnew insisted on his right to that the result would be a long period in which the Vice Presidency would be under a cloud. He did not think, Richardson said, the public interest would be served if the matter took this ordinary course. It was in the public interest that Agnew resign and be replaced quickly in the succession to the Presidency. That was the first factor in his recommendation. The second was his awareness of the effect of resignation plus subsequent conviction on a felony charge on a man who had been Vice President of the United States. The imposition of this penalty could not be measured against the normal penalties that could be imposed. Finally, he said, there did seem to be room for appropriate recommendation of Agnew's service to the nation in foreign policy, in federal-state relations, and as president of the Senate. (This last was a sop that had been urged on him earlier by Agnew's lawyers.) And so he was recommending that no jail sentence be given.

Hoffman said the attorney general's recommendation would be given great weight. All parties to the deal would be taken to task by the public, he warned them, but so long as the whole matter was on the record, that did not matter. Before he came to the meeting, the judge confessed, he had made up his mind to say that unless there was a strong recommendation from Beall or Richardson based on the national interest, he was going to treat Agnew as if he were a run-of-the-mill lawyer. He repeated he was giving no weight to the government's summary of nontax offenses or to Agnew's response. But the fact that the government was agreeing to drop further charges did not mean that Agnew's name would not or could not be used in connection with other defendants as an unindicted co-conspirator; nor could the judge bind the Maryland Bar Association, the American Bar Association, or any other from disbarring Agnew. Then, without fanfare, he asked: did they want to have the arraignment the next day?

The faster the better, Topkis put in quickly. His side was fearful of leaks. And it was not only the Justice Department that was considering the national interest, he said. So was his client. Judge Hoffman said he had no doubt of that. The Vice President, Topkis said, with that studied pomposity which so grated on the Justice team, yielded to no one in his concern that the matter be resolved in the national interest. Agnew, he said, meant to uphold his oath of office. To which Hoffman replied: he had sympathy for a man with a skeleton in his closet that was rattling.

The meeting then got down to mechanics. Judge Hoffman had no authority to impose resignation from office as a condition of any sentence, he reminded the lawyers, and some procedure should be established to have a copy of Agnew's letter of resignation to the secretary of state—the proper officer of the government to receive it—handed to the court. Some plans already had been worked out, Topkis reported. George Kaufmann, representing the Vice President, would be standing by in Secretary of State Henry Kissinger's office with instructions to turn over the letter at the appropriate time. A phone line would be held open from the courtroom in Baltimore to Kissinger's office and the instant it was clear that there were no last-minute snags in the deal, Kaufmann would submit the letter. Thus, Agnew would stand before the arraignment as a private citizen; history, technically at least, would not have to record that a sitting Vice President had pleaded to a felony.

There was then some discussion about sparing Agnew undue humiliation. Hoffman said there were certain questions that the law required be asked of a person making a *nolo* plea. It seemed foolish to have to ask them of a highly educated man, the judge said, but that was the law—questions such as whether he understood his rights. Those would be asked. But he was not going to insult Agnew by asking him whether he was or had recently been under the influence of drugs or alcohol, as also usually required.

Judge Hoffman said he didn't mind taking the brunt of criticism for the plea bargain, and would prepare a statement approving the joint recommendation of no jail. It would note that he had disregarded the government summary and Agnew's denials; it might add that he would ordinarily impose a jail sentence and probation but that this was an unusual situation, and it would spell out why.

Topkis continued to press for having the case disposed of expeditiously and with no humiliation to the Vice President and the nation. He again asked that the court not direct Agnew to be fingerprinted or photographed, and Petersen said the department had no objection. Hoffman agreed to that. Topkis also implored the court not to give a suspended jail sentence. It was functionless. Hoffman said he didn't care, though he generally did put a convicted man on probation, and asked the government side if it had any objection. Richardson said the government had no strong feelings about it. Again Topkis: he hoped that in the national interest—this was a favorite Topkis phrase—any probation would be unsupervised. Hoffman quickly agreed that there certainly was no need for supervision, the purpose of which was rehabilitation. He suspected, he said, that Agnew would be rehabilitated by the press.

The group then discussed the arraignment. There was to be a hearing at ten o'clock the next morning on the leaks issue, and the judge said he assumed the deal would moot the need for presenting depositions in that regard. Topkis interjected that he would love to get the answers on who had leaked the Agnew investigation stories but, smiling, said he would make the sacrifice. Petersen, angered by this remark and convinced that the first leaks had come from Agnew's lawyers, suggested that Topkis might have had something to tell the judge himself on that score.

Hoffman, predictably, was worried about how to handle the ever-present press. He was going to Baltimore that night and would prepare his statement there. The press would be told only that depositions on the leaks would be deferred pending a proceeding at two o'clock. Then, if the deal went through, the depositions would be canceled. The assumption would be, they guessed correctly, that the press would conclude that the two-o'clock session would be on the leaks issue, nothing more. It was also agreed to permit the Secret Service to exercise its usual precautions around the courtroom for Agnew's appearance. A courtroom at the end of the hall next to the grand jury room in the Baltimore courthouse was selected as most readily accessible from the elevators. It was agreed that Beall would introduce Richardson to state the government's position—this would be for an Attorney General of the United States a precedent-setting appearance for a *nolo* plea in a federal district court proceeding. Topkis then would state that Agnew had resigned, and Agnew would give his statement prior to sentencing.

At this juncture, there was a final ripple. Richardson, concerned to eliminate any eleventh-hour snags over the full-disclosure statement, advised Judge Hoffman that what he would file would be a lot longer than the summary he had already submitted. The estimate was that it would be sixty pages. Hoffman didn't like this. He would go along with seven or ten pages, but he didn't care for the idea of a full amplification, especially one that Agnew's lawyers hadn't seen. Topkis, who earlier had said he would go along, admitted he didn't care for it either.

For a moment, the whole deal looked as if it might be scuttled. Richardson himself might hold fast or, if he did not, which was very unlikely, the Baltimore prosecutors would certainly dissociate themselves from the settlement and cause a public uproar. Judge Hoffman finally said, well, don't change the spirit of the seven pages. Agnew's statement had been drafted in light of them, and he didn't want any new information inserted to complicate things. (Possibly Hoffman feared that the sixty pages would present material so incriminating that it would render the plea bargain—and the no-jail arrangement—vulnerable.) Topkis put in that Richardson had told him the longer statement would be just an amplification, and Richardson agreed; it would be more detailed in terms of what witnesses would have testified to, but it would be consistent with the shorter draft and Agnew's lawyers would see it in the morning. Hoffman seemed satisfied. He simply warned the Justice team to beware of prejudicing future cases with what was used in the longer statement. Richardson, along with Skolnik, who would be writing the longer version with Baker and Liebman, indicated they were aware of that problem.

Topkis was not finished. If Agnew's lawyers were to comment on the charges in the longer statement, he argued to the judge, they couldn't do so if they hadn't seen them. Maybe the government could hold off and file the full disclosure a week later? But now Judge Hoffman was getting impatient with the hassling over this point, which he did not seem to appreciate as Richardson and his team did. The seven pages had certainly been enough to convince him, Hoffman said, that a stiffer sentence ordinarily would be warranted. They painted Agnew as scoundrel enough to vindicate the Justice Department's actions, so why were sixty pages needed?

Richardson paused and measured his words very carefully, in his painfully deliberate way, controlling his anger but giving himself away with slight inflections of the voice. A bitter attack had been launched on the government for its conduct of this case, he said, without mentioning Agnew. He was referring not merely to criticism about the news leaks but to charges that the government had sought to take advantage of perjured testimony. These charges would subject the department to endless digging and worrying by investigative reporters if the full facts it had gathered were not disclosed now. Well, Hoffman said, he was not going to proceed with the two-o'clock arraignment until Agnew's lawyers saw what the long statement included, because he was not going to permit the government at the last minute to slip in a "mickey."

Richardson was a picture of controlled exasperation, as Topkis and the other Agnew lawyers sat back and listened to Hoffman carry their mail for them. The Vice President's attorneys had understood from the outset of plea bargaining that a more complete summary of evidence would be filed, Richardson said. They had agreed to that, subject only to viewing it first to see that it was consistent with the seven-page summary. Well, Hoffman interjected—by now also angrily—the Vice President would just say he denied it all. Then Petersen weighed in with a strong endorsement of Richardson's points. Hoffman grew more and more impatient. The whole disclosure business didn't concern his decision. It was only for the press that the government was doing it anyway.

But Richardson pressed on. A historic, unprecedented action was being brought before the court, he said, and it would have a historic, unprecedented result. The government had a responsibility to the American people to satisfy them that the result was based on all relevant factors, including the government's evidence. Because there undoubtedly would be questions about that evidence, it was vital that it be made clear it was substantial.

Judge Hoffman still wasn't buying. Wouldn't it come out in future trials? Richardson said that was unlikely, because many of the co-defendants would plead guilty and waive trial. Would it be agreeable if he had the more extensive statement in the hands of Agnew's lawyers by first thing in the morning? Hoffman said yes, but he wanted to hold a hearing after that and before the arraignment. Again Richardson stressed that Agnew's lawyers had already agreed that they would see it only to satisfy themselves that it was consistent with the seven-page summary.

Topkis said he trusted Richardson but was concerned because the statement would be drafted by individuals who were not present. And perhaps the statement wouldn't be ready until half an hour before they were all to go to court. Petersen volunteered that Beall and Skolnik would review the material before a final draft was written. It would not be an eleventh-hour mickey, he assured Topkis and the judge.

Without consulting with Beall and Skolnik (who with Baker and Liebman had to do the work), the attorney general promised he would have the document ready by eight o'clock the next morning. Agnew's lawyers adjourned to the bathroom for a conference, and came out, saying they agreed. The draft would be delivered to Best's office.

Skolnik, however, continued to worry that Agnew's lawyers might back out of the deal when they saw the full disclosure. He suggested to Petersen that Agnew or his lawyers be required to sign a letter saying that if that happened, the government was free to make public Agnew's earlier agreement to resign and cop a plea. Petersen passed on the idea to Richardson, but he balked.

After the meeting, Richardson, Beall, and Skolnik adjourned to the attorney general's private office to prepare for the next day's arraignment. It was agreed that Beall and Skolnik would return to Baltimore, help Baker and Liebman finish taking statements from Matz, Wolff, Green, and Hammerman, and write the summary of evidence. Richardson and Petersen said they would drive to Baltimore to read the final draft when it was ready, before dispatching it to Best's office. Skolnik dictated a draft of a letter for Topkis to sign, acknowledging the draft was being shown to him merely to verify it was only an amplification of the seven-page summary.

While the Justice team was making its final preparations, Topkis, London, and Best returned to Agnew's office in the Old Executive Office Building to convey the news to the Vice President that the deal had been struck. From about six o'clock until about 7:30 that night, Agnew composed his resignation and a letter to the President; only the lawyers, Art Sohmer, and Mike Dunn were present with him. The Vice President's secretary, Mary Ellen Warner, typed both letters, and arrangements were made for Kaufmann to deliver the resignation to Secretary of State Kissinger. Through all this, Agnew remained cool, dignified, restrained. These last, tragic documents having been written, the Vice President of the United States left his office, walked out of the building and across the way to the White House. Spiro T. Agnew, proud, erect, trim, was admitted to the Oval Office, where he personally informed the already beleaguered President of the United States that he would have one less burden to bear.

15 The Instrument of Resignation

The Baltimore-Washington Parkway, thirty-nine miles long, is a pleasant precursor of the antiseptic and boring federal expressways of the 1960s and 1970s. Tall, lush trees line its route, and an occasional rest stop with a picnic bench is tucked beneath the foliage. No billboards, no service stations, no snack bars or restaurants mar the gentle Maryland countryside. In the course of an hour driving south, you travel from deteriorating downtown Baltimore—a city that shows its age, despite attempts at architectural cosmetics and face-lifting—to a capital city whose monuments and public buildings project a sense of national history that coaxes the eye from the squalor of its overpopulated slums.

In the previous five years, Spiro T. Agnew had traveled this road, both literally and figuratively, out of his modest Baltimore beginnings to the very doorstep of the White House. When he took the oath of the Vice Presidency for the second time on January 20, 1973, he signaled to all who knew him that it was his intention to seek occupancy of that historic national house in 1976. There was no sense in being Vice President for a second term, he often told aides and even acknowledged publicly, unless he was going to go after the Presidency.

Now, in the late evening of October 9, 1973, and the early hours of October 10, the Baltimore-Washington Parkway was for Spiro T. Agnew a dismal road back from grandeur and power. While unsuspecting motorists cruised the Parkway in the early fall of an America not yet shackled by the energy crisis, the principal players in the deposing of a Vice President busily shuttled between the two cities.

George Beall and Barney Skolnik were the first. Their work in Washington done, they arrived back in Baltimore at around six o'clock, while Agnew, in Washington, was still preparing his letters of resignation. It was an indication of their extreme thoroughness that they brought with them a thick stack of stationery with the words "Office of the Attorney General" embossed across the top, for use in case the draft of Elliot Richardson's letter to Topkis had to be redone at the last moment.

Agnew's lawyers, after helping the Vice President with his letters, returned to Judah Best's office. Best, who shared Richardson's appreciation for the judgment of history, was troubled by what would turn out to be a footnote. The Vice President, he told his colleagues, should resign before pleading *nolo contendere,* so that history would be unable to record that a sitting Vice President was simultaneously a felon. Jay Topkis and Martin London, who thought this was one hell of a time to start nitpicking, offered the facetious suggestion that the clock in Henry Kissinger's office be stopped at two o'clock, so that the Vice President's resignation could be recorded as having been accepted by the secretary of state before the plea was announced in the courtroom. Finally, the lawyers worked out their strategy and Best went home. From his house in Arlington, he called George Kaufmann and went over the arrangements one more time.

Agnew's personal staff had some unfinished business too. Late that night, General Mike Dunn phoned David Keene at home. Keene, who had arranged a breakfast meeting with about a hundred congressmen for the next morning, was suspicious that something was wrong and had tried to call it off, but Art Sohmer— Agnew's chief of staff—had said no. Now Dunn told him: "Cancel the meeting." Keene said he couldn't, it was too late. "The boss wants you to call the Hill and cancel it," Dunn said. Keene refused, and hung up. Dunn had not told him why the meeting was to be called off, but he understood. With so few friends, Agnew could not afford to make enemies with so rude an act. It had to be the end of the line.

In Baltimore, Tim Baker and Ron Liebman were hard at work writing the all-important full-disclosure statement. Central to the preparation of that document were signed statements from the four principal witnesses—Matz, Wolff, Green, and Hammerman.

One by one, the lawyers for the four had been phoned and told they and their clients must come in that evening to write and sign the statements. With each one, the prosecutors hinted that the hurry-up routine had something to do with the issue of leaks and the court hearing scheduled for the next day. Allen Green's lawyer, Brendan Sullivan, was a bit mystified by this strange summons to Baltimore and he went to see his associate, Joe Califano, about it. Califano, however, had problems of his own. As chief counsel for The Washington Post Company, he was busy preparing his motion to quash the subpoenas served on *Newsweek*, its writer Stephan Lesher, and Richard Cohen of the *Post*. Along with two associates, Richard M. Cooper and Gregory B. Craig, Califano worked through most of the night.

As a matter of fact, Califano had been working on a crash basis ever since the subpoenas were served the Friday before, with two goals in mind: to quash the subpoenas served on Cohen and *Newsweek*, and to keep Cohen out of jail.[1] Califano's strategy had been dictated by Benjamin C. Bradlee, the *Post*'s executive editor, the same day the subpoenas were served. Dropping into a meeting in the office of managing editor Howard Simons, Bradlee announced that he had to catch a plane, but he had one observation to make before he left: "It goes without saying that *The Washington Post* will not reveal its sources. We will go to jail first." With that, Bradlee left the room, and Califano had his marching orders.

---

[1] Cohen's name, selected on an alphabetical basis, was given to the case. It was generally assumed that he would be the first reporter called to the witness stand—and the first to go to jail.

First, Cohen of course would answer no questions relating to the sources for any Agnew article. Second, Califano, in behalf of Katharine Graham, publisher of the *Post*, asserted in an affidavit that she had "ultimate responsibility for the custody" of Cohen's notes. In some ways, this was a bold tactic, although for the publishers of *The Washington Post* and *The New York Times* it had nearly become standard operating procedure. If Judge Walter Hoffman granted Califano's motion and recognized Mrs. Graham's ownership of Cohen's notes, the judge might then have to demand that she surrender the notes or face jail herself. Mrs. Graham was prepared for that eventuality.

Califano did not stop there. In his supplemental charge to the jury, Hoffman had given every indication that he wanted the leaks issue brought to a head and would not accept a motion to quash. Califano therefore girded for a long battle. He planned to confront the judge with fourteen affidavits—nine from *Post* reporters, editors, and executives; four from newsmen from other organizations; and one from Richard Neustadt, a professor of political science at Harvard—each stressing the importance of confidential sources to the gathering of news. In Neustadt's affidavit, the scholar and former adviser to presidents Truman, Kennedy, and Johnson maintained that news stories based on information gathered from confidential sources were invaluable to the government itself since they facilitated internal communication within the vast bureaucracy.[2]

While the affidavits and the motion to quash were being prepared, Califano planned for the worst. In concert with the lawyers for all but one of the other news organizations,[3] he retained a Richmond, Virginia, law firm in the event Judge Hoffman rejected the motion to quash and immediately ordered a reporter to jail for contempt of court. By Tuesday, the Virginia firm had scouted the locations of the appeals judges, ready to contact them

---

[2] Neustadt's affidavit had actually been written for an earlier suit in which the *Post* had been asked to reveal its sources. Neustadt updated it by telephone, and flew down from Cape Cod to a rendezvous with a *Post* lawyer at LaGuardia Airport in New York, signed the affidavit, turned around, and flew back to the Cape.

[3] *Time* was not included.

if necessary. A private plane was readied for Mrs. Graham in case she had to hurry to Baltimore from a speaking engagement in Hartford, Connecticut; rooms at the Lord Baltimore Hotel were reserved for Mrs. Graham, Cohen, and Osborne Elliott, the editor of *Newsweek*. In the end, this wasted effort would cost The Washington Post Company about $25,000 in legal fees and another $5000 in expenses. Similar expenses were incurred by the other news-gathering organizations whose reporters were subpoenaed. Little wonder, then, that Califano paid scant attention to Sullivan's bewilderment that Tuesday evening.

Sullivan and his client, Allen Green, were the first to arrive at the Baltimore courthouse that night. Baker began working with them even before Beall and Skolnik had returned from Washington, and he produced a revealing statement that with some editing eventually became a quarter of the full-disclosure summary of evidence filed with the court. Lester Matz and Jerome Wolff came in with their lawyers, Joe Kaplan and Arnold Weiner, at about 8:30, and Bud Hammerman with Sidney Sachs about an hour later. None was told of the momentous development that required this crash effort, nor were the men aware that the whole assemblage of heavy-hitters against Agnew was in the building. Hammerman, however, ran into Green in the hallway and gave him a wan smile.

An assembly-line procedure was established to write, edit, review, and type the statements and, from them, the summary of evidence. When Green's statement was completed, Baker checked it and reworked it for use in the summary. First-person references were changed to the third person, there was some reorganization of the paragraphs, but essentially the statement provided the raw material for the section relating to Green's dealings with Agnew. The same procedures were used to convert the statements of the other three to the text of the summary. Baker, having concluded with Green, next turned to Wolff and his lawyer, Weiner; in separate rooms Liebman worked with Matz and Kaplan, Skolnik with Hammerman and Sachs. Some preliminary drafts had already been approved, and much of the time was spent discussing words, nuances, changes that the lawyers thought ought to be made for the protection of their clients. The three assistant U.S. attorneys rotated the drafts, giving their approval or voicing objections to changes, until all four statements were hammered out. The U.S. marshals on duty were dispatched for cheeseburgers.

The pressure of time precluded a complete rewriting of the statements into the court summary, and so the prosecutors functioned like three editors on a newspaper desk—Xeroxing the statements, cutting paragraphs out with scissors, and pasting or stapling them back in more readable order. Four secretaries who had been sworn to secrecy worked through the night typing each new draft, which then would run the gamut of Skolnik, Baker, and Liebman.

There was not much time for literary flourish, but the sheer narrative force of the straightforward confessions was compelling, and the Baker-Skolnik team combined to provide a kicker that was worthy of the best short-story writer. The final paragraph, as written by Baker and edited by Skolnik, discussed Matz's refusal to give The Close Associate $10,000 for the 1972 Nixon-Agnew campaign, and ended: ". . . Matz complained about these solicitations to Mr. Agnew, who told Matz to say that he gave at the office."

At about midnight or so, the team had nearly completed the first draft. Beall phoned Richardson, at home in McLean, to report on the progress. The attorney general said he would contact Henry Petersen and the two of them would head for Baltimore in half an hour. Richardson's limousine picked them up and whisked them along the nearly deserted Baltimore-Washington Parkway to Beall's office. The limousine was parked in the basement garage of the building and Richardson and Petersen took an elevator upstairs. At this hour, no special precautions were needed to camouflage their arrival.

Skolnik, Baker, and Liebman were still at work when they arrived at about 2 a.m. About twenty-five of the forty pages were ready, and Richardson and Petersen began to read through them, eating doughnuts and drinking coffee brought in by the marshals. Richardson had a great deal riding on the summary of evidence;

if it failed to make a persuasive yet fair case against Agnew, he would be accused of railroading the Vice President out of office; if it were too strong, he would be accused of making too lenient a deal. In the end, the latter allegation was heard from many quarters anyway, but Richardson had made clear to the prosecutors that he wanted the disclosure to be as strong as they could legitimately make it, without distortion of evidence or testimony.

Sometime about three o'clock, Beall walked down to Skolnik's office and inquired how the final section was coming along. Skolnik told him he was nearly finished. "Good," Beall said, "because the Attorney General of the United States and the Assistant Attorney General of the United States are down the hall in my office. They've got coffee and doughnuts and they're reading our product, and they're having a nice time." Beall smiled.

When the last statement was ready, the three prosecutors repaired to Beall's office, there to find Richardson and Petersen at Beall's desk marking up the draft with pens. When he heard them walk in, Richardson turned, administered his broadest smile, and commended the authors profusely. If the three prosecutors did not realize it at the time, the statement constituted a very powerful indictment of the Vice President, exactly the sort of detailed, believable statement Richardson thought was required to satisfy the public of Agnew's guilt. "It's a good job," he said to them once, then again, and again. He praised its content, its objectivity, its length, its literary style. He and Petersen made only a very few minor corrections, and again the draft went to the four weary secretaries. (When everything was ready at about four o'clock, Richardson came down the hall and personally thanked the women—Baker's secretary, Joyce Kegley; Liebman's, Ann Cahill; Beall's, Dolores Furncase; and Skolnik's, Mary Herbert. Later, each received a letter from him thanking them again.)

Beall had reserved rooms for Richardson and Petersen at the Baltimore Hilton, but they decided instead to go back to Washington. Richardson wanted to be in his office in the morning to handle any last-minute details that might crop up, including possible complications raised by Agnew or his lawyers, or calls from the White House. He and Petersen went home for a couple of hours' sleep, a shower and shave, and then headed for the Justice Department.

Between four and seven o'clock in Baltimore, the prosecutors addressed themselves to a final technical chore, the proofreading of the forty-page statement, which was now in four parts: a summary of the contents; a description of Agnew's relations with Hammerman and Wolff; a detailed account of Agnew's dealings with Green; and a narrative of his relationships with Matz concluding with, "Say you gave at the office."

At about a quarter past seven, Beall called for the two U.S. marshals who had been on duty through the night—Al Smith and Gerald Testerman—and handed them two envelopes, one containing the statement, and the other containing the letter to Topkis from Richardson stating that the summary was being shown to the Agnew lawyers strictly for verification purposes. The documents were supposed to be in the hands of the lawyers by eight o'clock that morning. With Testerman at the wheel, the marshals radioed for a U.S. Park Police escort to meet them at the Baltimore end of the Baltimore-Washington Parkway. The police car made the rendezvous and with screaming siren and flashing emergency light cleared a path through the commuter traffic, through the early-morning congestion of Washington, down past the Old Executive Office Building, to the law offices of Colson and Shapiro on New York Avenue. Smith jumped from the car and scurried into the building. He handed Best the package and the lawyer signed the letter. It was 8:05.

Jud Best had already been up for a long time. At three o'clock that morning, he had given up on getting any sleep and had spent the rest of the night in his wood-paneled study, there alternating between pacing the floor and sitting on the couch, reading a history of the Greek wars. Over and over again he planned the approaching day, especially the words he would say to Agnew. The occasion demanded that he not speak casually. He was not one to function well without sleep, and none of them the melancholy intensely. Then, just after dawn, he heard the thump of *The Washington Post* hitting the front door. Best scanned the paper quickly, hoping he would not find a story about plea bargaining that would upset the deal at the last minute. The *Post* had an article reporting that the grand jury had subpoenaed records relating to Agnew's purchase of his home in Kenwood, and another saying that lawyers for the subpoenaed reporters and news organizations would move in court later that day to quash the subpoenas. Best was relieved. The *Post*, obviously, was oblivious to what was happening. Forsaking his Fiat sports car for the day, he borrowed his wife's Mercedes-Benz and drove to his office across the Potomac where he met London, Topkis, and Max Gittler, a lawyer who had helped Topkis in writing the briefs.

After receiving the documents from the marshals, the lawyers walked over to the Old Executive Office Building. Agnew was not there. Best picked up the letter of resignation and dispatched a copy of it to the White House, along with the letter to the President. Then he telephoned the White House to arrange for the admittance of Kaufmann later in the day. He wrote down the phone number in Kissinger's White House office, where Kaufmann would be waiting. The lawyers returned to the offices of Colson and Shapiro, handed Kaufmann the letter addressed to Kissinger, and then got into the Mercedes for the drive to Baltimore.

Now began a period of nail-biting, general anticipation, and apprehension. The deal was cut, in the prosecutors' parlance, but it could still become unstuck. In Baltimore, in the final stages of proofreading the statement, the other prosecutors had noticed that their colleague, Liebman, was becoming extremely irritable. He was not one to function well without sleep, and none of them had slept at all that night. They agreed, as soon as the marshals had left, to go home for an hour or two, just long enough to get cleaned up, and to return to the office for the historic events of the unfolding day.

Beall went home, took a shower, shaved, dressed, and came downstairs for a big breakfast. On the table, waiting for him, was a heart-shaped note of congratulations from his wife, Nancy. Skolnik saw his wife just before she went to work and told her to be sure to be in the courtroom at two o'clock that afternoon. He was beginning to relax when the phone rang.

It was Liebman. "Talk to me," he said to Skolnik, in a frightened voice. "I just want you to talk to me."

"Ron, what the hell's the matter?" Skolnik asked.

"I thought I was falling," Liebman said, "I thought I was falling."

"What are you talking about?" asked Skolnik, bewildered.

"I fell asleep," Liebman told him. "I knew I wasn't supposed to do it, but I lay down and I fell asleep and I was so scared because I was dreaming and I thought I was falling. And I woke up and I didn't know where I was. I knew I had to talk to somebody, so I just dialed. Just talk to me for a minute and I'll be all right."

"For Christ's sake," Skolnik said. "Now look, take it easy. It's Barney, and you're all right. You're very tired and you shouldn't have fallen asleep. When you haven't slept the worst thing you can do is sleep for five minutes." Skolnik continued on like that, and talked about being on the brink of a major event in American history. "Go slosh some water on your face and take a shower," he told Liebman. "Then calm down and you'll be all right." Later, Skolnik and Liebman, now in control, had breakfast together across the street from their office. They took the precaution of entering the back way, but photographers were there and took their pictures—not knowing that the photos would be used the next morning to help illustrate a momentous political news event.

All during the morning, Skolnik busied himself with mechanical matters, such as arranging the seating in the courtroom for Richardson, Petersen, and the prosecutors, and discussing security precautions with courtroom officials. Through all this, nothing was said about what would in fact happen at two o'clock. According to what most courthouse insiders, the press, and the world at large knew, there was simply to be a hearing before Judge Hoffman on the narrow issue of the briefs on leaks.

As a courtesy to Matz, Wolff, Green, and Hammerman, it was decided to advise them through their lawyers—without disclosing the purpose of the two-o'clock hearing—that something was about to happen that would reveal their involvement in the

Agnew case. At about noon, the three assistant U.S. attorneys placed calls to Kaplan, Weiner, Sullivan, and Sachs. Most took the warning with some gratitude, but Sullivan became irate and screamed at Baker for nearly twenty minutes, charging that he had been lied to, that he had been told his client would not yet surface publicly. He complained about more government leaks, and when Baker assured him he was not talking about a leak, he still was not satisfied. He issued what the prosecutors took to be a veiled threat to file a suit to enjoin them from taking whatever action it was they were warning him about. To deter him, Skolnik called back and engaged him in a long, mollifying conversation the purpose of which was to make it impossible for Sullivan to get to the court in time to disrupt the proceedings.

After a few hours' sleep in McLean, Richardson spent the morning in his Justice Department office preparing the statement he would make in court on the significance of the government's summary of evidence and why he was recommending that no jail sentence be imposed. He also took a number of phone calls from Agnew's lawyers, who by now had read the exposition of evidence and were pressing for several changes that Richardson told aides he regarded as incredibly petty. He held firm against any changes, noting that the statement itself was nonnegotiable so long as it did not go beyond an elaboration of the charges in the earlier short summary.

Shortly after noon, a somber Elliot Richardson, accompanied by Henry Petersen, J. T. Smith, and Richard Darman, climbed into his limousine and headed up the parkway once again. William Ruckelshaus and Jonathan Moore stayed behind to provide communications and to prepare statements for the press. They kept in touch with Richardson over his car telephone, watching the wire-service tickers to be sure there was no leak, and giving him information as he read over his prepared statement en route.

At the courthouse, Richardson and his party went to Beall's office. By now the courtroom had been opened to the press and to lawyers, and everyone flocked in—the reporters under the impression they would be covering a hearing on the leaks, the lawyers prepared to defend their newsmen clients.

Califano was one of the first. He and his associates had left Washington at 6:30 that morning by chauffeured limousine, arriving at the courthouse much too early to file their papers. After driving around for a while, Califano had gotten out in front of the courthouse and been mobbed by reporters. In all his years traveling with President Johnson, Califano had never been in such a crush. He elbowed his way into the courthouse and attempted to reach the elevators. Finally, he was rescued by a couple of marshals who escorted him to the clerk's office.

Now Califano was moving into the courtroom, wondering what the two-o'clock hearing would be about. By then, he had been notified that it wasn't about leaks but that Judge Hoffman might turn to them as soon as it was over.

A few minutes before two o'clock, Richardson, Petersen, and the four Baltimore prosecutors set out together with security men around them, down the hall to the courtroom. A sense of the drama now began to crowd in. Skolnik confessed later to have been momentarily mesmerized. He caught sight of the jammed courtroom ahead, with the doors open and a sea of faces expectantly looking toward the bench, and he glided along as if on air. "I don't remember to whom I was talking because my ears were full of 'Hail to the Chief,'" he said later. "I was just aware of history; we were striding down to history." Earlier, Richardson had shown Skolnik a draft of his statement and had asked for his opinion. Skolnik had made a suggestion and Richardson had incorporated it. Now, as they walked toward the courtroom, Richardson turned and asked him over his shoulder, "How is the statement now? Is it okay?" Skolnik replied, "Yes, great." Richardson smiled. "Good," he said. The capture of Barney Skolnik was complete.

The arrangement of chairs before the bench was such that the full prosecutorial team was obliged to file past the defense counsel's table, where Topkis, London, and Best already sat. They had arrived in Baltimore around noon, had eaten lunch, and then had gone directly to the courtroom, a marshal leading them through the crush of reporters, who immediately recognized them and peppered them with questions. As Richardson, Petersen, and the rest went by, they shook hands and exchanged pleasantries as if it were a class reunion—all, that is, except Skolnik, who stiffly shook hands but remained sober-faced and said nothing. For him, it was not a time for pleasantries, and some reporters who noted his demeanor later attributed it to bitterness over the agreement to let Agnew off without a jail sentence. They did not know that by now Skolnik had not only accepted Richardson's no-jail recommendation but had helped sell it to his colleagues.

Richardson, Petersen, and Beall sat at the prosecution table, with Skolnik, Baker, and Liebman in chairs just behind them. An unexpected problem had cropped up shortly before, with the appearance in the courtroom of John F. Banzhaff III, a George Washington University professor and self-styled public ombudsman, who had filed a brief seeking a special prosecutor in the Agnew case on grounds that Richardson as a potential 1976 presidential rival to Agnew had a conflict of interest.[4] Banzhaff had walked in and insisted on sitting at counsel's table. He was ousted by Best, but then moved first to the jury box and then to a seat reserved for Agnew, before he was finally shunted aside. But all was in readiness now.

As Richardson got settled, Best walked over to him and asked, "Are you prepared to honor the agreement?"

"Oh, yes, certainly," Richardson replied, and he showed Best the statement he was about to read in court.

Just then, a Secret Service agent approached Best and told him his client had arrived in the building. He had come up from Washington with only Art Sohmer and the driver. At precisely three minutes after two o'clock, Spiro T. Agnew, Vice President of the United States, strode briskly into the courtroom. He was dressed impeccably, as always, in a perfectly pressed blue suit and blue-and-tan striped tie, his graying hair slicked neatly back

---

[4] The day after the resignation of the Vice President, Richardson held a press conference and was asked whether he would accept nomination as Vice President to fill the vacancy created by Agnew's departure. Richardson said he would not; it "would be highly inappropriate for me as the government's accuser of the Vice President . . . to be for one moment considered as a potential successor to him."

off his tanned but now thin and tight-lipped face. There were murmurs as he made his unannounced entrance.

The Vice President shook hands with his three lawyers and then sat down with them. Best leaned over and whispered, "The attorney general has assured me he will honor the agreement. Do you authorize me to cause your resignation to be handed into the secretary of state?"

"Certainly," Agnew answered.

Best walked to the judge's chambers and got Kaufmann on the line being held open outside Kissinger's office in the White House. Then, using the precise language he had decided on in the sleepless early hours of the day—direct from the federal code—he said, "You are authorized to deliver into the secretary of state the instrument of resignation." [5]

Best held the phone and waited as Kaufmann went into Kissinger's office and handed him the one-sentence official resignation. It said:

"Dear Mr. Secretary: I hereby resign the Office of Vice President of the United States, effective immediately. Sincerely, Spiro T. Agnew."

Then Kaufmann returned to the phone and told Best:

"The instrument of resignation was delivered into the secretary of state at fourteen-oh-five."

"What?" Best asked.

"Two-oh-five," Kaufmann said.

Best walked back into the courtroom and went over to Agnew. "Sir," he said, "your resignation, sir, has been delivered." Agnew made no reply. Best then handed Topkis a note conveying the information for inclusion in Topkis's remarks to the court.

Now Judge Hoffman walked in. All rose, then sat again as the clerk announced his arrival and concluded with the traditional "God save the United States and this honorable court." Judge Hoffman first addressed the spectators and press, who thought

---

[5] Best's language was taken almost entirely from Title 3 of the U.S. Code: "The only evidence of refusal to accept, or of a resignation of, the Office of President or Vice President, shall be an instrument in writing, declaring the same, and subscribed by the person refusing to accept or resigning, as the case may be, and delivered into the office of the Secretary of State."

they were attending a hearing on the question of newspaper leaks. "You will not be permitted to leave at any time during the course of the proceeding," he told them firmly, "and there will be no disturbances or outcries of any kind from anyone. If so, the marshals have received instructions to take you into custody." Then he had the courtroom locked.

"I am advised that Spiro T. Agnew desires at this time to execute a waiver of indictment in open court," Hoffman said, addressing Topkis. The lawyer said the judge was correct. "Mr. Agnew," Judge Hoffman now remarked, looking at the defendant, "before executing the waiver of indictment, I am required to advise you that you have a right, under the Constitution of the United States, to require that an indictment be returned against you, charging you with the commission of any crime. Therefore, you should not execute the waiver form unless you do so freely, voluntarily, and with full knowledge of your rights in the matter. Do you fully understand your rights?"

"I do, your honor," Agnew said, standing at the defendant's table, tense and grim, but in a firm voice.

Each time the judge addressed him in the next few minutes, Agnew would stand, reply, and sit down again. It was a humiliation, a visible ebbing of power. "Down and up, down and up," one of the Richardson lieutenants recalled later. "He was obeying in the simple, polite way of a trained schoolboy."

Hoffman ascertained from Topkis that Agnew had seen the criminal information against him and was waiving formal arraignment. Then he asked, "Mr. Topkis, what plea are you advised does the defendant wish to enter in connection with the charge as stated in the criminal information?"

"On behalf of the defendant, your honor," Topkis replied, "we lodge a plea of *nolo contendere*."

Hoffman turned again to the ex-Vice President. "Mr. Agnew, is that correct and is that your plea?"

"That is my plea, your honor," Agnew said, again in a firm voice.

"I am required to advise you, Mr. Agnew," Judge Hoffman said, "that a plea of *nolo contendere* is, insofar as this criminal proceeding is concerned today, the full equivalent to a plea of guilty and that, while a plea of *nolo contendere* may protect you in certain collateral proceedings, it has no bearing upon the disposition of the present case. Do you thoroughly understand the consequences of a plea of *nolo contendere?*"

"I do, your honor," Agnew—struggling lawyer who became Vice President, voice of the law-and-order society—replied.

The judge then asked Agnew a series of questions required under court procedure. Each time, the answer came in a clear voice. Even as his political life crumbled around him, Spiro Agnew was as always projecting the image of a man in control.

"Do you fully understand the nature and the seriousness of the charge as stated in the criminal information?"

"I do."

"Have you had all the time necessary to confer with your counsel as to any possible defenses to the charge as set forth in the criminal information?"

"I have, your honor."

"Has anyone connected with the federal government persuaded or induced you to enter this plea of *nolo contendere?*"

"No one has."

"Totally aside from any plea agreement, has anyone held out to you any offer of leniency in connection with this matter?"

"No, sir."

"Congress has provided by law that a person convicted of federal income-tax evasion can be punished by a maximum fine of ten thousand dollars, a maximum term of imprisonment of five years, either or both. Have you been fully advised of the maximum sentence provided by law?"

"I have been so advised."

"Do you realize that, by pleading *nolo contendere*, you are not entitled to a trial by jury; whereas, if you entered a plea of not guilty, you would be entitled to a trial by jury?"

"I do."

"Do you realize that, by entering a plea of *nolo contendere*, the Department of Justice is not required to prove its case beyond a reasonable doubt; that is to say that your plea of *nolo contendere* is an admission by you that the Department of Justice is possessed of sufficient evidence to prove its case beyond a reasonable doubt?"

"I do."

"Do you realize that, by entering a plea of *nolo contendere*, you waive your rights under the Fifth Amendment with respect to testifying against yourself as the same pertains to the charge as stated in the criminal information?"

"I do so realize it."

Judge Hoffman then recited the terms of the plea agreement— resignation, no further federal prosecution, and a recommendation by the attorney general for an unsupervised probation and fine.

"Mr. Agnew," he asked, "do you thoroughly understand the plea agreement and do you now ratify and approve the same?"

"I do so," Agnew said, "and I understand it."

"Thank you, Mr. Agnew," the judge said, "and now you may take your seat. Subject to further proceedings, I will accept your plea of *nolo contendere*."

Agnew sat down and Topkis got up. "At two-oh-five p.m.," he told the court, "there was delivered into the office of the secretary of state a letter, subscribed by the Vice President, in which he resigns his office." Topkis said he and the attorney general had agreed to waive the requirement of pre-sentence investigation so that the judge could proceed at once to impose sentence.

Next it was Richardson's turn. He rose and read the statement he had written, a statement he hoped would make clear that the scope of the government's allegations against Agnew went far beyond simple tax evasion; that the national interest as well as justice was being served in the compromise struck.

"May it please the court," he said, "I am, like every other participant in these proceedings, deeply conscious of the critical national interests which surround them. The agreement between the parties now before the court is one which must be just and honorable, and which must be perceived to be just and honorable, not simply to the parties but above all to the American people.

"From the outset of the negotiations which have culminated in these proceedings," the attorney general continued, "the Department of Justice has regarded as an integral requirement of any agreement a full disclosure of the surrounding circumstances, for only with knowledge of these circumstances can the American people fairly judge the justice of the outcome. One critical component of these circumstances is the government's evidence. In accordance, therefore, with the agreement of counsel, I offer for the permanent record of these proceedings an exposition of the evidence accumulated by the investigation against the defendant conducted by the office of the United States Attorney for the District of Maryland as of October 10, 1973. Because this exposition is complete and detailed, it is sufficient for present purposes simply to state that this evidence establishes a pattern of substantial cash payments to the defendant during the period when he served as governor of Maryland in return for engineering contracts with the state of Maryland.

"Payments by the principal in one large engineering firm began while the defendant was county executive of Baltimore County in the early 1960s and continued into 1971. The evidence also discloses payments by another engineer up to and including December 1972. None of the government's major witnesses has been promised immunity from prosecution, and each of the witnesses who would testify to having made direct payments to the Vice President has signed a sworn statement subject to the penalties of perjury." Richardson was all too aware of the attacks that might be made on the credibility of the prosecutors' witnesses, and the fact that the case could reach this stage without formal immunity of any kind having been granted was a triumph of negotiations by Beall and his team.

Richardson now got to the core of his position. "In the light of the serious wrongdoing shown by its evidence," he went on, "the government might have insisted, if permitted by the court to do so, on pressing forward with the return of an indictment charging bribery and extortion. To have done this, however, would have been likely to inflict upon the nation serious and permanent scars. It would have been the defendant's right to put the prosecution to its proof. The Department of Justice had conceded the power of Congress, once an indictment had been returned, to proceed by impeachment. The Congress could well have elected to exercise this constitutional power. If the Congress chose not to act, the defendant could, while retaining office, either have insisted upon his right to a trial by jury or have continued to contest the right of the government to try an incumbent Vice President. Whichever of these courses were followed would have consumed not simply months but years—with potentially disastrous consequences to vital interests of the United States. Confidence in the adequacy of our fundamental institutions would itself have been put to severe trial. It is unthinkable that this nation should have been required to endure the anguish and uncertainty of a prolonged period in which the man next in line of succession to the Presidency was fighting the charges brought against him by his own government.

"On the basis of these considerations, I am satisfied that the public interest is better served by this court's acceptance of the defendant's plea of *nolo contendere* to a single count information charging income tax evasion."

Richardson then addressed himself to the one issue he had hoped to avoid, the one issue that he knew would put the fair administration of justice to its most severe and probably most lasting public test—letting Agnew off without imprisonment.

"There remains the question of the government's position toward the sentence to be imposed," he said. "One possible course would have been to avoid this difficult and painful issue by declining to make an affirmative recommendation [which, of course, he had much preferred to do]. It became apparent, however, in the course of the negotiations that without such a recommendation no agreement could be achieved. No agreement could have been achieved, moreover, if that recommendation did not include an appeal for leniency.

"I am firmly convinced that in all the circumstances leniency is justified. I am keenly aware, first, of the historic magnitude of the penalties inherent in the Vice President's resignation from his high office and his acceptance of a judgment of conviction for a felony. To propose that a man who has suffered these penalties should, in addition, be incarcerated in a penal institution, however briefly, is more than I, as head of the government's prosecuting arm, can recommend or wish." They were words of compassion, and Elliot Richardson made them sound as if they came from his heart.

"Also deserving of consideration is the public service rendered by the defendant during more than four and one-half years as the nation's second highest elected official," he added, in deference to a suggestion by Agnew's lawyers. "He has been an effective spokesman for the executive branch in the councils of state and local government. He has knowledgeably and articulately represented the United States in meetings with the heads of other governments. He has participated actively and constructively in the deliberations of the government in a diverse range of fields.

"Out of compassion for the man, out of respect for the office he has held, and out of appreciation for the fact that by his resignation he has spared the nation the prolonged agony that would have attended upon his trial," Richardson concluded, "I urge that the sentence imposed on the defendant by this court not include confinement." Then Elliot L. Richardson, Attorney General of the United States, took his seat.

Now it was Agnew's turn. A private citizen for minutes only, he rose again at the defendant's table, holding a single sheet of paper in both hands—the statement that had been written in conjunction with the prosecutors and approved by them word by word in what had been the prime issue for much of the plea bargaining. But before he started reading, Agnew turned toward Richardson and his colleagues—of whom he had been so very critical only days before. "May I say at the outset," he observed, "I want to express my appreciation for the courtesy and cooperation extended to me through my counsel in their deliberations with the prosecutors and throughout the consultations on this matter." The Justice team was surprised, and moved. Then Agnew began, reading in an even voice:

"My decision to resign and enter a plea of *nolo contendere* rests on my firm belief that the public interest requires swift disposition of the problems which are facing me. I am advised that a full legal defense of the probable charges against me could consume several years. I am concerned that intense media interest in the case would distract public attention from important national problems—to the country's detriment.

"I am aware that witnesses are prepared to testify that I and my agents received payments from consulting engineers doing business with the state of Maryland during the period I was governor. With the exception of the admission that follows, I deny these assertions of illegal acts on my part made by the government witnesses. I admit that I did receive payments during the year 1967 which were not expended for political purposes and that, therefore, these payments were income taxable to me in that year and that I so knew." [6] That was the meat of it: the single actionable admission on which the charge of income-tax evasion was based.

Next was the admission that those who had paid off benefited from the state—an admission couched in veiled phrases designed to take some of the curse off, in public-relations terms. "I further acknowledge that contracts were awarded by state agencies in 1967 and other years to those who made such payments, and that I was aware of such awards. I am aware that government witnesses are prepared to testify that preferential treatment was accorded to the paying companies pursuant to an understanding with me when I was the governor. I stress, however, that no contracts were awarded to contractors who were not competent to perform the work and in most instances state contracts were awarded without any arrangement for the payment of money by the contractor. I deny that the payments in any way influenced my official actions. I am confident, moreover, that testimony presented in my behalf would make it clear that I at no time conducted my official duties as county executive or governor of Maryland in a manner harmful to the interests of the county or state, or my

---

[6] In the formal plea Agnew acknowledged that he had evaded payment of $13,551.47 in federal income taxes for 1967. The government charged that in a joint return with his wife he had reported income of $26,099 on which he paid taxes of $6,416, when his actual income that year was $55,599, on which he should have paid $19,967.57 in taxes.

duties as Vice President of the United States in a manner harmful to the nation, and, further assert that my acceptance of contributions was part of a long-established pattern of political fundraising in the state. At no time have I enriched myself at the expense of the public trust." He did not deny being paid off, in other words, only that the payoffs had influenced him. And he was only doing what others before him had done.

"In all the circumstances," Agnew said, finally, "I have concluded that protracted proceedings before the grand jury, the Congress, and the courts, with the speculation and controversy surrounding them, would seriously prejudice the national interest. These, briefly stated, are the reasons I am entering a plea of *nolo contendere* to the charge that I did receive payments in 1967 which I failed to report for the purposes of income taxation." With that, Spiro T. Agnew, private citizen, sat down.

Now Judge Hoffman spoke, outlining his position on the arrangement made between Agnew and the Justice Department. "For the past two days," he said, "counsel for the defendant and the representatives of the Department of Justice have engaged in what is known as 'plea bargaining,' a practice which has received the judicial approval of the Supreme Court of the United States. As the judge of the court, I have refrained from making any recommendation to the parties involved as I was unaware of the facts involving the alleged charges. The agreement finally reached between the parties, and which has been fully set forth by Mr. Topkis, one of the attorneys for the defendant, and Mr. Richardson, the distinguished Attorney General of the United States, was the result of some relinquishment of rights on both sides. We are all aware of the fact that some persons will criticize the result and the sentence to be imposed but, in a case such as this, it would be impossible to satisfy everyone.

"Once the agreement was reached between the parties, it had to be submitted to the judge for his approval or disapproval. It was late yesterday afternoon when I learned the final details of the negotiations. I insisted that all details would have to be submitted in open court and in the presence of the defendant before any formal approval or disapproval could be given. Such has now been accomplished and it becomes my duty to proceed.

"The judge must accept the final responsibility as to any sentence, but this does not mean that he should disregard the negotiations and advices of the parties who are far more familiar with the facts, the national interest, and the consequences flowing from any sentence to be imposed." Here Hoffman made clear that he would sentence Agnew only on the one specific charge to which he was pleading; the rest, he implied correctly, was part of a public-relations battle between the Justice team and Agnew for public acceptance or rejection of Agnew's greater guilt.

"As far as the court is involved," Hoffman said, "the defendant is on trial for willful evasion of income taxes for the calendar year 1967, which charge is a felony in the eyes of the law. He has entered a plea of *nolo contendere* which, so far as this criminal prosecution is concerned, is the full equivalent of a plea of guilty. Such a plea frequently is accepted in income-tax-evasion cases as there are generally civil consequences flowing therefrom and the criminal court is not interested in the precise amount of taxes which may be due. The plea of *nolo contendere* merely permits the parties to further litigate the amount due without regard to the conviction following such a plea.

"A detailed statement has been filed by the Department of Justice and refuted by the defendant, all of which are wholly unrelated to the charge of income-tax evasion. These statements are a part of the understanding between the parties and are submitted merely because of the charges and countercharges which have received so much advance publicity. Of course, the agreement further provides that the federal government will take no further action against the defendant as to any federal criminal charge which had its inception prior to today, reserving the right to proceed against him in any appropriate civil action for monies allegedly due. Furthermore, neither this court nor the Department of Justice can limit the right of any state or organization to take action against the defendant. Since the Department of Justice, pursuant to its agreement, will be barred from prosecuting the defendant as to any criminal charge heretofore existing, the truth of these charges and countercharges can never be established by any judicial decision or action. It would have been my preference to omit these statements and end the verbal warfare as to this tragic event in history, but I am not inclined to reject the agreement for this reason alone.

"There is a fundamental rule of law that every person accused of a crime is presumed to be innocent until such time as the guilt is established beyond a reasonable doubt. It is for this reason that I must disregard, for the purpose of imposing sentence, the charges, countercharges, and denials which do not pertain to the single count of income-tax evasion. I have so advised counsel for the parties and they are in agreement that this is my duty.

"We come then to the charge of income-tax evasion which, as I stated, is a felony and a most serious charge in itself. In approving the plea agreement between the parties, I have not overlooked my prior writings and sentences in other income-tax cases. Generally speaking, where the defendant is a lawyer, a tax accountant, or a business executive, I resort to the practice of imposing a fine and a term of imprisonment, but provide that the actual period of confinement be limited to a period of from two to five months, with the defendant being placed on probation for the balance of the term. The reason for taking such action is that our method of filing income-tax returns is fundamentally based upon the honor of the individual reporting his income, and a sentence of actual confinement serves as a deterrent to others who are required to file their returns.

"But for the strong recommendation of the attorney general in this case, I would be inclined to follow the same procedure. However, I am persuaded that the national interests in the present case are so great and so compelling—all as described by the chief law-enforcement officer of the United States—that the ends of justice would be better served by making an exception to the general rule. I therefore approve the plea agreement between the parties."

Judge Hoffman then asked Agnew to stand, and offered him a chance to speak again.

"I have no further comment, your honor," he said.

"It is the judgment of this court," Hoffman told him, "that imposition of any sentence be suspended for a period of three years, conditioned that you, Spiro T. Agnew, at all times will be of uniform good behavior, that you will not violate the laws of the United States or any state; that, as a further condition of this probation, you are to pay a fine in the sum of ten thousand dollars within thirty days from this date or otherwise stand committed for nonpayment of said fine; and that you shall not be required to be under the supervision of the probation officer of this court unless otherwise ordered by the court."

Agnew turned, tight-lipped and somber, and strode quickly from the court—so quickly that Richardson and Petersen, each independently moving to express their condolences to him, could not catch up with him. Jud Best, encountering Art Sohmer at the curbside outside the courthouse, said, "Art, it isn't going to be easy from here on in."

"I know," said Sohmer. "But I've been with him all through his career and I'm not going to leave him now." He moved swiftly toward Agnew's gold-and-black Cadillac limousine and hopped in. Agnew, Sohmer, and the standard retinue of Secret Service agents headed out toward suburban Randallstown and the Byers Funeral Home, where the body of Agnew's half brother W. Roy Pollard, who had died a few days before, was awaiting burial. As the car pulled away, photographers leaned forward to snap the final pictures of Agnew on his last day as Vice President of the United States.

Agnew left behind a stunned group of bystanders. Joe Califano, mobbed going into the courthouse that morning, departed unnoticed. In the courthouse itself, reporters huddled on the stairs, thumbing through the forty-page exposition of evidence. Ripples of surprise came with every turn of the page. "This is incredible stuff!" exclaimed the courthouse reporter for a Baltimore newspaper, over and over again. Even the press corps was unprepared for the extraordinary document that just moments before had sunk Agnew. Almost at once, though, Agnew's home town seemed to accept the news. In a restaurant that night, the wife of a Baltimore state senator denounced not Agnew but rather the men who had been witnesses against him. An aide to Governor Marvin Mandel echoed the same theme, and to The Close Associate he awarded Baltimore's ultimate accolade: a stand-up guy.

At the Baltimore Hilton, a public-relations aide for the J. E. Greiner Company made the rounds of the rooms occupied by reporters, handing out a press release. Jerome B. Wolff was henceforth no longer an employee of the engineering firm.

The deposed Vice President that grim afternoon stayed at the funeral home for about an hour, then was driven with Mrs. Agnew, his son Randy and Randy's wife Conelia, and Susan Agnew to dinner at Sabatino's restaurant, a favorite haunt in the Little Italy section of Baltimore. Joe Canzani, the owner of the restaurant, was ready, having been alerted earlier that afternoon that Agnew might be stopping by. Canzani escorted the Agnews to a private room upstairs from the main dining area. The Secret Service routinely took up their positions. Agnew ordered the usual: linguini with clam sauce, garlic bread, salad—and a sirloin strip steak. The wine was Italian red. The Agnews stayed about two hours and then departed for their home in the Washington suburbs.

The news of Agnew's resignation went out to Washington and the world like an electric shock. Agnew's staff, which had been kept in the dark for so long and had persevered in loyalty and trust through it all, had had only a few minutes' warning. As Agnew was going into the courtroom, General Mike Dunn had summoned the full staff to a meeting—even secretaries were told to come and leave the phones unattended. Dunn announced without fanfare—and without adequate explanation, in the view of some of the aides—that the man for whom they had gone out on a limb was quitting. "Our leader is today resigning his high office," Dunn said, and the Vice President had asked him to convey his thanks to all of them for their service. A fist came pounding down on the conference table, shattering the silence—otherwise marred only by some women weeping.

"Don't you think the Vice President owes it to us to thank us himself?" a voice asked. The question went unanswered, and the meeting broke up.

A few minutes later, at about 2:20, the phone rang at the desk of Lisa Brown, Marsh Thomson's secretary. It was Richard Pyle of the Associated Press Washington bureau. An aide in the AP's Baltimore bureau, Roxanne Snead, had seen Agnew going into the courthouse a short time earlier and had phoned her office, which in turn notified Washington. Reporters on the scene were now in the courtroom and unable to get out. AP put out a bulletin saying only that Agnew was in the courthouse, purpose unknown. What, Pyle now asked Lisa Brown, was going on?

"I can't tell you very much about it," the secretary said, obviously upset. "The Vice President has just resigned."

"What?" Pyle asked, incredulously.

"We have just come from a meeting at which we were told the Vice President resigned as of two-oh-five this afternoon."

Pyle turned to the AP's assistant bureau chief and one-time top political reporter, Walter R. Mears. "Wally, Agnew's just resigned," he said.

Mears, without changing his stoical expression and barely raising his voice, swung around, and called across the room: "Clear the A wire" (the main AP national wire). Then he told Pyle to start writing. But the reporter's hands were shaking so much that he could not hit the keys. Mears, dead-pan, sat at the typewriter and told Pyle to dictate the story to him. In seconds, another bulletin went out that said: "Vice President Spiro T. Agnew resigned today, his secretary said."

It was a clean beat for the AP. Another nine minutes passed before the opposition, United Press International, reported the same startling news. Within seconds the word was flashed to the nation's newspapers and television networks, and millions watching the fifth game of the National League playoffs between Cincinnati and New York suddenly saw a legend spelled out across the bottom of their screens reporting the political end of Spiro T. Agnew.

At the White House, the customary exchange of letters between a resigning official and a grateful President was disclosed. Agnew had written:

Dear Mr. President:

As you are aware, the accusations against me cannot be resolved without a long, divisive and debilitating struggle in the Congress and in the Courts. I have concluded that, painful as it is to me and to my family, it is in the best interests of the Nation that I relinquish the Vice Presidency.

Accordingly, I have today resigned the Office of Vice President of the United States. A copy of the instrument of resignation is enclosed.

It has been a privilege to serve with you. May I express to the American people, through you, my deep gratitude for their confidence in twice electing me to be Vice President.

Sincerely,
Spiro T. Agnew

Nixon, who had wanted Agnew out and the quicker the better, replied:

Dear Ted:

The most difficult of decisions are often those that are the most personal, and I know your decision to resign as Vice President has been as difficult as any facing a man in public life could be. Your departure from the Administration leaves me with a great sense of personal loss. You have been a valued associate throughout these nearly five years that we have served together. However, I respect your decision, and I also respect the concern for the national interest that led you to conclude that a resolution of the matter in this way, rather than through an extended battle in the Courts and the Congress, was advisable in order to prevent a protracted period of national division and uncertainty.

As Vice President, you have addressed the great issues of our times with courage and candor. Your strong patriotism, and your profound dedication to the welfare of the Nation, have been an inspiration to all who have served with you as well as to millions of others throughout the country.

I have been deeply saddened by this whole course of events, and I hope that you and your family will be sustained in the days ahead by a well-justified pride in all that you have contributed to the Nation by your years of service as Vice President.

Sincerely,
Richard Nixon

It was all so courteous, so friendly, so tidy—and so final.

16 Was Justice Served?

With the same suddenness that the case against Spiro T. Agnew descended on the American consciousness, it seemed now to disappear. The tempest over the White House tapes on Watergate rushed in again; within ten days, the crisis broke that produced the firing of special Watergate prosecutor Archibald Cox and Elliot Richardson's own resignation as attorney general. Agnew's lawyers, brought together in a marriage of necessity during the case, went off on their separate paths. The U.S. attorney's office in Baltimore, after a few days' rest, returned to its usual labors in the less dramatic investigation of lesser Baltimore County officials. Some, like George Beall, could not shake the experience so easily. For nights thereafter, he awoke repeatedly, haunted by nightmares about all the things that could have gone wrong.

For the others, however, life went on. Even for Ted Agnew. Several nights after he surrendered the Vice Presidency to stay out of jail, he phoned James B. Reston, the *New York Times* columnist. Would Reston do him a favor? Of course, the courtly and gentle Reston said. Would he play tennis with Agnew? A

357

night or two later, Reston and his son Richard, a reporter in the *Los Angeles Times* Washington bureau, joined Agnew and the pro at Linden Hill, a private club in Bethesda, for an hour of concentrated tennis—and no discussion of Agnew's woes. Secret Service agents chased errant shots, and Mrs. Agnew sat waiting.

In the days and weeks immediately thereafter, Agnew spent his time not in some far-off hideaway contemplating the disastrous turn in his life, but across the street from the White House and his old vice-presidential suite. From an office on Jackson Place provided free by the government, Agnew put in normal work days—answering mail, occasionally lunching at a favorite restaurant. About three weeks after his resignation, the Agnews entertained about a hundred loyal staff people at their home in suburban Kenwood, Maryland—a kind of combination thankyou party and housewarming. The host and hostess greeted their guests at the door, served drinks and a buffet, and Agnew himself capped off the evening by playing the piano. It was a warm and friendly affair, again with no discussion of the recent trouble. Yes, life went on.

Agnew's trouble—and how it was resolved—was the subject of discussion, however, among others. Tim Baker's wife, Betsy, tempered her accolades with criticism of what she saw as the rank injustice of Agnew escaping without a jail sentence. It was a view held by many others. In contrast, Judah Best encountered a fellow lawyer on the street in Washington who came up and shook his hand, looked him squarely in the eye, and commended him for the great deal he had made for his client. It all depended on your perspective.

Both reactions—that of Baker's wife and Judah Best's lawyer friend—were predicated, however, on the same assumption: that Spiro Agnew was an exceedingly guilty man. So the lengthy summary of evidence had done its work. It had conveyed what Richardson insisted it had to—that Spiro Agnew's guilt went far beyond the commonplace count of tax evasion to which he confessed. There remained a few diehard supporters who accepted Agnew's dark hints that some sinister development, to be disclosed at some vague time in the future, had forced him to step aside. Agnew spent much time in the days and weeks after his removal from office conveying this message to old friends. Some, but not all, bought it. One of them, shocked as all others at the original charges and thoroughly disbelieving, listened to Agnew's hints, took another look at the summary of evidence, and reluctantly concluded the former Vice President had deceived him. "It's the oldest ploy in the book," the friend said later. "'There was a good reason, but I can't tell you what it is.'" The man went away sadder but wiser.

In the absence of an explanation, Agnew's supporters were doubly crushed at his capitulation because they had come to think of him as a fighter. In this most desperate moment of his life he refused to fight, and for that above all they could not forgive him. His willingness to surrender the Vice Presidency to stay out of jail bewildered them, doubting as they did that he could be guilty. The refusal to fight was itself taken by many of them finally, reluctantly, as an admission of guilt, for they could not see it in the character of the man to do anything but stand firmly against his foes.

So, it seemed, was the judgment of Agnew's supporters around the country. The absence of any public groundswell for him or any outpouring of financial support for his defense indicated persuasively that the great silent majority for which Spiro Agnew had been the venomous, relentless spokesman had no intention of breaking its silence in his behalf. In a time of great national disenchantment with politicians as crooks and dissemblers, Agnew had stood out to millions as the exception—a man of trust and candor. He who climbs highest risks the greatest fall, and so it was with Agnew, who encouraged great expectations and rewarded them with the admission that he was a felon.

One major psychological impact of the Watergate revelations, after the resounding re-election of Nixon and Agnew in 1972, was the related realization by millions of American voters that they had been duped. Agnew alone had seemed untainted by Watergate, and that in itself made his fall, when it came, all the more damaging to public confidence. His legions of admirers, like

Caesar, could ask without being accused of melodramatics: "Et tu, Brute?"

Much has been said and written about the collective wisdom and good sense of the American people; that somehow by some mysterious osmosis the voters sift through all the political propaganda and select the best men to lead the country. That notion has always been poppycock; the Nixon-Agnew experience merely documents it anew. Closer to the truth is the demonstrated fact that the American people—and the press that strives to discern for them who these men are who seek to lead—are poor judges of character, as vulnerable now to the trick mirrors of the television age as they have been to the age-old deceptions of men in politics. Spiro Agnew was a slick snake-oil salesman. Not everyone bought his product, but just about everyone bought him. The accepted wisdom, among political friend and foe alike, was that you might not agree with Agnew, but he was honest. The measure of his fall was in that misconception: in his greed, he squandered finally the one prime source of his political wealth, the belief that he was the exception in politics—an honest man.

The first objective of Elliot Richardson after Agnew's removal from the succession, that the man's guilt be perceived, appears to have been accomplished. But what of the second—that the disposition of the case be perceived as just? That is a more difficult question, and one not likely to be resolved in the public mind for some time to come. Inherent in Betsy Baker's anger was her belief that justice had not been served. "Mr. Attorney General," a reporter had asked in a press conference the day after the resignation, "you say that the moral of this whole episode is that the public should have confidence in the system of justice. Isn't the public going to gather that if a man is high enough, he gets off very lightly?"

Richardson replied: "I think this is a feeling that some people may have. It was the awareness that this would be the reaction, or might be the reaction, of some of my fellow citizens that led me to try to make as clear as I could, in my statement to the court yesterday, that the interests of justice, as well as the interests of the public, were better served in this instance by a disposition that did not involve confinement of the former Vice President in a penal institution. I can only say that I hope that these considerations prove persuasive to the majority of my fellow citizens."

Americans, however, have always been prone to believe that when the rich, the influential, the powerful are involved, justice keeps a thumb on the scales. Agnew's deal, for the very persuasiveness of the evidence that he was guilty of bribery and extortion as well as simple tax evasion, risked reinforcing that public cynicism. It was Richardson's hope and intent that, having convinced the public that Agnew was guilty and was not being railroaded, he would also be able to convince the people that the national interest was served by Agnew's speedy dispatch from office. That task over the long run may be the harder to achieve. The public throughout American history has questioned the importance of the Vice President; the political folklore is replete with ridicule of him and the roster with a few exceptions is a roll call of mediocrity and obscurity. Persuading the public that the preservation of the Republic is involved in what happens to the Vice President is especially difficult.

But Richardson tried to make this case, noting the instability of President Nixon's position in the climate of Watergate, the concurrent crisis in the Middle East, and the prospect of a drawn-out debate and trial on his Watergate culpability either in the courts or in Congress. Unlike the eager prosecutors from Baltimore, who were hunters after prey, Richardson sought to be at once prosecutor, politician, diplomat, and protector of the broad national interest. It can be said that the country could have withstood whatever Spiro Agnew could impose on it—a fight in the courts, impeachment, and trial in Congress, a public campaign of vilification against his accusers. That is an argument that can never be resolved. Only when history records the outcome of the Watergate affair, and the fate of Richard Nixon as President, will it be known whether the swift surgery that took Spiro Agnew out of the line of succession was necessary for the survival and recovery of the national patient.

In the broad assumption that Agnew would have been convicted or impeached or both if the investigation had taken its course, the vagaries of politics may have been underestimated. At the core of Richardson's fears was not only the specter of a sudden presidential disability projecting a felon into the White House, but also the realization that it was always possible Agnew could escape all punishment. A single recalcitrant juror could deadlock a jury. As for Congress, one third plus one of the United States Senate could block conviction in an impeachment trial, and they had a variety of reasons, ranging from party loyalty among Republicans to the desire of the Democrats to keep a sure loser in office until the next election.

In terms of the national interest, the foundering second term of Richard Nixon was already evidence of the perils of leadership bereft of public confidence. Richardson, a man motivated as attorney general to restore the people's belief in the administration of justice, could have rehabilitated it in a stroke by demanding jail for the Vice President. Instead, he sacrificed this opportunity in order to clear the line to the Presidency.

Elliot Richardson had to await history's resolution of the national turmoil in which the investigation and resignation of Spiro T. Agnew took place, before history could render its judgment of his actions. But for Agnew, there could be little doubt that history's judgment was already upon him, the first Vice President of the United States to have resigned in disgrace. All that he achieved or sought to achieve in his public life—and it certainly was more than the accumulation of secret wealth—had been buried in that tragic and irrefutable act. In the end, because he stood a heartbeat away from the Presidency in a time of great national uncertainty and crisis, his peers moved in fear and haste to expunge him from the line of succession for the common good.

For all his continued protestations of innocence, Agnew had to live with that realization in the quiet reflection of his own mind. In the first days of his exile from the Vice Presidency, he appeared to manage that very well. He seemed, in fact, more concerned with maintaining the high standard of living he had enjoyed at the taxpayers' expense than any remorse over what he had done. With Secret Service protection ordered by the President for months afterward, Agnew continued to live and travel in style. Indeed, he seemed to flaunt the decision that gave him his freedom in exchange for his high office, with neither his conscience nor any visible sense of shame inhibiting him. If, however, Spiro T. Agnew was really the introspective man he had always claimed to be, the knowledge that he was considered unfit and unworthy to be President could well become for him, eventually, a self-imprisonment as confining as any physical incarceration.

Index